Inclusive Early Childhood Education

Merging Positive Behavioral Supports, Activity-Based Intervention, and Developmentally Appropriate Practice

David Dean Richey

John J. Wheeler

Tennessee Technological University
With Selected Invited Contributions

Africa • Australia • Canada • Denmark • Japan • Mexico • New Zealand • Philippines
Puerto Rico • Singapore • Spain • United Kingdom • United States

Delmar Staff:

Business Unit Director: Susan Simpfenderfer
Executive Editor: Marlene McHugh Pratt
Acquisitions Editor: Erin O'Connor Traylor
Editorial Assistant: Alexis Ferraro
Executive Marketing Manager: Donna Lewis
Executive Production Manager: Wendy Troeger
Production Editor: Sandra Woods

Delmar Publishers
3 Columbia Circle, Box 15015
Albany, New York 12212-5015
International Thomson Publishing Europe
Berkshire House
168-173 High Holborn
London, WC1V7AA
United Kingdom
Nelson ITP, Australia
102 Dodds Street
South Melbourne,
Victoria, 3205 Australia
Nelson Canada
1120 Birchmont Road
Scarborough, Ontario
M1K 5G4, Canada
International Thomson Publishing France
Tour Maine-Montparnasse
33 Avenue du Maine
75755 Paris Cedex 15, France

International Thomson Editores
Seneca 53
Colonia Polanco
11560 Mexico D.F. Mexico
International Thomson Publishing GmbH
Königswinterer Strasbe 418
53227 Bonn
Germany
International Thomson Publishing Asia
60 Albert Street
#15-01 Albert Complex
Singapore 189969
International Thomson Publishing Japan
Hirakawa-cho Kyowa Building, 3F
2-2-1 Hirakawa-cho, Chiyoda-ku,
Tokyo 102, Japan
ITE Spain/Paraninfo
Calle Magallanes, 25
28015-Madrid, Espana

Library of Congress Cataloging-in-Publication Data
Richey, David Dean.
    Inclusive early childhood education : merging positive behavioral supports,
activity-based intervention, and developmentally appropriate practice / David Dean
Richey & John J. Wheeler.
        p. cm.
    Includes bibliographical references and index.
    ISBN 0-7668-0273-6
        1. Handicapped children—Education (Early childhood)—United States. 2. Inclusive
    education—United States. I. Wheeler, John J. II. Title.
LC4019.3.R53 1999
    371.9'047—dc21   99-046299
                                        CIP

Brief Contents

Foreword   vii

Preface   ix

SECTION   I   **Principles Overview   1**

Chapter   1   *Introduction (D. Richey)   3*

Chapter   2   *Family/Professional Collaboration: A Parent's Perspective (C. Russell)   31*

Chapter   3   *Principles of Positive Behavioral Supports (PBS) (J. Wheeler)   72*

Chapter   4   *Principles of Activity-Based Intervention (ABI) (D. Richey)   103*

Chapter   5   *Principles of Developmentally Appropriate Practice (DAP) (L. Richey)   127*

SECTION   II   **Procedures Overview   145**

Chapter   6   *Assessment (J. Wheeler)   148*

Chapter   7   *Effective Teaching and Intervention Practices (J. Wheeler)   174*

SECTION   III   **Issues Overview   205**

Chapter   8   *Respecting Cultural Diversity (E. Jackson)   207*

Chapter   9   *Future Directions in Inclusive Early Childhood Education (D. Richey, L. Richey, C. Russell, J. Wheeler)   224*

SECTION   IV   **Applications Overview   247**

Chapter   10   *Applying PBS, ABI, and DAP in Inclusive Infant/Toddler Settings (D. Richey)   249*

Chapter   11   *Applying PBS, ABI, and DAP in Inclusive Preschool and Kindergarten Settings (L. Richey)   276*

Chapter   12   *Applying PBS, ABI, and DAP in Inclusive Early Elementary Grades (C. Russell, J. Wheeler)   297*

Appendix A   *Individualized Family Service Plan   331*

Appendix B   *Sample Format for an Individualized Family Service Plan   339*

Index   355

Contents

SECTION I PRINCIPLES 1

Chapter 1   Introduction 3

Introduction 3

Key Terms and Concepts 3

Inclusion 4

Positive Behavioral Supports 5

Activity-Based Early Intervention 5

Developmentally Appropriate Practice 5

Collaboration 6

Partnerships with Families 7

Family-Centered Services 8

Transdisciplinary Teaming 8

Self-Determination 9

Ecological Approach 10

Transitions 10

Person and Family-First Language 11

Why Inclusion? 12

Ethical and Commonsense Arguments 14

Positions Taken by Advocacy Groups and
Professional Organizations 14

Legal Mandates 16

Research Support for Early Inclusion 19

Merging Disciplines 21

Summary 23

Chapter 1 Suggested Activities and
Resources 25

References 26

***Chapter 2   Family/Professional
Collaboration: A Parent's
Perspective 31***

Introduction 31

Impact of a Child with a Disability on
the Family and Need for Professional
Partnership and Support 32

Stages toward Adjustment 32

Bewildering Times 32

Artistic Avenues for Expression 36

Impact on Siblings 37

Grandparents and Extended Family 46

The Family as a System 49

Sandler's Three R's: Roles, Relationships,
and Responsibility 50

Utilizing a Family-Centered
Approach 50

Characterizing and Defining Family-
Centeredness 51

Collaboration for Successfully Working
with Young Children with Special
Needs and Their Families 51

Effective Communication 54

Negotiation and Conflict Resolution 54

Mediation 55

Due Process 56

Implementing Effective Collaborative
Practices 57

The Importance of Empowering Families
to Assist Them in Making Informed
Decisions 60

Recognizing Family-Centered
Support/Services and Collaboration
as a Foundation for Positive
Behavioral Supports and Activity-
Based Intervention 65

Summary 65

Chapter 2 Suggested Activities and Resources   66

References   68

Chapter 3   Principles of Positive Behavioral Supports (PBS)   72

Introduction   72

Ecological Influences on Behavioral Development   74

Parental Influences   76

Sociocultural Influences   78

Developing Age and Behavior   80

Principles of Positive Behavioral Supports   82

Functional Assessment and Positive Behavioral Supports   83

Methods of Recording Behavior   87

Merging PBS, ABI, and DAP   96

Summary   97

Chapter 3 Suggested Activities and Resources   97

References   99

Chapter 4   Principles of Activity-Based Intervention (ABI)   103

Introduction   103

Theoretical Foundations of Activity-Based Intervention   103

Defining Activity-Based Intervention   104

Considerations for Activity-Based Intervention in Various Early Childhood Settings   109

Some Concerns Regarding Activity-Based Intervention   121

Summary   123

Chapter 4 Suggested Activities and Resources   124

References   124

Chapter 5   Principles of Developmentally Appropriate Practice (DAP)   127

Introduction   127

Developmentally Appropriate Practice   128

Developmentally Appropriate Programs   139

A Shared Philosophy Results in Similar Recommended Practices   139

Environment and Experiences   141

Summary   141

Chapter 5 Suggested Activities and Resources   141

Selected Resources   142

References   144

SECTION II   PROCEDURES   145

Chapter 6   Assessment   148

Introduction   148

The Diagnosis of a Developmental Disability   148

Importance of the Assessment Process   153

Models of Assessment   155

Family Participation in the Assessment Process   167

Translating Assessment Information into Meaningful Educational and Intervention Programs   168

Summary   169

Chapter 6 Suggested Activities and Resources   170

References   171

Chapter 7   Effective Teaching and Intervention Practices   174

Introduction   174

Selection of Socially Valid Goals and Objectives   175

Analysis and Summary   178

Longitudinal Educational Planning   180

PBS, ABI, and DAP Teaching and Intervention Methods   181

Developing Goals and Objectives   189

Designing Child-Centered Learning Environments   193

Promoting Successful Inclusion   195

Methods of Evaluating Intervention Effectiveness and Outcomes   198

Summary   199
Chapter 7 Suggested Activities and
    Resources   200
References   201

SECTION III   ISSUES   205
Chapter 8   Respecting Cultural
    Diversity   207
Introduction   207
What is Cultural Diversity?   208
Cultural Diversity: In Schools and in
    Early Childhood Education   209
Cultural Diversity and Contemporary
    Issues   212
Meeting the Challenges of Diversity in
    Inclusive Early Childhood
    Education   217
Summary   219
Chapter 8 Suggested Activities and
    Resources   219
References   220

Chapter 9   Future Directions in Inclusive
    Early Childhood Education   224
Introduction   224
Foundations for Future Directions   224
Research   227
Public Policy   229
Future Directions in Service Delivery
    Practices   231
Families   236
Personnel Preparation   238
Summary   242
Chapter 9 Suggested Activities and
    Resources   242
References   243

SECTION IV   APPLICATIONS   247
Chapter 10   Applying PBS, ABI, and DAP
    in Inclusive Infant/Toddler
    Settings   249
Introduction   249
Summary History of and Legislative Basis
    for Early Intervention   249
Introduction to the Five Vignettes   251
Summary   271
Chapter 10 Suggested Activities and
    Resources   272
References   274

Chapter 11   Applying PBS, ABI, and DAP
    in Inclusive Preschool and
    Kindergarten Settings   276
Introduction   276
Summary   293
Chapter 11 Selected Activities   294
References   296

Chapter 12   Applying PBS, ABI, and DAP
    in Inclusive Early Elementary
    Grades   297
Introduction   297
Summary   327
References   329

Appendix A   331

Appendix B   339

Index   354

Foreword

The authors wish to dedicate this book to their children, Benjamin Wheeler, Allison Wheeler, Adam Richey, Patrick Richey, and Amanda Richey. They have truly been, and continue to be, our most important teachers. The privilege and responsibility of fatherhood are guiding principles in our lives. We trust that the love for our children and our feelings of the importance of the family are evident in this book.

Obviously completion of a project like the writing of a book requires the support, commitment and combined talents of a number of individuals. We would first like to extend our thanks to our invited contributors, Dr. Linda Richey, Associate Professor of Child and Family Studies at Tennessee Technological University, Dr. Elouise Jackson, Associate Professor of Early Childhood Special Education at Tennessee Technological University, and Dr. Carol Russell, Assistant Professor of Early Childhood Education at Emporia State University. The commitment of these contributors to the mission of the book, and their expertise and eagerness to work as a team assisted greatly in the completion of this text. We would also like to thank our patient and very capable Editor, Erin O'Connor whose guidance made this project possible, along with the many other staff members at Delmar who were a delight to work with and whose expertise facilitated the process and enhanced the final product. Additional thanks are extended to the reviewers of this text whose insightful comments and suggestions made our job as authors much easier. You will find their names and affiliations listed elsewhere.

A number of people at our University played a significant role in contributing to the completion of this book. Ms. Lucinda Myers is acknowledged for her preparation of the manuscript. Ms. Tiffany Short, Executive Aide in the College of Education Dean's Office and Mrs. Pat Eaves, Secretary in the Associate Dean's Office provided a variety of supportive functions, not the least of which was attempting to keep us organized and on task. Mrs. Cindy Mayer is responsible for much of the photography and art work in the book. She took the lead in identifying the pictures needed for each chapter, taking additional pictures and following through on the finalizing of captions and securing permissions. Cindy's giftedness as an artist, along with her ability to communicate and her knowledge of what is being communicated to the reader by what is represented graphically, was invaluable and greatly appreciated by the authors. The vignettes about very young children with disabilities and their families, in most instances, relate real experiences of children and families. These life stories were contributed by many, including personal friends, our own extended families, families we have served, and professionals from our district office of Tennessee's Early Intervention System. The service coordinators from TEIS, including Mary Ebersviller, Susan O'Connor, and Filomena Walker were also helpful to the authors in determining and focusing some areas of content. Their outstanding, heartfelt, family-centered work every day on behalf of young children and their families in implementing the philosophy and practices detailed in the book continue to be an inspiration to us. To Crystal Amirkhanian and Jill Lively we extend a big professorial thank you! As advanced undergraduate students in early childhood education approaching student teaching and reviewing the chapter drafts as a part of your independent study in early childhood special education, your comments and suggestions were very helpful and were incorporated.

A special thanks is due to Dr. Carol Russell's family and extended family. Her chapter on families (chapter 2) and her contributions elsewhere were really "family affairs" reflecting very much personal experiences and interactions with various professionals over time. Carol, we are grateful for you and your family's willingness to share so much. The authors have been privileged to partner with a number of wonderful family members over the years. For people like Janey Bassett, Glenda Bond, Perry Melton, Lisa Miller, and Melinda Swafford, you have had a role in determining that this book would be written and in shaping what it says. Finally, we are blessed if we have wise and learned mentors for our professional lives. It happens that the authors have had several. Some of these include Don Bailey, Paul Bates, Diane Bricker, James Gallagher, Ray Heubschmann, Nicholas Hobbs, Kathleen Marshall, Sidney Miller, Roger Poppen, Bob Slagle, and Donald Stedman. Each of these prominent professionals has, sometimes unbeknownst to them, had a substantial influence on what we have included in the textbook and why it is important to the future of our disciplines.

Preface

Well, here we go! You are probably starting out at the beginning of a term with this text as a required, supplementary, or recommended reading, and you are wondering as with other textbooks if it is going to be readable, useful, interesting, relevant, and reasonably jargon-free. The authors begin this endeavor with you by noting that we have been on the receiving end of many textbooks and journal readings that seemed to be designed to confuse and aggravate. We have also been guilty on occasion of selecting and requiring of our students texts and other readings lacking in the attributes noted above. We intend for this book, beginning with Chapter 1, to be as "reader friendly" as possible. That of course does not mean you will not be challenged with new ideas and concepts, some of which you may find confusing or troublesome. We will strive to present this information in a clear and logical manner. You and your professor are the ultimate judges of whether or not we were successful.

The tie that binds us is our common concern for the well-being of all young children and their families. It is likely that you are reading this book because you are preparing yourself to work in service to young children and their families. Possibly you are already on the job and seeking to enhance your knowledge and skills. Or maybe you are a parent or other family member of a young child. At any rate, our common denominator is that we desire to develop, improve, or enhance our knowledge of this population and to further our professional abilities as teachers, caregivers, and interventionists. We encourage you to engage this text, study these concepts, and integrate this material into your professional development.

Organization of the Text

This book is divided into four sections, from two to five chapters each. The chapters range from fifteen to thirty pages in length. Each chapter is organized in somewhat the same fashion. That is, at the beginning of the chapter several objectives for that specific chapter are presented. A paragraph or so is provided early on, making a transition from the previous chapter. The body of the chapter includes multiple subheadings detailing the content. At the end of each chapter, you will find a summary section, references, and when relevant and useful application examples, resource listings, and/or suggested activities to extend your learning of the chapter content. The authors attempted to keep charts, tables, and graphs to a minimum and to provide pictures and illustrations in each chapter. In some chapters, you will find vignettes provided by the families with which the authors were privileged to work and partner. These vignettes illustrate experiences of families with the process of inclusion. A one- or two-page overview of the subsequent chapters is at the beginning of each section. You should actively use the goals presented with each chapter as a general measure for yourself of whether or not you understand the main ideas conveyed in the chapter.

With regard to content, *Inclusive Early Childhood Education: Merging Positive Behavioral Supports, Activity-Based Intervention, and Developmentally Appropriate Practice* is organized in a manner that moves the reader through four levels. The first is Section I: Principles. It provides the foundation for understanding and using the rest of the text. This section (Chapters 1 through 5) defines and describes the central themes and principles including early childhood inclusion, positive behavioral supports, activity-based intervention, and developmental appropriateness. Section I also introduces the historical development and current status of these principles and related practices in service programs. In Section II: Procedures, the focus is on assessment and intervention/instructional practices that support the inclusion of young children in natural settings (e.g., child care centers, Head Start classes, kindergartens, and early elementary classrooms) using the principles of positive behavioral supports and activity-based intervention. Section III: Issues relates some of the most important issues currently faced by those working on behalf of young children and their families toward the goal of inclusion using positive behavioral supports and activity-based intervention. Examples of issues included are: respecting and accommodating cultural diversity, future applications of technology in early childhood programs, directions for research, merging traditional approaches among early childhood education, child and family development, and early childhood special education and ways to train professionals to collaborate and partner in order to successfully use the methods advocated in this textbook. Section IV consists of fifteen vignettes over three chapters (Chapters 10 through 12) that illustrate the specifics of how to apply positive behavioral supports and activity-based intervention in inclusive settings: infant and toddler programs, preschool programs, kindergartens, and grades 1 through 3.

Terminology

A few comments about terminology will be helpful here. The focus of this textbook is to provide a variety of high-quality services to young children, primarily from birth through third grade, and to their families. So when we refer to early childhood, we mean birth through third grade. The term *early intervention* refers to the specialized services provided to infants and toddlers, birth to thirty-six months, and their families. Preschoolers are those young children aged three through five. When the term *early childhood special education* occurs, it refers to the specialized services provided to children with disabilities birth through third grade, including those delivered in other than inclusive settings. The reader may become weary of our chronic use of the phrase "and their families" when we discuss services to young children. We must convey in the strongest of terms that services to young children, disabled or not, impact the family as a unit; we trust you will bear with us. Another term the reader will encounter frequently is *natural setting* (or *natural environments*). A natural setting is a place like a kindergarten classroom, a day care center, a mother's day out program, a Head Start center, or a family day care home. Natural setting also refers to the variety of places most young children might be found, such as a Sunday school class, the mall, or a restaurant. It might be helpful, at least for a few weeks or so, for you to have index cards or other forms of noting the definitions of these terms for reference as you begin studying this textbook. One final word before you launch into Chapter 1. The authors assumed a moderate level of education and/or experience related to child development, early childhood education, and special education in determining the content and extent of detail to cover in this text. If you do not have this background, the text will be a greater challenge for you, but we trust for the most part still manageable.

Acknowledgments

We would like to thank the reviewers for the insight they have provided:

- Elaine Boski, Collin County Community College, Plano, TX
- Craig Boswell, Ph.D., University of Central Oklahoma, Edmond, OK
- Frances Joyce Gerber, Housatonic Community-Technical College, Bridgeport, CT
- Mary Frances Hanline, Florida State University, Tallahassee, FL
- Barbara Lowenthal, Ed.D., Northeastern Illinois University, Chicago, IL
- Amy Sue Reilly, Auburn University, Auburn University, AL
- Marcia Ryztag, Lansing Community College, Haslett, MI
- Kristine L. Slentz, Ph.D., Western Washington University, Bellingham, WA

About the Authors

Dr. David Dean Richey currently serves as Interim Dean of the College of Education and Professor of Early Childhood Special Education at Tennessee Technological University in Cookeville, Tennessee. He received his Ph.D. in Education with emphasis in early intervention and child development from the University of North Carolina–Chapel Hill in 1975. Dr. Richey has thirty-four years of experience in teaching including twenty-five years in higher education. He has authored a number of professional journal articles and has developed curriculum resources and directed model programs for young children with special needs and their families. His research and program development interests have focused on family-centered intervention, inclusion processes in early childhood, and cross-disciplinary models of personnel preparation. Dr. Richey and his wife Linda (a contributor to this textbook) are the parents of three young adult children: Amanda, Patrick, and Adam.

Dr. John Wheeler currently serves as Interim Associate Dean of the College of Education and Professor of Special Education at Tennessee Technological University in Cookeville, Tennessee. He received his Ph.D. in Education with emphasis in Special Education from Southern Illinois University at Carbondale in 1989. Dr. Wheeler has twenty years of experience in education that has included service as a teacher of children with severe disabilities and as a university faculty member. He has written numerous research articles and has specialized in the development of programs to serve children with severe disabilities and their families. His research and publications have included the areas of positive behavioral supports and interventions with children with severe disabilities, autism, and severe behavior disorders. Dr. Wheeler is the parent of two young children, Alli and Ben.

Section I
Principles

OVERVIEW

The first section of your text consists of Chapters 1 through 5. The intent of Section I: Principles is to get you off to what the authors hope will be a good start by providing the foundation for the early childhood inclusion ideas, practices, processes, and issues advanced in the book. Generally the message of Section I is that effective and responsible inclusive early childhood education is based on a family-centered approach, in which professionals are in partnership with families, and on the meshing of the principles of and actions associated with developmentally appropriate practice positive behavioral supports, and activity-based intervention. Chapter 1 is an introduction to the terms, themes, or concepts that will be carried throughout the text. You will note in Chapter 1 an emphasis on "people first" language and the goal of fostering self-determination, the necessity for the collaboration and teamwork among professionals, transitions over time for children and parents regarding the location and types of services received, and the ecological perspective applied to better understand how to foster early inclusion.

Chapter 2 describes the partnership between families and professionals in general and in particular as it impacts the delivery of early childhood special education services in inclusive classrooms and other natural environments. The author of Chapter 2 is a professional special educator, but she is also the parent of a child with special needs. The intent is that the reader will not only get the professional content that establishes the roles of families in inclusive early childhood programs and services but also understand to some extent how it feels to be part of a family in which there is a young child with a disability and to interact with teachers and other service providers. It is accurate to "read into" the chapter one of the central assumptions of this text, which is that professionals, in special education and related disciplines, have historically too often tended to create an unnecessary distance between themselves and the parents of their students, even as they were focusing intently on an individualized, supportive, and nurturing relationship with the children.

Chapter 3, Principles of Positive Behavioral Supports (PBS), provides an introduction to the historical development and theoretical underpinnings of PBS as a best and effective means of supporting, encouraging, and guiding the behavior of young children, in particular for children in inclusive learning environments. You will find PBS sometimes referred to elsewhere in the literature as child-centered behavioral supports, and you may take the meaning to be the same. In understanding the theory and concepts of PBS it is useful to think about how traditional behavioral theory is complemented by both an ecological and developmental perspective. Positive behavioral supports refer to the things that we as adults (teachers, caregivers, parents, or others) can do, provide for, and plan to foster the behaviors that we desire in young children, to prevent the occurrence of undesirable behaviors, and to effectively intervene to manage challenging behaviors. The emphasis of PBS is clearly on avoiding punishment strategies to affect the behavior of children and on the use of naturally occurring antecedents and consequences rather than those that are contrived.

Chapter 4, Principles of Activity-Based Intervention (ABI), establishes the role of ABI as a primary structure for how to embed the specialized goals and objectives that we must address for young children with disabilities, in inclusive and natural environments. Using these principles (ABI), it is possible to take advantage of the normally occurring routines, child initiations, and teacher-directed activities in inclusive settings, such as a kindergarten classroom, to enhance the child's skills in a way that is more likely to carry over to other settings. Activity-based intervention is described as a means of bringing together the traditional focus of special educators on highly intensive, individualized, and controlled teaching with the advantages of inclusive settings, such as peer modeling and incidental learning, and developing independence and coping strategies associated with "real world" circumstances.

Finally, the last chapter of Section I (Chapter 5) is a description of developmentally appropriate practice (DAP) and its place along with positive behavioral supports and activity-based intervention as the foundations for successful inclusion of young children with disabilities. The leadership of the National Association for the Education of Young Children (NAEYC) in defining, describing, and advocating DAP is detailed, and the collaboration between NAEYC and the Division for Early Childhood of the Council for Exceptional Children is introduced. This collaboration, along with attention in both the early childhood and early childhood special education literature, has helped bring into focus the relevance of DAP for early intervention and early childhood special education services and has addressed concerns, such as the distinction between age appropriateness and developmental appropriateness.

Introduction

Chapter

1

INTRODUCTION

This chapter provides a brief review of the evolution of inclusive programs and services for young children and their families. The current status of the field is summarized, with particular attention given to recommended practices. The fundamental themes are defined, and their relationships and relevance to the mission of the textbook are explained. Here are the objectives the reader will address in Chapter 1. You should be able to:

- Define and give examples of the following themes/terms/concepts: inclusion, positive behavioral supports, activity-based early intervention, developmentally-appropriate practices, collaboration, partnerships with families, family-centered services, transdisciplinary teaming, ecological approach, person and family-first language, self-determination, and transitioning.
- Briefly state the rationale for inclusive programs for young children with disabilities, from the vantage point of professional organizations, from an ethical and commonsense perspective, from legislative mandates, and from the evidence in current literature regarding the extent to which inclusion works.
- List and give examples of five factors that are practical considerations in the implementation of inclusion in early childhood education.
- Discuss the relationship, in general terms, among the disciplines of early childhood, early childhood special education, and child and family science, as it developed historically and how it presently affects inclusion.
- Describe how positive behavioral supports, activity-based intervention, and developmentally-appropriate practices are central to successful inclusion programs.

Key Terms and Concepts

The following twelve themes/terms/concepts are critical to your ability to find meaning in and make effective use of your text: inclusion, positive behavioral supports, activity-based early intervention, developmentally appropriate practice,

3

collaboration, partnership with families, family-centered services, transdisciplinary teaming, self-determination, ecological approach, transitions, and person and family-first language. They continually occur throughout the following chapters. It will serve you to carefully study each of them and be able to relate them to a variety of circumstances and settings, especially those child care, preschool, and school-aged classrooms with which you are most familiar. The primary focus of this textbook is on practices of inclusion for children from birth through the early elementary grades and for their families. Think of each of the following concepts/themes as applying to little ones and their families, whether they are infants, toddlers, preschoolers, or six- to eight-year-olds.

Inclusion

Inclusion has been defined in numerous ways. For our purposes, we draw upon several definitions that seem to capture the spirit and intent of the practice and process of inclusion. Abraham, Morris, and Wald (1993), in describing a model for inclusive early childhood classrooms, define such a classroom as "one in which children with and without disabilities learn and play together." Bowe (1995) defined inclusion as "an approach in which children with disabilities (including those with severe disabilities) are placed in rooms with, and receive services side-by-side with, children who have no disabilities." Kerzner-Lipsky and Gartner (1994) provide a third definition, focusing more on school-aged children. Their definition states that "inclusion is the provision of services to students with disabilities, including those with severe disabilities, in their neighborhood schools, in age-appropriate regular education classes, with the necessary support services and supplementary aids for both children and teachers."

Finally, with regard to gaining an understanding of this concept, we turn to the position statement on inclusion from the Division for Early Childhood of the Council for Exceptional Children (April 1993). It is as follows: "inclusion, as a value, supports the right of all children, regardless of their diverse abilities, to participate actively in natural settings within their communities. A natural setting is one in which the child would spend time had he or she not had a disability. Such settings include but are not limited to home and family, play groups, childcare, nursery schools, Head Start programs, kindergartens, and neighborhood school classrooms." You may wonder how this concept fits, or does not fit, with previously used terms such as mainstreaming and early integration. We take up this question a bit later in Chapter 1, along with a consideration of the rationale for inclusion.

One final word about inclusion, however, is useful here. In a review of work done earlier (McLean & Odom, 1993), LaMontagne, Danbom, and Buchanan (1998) point out that one of seven common threads between the National Association for the Education of Young Children and the Division for Early Childhood of the Council for Exceptional Children is a focus on inclusion. They suggest that as we gain more experience and success with inclusion, families will choose it for their young children with special needs as a rule rather than the exception. These choices for inclusive settings and processes will certainly become more of a reality because of the requirement in the 1997 reauthorization of the Individuals with Disabilities Education Act (IDEA) (Part C, Early Intervention) that natural environments (largely inclusive) must be used, unless there is a clear and defensible reason not to do so.

Positive Behavioral Supports

The approach of providing positive behavioral supports (PBS) is fourfold. First, responses to young children's behaviors are nonpunitive. Second, the emphasis is on understanding what is developmentally appropriate for an individual so that inappropriate behavior is lessened, or prevented, by having behavioral expectations that match developmental abilities. Third, the play/learning environments of young children are designed and managed to facilitate desired behaviors. And last, responses to children's undesirable behavior are positive, specific to the behavior, and intended to teach and nurture. The principles of this approach to influencing the behavior of young children are detailed in Chapter 3. Look for references to and applications of PBS throughout the text.

Activity-Based Early Intervention

The primary source for understanding this innovative approach to including young children with disabilities in natural settings is the landmark work of Diane Bricker and Juliann J. Woods-Cripe (1992) in their book entitled *An Activity-Based Approach to Early Intervention*. They defined the activity-based intervention (ABI) approach as "a child-directed, transactional approach that embeds intervention on children's individual goals and objectives in routine, planned, or child-initiated activities and uses logically occurring antecedents and consequences to develop functional and generalizable skills." Another way of saying this is that ABI allows the teacher, caregiver, or interventionist to address the special needs of a child with a disability in the context of the regular routines, activities, and materials in the inclusive setting.

Historically, our willingness and ability to be inclusive has been hindered to some extent by traditional views and misconceptions held by special educators as well as by regular educators, caregivers, early childhood educators, and parents. Special educators working on behalf of young children often focused on the need for highly specialized one-to-one instruction emphasizing specific measurable objectives and retaining much of their control of the reinforcement choice and administration. On the other hand, professionals not trained in special education believed that the needs of children with disabilities were beyond their training and capabilities. ABI is an approach that promises to "close the gap" between these divergent points of view and make it possible in a practical way to include most young children with disabilities in natural settings. We undertake a thorough consideration of ABI and its necessity as a foundation for inclusion in Chapter 4.

Developmentally Appropriate Practice

Developmentally appropriate practice (DAP) represents a significant national trend that, over the past fifteen years, has focused attention on ensuring that programs and services provided to young children birth through age eight take into account their developmental status and individual needs. The concept of DAP has been formulated and expressed by the National Association for the Education of Young Children (NAEYC). It originated from a growing concern that programs for young children were failing to provide for the developmental needs of young children, due partly to pressures for specific skill development and academic readiness and content. NAEYC provided a definition of developmental appropriateness (Bredekamp, 1987) that has two dimensions: age appropriateness and individual appropriateness. Age appropriateness states that those who work with young children should have a thorough understanding of their typical development (growth and change) and that learning and play environments and experiences should be planned to address their developmental needs. Individual appropriateness requires that the unique developmental differences of young children be recognized and that the experiences which children receive in programs match their developmental abilities.

In the revised edition of *Developmentally Appropriate Practice in Early Childhood Programs* (Bredekamp & Copple, 1997), NAEYC provides a position statement and guidelines for implementing DAP is early childhood settings for young children from infancy through age eight. The necessity of making accommodations and adaptations for children with disabilities in early childhood programs and the importance and relevance of the inclusion movement are highlighted in the document. NAEYC provides important guidelines for implementing developmentally appropriate practice that may all be viewed as consistent with successful inclusion. One in particular that was included in the first edition of the NAEYC document is presented here because of its specific relevance: "programs provide for a wider range of developmental interests and abilities than the chronological age range of the group would suggest. Adults are prepared to meet the needs of children who exhibit unusual interests and skills outside the normal developmental range." Keep in mind that DAP is an important theme throughout this book. Also remember that developmental appropriateness must be viewed in the context of cultural diversity (see Chapter 8). Developmentally appropriate practice is addressed in detail in Chapter 5.

Before we move on to a consideration of collaboration, a point should be made here about the relationship among the last three terms/concepts: positive behavioral supports, activity-based intervention, and developmentally appropriate practice. Novick (1993) summarized the relationship among them by suggesting that activity-based intervention and developmentally appropriate practice converge because they put the child at the center (child-centered). She points out: "Both approaches view children as self-directed human beings, and emphasize choice and the development of problem-solving skills and curiosity." (See Figure 1–1.)

Collaboration

To collaborate means to work together toward a common goal. Parents and other family members of children with disabilities, when asked what has been their greatest challenge in getting services, often say that it was getting various professionals and agencies to share information, to work together, and to relate to the child and family as a unit. Including children with disabilities in natural settings (child care centers, nursery and preschools, kindergartens and early grades) makes collaboration even more important, while increasing its complexity. Special educators, therapists, and other specialists must communicate and coordinate with caregivers, early childhood educators, and teachers. Hanson

Figure 1–1 Young children thrive in supportive, developmentally appropriate settings.

and Widerstrom (1993) reviewed the importance of collaboration to successful integration and noted that collaboration is essential in efforts to include especially young children with disabilities in natural settings. Bruder (1998) has discussed the necessity of providing support and training related to collaboration for child care providers, along with other assistance, if we are to expect them to include young children with diverse needs in their programs.

Partnerships with Families

While collaboration is the process that should occur among professionals who serve the same young child and that child's family, partnerships are relationships between families and professionals. Members of a partnership assume a somewhat equal voice and influence, and each party has an opportunity to make significant contributions to a common goal. The existence of a partnership with a family suggests the need for family members to be empowered and enabled. Family empowerment is the belief by professionals that the family's expertise about their needs and their child's needs should be recognized, supported, and nurtured (Dunst, Trivette, & Deal, 1994). Partnerships with families and family empowerment are consistent with our federal legislative mandates to provide early childhood special education services that are "family-centered" and that expect us to view a young child with a disability in the context of her/his family unit. As professionals in the disciplines of early childhood education, early childhood special education, and child and family studies, we have long had as a part of our training an emphasis on parents and families. However, that training, both preservice and in-service, tended to focus more on family development and change, the importance of parent involvement, and our legal responsibilities, rather than learning to actively engage families as partners in the process of caring for and educating their young children.

One promising strategy to improve the abilities of professionals to partner with the families of infants and toddlers with disabilities was offered by Winton and DiVenere (1995). They suggested that we must not fail "to model what we preach"; that is, we must find innovative ways to have families be partners in our programs for the preparation of personnel. If you do not become comfortable with, learn methods for, and gain experience in partnering when you are in your training program, then you are ill prepared to practice it on the job. We are concerned in particular with young children, including the beginning of their formal schooling in kindergarten and first grade. While the partnership between parents/families and school personnel is important throughout the school years, it may be especially important early on. In a review of the history and current status of parent and school partnerships, Connors and Epstein (1995) point out that "the roles of families and schools have evolved from separate functions to shared and overlapping functions and responsibilities for children's learning and development." They further note that we must develop new approaches for all participants (teachers, family members, and students).

Family-Centered Services

This approach to the delivery of early intervention (birth to thirty-six months) is rooted in federal legislation (PL 99-457, Part H) and its subsequent implementation (Part C of 1997 IDEA). The fundamental idea behind family-centered services is that services to infants and toddlers with disabilities must not be delivered in a way that fails to consider the child as a part of the family unit, and that the family's participation—in ways that take advantage of their strengths, needs, and wishes—is essential. Family-centered services recognize that families are at different places developmentally, and that professionals are obligated to assist them to become more active partners, if they desire, and to foster the empowerment and enablement of families. So the delivery of family-centered services requires us to partner with our families at every level, from planning and intervening to evaluating effectiveness of our services. While the concept of family-centered services has been applied primarily to the services provided to infants and toddlers with disabilities and their families, for our purposes, we expand the concept to directly relate to the families of preschoolers and young children beginning their formal schooling in kindergarten and beyond. This text illustrates the close connection between family-centered service and partnerships with parents/families. Pearl (1993) emphasizes that family empowerment is an important part of the family-centered approach to caring for young children with special needs. (See Figure 1–2.)

Transdisciplinary Teaming

The next key term/concept that we will address in this section of Chapter 1 is transdisciplinary teaming. The transdisciplinary approach to assessing children, planning services for them, and providing intervention and care is important for successful inclusion. Bruder and Bologna (1993) suggest that on a transdisciplinary team "the members share roles and purposefully cross discipline boundaries. The communication style in this type of model involves continuous give and take between all the members of the team (especially the parents) on a reg-

Figure 1–2 The family-centered approach empowers families as partners with professionals in planning and carrying out early childhood education and intervention.

ular, planned basis." There is no doubt that we have professional growth and changes to make before we are able to say that transdisciplinary teams are prevalent in the delivery of services to young children with disabilities. Transdisciplinary teams are groups of professionals, as well as family members, who work closely together for the good of the child and family. McGonigel, Woodruff, and Roszmann-Millican (1994) highlight the importance of the transdisciplinary team for the delivery of family-centered early intervention. They remind us, however, that while Part C of IDEA requires a team approach for some early intervention services, it does not specify how that team must work together (e.g., in a transdisciplinary fashion).

Self-Determination

A fundamental goal that we have as parents of young children, or as caregivers or teachers, is to provide experiences and opportunities that foster the development of independence, self-reliance, and self-determination. Much of what we view as developmentally appropriate and best and effective practice has to do with facilitating the abilities of young children to initiate behaviors (such as expressive language development or social interactions), to make sound choices, and to assume responsibility for their actions. Wehmeyer, Martin, and Sands (1998) define self-determination as "acting as the primary causal agent in one's life and making choices and decisions regarding one's quality of life free from undue external influence or interference." A frequently expressed criticism of special education has been that it fails to provide adequate opportunities for children to develop self-determination because it tends to be highly teacher controlled and directed, with regard to both what the activity is and what the consequences and reward structure will be. Whether you view this as a fair criticism or not, it is clear that responsible and effective inclusive settings are more likely to provide most children with disabilities opportunities to develop self-determination. This is contingent upon the willingness of caregivers or teachers to provide positive behavioral supports at the level needed by individual children, including those who may not initiate as much because of their level of disability.

Ecological Approach

The fundamental tenet of the ecological systems perspective, developed and described by Bronfenbrenner (1994), is that a child's development is inseparable from her/his surroundings and the settings in which she/he functions (the ecology). If we are to understand how children, including children with special needs, develop and what educators can do to enhance their learning, we must take into account the interactions between and among five systems. Bronfenbrenner has conceptualized them as a concentric circle, with the individual (child) at the center, including the microsystem, the mesosystem, the exosystem, the macrosystem, and the chronosystem. Microsystems refer to a child's most immediate settings where interactions with other people occur, such as home for a young child or peer group for an adolescent. The mesosystem is the interrelations among contexts of the microsystem in which children actively participate. The relationship between the school and home would be a good example. The exosystem includes settings that influence a child's development but in which the child does not play a direct role, for example, the executive board of a child care center or the parents' workplaces. The macrosystem represents a set of ideological and institutional patterns of a particular culture or subculture. For example, how is a young child affected by living in a society that does not give priority to prenatal care? The last of the five contexts is the chronosystem, which refers to changes that occur over time specific to the child and the environment. An example of this is the impact of divorce on children, or the effect on the availability and quality of early intervention services when a family moves from one state to another.

For a comprehensive review of the ecological systems perspective as it relates to the delivery of early childhood special education services, the reader is referred to a work by Thurman (1997). Also in several of the following chapters in your book you will encounter references to and examples of how ecological factors impact the planning and delivering of inclusive early childhood education. (See Figure 1–3.)

Transitions

Transitions refer to the changes made by children as they move from one type of service delivery setting or program to another. Thinking in terms of young children with special needs, these transitions might be, for example, from a neonatal intensive care unit (NICU) to home, from home and a home-visiting program to an early childhood intervention program, from home to a family day care home, from a segregated early intervention, clinic-based program to an inclusive infant or toddler group child care program, from an early intervention program guided by an individualized family service plan (IFSP) to a public

Figure 1–3 An important part of Kyle's, his sister's, and his Mother's ecology is the swimming pool.

school preschool classroom guided by an IEP, or from a preschool setting to kindergarten.

Successful inclusion is dependent upon careful and systematic planning for transition (Fowler & Hazel, 1996), taking into account the perspectives, needs, and concerns of all the stakeholders, including the child, family, and both the sending and receiving programs. At various points in the book you will be provided examples of how transitions are carried out effectively, resulting in a successful and responsible inclusion process. You will also read about how a lack of attention to transitions can interfere with the delivery of early childhood education. Transitioning planning as a formal process is required as a part of the IFSP as children and their families move from early intervention to preschool services. However, formal planning is not legally mandated for transitions from preschool to kindergarten, or from one early childhood grade level to another. Fowler and Hazel (1996) suggest that the biggest barrier to transition planning often is the lack of time available for staff to meet, communicate, and develop systematic plans. Assume that you are applying for a kindergarten teaching position in which there is a clear expectation that you will include several children with varying types and levels of severity of disability. An appropriate question, along with what types of ongoing training and support can you expect, would be to what extent will you be provided the opportunity, time, and resources necessary to be a part of transitioning planning, as either the sending or receiving teacher?

Person and Family-First Language

The last of our twelve themes/concepts/terms is person and family-first language. In 1990, Public Law 101-476: Education of the Handicapped Act

Amendments was passed, making the third amendment to the original legislation enacted in 1975—Public Law 94-142: Education for All Handicapped Children Act. This amendment changed the title of the law to Individuals with Disabilities Education Act (IDEA). The change in name represented the culmination of a growing awareness on the part of professionals as well as consumers (families and persons with disabilities) that the time had come to formally and legally recognize that a person is a person first, and that the disability is secondary. The use of "person first" language leads us to avoid terms such as "Down syndrome girl," "blind child," or "crack baby." Rather, we will put the person first, for example, "child with a disability," "little sister with autism," or "my son has spina bifida." While this may sound like "political correctness" to some, to persons with disabilities and to those who advocate for them, it represents an important milestone in the evolution of our society's understanding of and response to persons with disabilities.

Additionally, we want to add a dimension to person first language specific to families. Families in which there are members with disabilities are families first. Like all families, they are diverse, but they have more in common with other families than attributes that separate them. So it is desirable to think about and refer to families in that manner, rather than to use terms such as "dysfunctional," "troubled," or "case." Certainly, as you will read in Chapter 2, there are issues and stressors that are frequently associated with families in which there is a young child with special needs. The point is that we are better served as professionals if our starting point in thinking about and serving families is to view them first as families (like our own families), and then as having uniqueness based on their individual circumstances, including the accommodations needed for a family member with a disability.

We presented twelve separate but related key terms/concepts that are themes throughout the book. Successful inclusion of infants, toddlers, preschoolers, and young, school-aged children in natural settings is made possible by the use of the strategies inherent in both activity-based intervention and child-centered behavioral supports. Developmentally appropriate practice emphasizes the importance of understanding the growth and development of young children, respecting individual differences, and seeing young children have experiences that are appropriate for their developmental needs. Family-centered services result when professionals collaborate and work as a transdisciplinary team and when they see themselves in a partnership with families. Now let us take a closer look at the justification, or rationale, for inclusion.

Why Inclusion?

Earlier we defined inclusion and noted that, while it does not mean exactly the same thing, its meaning evolved largely from the historical concepts in early childhood special education, that is, mainstreaming and integration. Bricker (1995) discusses the evolution of these terms, noting that mainstreaming refers to the "reentry of children with mild disabilities into regular classrooms." She notes that this term has not served very well when referring to young children. Integration has been used to describe "the systematic and careful combining of toddlers and preschool-aged children who had disabilities and those who did not in the same classroom setting," as opposed to segregation. Over the past few years, inclusion has gained broad acceptance as a term and process to replace mainstreaming and integration.

We begin our consideration of why inclusion is desirable by acknowledging that there are those who have strong reservations about the practice, particularly with regard to what has been referred to as full inclusion. Full inclusion would require that all children with disabilities, no matter how severe and regardless of their ability to function in natural settings, be included in those settings. Addressing in particular the inclusion of school-aged children, Shanker (1994, 1995) and Fuchs and Fuchs (1995) caution that those who advocate full inclusion do a disservice to some children with disabilities, as well as to their parents. They point out that the concept of "least restrictive environment," where children with disabilities are educated in the most normalized setting from which they can benefit, is more appropriate. For our purposes, we do not see inclusion as the best option for all young children with disabilities at all times. However, we will view an inclusive setting as desirable for many and a goal to work toward for most children and the inclusive process as desirable for all children with special needs. Certainly the wishes of the family are central to any decisions about placement. Simply stated, the family wants the specialized needs of their child met and they want their child seen as a child—not as a disability.

The rationale, or source of support, for inclusion of young children with disabilities in natural settings may be divided into four separate but related categories. Those categories are: ethical and commonsense arguments, positions taken by advocacy groups and professional organizations, legal mandates, and professional literature and study in support of inclusion. We will discuss each of these briefly. (See Figure 1–4.)

Figure 1–4 There are many strong arguments for including young children with disabilities in activities with their typically developing peers.

Ethical and Commonsense Arguments

Many of us have discovered that the more we know someone as a person the less noticeable their disability becomes. Think of a friend, family member, colleague, or child with whom you live, work or play who has a disability. Probably you think of many characteristics about this individual before you think of their disability. This perspective comes from experience and familiarity. For those of you who have had limited experiences with persons having disabilities, this point of view is more difficult to comprehend. Generally, the authors expect those of you who have will agree. While some wish to dismiss it, the distinction between handicap and disability is very meaningful to persons with disabilities, professionals, and family members who advocate for them. Many people have varied types and severities of disabilities. The extent to which these disabilities become handicaps is dependent to a large degree upon how individuals and society relate to them. Bicklen and Bogdan (1977) point out that we have a history in the United States of handicapping persons with disabilities by, for example, presuming that they must be sad, pitying them, overfocusing on their disability, treating them as children (when they are adults), avoiding them, making them the source of humor, or speaking for them.

How then are we to get to know people with disabilities as persons and avoid some of these handicapping behaviors? One fundamental answer to this question is for persons with disabilities to be included in, rather than excluded from, the typical activities and settings that people without disabilities experience. Common sense indicates that this should begin with young children, so they learn tolerance and understanding of differences. It is ethical to treat every person, including those with disabilities, with respect, kindness, and understanding. When people lack experience with and exposure to persons with disabilities, they have difficulty learning how to behave ethically toward disabled persons. Finally, the authors hasten to add that this argument for inclusion does not mean in any sense that persons with disabilities do not often have very specialized needs, sometimes extensive and complicated, making inclusion (as a setting as opposed to a process) difficult or impractical.

Positions Taken by Advocacy Groups and Professional Organizations

Over the past few years, a variety of organizations formalized their positions on the practice of inclusion. This is our second category for stating the rationale for inclusion. Professionals (and frequently families of children with disabilities) look to these organizations for leadership and guidance with regard to what represents desirable and effective practices. Essentially all of the relevant professional organizations and advocacy groups for persons with disabilities appear to support inclusion. However, they frequently express concern that it not be applied as an absolute (full inclusion), that it be guided by the individual needs of children and their families, and that it be viewed as a process rather than a form of service or environment.

The Council for Exceptional Children (CEC) is the primary national organization for persons concerned with the delivery of services to children and youth with special needs. There are several divisions within the CEC. One of those divisions, the Division for Early Childhood (DEC), focuses particularly on young children and their families. DEC (1993) provides a position statement on inclusion, an excerpt of which reads as follows: "Inclusion, as a value, supports the right of all children, regardless of their diverse abilities, to participate actively in natural settings within their communities. A natural setting is one in which the child would spend time had he or she not had a disability." Another document provided by this organization, *DEC Recommended Practices: Indicators of Quality in Programs for Infants and Young Children with Special Needs and Their Families* (1993), states that one indicator of quality intervention is that "natural community settings are developed and accessible as an option for early intervention."

As was noted earlier when developmentally appropriate practice was defined, the National Association for the Education of Young Children (NAEYC) provides guidelines and a position statement (Bredekamp, 1987) that defines developmental appropriateness as having two dimensions: age appropriateness and individual appropriateness. The importance placed on viewing young children as unique and individual in their growth and development can, at least generally, be considered consistent with the concept of inclusion. Specifically, one of the guidelines states that "some mainstreamed (inclusive) situations will demand a wider range of expectations." That is, the caregivers and early childhood educators need to be prepared to address a wider range of developmental interests and abilities of young children.

While inclusion was not addressed specifically in the original NAEYC document on developmental appropriateness, a subsequent publication (Bredekamp & Rosegrant, 1992) clarified that developmentally appropriate practice was intended to apply equally to children with disabilities (special needs). McLean and Odom (1993) compared the positions taken by the two organizations noted above, DEC and NAEYC, with regard to their recommended practices for serving young children with and without disabilities. On the subject of inclusion, they found substantive agreement between the National Association for the Education of Young Children and the Council for Exceptional Children. McLean and Odom point out that one potential source of disagreement is resolved. Both groups view the notion of age as meaning chronologically age appropriate for children with disabilities. That is, children with disabilities will more likely be included in settings with other young children similar in chronological age rather than developmental age.

More recently in the revised version of the NAEYC document on developmentally appropriate practices (Bredekamp & Copple, 1997) the trend toward inclusion is specifically acknowledged and supported as it relates to guidelines for providing services to all young children. Also recently Smith, Miller, and Bredekamp (1998) have reviewed the collaborative work done by NAEYC and DEC over the past few years in support of quality inclusion and have described how it fits with the early childhood theories of Vygotsky. Vygotsky emphasized that for young children with disabilities it is important to stress the development of social skills with adults and more capable peers. He noted that for children with disabilities the most significant difficulty is their isolation from peers who do not have disabilities.

While the organizations noted above focus on young children, there are organizations, concerned with the needs of school-aged children, providing considerable support for inclusion. We give only two examples here, although support is broad-based and expanding. The National Association of State Boards of Education published a report (1992) entitled *Winners All: A Call for Inclusive Schools*. In this report, the association advocates restructuring of schools to facilitate inclusion, while protecting the rights of students with disabilities to receive the specialized and support services that they frequently require. The second example of support from an organization with emphasis on school-aged children is a monograph entitled *Inclusion: Moving beyond Our Fears* (1994), published by the Phi Delta Kappa professional organization. One key theme in the series of articles presented in this monograph is that a "can do" attitude on the part of educators, along with support and positive experiences, can go a long way toward making inclusion a successful process in schools.

Bowe (1995) points out that the positions taken by various advocacy organizations for particular disabilities are mixed with regard to their support for inclusion. Some are highly supportive, while others are skeptical. One concern is that full inclusion might be implemented and that the highly specialized needs of some children with disabilities would be ignored or minimized. Organizations with emphasis on sensory disabilities (hearing and vision) in particular appear to have concerns about inclusion. The United Cerebral Palsy Association and the National Down Syndrome Society have taken positions strongly in favor of inclusion. The concern and disagreement present among these advocacy groups comes in large part from the belief that, as Bowe points out, "inclusion places the location of services above their appropriateness." In other words, placing children in a setting that is inclusive could become the goal, rather than placing children in the "least restrictive" and most "normal" setting to their needs. Progressing through this text complements your own experiences and your previous education. You will enhance your understanding of how the positions taken by various professionals and advocacy groups fit into the broader framework of inclusion in services for young children and their families.

Legal Mandates

There are no laws—state, federal, or otherwise—which absolutely require that young children with disabilities be served in inclusive settings. However, laws exist which require that inclusive settings (e.g., child care programs) not discriminate against the involvement of children with disabilities. These laws support the rights of young children with disabilities and their families to have access to services in inclusive settings, when those settings meet the criteria of being most appropriate and least restrictive for an individual child's special needs. While we don't intend to explore this subject in great detail here, there are three areas of legislation particularly important. They include legislation that: (1) prohibits discrimination against children with disabilities in various public and private service delivery settings; (2) establishes the right of infants, toddlers, preschoolers, and school-aged children to a free and appropriate education delivered in the least restrictive and most natural and normal setting, along with peers who do not have disabilities; and (3) requires the enrollment of children with disabilities in the Head Start program.

The Americans with Disabilities Act (ADA) (1990) was implemented on July 26, 1992. This fundamental civil rights legislation prohibits private employers, state and local governments, employment agencies, and labor unions from discriminating against qualified individuals with disabilities in job application procedures, hiring, firing, advancement, compensation, job training, and other terms, conditions, and privileges of employment. Perhaps you know individuals who benefited from this legislation, or maybe you know of agencies that struggled to comply with ADA. One of the sections of ADA addresses public accommodations that specifically include child care centers and programs. In a paper provided by the Child Care Law Center (1992) the ADA provision related to eligibility for services states:

> A child care center may not use eligibility requirements that exclude or segregate individuals with disabilities unless they are necessary for the operation of the business (a very high standard to meet) or necessitated by safety considerations, and even then they must be based on actual risks and not generalizations or stereotypes. A childcare center may exclude individuals with disabilities if they pose a direct threat to themselves or others that cannot be mitigated by modifications in policies, practices, or procedures or by the provision of auxiliary aids. The services must be offered in the most integrated setting appropriate to the needs of the individual.

We have now had sufficient time for the law to be tested in the courts. Gil-de Lamadrid (1996) reviewed several cases and found, for example, that toileting skills may not be used as a criteria for admission to Head Start centers. She also reported on a case in which a child care center refused to make certain accommodations (assistance with leg braces and diapering and architectural barriers) for a four-year-old child with cerebral palsy. In the settlement, the dismissed child was readmitted, placed in an age-appropriate class, and provided the assistance and accommodations requested.

In 1972, Head Start began operating under a congressional mandate requiring that a minimum, often 10 percent, of the children served by a grantee have diagnosed disabilities. In their extensive historical review of Head Start, Zigler and Muenchow (1992) state that the services provided to children with disabilities have become one of Head Start's most commendable features. While some disagree with this supposition, they also assert that Head Start's inclusion of children with disabilities inspired PL 99-457, requiring special education services for three- to five-year-olds as well as the emphasis on mainstreaming and the parent involvement and family support focus in Part C of the infant and toddler section of the law. New regulations and performance standards set the stage for Head Start to continue serving as a primary, least restrictive environment placement for preschoolers. Under IDEA, local school systems may designate a Heard Start program as a primary service for these children, or families may choose a Heard Start program for their preschooler over what might be offered by their school system. We will examine more specifically how Head Start programs address the needs of young children with disabilities in Chapter 11. (See Figure 1–5.)

As noted above, it is not our intention here to undertake a thorough review of the legislation, occurring over the past three decades, that shaped public policy in the delivery of special education services to young children and their families. The reader, if not already familiar with these laws, will find numerous

Figure 1–5 Head Start has a mandate to include young children with special needs.

references to them in the early childhood special education literature and in the current literature in early childhood education and child care. For example, Hebbeler, Smith, and Black (1991) provide a historical review of legislation specific to early childhood special education occurring from 1965 to the early nineties. Bowe (1995) includes a chapter in his text on early childhood special education, which explains the Individuals with Disabilities Education Act (IDEA) and its implications for young children with special needs. Five laws are briefly introduced here. Public Law 94-142: The Education of the Handicapped Act was passed in 1975. This landmark legislation established the right of children and youth with disabilities to a free and appropriate public education, designed to meet their individual needs and delivered in the least restrictive environment. While the law covered children and youth aged three to twenty-one years, it allowed an exception whereby states, if their state laws did not so mandate, could choose not to serve preschoolers with disabilities. Most states did not, therefore, serve that population.

As Noonan and McCormick (1993) point out, PL 94-142 is important to early childhood special education because it represented a formal endorsement of the importance of and need for services for young children. In 1986 Public Law 99-457 amendments to PL 94-142 were passed. This legislation, which resulted from the long and determined advocacy of professionals and family members concerned especially for young children with special needs, required that states provide special education services to preschoolers. It also included Part H (renamed to be Part C in the 1997 IDEA reauthorization), a program designed to support states in the development over a five-year period of comprehensive services to infants and toddlers with disabilities and their families.

In 1990, PL 94-142 was again amended to be titled the Individuals with Disabilities Education Act (IDEA). This amendment was PL 101-476. IDEA was amended again in 1991, entitled PL 102-119. In this amendment, the requirement for provision of services to preschoolers with disabilities and infants and toddlers with disabilities and their families (Part H, now Part C) was continued and strengthened. Support was provided under PL 102-119 for states to continue their efforts for infants and toddlers and their families beyond the five-year planning period and into actual implementation and delivery of services. Part H of IDEA says that early intervention services are to be provided in "natural environments, including the home and community settings in which children without disabilities participate." This text frequently references Part C (formerly Part H) services for infants and toddlers and their families and Part B services for preschoolers with disabilities aged three to five.

This textbook highlights the relevance of these services to state and local education agency policies and practices in planning and delivering services, particularly the option of inclusion. Noonan and McCormick (1993) point out, specific to the mandates from legislation and subsequent court cases, that "the burden of proof rests with the educational agency in adjusting any placement other than a regular classroom for a child with a disability. Young children with special needs should be educated in a regular preschool or kindergarten unless there is substantial evidence that instruction in the regular environment cannot be effective." Lastly with regard to legislation, on June 4, 1997, the Individuals with Disabilities Education Act (IDEA) Amendments of 1997 were enacted into law as Public Law 105-17. Under this legislation Part H (the early intervention part) became Part C on July 1, 1998, and a requirement was made that IFSPs must specify natural environments (settings) in which services will be delivered, specify when they are not, and justify why they are not being provided to Part C eligible infants and toddlers and their families. Turnbull and Cilley (1999), both attorneys concerned with legal issues related to persons with disabilities, have provided a useful summary guide to understanding the 1997 amendments to IDEA. Specific to inclusion they have noted in the recent amendment to IDEA the emphasis on access by students with disabilities to the general curriculum, the role of the general educator in individualized education program (IEP) development, the requirement to justify in early intervention why natural environments are not used for services, and the strengthening and extending of the principle of least restrictive environment.

Research Support for Early Inclusion

Since the emphasis for least restrictive environment that came with PL 94-142 and the subsequent focus on mainstreaming and then integration in early childhood special education, we have had a substantial amount of research aimed at determining the effects of inclusion on the well-being of children with disabilities, children without disabilities, parents/families, and professionals. There is now a history of some twenty years of research and evaluation of the impacts of inclusion. Peck (1993) points out that the field of early intervention clearly demonstrated "the value and feasibility of integrating young children with disabilities into programs with their non-disabled peers." The preponderance of evidence indicates that inclusion has the potential to be a positive practice for all involved, that is, all young children, parents and family members, and professionals. Now, attention focuses on successfully implementing inclusion (Baker, Wang, Walberg, 1995; Bricker, 1995; Peck, 1993), rather than researching whether or not programs for young children should be inclusive. Let us turn our attention to some general guidelines regarding the implementation of inclusion. Certainly this topic, using activity-based intervention and child-centered behavioral supports as the foundation, is the heart of the text—how to make inclusion a successful process.

One question asked when implementing inclusion is: What are the "pieces of the puzzle" we need in order to make inclusion work? Bricker (1995) suggests that there are three factors including attitude, resources, and curricula. Positive and constructive attitudes about young children with disabilities on the part of teachers, caregivers, family members, and children must be developed and nurtured. Those responsible for implementing inclusion must have access to resources, including specialists, opportunities to collaborate and function as team members, and the right kinds of environments and equipment. Activity-based curricula and naturalistic teaching and caregiving approaches not only support interaction among children but increase the comfort level caregivers and early childhood educators feel.

In an article describing the successful inclusion of a young child with Down syndrome, the authors (Guida, Pirsos, Schempp, & Cuthbertson, 1994) emphasize preparing children before inclusion begins, building a team, and identifying resources (such as personnel, environments, and peers). Richey, Richey, and Webb (1996) identify eight elements that assist in reducing stress and concerns in preparing caregivers and families for inclusion of children, infants, and toddlers in child care settings. These elements are planning and preparation, support and information meetings for families, use of experts as resources, applying activity-based intervention, providing resource materials on disabilities, fostering communication and experiences with people having disabilities, using people resources such as volunteers, and knowing when and why inclusion may not be appropriate. Stainback, Stainback, and Stefanich (1996) examined inclusion with particular attention to curriculum. They point out that learning objectives should be flexible, activities must be modified, a team approach is essential, and peer involvement is needed.

A synthesis of the sources of information noted above regarding what is important for inclusion yields several major points:

1. Positive attitudes on the part of all those involved are of great importance. They are engendered by knowledge of disabilities, exposure to people with disabilities, feelings of being collaborators and partners, and open communication. Positive attitudes are fostered by beginning the inclusion process early (see Figure 1–6.).
2. Planning and preparation are central to successful inclusion. Caregivers and teachers should have opportunities to plan with families and specialists for the inclusion of a child with special needs. Children, both those having disabilities and those who do not, should be prepared for inclusion.
3. All professionals and family members must invest themselves in the collaborative process. We discussed previously in the chapter the importance of partnerships, collaboration, and teaming.
4. Using the various resources that are often available—including, for example, specialists, Part H (C) services for infants and toddlers, volunteers, students,

Figure 1–6 The inclusive process often begins in infant and toddler child care programs.

specialized equipment, and print and video resources specific to inclusionary practices and disabilities—is beneficial. Journals in early childhood special education as well as in early childhood/child and family science and magazines, such as *Exceptional Parent,* are further examples of resources.

5. Collaborators must review curriculum, and program activities must be reviewed so that individual needs (objectives) of children with disabilities can be met in the context of the regular routines and activities of the inclusive setting. Activity-based intervention is a primary means of addressing curricular issues.

Taken together, these five interrelated factors are seen as significant contributors to successful inclusion of young children with disabilities, whether the setting is an infant-toddler child care program, a preschool, or a kindergarten classroom.

Merging Disciplines

Parents and other family members of young children with disabilities want their children to have the specialized services that will allow their disabled children to develop competence and independence and will help them either remove or minimize the negative impacts of the disability. Parents hope (and more recently demand) that the services needed and received by their children are planned and delivered in a way that makes them "fit" together in the best interest of the child and the child's family. Parents and families want professionals to function collaboratively; they want those collaborators to treat them (the family) as equal partners. While the history of the development and delivery of quality services to children with disabilities is significant, it is only in the last decade or so that emphasis shifted to the necessity of professionals working together. Professionals must synthesize their divergent views of a child and formulate a unified plan—paying attention to what is common in their philosophies and practices, rather than what makes them "special." Another way to put this is that parents and families care little about which professional knows what, as long as the collective expertise of the professionals who serve them and their child adds up to services that address the needs of their child.

Various disciplines play a part in the delivery of services to young children with disabilities. With regard to infants and toddlers, Part C of IDEA indicates that there are eleven distinct disciplines, or categories of personnel, that may be required for meeting the needs of a particular child. They are special educators, speech and language pathologists and audiologists, occupational therapists, physical therapists, psychologists, social workers, nurses, nutritionists, family therapists, orientation and mobility specialists, and pediatricians and other physicians. Note that early childhood educators, caregivers, infant specialists, or child and family specialists are not included. While the list of professionals who may be involved is not extensive for preschoolers and children beginning their formal schooling, there are still various disciplines whose expertise may be necessary for meeting the individual needs of the young child with a disability. For example, the kindergarten teacher who has a student who is blind included in her classroom will probably need support and technical assistance from a vision specialist in order to manage such things as mobility, classroom arrangement, adaptation of materials, and the like.

The challenge we face is how to ensure that young children with disabilities receive the specialized services they require in the context of an inclusive (natural) setting. Traditional "pull out" services—where children were removed from, for example, the classroom in order for them to receive therapies or other specialized services—do not typically fit well with the process of inclusion. The notion of embedding specialized services in the context of typical routines, plans, and child-initiated activities of an inclusive setting (activity-based intervention) continues to be foreign to many professionals; their training and experience have not prepared them to merge their disciplinary expertise with that of others for the purpose of advancing the development of a young child with a disability in an inclusive setting. It is certainly true that many professionals feel strongly that one-on-one intervention in therapeutic settings away from natural settings is necessary for many children with disabilities, especially those with severe and comprehensive disabilities. The position taken by the authors of this textbook is that when an inclusive setting is deemed by families and professionals as desirable and appropriate for the individual needs of a child, it is critical that professionals transcend (transdisciplinary) their disciplines and merge their expertise to facilitate inclusion.

In particular, we address the need for a merging of and collaboration among early childhood educators, early childhood special educators, and child and family specialists. It is, of course, most difficult for professionals in these disciplines to work together when they lack experiences, models to observe and emulate, and training in which collaboration is valued and taught. For example, if you use this textbook for a class in which there are students preparing to serve young children and/or their families through various disciplines and in varied capacities, then you have an excellent opportunity to consider these issues and concepts related to collaboration and merging of disciplines. You may even have the opportunity in conjunction with the class to practice collaborative teaming through participation in field and practicum experiences in inclusive settings. However, if all students of this class (or a significant majority) share the same disciplinary major, you and your classmates will have difficulty studying and evaluating the process of merging multiple disciplines specific to the provision of services and programs for young children with disabilities and their families.

An appropriate question for any individual engaged in a graduate or undergraduate preservice training program or an in-service program in which they are preparing to better serve young children and their families is: When and how will I have the experiences that will help me know how my discipline fits with others and how to be a collaborator? For example, students in child and family studies need to know something about managing groups of young children and about curriculum. Students in early childhood education need a thorough understanding of child development and family influences. Students in early childhood special education need to know about typical development, developmentally appropriate practice, and early childhood curricula and methods.

Stedman (1990), in a summary of research on quality programs for young children, asserts that the key to quality programs has more to do with the attributes of the teacher than the setting or program model. If the early childhood educators, early childhood special educators, or caregivers are prepared in a manner that allows them to think and behave in ways consistent with inclusion, then they will be better prepared to meet the challenges of their chosen profession. Miller (1992) argues that the time has come for personnel preparation programs to cease training professionals in early childhood and early childhood special education through segregated programs. She suggests that doing so is both immoral and inefficient, and that categorical certification (licensure) programs may foster the continuation of segregated (noninclusive) services for young children and their families. Stayton and Miller (1993) describe how some states combined the standards established for the preservice preparation of early childhood and early childhood special educators in a manner that better prepares individuals from both disciplines to manage the process of inclusion.

Summary

Twelve themes/terms/concepts, considered central in making use of this textbook, are presented in Chapter 1. Several definitions of inclusion were given, and taken together, they define inclusion as an approach and process of including young children with various types and levels of severity of disabilities in the same services, programs, and settings as young children without disabilities. For our purposes, that includes such places as family day care homes; child care programs for infants, toddlers, and preschoolers; nursery schools; mother's day out programs; Head Start centers; and kindergarten/first through third grade classrooms. These settings facilitate inclusion by applying developmentally appropriate practices, principles of positive behavioral support, and activity-based early intervention. Positive behavioral supports (see Chapter 3) are nonpunitive methods intended to foster desirable behavior and prevent undesirable behavior by understanding the developmental needs of young children, designing and managing appropriate play and learning environments, and lifestyle enhancements.

Activity-based intervention is "a child-directed, transactional approach that embeds intervention on children's individual goals and objectives in routine, planned, or child-initiated activities and uses logically occurring antecedents and consequences to develop functional and generalizable skills" (see Chapter 4). Developmentally appropriate practice is a concept originated by the National Association for the Education of Young Children. It includes guidelines and standards intended to support the provision of services to young children that are appropriate for their developmental and individual needs (see Chapter 5).

In order to accomplish inclusion, professionals from various disciplines must collaborate and partner with parents/families. The idea of family-centered services closely relates to the notion of partnerships between professionals and parents/families. Family-centered services view the child as an integral part of the family unit. These services provide opportunities for families to participate and partner in ways that fit their unique needs and that assist family members in becoming "empowered." Transdisciplinary teaming requires that professionals cross their disciplinary boundaries and share their expertise to focus on the needs of young children with disabilities and their families.

The rationale, or justification, for inclusion is described as having four parts. The first is the ethical and commonsense argument. Second, we now have a foundation of support for inclusion from relevant professional organizations, such as NAEYC and the Division for Early Childhood of the Council for Exceptional Children, and from many disability advocacy organizations. The third rationale is legislation. It includes laws that emphasize the importance of children with disabilities receiving services in the "least restrictive" and "natural settings" as well as laws prohibiting discrimination against persons with disabilities, including the access of young children with disabilities to child care programs. The fourth rationale is the empirical support (research) for inclusion. The preponderance of evidence indicates that inclusion, implemented correctly, is highly desirable and has the potential to positively impact all participants.

Some general guidelines for successful inclusion are provided in the chapter. Five categories were discussed, including (1) the importance of fostering and maintaining positive attitudes about inclusion; (2) careful planning and preparation; (3) collaborating and partnering with families; (4) making use of the various resources often available; and (5) using approaches, like activity-based intervention and child-centered supports, that make the ability to embed the specialized goals and objectives of young children with disabilities in the normal routines and activities of inclusive settings practical.

The last topic addressed in Chapter 1 focused on the need for merging the various disciplines central to the success of inclusion. Specifically, if early childhood educators, early childhood special educators, child and family specialists, and the professionals from disciplines are to collaborate and facilitate inclusion, then training programs must prepare them for collaboration and teaming and they must see and participate in models of successful merging of disciplines. Preservice training programs—particularly in early childhood, early childhood special education, and child and family studies—at present often have unnecessary barriers and distinctions that are inconsistent with the goal of preparing professionals in those disciplines who are committed to and prepared for collaboration.

Chapter 1 Suggested Activities and Resources

Activities

1. Read and synthesize a journal article (from the list of journals given under Selected Resources) on one of the key terms/concepts presented in this chapter. Share the article with other class members, review the information, and compile a resource packet.

2. Conduct an in-class debate on the topic of "full inclusion" for young children with disabilities. Require teams (two to four members each) to prepare their arguments based on what they find in the professional literature, rather than opinions.

3. Visit an infant/toddler, preschool, Head Start, or kindergarten that is inclusive. Interview the caregivers or teachers about their inclusion experiences. Report your observations and interview findings to the class. For your observation, you might simply make notes or you may use an observation instrument—if you have access to one. In your interviews of the caregivers or teachers, be sure to ask them how their attitudes were shaped over time with regard to inclusion. What made them feel OK or not so good about inclusion?

4. Invite a panel of five to seven family members (include if possible fathers, grandparents, and siblings) to class to discuss their experiences with inclusion. Include family representatives whose children have been, are presently, and will in the future be in inclusive settings.

5. If you have classmates representing different disciplines, create small groups (three to five members each) in which members from different disciplines are represented. Discuss the advantages related to collaboration, teaming, and merging of disciplines.

6. Interview faculty members in various disciplines (for example, early childhood, early childhood special education, child and family studies, psychology, physical therapy, or speech therapy) about their views on training individuals to accomplish inclusion. You might do this in pairs, to share notes and then present your findings to the class.

7. Using the documents from NAEYC and DEC (see Selected Resources) review the guidelines, standards, and quality indicators paying particular attention to those that relate in your opinion most closely to inclusion, natural environments, and least restrictive environments.

8. Invite a representative or representatives from a local, district, or state level advocacy organization, such as the United Cerebral Palsy Association or the Down Syndrome Society, to come to class and share their position on and experiences with inclusion.

9. Contact your area Infant and Toddler Program (Part C) and share how they are organized, how the service coordinators help families find and use inclusive programs, and how they work toward the transition of children to preschool programs, particularly with regard to the continuation of inclusionary practices.

10. Contact your local education agency and ask them to come to class and share how their system is organized to provide services to preschoolers and kindergartners and first graders with disabilities, particularly when the need is for an inclusive setting.

Selected Resources

1. For an overview of activity-based early intervention, see the book authored by Diane Bricker and Juliann J. Woods Cripe entitled *An Activity-Based Approach to Early Intervention,* published by Paul H. Brookes Publishing Co. in 1992.

2. While there are numerous journals in which you will find articles specific to inclusion and young children, here are some that are prominent: *Journal of Early Intervention, Topics in Early Childhood Special Education, Exceptional Parent, Young Children, Dimensions, Teaching Exceptional Children, Exceptional Children,* and *Childcare Information Exchange.*

3. For a complete list of the guidelines for developmentally appropriate practice, see *Developmentally Appropriate Practice in Early Childhood Programs Serving Children from Birth through Age Eight: Expanded Edition,* edited by Sue Bredekamp and published by NAEYC in 1987.

4. For information about recommended practices in early childhood special education, see *DEC Recommended Practices: Indicators of Quality in Programs for Infants and Young Children with Special Needs and Their Families,* available from the Division for Early Childhood of the Council for Exceptional Children, and published in 1993.

5. To find how services to infants and toddlers with disabilities and their families are organized and delivered in your state, see the *1996 Resource Guide of the Exceptional Parent* magazine. *Exceptional Parent* publishes an annual guide that includes this information, along with a great deal of additional information of particular interest to families of children with disabilities.

6. For definitions of terms in early intervention/early childhood special education, see *The Early Intervention Dictionary: A Multidisciplinary Guide to Terminology* by Jeanine G. Coleman, published 1993 by Woodbine House.

7. For a helpful and current review of the status of inclusion in programs for young children, see Diane Bricker's article in the *Journal of Early Intervention,* Vol. 19, No. 3, 1995, entitled "The Challenge of Inclusion."

References

Abraham, M. R., Morris, L. M., & Wald, P. J. (1993). *Inclusive Early Childhood Education.* Tucson, AZ: Communication Skill Builders.

Baker, E. T., Wang, M. C., & Walberg, H. J. (1995). The effects of inclusion on learning. *Educational Leadership, 52*(4), 33–35.

Bicklen, D., & Bogdan, R. (1977). Handicapism in America. In B. Blatt, D. Bickler, & R. Bogdan (Eds.), *An Alternative Textbook in Special Education:*

People, Schools, and Other Institutions (pp. 205–215). Denver, CO: Love Publishing Company.

Bowe, F. G. (1995). *Birth to Five: Early Childhood Special Education*. Albany, NY: Delmar Publishers.

Bredekamp, S. (Ed.). (1987). *Developmentally Appropriate Practice in Early Childhood Programs Serving Children from Birth through Age Eight: Expanded Edition*. Washington, D.C.: National Association for the Education of Young Children.

Bredekamp, S., & Copple, C. (Eds.). (1997). *Developmentally Appropriate Practice in Early Childhood Programs* (revised ed.). Washington, DC: National Association for the Education of Young Children.

Bredekamp, S., & Rosegrant, T. (1992). *Reaching Potentials: Appropriate Curriculum and Assessment for Young Children (Vol.1)*. Washington, DC: National Association for the Education of Young Children.

Bricker, D. (1995). The challenge of inclusion. *Journal of Early Intervention. 19*(3), 179–194.

Bricker, D., & Woods-Cripe, J. J. (1992). *An Activity-Based Approach to Early Intervention*. Baltimore: Paul H. Brookes Publishing Co.

Bronfenbrenner, U. (1994). Ecological models of human development. In T. Husen & T. N. Postlehwaite (Eds.), *International Encyclopedia of Education* (2nd ed., Vol. 3). Oxford: Pergamon Press/Elsevier Science.

Bruder, M. B. (1998). A collaborative model to increase the capacity of childcare providers to include young children with disabilities. *Journal of Early Intervention, 21*(2), 177–186.

Bruder, M. B., & Bologna, T. (1993). Collaboration and service coordination for effective early intervention. In W. Brown, S. K. Thurman, & L. F. Pearl (Eds.), *Family-Centered Early Intervention with Infants and Toddlers: Innovative Cross-Disciplinary Approaches* (pp. 103–127). Baltimore: Paul H. Brookes Publishing Co.

Child Care Law Center. (1992). *Implications of the Americans with Disabilities Act on Child Care Facilities*. San Francisco, CA: Author.

Connors, L. J., & Epstein J. L. (1995). Parent and school partnerships. In M. H. Bornstein (Ed.), *Handbook of Parenting: Volume 4 Applied and Practical Parenting* (pp. 437–458). Mahwah, NJ: Lawrence Erlbaum Associates, Publishers.

The Council for Exceptional Children. (1993, April). *DEC Statement on Inclusion*. Reston, VA: Author.

Dunst, C., Trivette, C., & Deal, A. (1994). *Enabling and Empowering Families: Principles and Guidelines for Practice* (2nd ed.). Cambridge, MA: Brookline.

Education of the Handicapped Act Amendments of 1986, PL 99-457. (October 8, 1986). Title 20 U.S.C. 1400 et seq: U.S. Statutes at Large. 100. 1145–1177.

Fowler, S., & Hazel, R. (1996). Planning transitions to support inclusion. In K. E. Allen & I. S. Schwartz, *The Exceptional Child: Inclusion in Early Childhood Education* (pp. 171-186). Albany, NY: Delmar Publishers.

Fuchs, D., & Fuchs, L. S. (1995). Sometimes separate is better. *Educational Leadership, 52*(4), 22–26.

Gil-de Lamadrid, M. (1996). Child care and the ADA: Litigation updates. *Exceptional Parent, 26*(2), 40–43.

Guida, J., Pirsos, S., Schempp, K., & Cuthbertson, D. (1994). Making inclusion work: Angela is supported by a circle of friends. *Exceptional Parent, 24*(10), 43–46.

Hanson, M. J., & Widerstrom, A. H. (1993). Consultation and collaboration: Essentials of integration efforts for young children. In C. A. Peck, S. L. Odom, & D. D. Bricker (Eds.), *Integrating Young Children with Disabilities into Community Programs: Ecological Perspectives Research and Implementation* (pp. 149–168). Baltimore, MD: Paul H. Brookes Publishing Co.

Hebbeler, K. M., Smith, B. J., & Black, T. L. (1991). Federal early childhood special education policy: A model for the improvement of services for children with disabilities. *Exceptional Children, 58*(2), 104–111.

Kerzner-Lipsky, D., & Gartner, A. (1994). Inclusion: What it is, what is it not and why it matters. *Exceptional Parent, 24*(10), 36–38.

LaMontagne, M. J., Danbom, K., & Buchanan, M. (1998). Developmentally and individually appropriate practices. In L. J. Johnson, M. J. LaMontagne, P. M. Elgas, & A. M. Bauer, *Early Childhood Education: Blending Theory, Blending Practice* (pp. 83–108). Baltimore, MD: Paul H. Brookes Publishing Co.

McGonigel, M. J., Woodruff, G., & Roszmann-Millican, M. (1994). The transdisciplinary team: A model for family-centered early intervention. In L. L. Johnson, R. J. Gallagher, M. J. La Montagne, J. B. Jordan, J. J. Gallagher, P. L. Huttinger, & M. B. Kames (Eds.), *Meeting Early Intervention Challenges: Issues from Birth to Three* (pp. 95–131). Baltimore, MD: Paul H. Brookes Publishing Company.

McLean, M. C., & Odom, S. L. (1993). Practices for young children with and without disabilities: A comparison of DEC and NAEYC identified practice. *Topics in Early Childhood Special Education, 13*(3), 274–292.

Miller, P. S. (1992). Segregated programs of teacher education in early childhood: Immoral and inefficient practice. *Topics in Early Childhood Special Education, 11*(4), 39–52.

The National Association of State Boards of Education. (1992, October). *Winners All: A Call for Inclusive Schools*. Alexandria, VA: Author.

Noonan, M. S., & McCormick, L. (1993). *Early Intervention in Natural Settings: Methods and Procedures*. Pacific Grove, CA: Brooks/Cole Publishing Co.

Novick, R. (1993). Activity-based intervention and developmentally appropriate practice: Points of convergence. *Topics in Early Childhood Special Education, 13*(4), 403–417.

Pearl, L. F. (1993). Providing family-centered early intervention. In W. Brown, S. K. Thurman, & L. F. Pearl (Eds.), *Family-Centered Early Intervention with Infants and Toddlers: Innovative Cross-Disciplinary Approaches* (pp. 81–101). Baltimore, MD: Paul H. Brookes Publishing Company.

Peck, C. A. (1993). Ecological perspectives on the implementation of integrated early childhood programs. In C. A. Peck, S. L. Odom, & D. D. Bricker (Eds.), *Integrating Young Children with Disabilities into Community Programs: Ecological Perspectives on Research and Implementation* (pp. 3–15). Baltimore, MD: Paul H. Brookes Publishing Co.

The Public Health and Welfare, Americans with Disabilities Act, U.S. Code, Title 42, Pts. 1201 et seq. 1990.

Richey, D., Richey, L., & Webb, J. (1996). Inclusive infant-toddler groups: Strategies for success. *Dimensions, 24*(4), 10–16.

Rogers, J. (Ed.). (1994). Inclusion: Moving beyond our fears. *Phi Delta Kappa Hot Topic Series.*

Shanker, A. (1995). Full inclusion is neither free nor appropriate. *Educational Leadership, 52*(4), 18–21.

Shanker, A. (1994). Inclusion and ideology. *Exceptional Parent, 24*(10), 39–40.

Smith, B. J., Miller, P. S., & Bredekamp, S. (1998). Sharing responsibility: DEC-, NAEYC-, and Vygotsky-based practices for quality inclusion. *Young Exceptional Children, 2*(1), 11–20.

Stainback, W., Stainback, S., & Stefanich, G. (1996). Learning together in inclusive classrooms: What about the curriculum? *Teaching Exceptional Children, 28*(3), 14–19.

Stayton, V. D., & Miller, P. S. (1993). Combining general and special early childhood education standards in personnel preparation programs: Experiences from two states. *Topics in Early Childhood Special Education, 13*(3), 372–387.

Stedman, D. J. (1990, January). *The Professional Preparation of Teachers and Early Childhood Educators: Changes in the Wind.* Paper presented at the South Pacific International Conference on Special Education, Auckland, New Zealand.

Thurman, S. K. (1997). Systems, ecologies and contexts of early intervention. In S. K. Thurman, J. R. Cornwell, & S. R. Gottwald (Eds.), *Contexts of Early Intervention: Systems and Settings* (pp. 3–17). Baltimore, MD: Paul H. Brookes Publishing Co.

Turnbull, R., & Cilley, M. (1999). *Explanations and Implications of the 1997 Amendments to IDEA.* Upper Saddle River, NJ: Prentice Hall, Inc.

Wehmeyer, M. L., Martin, J. E., & Sands, D. J. (1998). Self-determination for children and youth with developmental disabilities. In A. Hilton & R. Ringlaben (Eds.), *Best and Promising Practices in Developmental Disabilities* (pp. 191–201). Austin, TX: Pro-ed.

Winton, P. J., & DiVenere, N. (1995). Intervention personnel preparation: Guidelines and strategies. *Topics in Early Childhood Special Education, 15*(3), 296–313.

Zigler, B., & Muenchow, S. (1992). *Head Start: The Inside Story of America's Most Successful Educational Experiment*. New York: Basic Books.

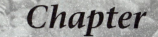

Chapter

2

Family/Professional Collaboration: A Parent's Perspective*

INTRODUCTION

This chapter includes a topic that is at the heart of our work with young children. Strong family/professional collaboration and partnerships are the foundation of the child's success. Here are the objectives the reader will address in Chapter 2. You should be able to:

- Express an awareness of the impact of a child with a disability on the family and especially on siblings as a basis for facilitating the family/professional partnership.
- Describe a systems perspective and ecological approach as fundamental to working with young children with special needs and their families.
- Provide a rationale for the significance of collaboration for successfully working with young children with special needs and their families; families need professionals and professionals need families.
- Begin demonstrating skills for implementing effective collaborative practices.
- Describe the importance of empowering families to assist them in making informed decisions for their children.
- Understand the need for functional family supports and assists to families in determining their priorities and concerns.
- Recognize that family-centered supports/services and collaboration among professionals make a difference in improving the lives of children with disabilities and their families.
- Understand the place of family-centered supports/services and collaboration as a foundation for developmentally appropriate practices, positive behavioral supports, and activity-based intervention in inclusive early childhood education.

*Written by Carol L. Russell, Ed.D., assistant professor in the Division of Early Childhood/Elementary Education at Emporia State University in Emporia, Kansas. She and her husband Fletch are the parents of three daughters: Cassie, 15; Mikelle, 12; and Tally, 9.

Impact of a Child with a Disability on the Family and Need for Professional Partnership and Support

The birth of a baby with a disability can be a parent's dreaded nightmare coming true. Their reaction and response depends upon several factors, including their personalities and individual attributes as well as the supports available to them. The reactions may also be based on how family members have dealt with past crisis. The parents and extended family often must first grieve for the healthy child that was not born, and start a different and altered dream for their child with special needs as well as the future for the rest of the family. Some parents write about their "shattered dreams," "constant grief," or "joyless lives." Some describe a feeling of functioning on the surface, yet being "eaten up from the inside-out." Others view their journey as altered, yet finding joy, beauty, and a promising future. Such a perspective reflects resiliency in families and is well illustrated in "Welcome to Holland" (see Figure 2–1).

Stages toward Adjustment

A variety of models have been developed describing the impact of a child with a disability on the family. It is important to note here, prior to our consideration of these stages, that professionals should understand that all families and the individual members within families are unique. They will all experience the process differently. Some will go through all of the stages, and maybe for prolonged periods of time. Others may not experience particular stages or may progress through them quickly. Also, as families change over time, specific grief reactions may be repeated. For example, grieving for the "perfect" healthy infant may be resolved, but the grief may resurface when the child at a later date does not meet certain child development milestones, does not engage in typical age-appropriate activities, or is surpassed by a sibling on certain developmental skills. Keep in mind that any system of parental reactions and phases is only a general guide and should not be used in a lockstep fashion. Among them are the stages that often correlate with the stages one may go through after the death of a loved one. Stages of: (a) shock, disbelief, denial; (b) anger and resentment; (c) bargaining; (d) depression and discouragement; (e) acceptance and adjustment have been attributed to the common responses of parents with children with special needs (Kantos & Dunham, 1987). These authors suggest understanding of the stages, describe parental feelings/actions that correlate with the stages, and suggest appropriate professional responses (Kantos & Dunham, 1987).

Bewildering Times

Perske (1987) refers to this adjustment process as "Bewildering Times." As noted earlier, many experts have listed detailed stages that parents are expected to face. These stages have often correlated to the stages of accepting and adjusting to the death of a loved one. Families who are adjusting to the special needs of their child do not necessarily follow a prescribed course. According to Perske

Welcome to Holland

I am often asked to describe the experience of raising a child with a disability—to try to help people who have not shared that unique experience to understand it, to imagine how it would feel. It's like this:

When you're going to have a baby, it's like planning a fabulous vacation trip—to Italy. You buy a bunch of guidebooks and make your wonderful plans. The Coliseum. The Michelangelo David. The gondolas in Venice. You may learn some handy phrases in Italian. It's all very exciting.

After months of eager anticipation, the day finally arrives. You pack your bags, and off you go. Several hours later, the plane lands. The stewardess comes in and says, "Welcome to Holland."

"Holland?!?" you say. "What do you mean, Holland? I signed up for Italy! I'm supposed to be in Italy. All my life I've dreamed of going to Italy."

But there's been a change in the flight plan. They've landed in Holland, and there you must stay.

The important thing is that they haven't taken you to a horrible, disgusting, filthy place, full of pestilence, famine, and disease. It's just a different place.

So you must go out and buy new guidebooks, you must learn a whole new language, and you will meet a whole new group of people you would never have met.

It's just a different place. It's slower-paced than Italy, less flashy than Italy. But after you've been there for a while and you catch your breath, you look around and begin to notice that Holland has windmills, Holland has tulips, Holland even has Rembrandts.

But everyone you know is coming and going from Italy, and they're all bragging about what a wonderful time they had there. And for the rest of your life, you will say, "Yes, that's where I was supposed to go. That's what I had planned."

The pain of that will never, ever, ever go away because the loss of that dream is a very significant loss. But if you spend your life mourning the fact that you didn't get to Italy, you may never be free to enjoy the special, the very lovely things about Holland.

by Emily Perl Kingsley

Figure 2-1 Welcome to Holland reflects the resiliency of families.

(1987) the process is very individual. Family members, particularly parents, may feel any of these ways at different times for a shorter or longer time.

Perske (1987) lists the following stages that parents may or may not experience, that is, the drags, the speeds, the blocks, the hurts, the guilts, the greats, the hates, and the escapes. Each stage is characterized by parents' feelings and behaviors. For example, the "drags" include feelings of tiredness and withdrawal. A flurry of activity, both useful and wasteful, characterizes the "speeds." The "blocks" may include a denial response to unwelcome news, for example, the diagnosis.

The "hurts" include indescribable pain and anguish that leave some parents feeling weak and vulnerable and others feeling stronger and more proactive. Guilty feelings and an examination of past behavior force parents to question their lives in the "guilts." The "greats" is a stage where parents may be placed on a pedestal by others; that is, parents are assigned superhuman qualities or considered very special. In reality parents of children with special needs are no different from parents of typical children. They have strengths and weaknesses like everyone else. Some meet the challenge and some do not. During the "hates" stage, parents may blame and lash out at others. Learning to safely release anger and hurt is necessary at this stage, as is channeling energy in a positive direction. Finally, the "escapes" may be a private, individual reaction to the experience of parenting a child with special needs. Many parents feel the urge to escape the situation.

Perske (1987) also offers options for consideration with such feelings associated with the eight stages of "Bewildering Times." These might be helpful to share with families, in addition to the description of feelings just discussed. Consider these options:

- "If you feel like ending it all . . . wait. In time you will realize that such escapes are stupid. They create more problems than they solve.
- Do not divorce your mate this week. Better to wait, even though you harbor fears that your spouse has rotten genes . . . or that it is all his or her fault. (They may share the same fears.) Contain such fears for the present and try to work together as a team.
- Shout epithets if you must. It may be wiser to utter them under your breath, to save wear and tear on your throat.
- If you find yourself in the drags, enjoy the misery only for a limited time. Then grit your teeth and get going.
- When the speeds come on, stop. Sit down for a moment. Then talk slowly, walk slowly. Pick only one of the 241,000 things you feel you should do that day, and do it.
- Learn to admit that no matter how real these feelings may seem, they are strange and irrational. They will pass.
- Know that time is your best friend. In time, beautiful sanity can grow out of the terrible chaos.
- Look around and choose genuine support-persons—key professionals, advocates, relatives, friends—who are capable of entering your struggle in a helpful way. Try not to "go it alone."
- Try to keep the 'unbearables' you experience from overflowing onto your child with special needs." (Perske, 1987, pp. 12–13)

Barry (1977) has suggested that there are adjustment tasks facing families. These tasks present the reality of struggles and opposition in feelings and life, in general. For example, the task "necessity of asking for financial assistance and the possibility of dealing with a welfare system" presents a contrast in feelings for parents. Parents know they need to seek support, but it may be difficult to ask for help. For some, asking for help is a sign of weakness. It is important to assist families to go beyond the stereotypes and view asking for help as a sign of strength. Yet, dealing with the welfare system is a unique experience. As professionals, we must take care to avoid stereotypes of individuals who utilize Medicaid and other programs that might be available for children with special needs and their families.

Another adjustment task that many families may relate to is "dealing with total lack of knowledge of this birth defect in the community" (Barry, 1977). It can be quite a lonely feeling for a parent to sit down with a team of professionals who know very little about their child's disability. Perhaps they have heard of the disability but have never worked with a child with that special need. It can be a continual trial and error process. We must, as professionals, take the responsibility to educate ourselves regarding a child's condition and specific needs and to work with medical professionals to understand and identify needs and collaborate to develop the most appropriate plan for a child.

It is important to examine how families cope and adapt to stressor events over time, for example, the birth and parenting of a child with a disability. In addition, existing stressors, such as responsibility for other family members and meeting financial obligations, must be factored into a study of a family's ability to function optimally. Family resources and family supports may bolster a family's ability to meet the needs of each individual in the family and realize the goals of the family. The perception of the stressor event by the family is also critical in determining how it will adjust to stressor events. McCubbin and Patterson (1982) provide a model that helps us understand these issues related to families' responses to stressor events, including adjustment and adaptation responses. Sandler (1997) has provided a useful summary of the realities of families with children who have special needs:

> Romantics like to portray members of such families as saints who can do no wrong. Skeptics seek psychopathology, offering stereotyped stories of overprotective, enmeshed mothers, interfering in-laws, isolated and rejected husbands, and angry siblings. Well, here is the truth! About 10 percent of American families include a child with special needs, and the overwhelming majority of these families are ordinary families . . . who make mistakes, win some important battles, lose others, and strive to do better. They go through some predictable transitions and experience some unpredictable stresses. They cope.

Perske (1987) offers options for consideration with the feelings and behavior associated with the eight stages. These might be helpful to share with families, in addition to the description of feelings just discussed.

Impact on Siblings (Meyer & Vadasy, 1994)

Unusual Concerns	Unusual Opportunities
Overidentification	Maturity and Insight
Embarrassment	Self-Concept and Social Competence
Guilt	Tolerance
Isolation, Loneliness, and Loss	Pride
Resentment	Vocational Opportunities
Increased Responsibilities	Advocacy
Pressure to Achieve	Loyalty
	Strength, Resiliency, and Sense of Humor When Coping

Artistic Avenues for Expression

Some (including the author of this chapter) have utilized art forms to depict the impact the birth/diagnosis of the child with a disability has on a family. One such form is interpretive dance and can be observed on the video entitled *When the Bough Breaks* (Wisconsin Department of Public Instruction, 1991). In this dance each stage of grief and adjustment process is demonstrated. The dance concludes with a very unique looking older individual in what appears to be the "helping profession" supporting the parents through this process. The visual arts are another art form. Refer to Figures 2-2 and 2-3 for photographs of two artworks by a father and grandfather of a child born with spina bifida. "Cradle of Tears" was created within the first three months after the artist's child was born. "Father and Daughter" was created by the same child's grandfather. These works, although very contrasting, depict the need for expression that may not necessarily be through words. We must listen . . . not only with our ears.

In summary, whether you remember the impact of the child with a disability as a cycle, stages, puzzle of feelings, or through an art form, acknowledgment and validation of feelings is extremely important. The stages and feelings can occur and reoccur with each new diagnosis and/or each developmental milestone missed, or for no apparent reason at all. Appropriate supports are essential. Parent and family counselors, family therapists, and psychologists can be very helpful to both parents, family, and staff. When par-

Figure 2-2 Cradle of Tears. Artist: Fletcher L. Russell

Figure 2-3 Father and Daughter. Artist: Fletcher L. Russell

ents and family are supported in dealing with issues and their feelings, they can be better parents, more effective team members, resulting in benefits for the child.

Impact on Siblings

A mother of three daughters, one with special needs, reports the following:

> When our third daughter, Tally, was born with spina bifida, my first two thoughts were: "Is she going to live?" and "What will life be like for her two older sisters?" (then, ages 5 and 2) Throughout the first year of Tally's life (and nine surgeries later) I found a partial answer to my first question—yes, my daughter would experience life beyond the IV tubes, needles, constant CAT scans, MRIs, X rays and the hospital environment. Although we must stay vigilant, continually preventative and advocating in our care for her, she is thriving.
>
> The answer to my second question . . . on that life-changing-day . . . continues to be answered—a little more each day. I observe our daughters grow, mature, love, fight with each other, and learn from our struggle as parents advocating for the rights of our child and of other children with disabilities and their families. The future looks promising for

Tally to grow up and become more independent. I also realize that our older two daughters will probably outlive my husband and me. Therefore we may need to all look ahead to the future and together make decisions that will affect all of us. In the meantime, there are and have been stresses as well as opportunities for our older daughters, as siblings of Tally.

Meyer and Vadasy (1994) note how "sibs" of children with disabilities experience both good and bad feelings about having a sibling with special needs. These are summarized below, along with suggestions based on siblings' concerns. Opportunities for sibling growth and maturing are also provided by the ongoing sibling relationship. These opportunities are also discussed.

Special Concerns and Needs of Siblings

Overidentification. Siblings sometimes wonder if they share—or will share—the special need. Sisters and brothers need accurate information about their sib's condition. They need information repeated and updated periodically. Try to give details at the child's level without frightening them. Siblings often have a desperate need to know what is going on, what is going to happen next, and what is the plan (see Figure 2–4).

Embarrassment. Siblings may be uncomfortable with the, perhaps, unwanted attention their sibling and family may experience. The authors suggest giving siblings "permission" to be embarrassed, allowing the sibling some control over the situation. Validate their feelings and give them space.

Guilt. Siblings may feel responsible for their sibling's disability or illness or feel guilt for being the survivor, being healthy or having the abilities their sibling lacks. "Sibs" may feel guilt over sibling conflicts, over caregiving or not

Figure 2-4 These children are getting to know their sibling through a viewing window. For many siblings of children born with disabilities, this is their only relationship for weeks and sometimes months.

wanting to caregive. Siblings may also feel shame or may even be "shame-driven" in their actions or even choice of profession. This is not to say that siblings are "shame-driven" into helping professions (as a great percentage of siblings do choose helping professions). Yet the risk exists.

Isolation, Loneliness, and Loss.

Siblings need attention from their parents especially during times of stress (such as when their sibling is hospitalized,

---

Suggestions for Parents from Parents

- Keep responsibility for sibling a choice. Do not force the sibling to help with your child with special needs; they will resent it.
- Communicate. Talk with your children about whatever is going on—at their level. Be open and honest. Get support with this, if needed.
- Allow and encourage sibling's expressions of feelings. Feelings of hate, jealousy, resentment and even depression are not uncommon for siblings. Assist them in finding avenues to share feelings and minimize the "unusual concerns" they experience and maximize their "unusual opportunities." Counselors, psychologists and family therapists can be supportive. SIBSHOPS and similar programs can be very helpful. Help them explore and cultivate their own interests, outlets, and the like.
- Include siblings in decision-making processes, IFSP/IEP meetings, clinics, and so on.
- Issues can "swallow us up" as parents. Keep challenges in perspective and try not to let them "swallow up" siblings too.
- Try to read your child's cues when they are needing extra attention. This may be in times of stress when you, yourself, are needing the extra attention too. Tell your children without special needs to let you know—in a positive way—when they're feeling that they're not getting enough attention. Perhaps you could develop some positive cue to indicate this (rather than negative attention-seeking behavior). Parents sometimes need "reality checks" from their children.
- Make special time for each child. Plan—or even make special dates with your child/children without special needs. Put it on the calendar. Recognize when siblings may get "cut short" and try to make special times for them.
- Encourage each child's independence and foster individual interests.
- Celebrate each child's accomplishments. Have parties and invite family and friends.
- Talk about the future. Sometimes this can be pretty frightening—for everyone. But there is less fear of the future if we can talk, plan, and problem-solve. When you talk about plans or procedures or even diagnosis, have children repeat to you what they are understanding. Reflective listening and repeating what is understood is a helpful tool.
- Reinforce positive behavior, advocacy, compassion, and love. Surround yourself with people who are positive. Encourage your children to do the same. It trickles down. ATTITUDES MAKE THE DIFFERENCE.

diagnosed, times of increased advocacy, due process). Unfortunately these are times when parents are very occupied with their child with special needs. Siblings may feel alone because they are not getting or understanding information. They are needing clear information and emotional support. Siblings need to participate with the process as much as they are comfortable. If siblings agree, include them in IFSP/IEP meetings, clinics visits, and therapy sessions.

Isolation from peers may occur frequently. When parents are dealing with hospitalizations, special treatments, extra time for therapies, evaluations, IFSPs/IEPs, the additional arrangements for time with friends sometimes take a "back seat" to other pressing issues. Arranging time with friends takes more planning.

Resentment.　The feeling of resentment is quite prevalent in siblings of children with special needs. These feelings may result from loss of parent attention, feelings of unequal treatment and excessive demands, and resentment regarding failure to plan for the future.

> I can still envision our then 2-year-old, needing something and having to wait, as my husband and I were gowned, gloved, and masked, completing the medical procedures for our month-old baby, which took both of us 1 1/2 hours! An adult would even resent having to wait that long! And here was my sweet little 2-year-old trying to figure this out. And how long 1 1/2 hours must have felt to a 2-year-old. Sometimes growing up and maturity comes all too soon for sibs.
>
> —Parents of a child with spina bifida

Parents of children with disabilities may often hear from their children without similar challenges, "It's just not fair. Why doesn't he/she need to do this?" "You let him/her get away with anything!" Parents, too, may feel like saying, "Yes, you're right, it's not fair. You can walk up the stairs and get what you want. He/she can't." "You have friends that call you and ask you over; it's not that simple for your sibling."

Making special time to be with the children without these challenges is important. Talking about feelings and developing strategies for all to help the

---

Suggestions from Sibs to Parents

- Give responsibilities to all children—based on abilities.
- If you are going to an appointment that includes a lunch out, take the siblings out to lunch or on a special outing another time.
- Recognize each child's cues for extra attention.
- Healthy conflict is part of being siblings. Try not to overprotect or overhelp.
- Find SIBSHOPS or something like it for "sibs."
- Talk about how you're feeling. Find another sib to talk to, write, or e-mail. You're not alone!
- Plan together for the future. You can't live forever. Siblings need to be informed and involved in these plans.

child with special needs be more independent is important. A counselor might be helpful in this process.

Increased Responsibilities.   Research suggests that caregiving demands are often assumed by siblings of children with special needs. Meyer and Vadasy (1994) state that sisters, especially oldest sisters, appear to be at greater risk for heavy caregiving responsibilities, resulting in being at risk for other problems, such as educational failure, increased disturbances, and stress (Cleveland & Miller, 1977; Farber, 1960; Fowle, 1973; Gath, 1974; Labato, Barbour, Hall, & Miller, 1987). There is no question that parents of children with special needs are typically in need of supports. And the natural supports from within the family are appropriate and beneficial. However, when this support becomes a burden to the person providing it— and when it causes "burn out," guilt, and resentment—then the supporter (sibling) ends up needing the support. A balance is needed. These feelings and needs must be communicated. Other supportive possibilities should also be explored. Professional help such as family therapists, counselors, psychologists, and social workers could be supportive to assist siblings and their families. Funding is often available from state agencies to access such services for a child with a disability and his/her family. This includes siblings and their issues.

It is important to note that the child with special needs must also have responsibilities that are appropriate to their abilities and to environmental accessibility. Self-help is often an issue. The author has observed many siblings who know what their brother or sister with special needs can do. Siblings may promote independence more than we parents do at times. Parents tend to be the ones who overhelp. Parents, also, may interpret siblings' behaviors as cruel when they state, "I know he or she can do it. You do too much for him or her." An individual with spina bifida relayed an experience about her sister leaving her in the school bathroom on the toilet telling her, "You can get off by yourself. I know you can." She did, and, needless to say, she was extremely frustrated with her sister! Yet, she did it on her own. This is not to say it is permissible to put siblings in nonsafe situations, but to illustrate how well siblings understand the abilities of their sibling with special needs.

Pressure to Achieve.   Meyer and Vadasy (1994) suggest that pressure to achieve may be placed on siblings of children with special needs by their parents (as if to compensate for the disabilities of their child with special needs). Siblings may also put pressure on themselves. The pressure may be "shame-driven" or attention-seeking. This need to achieve may also be an "unusual opportunity." Siblings are often "overachievers." There are numerous examples of families who have a sibling excelling academically or in gifted education programs.

Unusual Opportunities

Maturity and Insight.   The experience of siblings of children with special needs is often different from that of their peers (see Figure 2–5). Their experience may have occurred as a result of their parents' negotiation, mediation, and advocacy for their children with special needs. It may have occurred as a result of

Figure 2-5 The "sib" relationship is the first and most intense peer relationship.

required activities to care for the child with special needs, for example, extensive and frequent hospitalizations. It may have been painful, but invaluable at times. For example, one mother reports the following:

> Because of my youngest child's spina bifida, my two oldest children spent much of their sibling's first year of life in and out of the hospital because of nine surgeries. After this experience, the two older siblings were making CAT scans and MRIs out of oatmeal boxes, creating IVs and monitors out of boxes and tubing, and spending at least 95% of their dramatic play in hospital play. (Russell, 1997)

Siblings often become advocates for their sibs and ultimately for the ADA and IDEA. An example of this advocacy is a paper written by an eleven-year-old sibling of a child with disability.

Meyer and Vadasy (1994) also discuss maturity due to loss of innocence, increased responsibilities, and greater insight. Parents need to openly share with siblings information about their children with disabilities in a developmentally appropriate manner. The life and death issues that may arise need to be discussed because children sense when something is wrong. The fragility of the human condition is very apparent to many siblings of children with special needs. Because of this experience many siblings tend to not take life and health for granted. Depending on how evident a child's disability may be, siblings must often deal with stares, ignorance about special needs, and even rudeness. Siblings may be tempted to stare back, make quick remarks, even respond with rudeness. It is suggested that the best advice is to be yourself. Let others see the family engaging in laughing, loving, sharing, and even healthy sibling rivalry. This demonstrates and models positive, normal family interaction and cohesiveness.

Persuasive Paper

Building Ramps, Elevators, and Curb Cuts in Front of Buildings

In this paper I am going to write about building ramps, elevators, and curb cuts in front of buildings to make them accessible. I'm going to talk about why ramps, elevators, and curb cuts are important to other people not just people in wheelchairs. And I'll also talk about how businesses and restaurants can benefit. Also I'll talk about how it will be easier for families to do more things together. Also it is the law!

Ramps, elevators, and curb cuts not only help people with disabilities, but they also help other people too. They help people who have strollers or carts. Older people who can't use their legs very well can also take advantage of ramps, elevators and curb cuts. People who have a broken leg or other problems with stairs can also benefit from these adaptations.

If there is a restaurant, store or any business, they are opening their store for more business if they put in ramps, elevators and curb cuts in front of their store. There are almost 50 million Americans with disabilities. If they open their store doors to them they could make a lot more money.

Ramps, elevators and curb cuts make it easier for people to get around and spend time with their families. If some places aren't accessible you cannot go in with your whole family. So either you go to a different place that is accessible or you would have to split up your family and go different places. I don't think that is fair because you should always be with your whole family in one place, no matter where you want to go.

I know what this is like because I have a sister that uses a wheelchair. So this is important to me. I remember a time when we went to a restaurant and the main entrance was just stairs, so she had to go up an extra steep ramp and through the kitchen to get to the place that we were eating. Another time we went to a play and they wouldn't let her sit in the [a]isle. We had to sit way in the back or not together. Another restaurant would not put any ramp in, so we stopped going to it. My family worked for seven years to get an elevator in an art building, so my family could all go see my dad's artwork in the building and take art classes there. I could go on a lot more, because it's an everyday thing for me.

If you don't build ramps, elevators and curb cuts you would be breaking the law. The Americans with Disabilities Act, passed in 1990 says that public places need to be accessible for ALL! Some people say that they don't have enough money to build ramps, elevators and curb cuts. But it is the law and if you don't do it, then you could be fined a lot more money than it would take to build ramps, elevators and curb cuts. IT'S THE LAW AND THE RIGHT THING TO DO!!!

There's a lot of work to be done!

By Mikelle Russell, age 11

It is possible the "starers" will learn something from their observations. Some families have experienced a direct smile in the "starers" direction is often returned with a smile.

Self-Concept, Social Competence, Tolerance, and Pride. Studies
on self-concept and siblings of children with special needs are inconclusive, with the majority of recent information indicating that the self-concepts and social competence of siblings compare favorably with that of their peers who do not have siblings with special needs (Meyer & Vadasy, 1994). These studies list flexibility, compassion, understanding of people, awareness of prejudice and its consequences, greater tolerance, and even being intolerant of intolerance as some characteristics of siblings. Families with a child with a disability often appreciate and even celebrate diversity in themselves and others around them. Children observe the strength and struggles of their sibling with special needs. They share in the celebration of their lives and accomplishments. When children are exposed to therapy sessions, teaching strategies, styles of learning, and even medical procedures that are routine for their sibling with special needs, they realize the magnitude of their sibling's accomplishments. Keeping children involved with their sibling with special needs and the services they receive will enhance their understanding of the need to celebrate accomplishments.

One family described how their child with special needs was intensely afraid of large things. The family made up the term *megaphobia* to describe it. The child would basically gag and throw up in such situations. The two older siblings lived through many times where the family had to separate to experience places, for instance, the Arch in St. Louis, dinosaur skeletons in museums, even large buildings in cities. This family attended a hot air balloon display where the process of unfolding to "hot airing" the balloons took place. By the end of the evening (to their surprise), the fearful child was looking up inside one of the hot air balloons! The family followed with an "overcoming megaphobia celebration!"

Vocational Opportunities. Siblings' vocational choices are often in the
helping professions (Cleveland & Miller, 1977; Grossman, 1972; Meyer & Vadasy, 1994). Is it any wonder? They have much to share from their own experiences. Adapting, problem solving, advocating, knowledge of medical issues, and the like, are often second nature to them. They feel comfortable with diversity and with the naturalness of helping others. We can help children explore professions even at an early age and facilitate children's professional inquiries.

Advocacy. Siblings can have an active role in IFSP/IEP meetings, negotia-
tion, mediation, and advocacy. The MAP process (referred to later in this chapter) is an excellent tool to involve siblings and other family members and friends in the process of looking to the future and facilitating the child's road to independence and reaching goals. The Americans with Disabilities Act and IDEA are household words in many homes of children with special needs. Mikelle's "Persuasive Presentation" (see page 43) on the need to build more

ramps, curb cuts, and elevators certainly illustrates the importance of even young children understanding the law and advocating for the rights of their family members and others needing accessibility. This advocacy role must be a choice, not forced. Opportunities are available on a daily basis. Siblings must initiate when, where, and if to advocate from the heart, not out of guilt.

Loyalty.   This can be a problem for some siblings (Binkard et al., 1987; Meyer & Vadasy, 1994). Feeling obligated to defend their brother or sister from rudeness and stares can be uncomfortable. It is healthy if these feelings can be communicated and ways to deal with such situations openly discussed. Counselors can also be very helpful with these and other feelings. Many children appreciate keeping friendships with those who also appreciate the diversity of themselves and their sibling. Sibling support programs, for example, SIBSHOPS (Binkard, 1987), are an excellent avenue for such discussions and sharing. SIBSHOPS offer opportunities for siblings to meet and talk with their peers who are experiencing similar situations and feelings.

Strength, Resiliency, and Sense of Humor When Coping.   The experiences of siblings of children with special needs are often complex and intense. They have practiced many skills and coping strategies, demonstrating strength and resilience (Grossman, 1972; Meyer & Vadasy, 1994; Skirtic, Summers, Brotherson, & Turnbull, 1983;). For example, a mother of two daughters relates the following:

> I recall, whenever things were really looking low for Cindy (our daughter with special health care needs), it was as if Jenny's (her older sister) super humor side came to life. She would often have us laughing instead of crying. Jenny could get Cindy to do things we could never get her to do. Jenny had a knack for redirecting the mood and situation with "one liners." This is also evident in other aspects of her life.
> —Cindy and Jenny's Mother

SIBSHOPS is the award-winning program that brings together siblings of children with special needs to share and express their good, and not so good, feelings about having sisters and brothers with special needs. The following is a description of SIBSHOPS from a participating sibling (Russell, 1997):

> SIBSHOPS are fun! You get to make your own food. You get to play games and do lots of fun stuff. It's a good way to share feelings about what's going on or how you're dealing with things with your sibling. It's not hard to share feelings because they're going through some of the same stuff and might feel some of the same things you do. You can relate with other siblings that may have similar situations. You can relate to each other, instead of talking to a counselor—you get to talk to someone else that might feel the same way you do. And if you don't want to talk, that's OK too—it's interesting to listen to others. Just by listening you might learn about a situation or feeling that you might face later on.
> —Mikelle, age 12

"Sibnet" (for teens and adult siblings) and "Sibkids" (for younger siblings about 12 and under) are available listserves and are quite supportive and interesting for parental awareness of sibling issues. Many children have utilized these resources on a weekly, sometimes daily, basis. Other resources for siblings include Siblings for Significant Change ([212]420-0776) and Siblings Information Network([203]648-1205). Professionals must be aware of resources and refer siblings and families to the supports available. Often teachers and other professionals may not be aware that their students are siblings of children with special needs unless families offer the information.

Parents and professionals cannot totally understand sibling issues. They are different in many ways from adult issues. Parents, teachers, and counselors must be aware of and acknowledge the issues and concerns of siblings. Resources must be found and used to support them. Suggestions are offered from both the parental and sibling perspectives (see Collaboration Works following).

Grandparents and Extended Family

When grandparents are told of the birth of their grandchild with special needs, they frequently experience dual hurt (see Figure 2–6). They hurt, not only for their grandbaby but also for their adult child. This pain may lead to feelings of denial, anger, hurt, and blame, which can result in intergenerational stresses (Sandler, 1997). Feelings and stresses must be dealt with and resolved in order for family members to be supportive of each other. The role of many grandparents of children with special needs may include additional supports that were not needed prior to the birth of a grandchild with special needs. Many

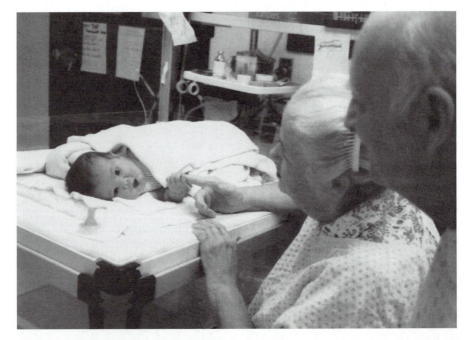

Figure 2–6
Grandparents often need special supports and opportunities to bond with their new grandchild.

Collaboration Works . . . It's a Fact

(Recommendations from Parents)

FOCUS ON CHILD
ACCOUNTABILITY
COMMUNICATION
TRUST

FOCUS ON CHILD (WELCOME OUR CHILD)
- Know our child, acknowledge and learn about his/her disability, individualize (e.g., MAPS).
- Use person first language and philosophy.
- Treat us as people (not just "mom" or "dad"—we have names).
- Reality, most disabilities don't just "go away."
- Use active/reflective listening.
- Join us in advocacy efforts. Help develop a supportive system for our child. "Walk in our moccasins."

Attitude makes the difference!!!

ACCOUNTABILITY (ASKING FOR HELP IS A SIGN OF STRENGTH)
- Welcome questions and be ready to find answers if you do not have them.
- Use us as resources. We are the professionals of our child. We may know more about our child, his/her special strengths and needs, and perhaps even about our child's rights.
- Use your resources; request training and outside help as needed.
- Additional training is essential; know what you're doing. Know the law and follow it.
- Accept the responsibility.
- Be creative and flexible; plan ahead.
- Monitor, justify how meeting goals, keep accurate records, share information with parents.
- *We are the consumer*—value our input—let us know we're heard—think about advisory groups or some method to welcome and utilize feedback from parents.

Attitude makes the difference!!!

COMMUNICATION (IT'S THE KEY!)
- *Listen, listen, listen*—"open door policy" in reality, not just "lip service."
- Courtesy of sending parents all information (assessment results, reports, etc.) at least one week prior to meeting. Questions can be addressed prior to or during the IEP/IFSP meeting. Our time is valuable too.
- Allow parents to digest information . . . before signing the IEP.
- We want what is best for our child, based on his/her needs.
- *Learn and practice negotiation and conflict resolution skills*. "Sweeping it under the carpet;" gets us nowhere. Try not to get on the system's "bandwagon" when it doesn't feel right. (KS ADVOCACY is a good resource if you have questions.)

continued on page 48

continued from page 47

COMMUNICATION (IT'S THE KEY!), *continued*
- We are the advocate for our child; hopefully we will not offend you in our role as parents and advocates.
Attitude makes the difference!!!

TRUST (CONFIDENTIALITY)
- Show us we can trust you. Listen, follow through, work with us. Trust is difficult to reestablish, once it has been broken.
- We have the right to due process. There are repercussions for everyone. It is preventable.
- Mutual respect and courtesy.
Attitude makes the difference!!!

—Carol and Fletcher Russell, 1996

grandparents are primary caregivers and very involved in the lives of their grandchildren with special needs (Sandler, 1997). These feelings, stresses, and dual hurts may also hold true for extended family members (aunts, uncles, cousins) depending on their relationship with the family. Such supports may also be needed for extended family. (See Figure 2-7.)

Figure 2–7 Family-centered services must foster the involvement of dads. Fathers today take a more active role in the care of their children.

The Family as a System

Bronfenbrenner's Bioecological Theory

The family system is a natural environment for young children. According to Bronfenbrenner (1995) the family is a child's microsystem. For infants it is their primary natural environment and most immediate setting for development. Over time other natural environments influence a child's development, for example, child care center, preschool. A hospital could be viewed as a natural environment or microsystem for a child with a disability or chronic health problem. The family, however, continues to be the most important natural environment for the young child.

Bronfenbrenner's bioecological model includes four other ecosystems or environmental systems, in addition to the microsystem. Those four environmental systems include the mesosystem, the exosystem, the macrosystem, and the chronosystem.

The mesosystem is the interrelationship between microsystems. The partnership between a child's home and preschool, as evidenced through shared communications and activities, would be an example of a mesosystem. Another example would be the relationship between a child's pediatrician and the parents of a young child with a chronic health condition.

Exosystems are the contexts and settings where a person is never "an active participant but in which events occur that affect, or are affected by, what happens in that setting" (Bronfenbrenner, 1979, p. 237). A child may not be present in a parent's workplace but is affected by the decisions made and events experienced by the parent in that setting. A parent who has the advantage of a flexible schedule may be able to provide at-home care to a sick child and still be able to complete work responsibilities. A parent who clocks in and out on a rigid schedule may need to either be absent from work with a loss of wages or find substitute care for the child. A child's experience when sick may be determined by the policies of the parent's employer.

The macrosystem refers to the cultural contexts of individuals, families, and other systems. Included in the macrosystem are cultural values, ideologies, and belief systems. Socioeconomic status and prevailing laws will also impact the development and functioning of individuals and families. Examples of macrosystems include legislation affecting special education and services for young children and families, local government policies, and societal attitudes.

The chronosystem is not an environmental system per se, but a temporal dimension highlighting changes to individuals or environments over time. In the last century in the United States, the attitudes toward institutionalization of children with disabilities have changed. For example, the attitudes associated with the eugenics movement in the first decades of the twentieth century have evolved into the policies and best practices of PL 94-142.

Family members have specific roles and are connected by different relationships. The balance of this family system is unique and delicate. A significant change in one family member can affect all others (Sandler, 1997). For example, if the primary caregiver (be it mother or father) becomes seriously ill, not only does his or her health concern other family members, but another member of the family must cover the responsibilities of that person or make other arrangements to care for the children. It is important to note the influence of the family on the ultimate outcome of the child with a disability.

Sandler's Three R's: Roles, Relationships, and Responsibility

As we understand the importance of the family as a system, we try to understand the roles of various family members. Role examples might be caregiver, organizer, victim, protector, friend, disciplinarian, or decision maker (Sandler, 1997). Professionals can assist families to note roles they each play, to discard the roles that are no longer useful, and to take on new roles that will support their family and will move them forward. Sandler (1997) also notes the importance of relationships in the family system. The basis of relationships is good communication such as providing "I" statements and being more skilled at listening and asserting our viewpoints when needed.

Families have important responsibilities. Some are essential, such as providing food, shelter, warmth, and safety. Economic realities make even these essential family functions difficult to carry out, particularly when families face enormous health care costs. Sandler (1997) presents two important responsibilities of families with children with disabilities. One of these is to overcome isolation. When families deal with many other systems (medical, professionals, numerous specialists, educators, therapists, Medicaid, Supplemental Security Income, and the list goes on), in addition to their own professional efforts, they may have little energy left. Families often withdraw socially. They may keep to themselves because of time, energy, and also the attitudes of others.

> I can recall a few days after my daughter was born with spina bifida, hydrocephalus, and other medical complications. I had a conversation with another father whose son was 5 years old with similar challenges. He shared his insights, looking back over the first years of his son's life. He said, "Your life will change. You'll lose some friends who may not have really been your friends to begin with. You'll make some new ones." Sometimes I think people don't call us because they feel we have too much to handle already, or they are afraid to approach us—especially during the first year. They don't know what to say. Friends are lost. We don't have the time or energy for the commitment of friends.
>
> —Father of a child with special needs

Using the family systems framework and an understanding of roles within the family system, we can conceptualize an approach that might be most supportive to the child with special needs and his or her family. The family-centered approach is one such approach. It is flexible and as individual as each family. Sensitivity to culture and family values are embedded throughout this approach.

Utilizing a Family-Centered Approach

"Family-centeredness values parental knowledge and experience" (*Families and Disability Newsletter,* 1997). Professionals who respect and utilize the vast knowledge that family members can offer can provide more effective interventions and supports to children with special needs and their families. Family-centeredness is at the core of the IFSP and is considered best practice with the IEP process. It has been described by many professionals in the field of early childhood special education. Features of family-centeredness are described in the following section. You may recall that we introduced this concept in Chapter 1.

Characterizing and Defining Family-Centeredness

Dunst, Trivette, and Deal (1994) characterized family-centeredness by eight interrelated features that together are the foundation for working with families who have children with disabilities. The features include (1) adopting the family systems perspective and expanding the definition of intervention; (2) moving beyond the child as the focus of intervention toward the family unit as the focus; (3) family empowerment as a major goal of intervention; (4) a proactive approach, placing emphasis on promotion of family growth producing behavior rather than treatment of problems; (5) focus on family, rather than professionally identified needs and concerns for targets of intervention; (6) emphasis on identifying and building capabilities of families in order to strengthen family functioning; (7) emphasis on strengthening the family's personal social network as a primary support and resources for needs; and (8) a philosophical shift in professional roles when working with families of children with special needs. Family-centeredness has also been described by other terms such as *family-focused, family-oriented, family referenced,* and *family empowerment.*

Collaboration for Successfully Working with Young Children with Special Needs and Their Families

Families Need Professionals, and Professionals Need Families

Families play a key role in early intervention and the future development of their children. In fact, early intervention does not separate the child from the family in planning and delivering services. The family is the hub of the child's life. "Without the active involvement of parents, the effects of early intervention are not as positive" (Dunlap, 1997). Collaboration is central to successful family/professional partnerships. It does not come easily and is not to be taken for granted. It takes work. It is most beneficial to the child with special needs.

Collaboration

According to Swan and Morgan (1993), collaboration describes efforts to unite people or organizations to achieve common goals. They suggest viewing cooperation, coordination, and collaboration (relating to a team or interagency efforts) within a developmental sequence. The lowest level of the hierarchy is the least complex: cooperation. It is a process of working together to achieve the day-to-day goals and general organization. Coordination is at a more sophisticated level of interaction, "a more formalized process of adjustment or utilization of existing resources than cooperation" (Swan & Morgan, 1993, p. 21). Cooperation or even coordination could occur without moving to a more intricate level that characterizes team collaboration. Collaboration, the most sophisticated level of team relationships, is defined by Bartel (as cited in Swan & Morgan, 1993) as a relationship "in which the parties share common goals, mutual commitments, resources, decision making, and evaluation responsibilities" (p. 22). Collaboration best describes the teamwork required to implement the complexity within Part C of Reauthorized IDEA (formerly, Part H of PL 99-457).

An important goal for professionals is to select, design, and communicate information and resources to parents that are "parent friendly" and easily understood. However, this requires individualizing. One should not assume that parents are coming with limited knowledge. Some may come with more expertise on their child's disability than many professionals have had the opportunity to gain. Although parents want the best for their child, other parents may be resistant to information at first or may need some time to adjust. As discussed at the beginning of this chapter, under the section on family impact, we must be sensitive to "emotional roller coasters" that parents are often riding. They may be on "information overload" and overwhelmed with diagnosis, interventions, schedules, constant direct care, medical appointments, medical bills, and generally striving for sanity. But they do care about their child.

Many parents take the time and energy to be immersed in their child's medical and educational well-being. These are parents who may be well versed in the laws, and perhaps actually impacting the laws through their advocacy efforts. Professionals may sometimes label these parents as "troublemakers." Professionals may be intimidated by the parents' efforts to do what they believe is best for their child. Here are the thoughts of a mother to the professionals who work with her child—written in the "wee hours" of the morning.

❧❧❧❧

You Don't Have to Like Me, But I Wish You Would
—Mother of a child with special needs

We both look at my child with loving eyes
We have her best at heart.
You have her a short time,
I have her for life.

We have my child in common.
I must be faithful to her,
Even if it means being unfaithful to you.
You have her a short time,
I have her for life.

Please put yourselves in "our moccasins."
Try to view her road ahead.
As you join for a brief time on her journey,
Don't lose sight of what's ahead.
You have her a short time,
I have her for life.

I am strong.
You know I will do anything for my child.
Please respect my advocacy.
You have her a short time,
I have her for life.

We're better together,
This can work!
Please trust my intuition.
I know her better than you.
You have her a short time,
I have her for life.

Professionals come and go,
Sometimes all too soon.
Even if your stay with us is short,
Won't you please join us in advocacy,
reaching for dreams
and celebration of her life?
You have her a short time,
I have her for life.

You don't have to like me, but I wish you would.
Because although you have her a short time,
we are better together,
And WE can impact her life!

❧❧❧❧

Professionals who respect and accept the various levels of parental participation and "take into account the individual needs of all family members, and avoid placing demands on parents that are likely to add more stress to a stressful life, will be more successful. Parents who are overstressed cannot effectively help their child" (Dunlap, 1997, p. 121). Parents and other family members have expectations of professionals, for example, to be understanding, supportive, knowledgeable, kind, cooperative, organized, and enthusiastic. They want professionals to plan and implement the best program for their child. They want open communication and availability to discuss their child's progress. Kept in perspective, these are reasonable expectations.

Generally, professionals have expectations of parents. They want parents to be supportive, involved, appreciative, enthusiastic, and cooperative.

Professionals also expect parents to understand time constraints, limitations, and their busy schedules (Dunlap, 1997). Professionals also expect parents to confirm their professional recommendations. When there is not mutual agreement regarding these recommendations, conflicts emerge. The need for more effective communication, negotiation, conflict resolution, and perhaps mediation becomes apparent. Information regarding due process must also be discussed. The following section discusses these methods for resolution of conflict.

Effective Communication

Effective interpersonal communication skills are probably the most important professional attribute, besides, of course, being professionally competent in your discipline. Development of these skills is an ongoing process that hopefully results in the attainment of increased competence in this area. Although the importance of family/professional communication and collaboration is discussed later in this chapter under implementing effective collaborative practices, students may wish to consult Turnbull and Turnbull (1996) for further information on this topic.

In addition to effective communication techniques discussed above, traditional and nontraditional communication strategies that are family-centered include conferences (formal or informal), handouts, handbooks, bulletin boards, message boards, newsletters, letters/notes/journals/logbooks, progress reports, positive reports (e.g., "happy grams," certificates of recognition) electronic mail, and telephone conversations/messages. Although these will not be expanded upon here, many resources exist for further information on these and other family-professional communication strategies.

Negotiation and Conflict Resolution

Coming to agreement, finding a solution, resolving differences are all outcomes of any negotiation or conflict resolution process. Although less formal, we do this on a daily basis at home, school, or work. The steps in resolving conflict are quite simple. Putting it into practice takes some practice. The goal is mutual gain. According to Fisher and Ury (1981), we must start with some basic principles: (1) the participants agree to be problem solvers, and (2) the goals are a best outcome through a friendly/efficient process. These authors describe four steps in the solution process. The first step is to separate the person from the problem. This means we must leave differences with people aside and focus on the problem. The second step is to focus on interests, not positions. In doing this we must explore interests, brainstorm, keep an open mind, look at the need. This means that even if feelings, such as "we've always done it this way" or "that has never been available before" come into mind, we must put them aside. Avoid having a bottom line. The third step is to invent options for mutual gain. Here again, the openness and brainstorming power of the group offer great potential. The authors advise to develop multiple options to choose from. This should be a flowing process without dead ends. This is not yet the decision step; that comes later. The final step is to insist on using objective criteria. This involves reasoning and being open to reason, and yielding to principle, not pressure.

Conflict can be constructive or destructive. The process discussed above is a constructive example, as it focuses energy on the issues and relevant activities. Destructive conflict results when there is disagreement with no effort to resolve conflicts and negativity grows. Conflict is usually handled passively, aggressively, or assertively. Parents who do not agree, yet choose to accept the situation without resistance or frustration, illustrate a passive response. When parents become hostile or attack the teaching staff, this is an aggressive approach. The most productive approach is assertive. When assertively responding, the parent would clearly state the issues in a nonhostile way.

Parents and professionals need to be familiar with this or a similar solution process and styles of dealing with conflict in order to progress when there is disagreement. This process can perhaps prevent mediation or due process. We encourage practicing these skills and role-playing simulated situations. An excellent resource is Fisher and Ury's (1981) *Getting to Yes: Negotiating Agreement without Giving In*. Still, there are times when agreement is not successful within the local system. Sometimes we need help from outside the system to resolve differences. Negotiation and conflict resolution are at the core of the mediation process. Although mediation is more formal, it involves, basically, the same process discussed above.

Mediation

According to the reauthorization of IDEA (in June 1997), mediation must now be available in all states, at no cost to the local school district. Mediation is a voluntary process. Both parties must agree to mediate. The mediator (a trained neutral third party) facilitates communication and negotiation between the disagreeing parties. "The goal of mediation is to reach a mutually satisfactory agreement and settle the dispute" (Swartz, 1997). Mediation is conducted in a nonthreatening, informal environment. Each party exchanges information regarding the issues in dispute. With the mediator, the parties collectively build an agenda, identify the issues, define the interests of each party, and build an agreement. Parties control the outcome, and the mediator controls the process (Swartz, 1997).

> Overall, we have found mediation to be a very positive, non-adversary method to resolve disagreements between the school district and our perspective, as parents. We went through the process on two different occasions, in two different states. One was much more positive than the other. Both had positive results. They took both time and work. During our more positive mediation, the informal and open communication set us in a positive direction. Having the agreement put in writing, with signatures, validated our willingness to work together on behalf of our child, even when there are gaps between our recommendations.
>
> —Parents of a child with special needs, who had recently completed a mediation process on behalf of their child.

Ideally, parents and schools will work through their differences through negotiation, conflict resolution, or mediation. Although due process is usually viewed as a last resort, it can result in a more appropriate plan and needed related services for the child with special needs. The following discussion describes the process and the possible repercussions.

Due Process

Due process is a right under the law, allowing parents or schools to protest what each other does. It is "a procedure which seeks to insure fairness of educational decisions and accountability of both parents and the educational professionals making these decisions. It can be viewed as a system of checks and balances concerning the identification, evaluation and provision of services regarding children with special needs" (*Kansas Parent and Professional Resource Manual,* 1995, p. 97). Within the process parents may be advised by an attorney or expert in the field. They may present evidence, cross-examine witnesses, obtain written records of the hearing and findings/decision. The due process hearing is conducted by an impartial hearing officer (to ensure no conflict of interest). The child involved may be present. Being open to the public is optional. Time lines are set by law, although extensions may be granted. Either party may appeal the decision and bring civil action in either state or federal court levels (*Kansas Parent and Professional Resource Manual,* 1995). Pursuing a due process impacts professionals as well as the entire family. Open dialogue regarding the due process, repercussions, and coping strategies utilized by family members may assist professionals and families in better understanding the intensity of such a process. Resources and recommendations for professional/family collaboration and suggestions for promoting the healing process after due process may benefit professionals and parents, but most importantly, the child.

You currently are or will be working with many parents who are more educated and informed consumers. They require more accountability and answers from professionals. We tend to question more today than in the past. We are more informed consumers. For example, you may question the grade an instructor gave you or question a doctor about a medical procedure being the most appropriate. This was not an accepted pattern in past generations. Families of children with special needs advocate and question more than ever before. Turnbull and Turnbull (1996) discuss the positive and negative effects of due process. Among the positives, they list assurance of the child's free and appropriate public education, accountability, a balance of power between schools and parents, appropriate changes in relationships with parents and children, and a focus on the child's rights and needs. The negative effects include financial and emotional costs, reduced confidence, and perhaps more conflict. Here are some reflections from parents after a due process hearing on behalf of their child.

- The due process itself was a horrible and terrifying experience—but we'd do it again in a heartbeat. It demonstrated to us how the system's safeguards can work for your child, but not without cost. We spent approximately 40 hours in direct contact (mediation and due process) meetings. In addition there were many hours spent with our lawyer, various calls, letters, and various documentation. We had twelve issues and mediated on all but one. We utilized a state advocacy service, so it was not a financial cost for us. We did prevail, and our daughter received most of the services we agree to, which were within her legal rights.

- Besides time, another cost was emotional. It impacted the entire family. We were swallowed up. We were treated as though we had committed a crime. We felt like victims. We were asked for phone bills, copies of calendars, notes, etc. The depositions were difficult. People testified information that was false—and we had proof! We wondered how they could sleep at night. We felt at times that it was a "Damned if you do, damned if you don't" or lose-lose situation. We were afraid of repercussions on our child.

- We lost "friends" or those we thought were friends. Worst of all, at times, our child was lost in the process. We certainly grew from this process—a painful growth. And we did make change.

- We are still healing. It was a struggle to return to the same team. Our trust was not there. Several people quit and we eventually moved. There is no winning, but sometimes you have no choice. We would not hesitate to do it again, if needed. We are stronger for this process.

"When parents and professionals work together to address the individual needs of children in a cooperative rather than adversarial manner, children benefit" (Dunlap, 1997, p. 119). Some conflict between parents and schools/professionals is unavoidable. But if we view due process as a means for working through conflicts, it can definitely have its positive effects. It may become a more adversarial means, and it is avoidable. In other words, some conflict is unavoidable, but due process is. Use of effective communication skills, negotiation/conflict resolution, and mediation are all means to avoid due process.

Implementing Effective Collaborative Practices

Guidelines for implementing effective collaboration are available in the literature (Anderson, 1985; Bailey,1987; Barnard, 1985; Bishop, Woll, & Arrango, 1993; Turnbull & Turnbull, 1996). The following information coincides with several of these but is written from your chapter author's personal and parental perspective.

These recommendations were compiled by two parents and edited by other parents and professionals. A major focus of this list is attitude. As noted, each section ends with "Attitude makes the difference." And it does! From the first diagnosis given to parents to the daily family/professional partnership, attitude is the key, along with good communication.

Focus on Our Child

I can recall when our youngest daughter, Tally (who has spina bifida and uses a wheelchair), was finishing kindergarten and about to enter first grade. She had also been a part of three preschool classes prior to kindergarten. We had not yet decided in which first grade class she would be. Transitioning her into the school system and kindergarten was quite an "eye opener" for everyone, and not a pleasant one for some. I will never forget one of the first grade teachers (who had also been a teacher for our older two daughters). She came up to me and sincerely said, "Is Tally going to be in our class next year? I would love to have her in my class. She's such a delightful girl!" I almost fell over. And then I nearly cried. This teacher was actually welcoming my child! She wanted her to be in her class. Tally's challenges did not outweigh this teacher seeing her as a child first. A child that she was even requesting to be in her class! We had not yet sensed this before, much less had anyone verbalize it. What a breath of fresh air!

—Mother of child with spina bifida

Focusing on the child means welcoming them and their family into a classroom or program. Welcoming a child into a classroom seems to be most appropriate and, of course, best practice. For some families this is not the experience. But the sense of being welcomed and belonging adds to the potential of success. Getting to know the child—as a child first—is important in not only language but, more important, philosophically. This does not mean that the child's disability should go unnoticed. Most disabilities don't just "go away." On the contrary, it is the responsibility of every professional working with the child to acknowledge, validate, and learn about his/her disability and how it affects this individual child.

Focus on the child cannot be achieved without partnership with the family. The family members are not just an extension of the child; they are individuals as well. Treat family members as individuals, not just "Tom's mom and dad" or "Jenny's sister." That would be like referring to a specific professional only as "Tom's teacher" or "Jenny's OT." Parents do have names. Try to use them, even if it means referring to the child's file in front of you. This partnership can also be enhanced with use of active/reflective listening. These specific skills will be discussed under the communication heading below. Active/reflective listening will cue professionals in to important information about the child as well as the concerns, needs, and resources of the family.

Many families "live advocacy" on a daily basis. It is a part of their family's way of life. This was evident in Mikelle's Persuasive Paper. Families welcome professionals in advocacy efforts. Parents sometimes feel that professionals would be more aware of their perspective if they could "walk in our moccasins" or "roll in our wheels" for a while. Professionals are increasingly recognizing the importance of family input and collaboration in their advocacy efforts. For example, the Division of Early Childhood (DEC) of the Council for Exceptional Children (CEC) established a Family Concerns position, to be held by a family member in each state, as a part of each state's DEC Executive Board. They look to parents as professionals of their children and appreciate their consultation. Another example of parent/professional collaboration is Family Voices, which is a coalition of families and professionals working together on behalf of children with special health care needs. Families need professionals to help develop a supportive system for their child.

Accountability

Parents of children with disabilities soon learn that they cannot "do this alone" and that asking for help is a sign of strength, not weakness. When professional, welcome questions and be ready to find answers if you do not have them. Utilize parents as resources. Parents are the professionals of their child. Parents know more about their child, his/her special strengths and needs, and perhaps even about their child's rights. Utilize your professional resources. Attend conferences on relevant issues; request training and consultation as needed. Additional training is essential: know what you're doing. Seek knowledge regarding special education and civil rights laws. Accept the responsibility. Be a creative and flexible planner. Plan ahead. This means looking ahead at a field trip sight for accessibility or collaborating with a therapist and parents on how a child can maximally participate in an activity. Monitor and justify how the child is meeting goals and objectives. Keep accurate records and share information with parents. The Reauthorization of IDEA in 1997 requires parents to receive updates on progress towards IEP goals (in all areas served) as often as typical educational progress reports. In other words, when a child gets a report card from school, the child on an IEP would also receive a progress report on related services, such as adapted physical education, physical therapy, and counseling. Value the input of parents. Let us know we're heard. Consider an advisory group or another means of attaining feedback from parents. Find some method to welcome and utilize feedback from parents. The reality is that the child and his/her family are the consumer. Their input may be very valuable.

Communication

Make genuine and two-way communication a reality, not just "lip service." For example, practice the courtesy of sending parents all information (assessment results, reports, etc.) at least one week prior to meeting. Questions can be addressed prior to or during the IEP/IFSP meeting. Here is a parent perspective on communication.

> Our time is valuable, too. Allow us time to digest information . . . before signing the IEP. We want what is best for our child, based on his/her needs. Yes, we do want what is educationally relevant. *Learn and practice negotiation and conflict resolution skills.* We will try to learn and practice them too. We may need some help. "Sweeping it under the carpet" gets us nowhere. Try not to get on the system's "bandwagon" when something doesn't feel right. We have known several professionals who knew something was wrong, but were afraid to speak out. There are many good resources in each state to assist with questions. We are the advocate for our child; hopefully we will not offend you in our role as parents and advocates. Please join us in advocacy.

Trust and Confidentiality

Here is a parent perspective on trust and confidentiality. Please show us we can trust you. Listen, follow through, work with us. Trust is difficult to reestablish, once it has been broken. Please don't talk about our child and family in the lounge or any other inappropriate place. We have the right to due process and pursuing our child's rights. There are repercussions for everyone. It is preventable. Mutual respect, honesty and courtesy are keys to our success in collaborating on behalf of our child.

The Importance of Empowering Families to Assist Them in Making Informed Decisions

Supporting and empowering families to make them stronger can only assist them in parenting. As discussed in Chapter 1, the empowering of families is important to establishing and maintaining a partnership. Family empowerment can also assist professionals with more effective intervention results. The family empowerment model and its potential impact is introduced below.

Family Empowerment Model

The child's needs are not in isolation of the family. Family empowerment and family-centeredness mean building upon the family's strengths and concerns based on their needs (within the context of the child). This model also offers families the tools to move forward and make educated choices, with respect to their individuality and diversity.

And we must realize that, as Bailey (1991) states, "true collaboration requires that programs move beyond token representation of families in planning and evaluating services" (p. 29). The service provider consults with the family, giving them information that serves to empower their decision making and involvement. Everyone on the child's team collaborates in the final decision-making process. However, it is the family that should make the final decisions (*Families and Disability Newsletter,* 1997). "By trying to give families what they want, professionals facilitate families' own power" (*Families and Disability Newsletter,* 1997). Giving families the ownership in decision making for their child can only strengthen them as a family and benefit the child. Parents need reminding that their ideas, solutions, and feelings are important and are implemented into their child's educational plan. "For most children in this country, the best investment in their future is an investment in a strong family" (M. L. Allen, social work educator in *Families and Disability Newsletter,* 1997). Program evaluations and parent/professional partnership checklists have been developed for the purpose of evaluating the family centeredness of a program, or the extent to which a program's philosophy promotes family empowerment (Bailey, McWilliam, Winton, & Simeonsson, 1992).

Parental Advocacy

Another empowering mechanism is advocacy. Parents typically have an innate need to protect their children. In other species, protection of the defenselessness of little ones is demonstrated with teeth, claws, cunningness, and ferocious strength (Sandler, 1997). Although some parents may display similar behavior, they have an empowering and more potent form of protection—namely, knowledge.

Families benefit from the supports and services that assist them in their role as parents in nurturing the development of their child. Parents need to be supported in the decision-making process on behalf of their child. Families need choices in services for their child and the family supports. Professionals must facilitate families in identifying their needs, concerns, and accessing their resources to address their needs and concerns. Professionals must assist families in getting the information needed to make knowledgeable choices. This information may vary, depending on the family, and must be "family friendly," that is, readily understandable. Families need to learn about and have access to support from other families, if they choose. Family support should be functional and appropriate to the individual family. The individualized family service plan (IFSP) serves to support the family in the way the family sees as appropriate. Through the facilitation from the team, the family identifies their strengths, needs, and concerns, as they choose. It is important to remember that this process is totally voluntary on the family's part. Several more formal interviews, surveys, and assessment forms exist to assess the strengths, needs, concerns, and resources of the family. Some are more appropriate than others. Some get downright personal and invasive. Some professionals prefer a less formal, more natural process of determining the priorities, concerns, and resources of families such as a family portfolio.

Part C of Reauthorized IDEA (formerly Part H of PL 99-457) and its accompanying regulations require that the IFSP identify family strengths and needs. Since the beginning of the Part H program, both families and professionals have been concerned about the potential intrusiveness of family assessment and identification of family strength and needs (Kaufman & McGonigel, 1991). According to McGonigel and colleagues (1991), many professionals and families prefer a more family-centered concept, that of identification of family concerns, priorities, and resources. Within activity-based intervention we must be sensitive to and implement methods in response to family concerns, priorities, and resources.

Family Concerns

Family concerns are defined as "areas that family members identify as needs, issues, or problems they want to address as part of the IFSP process" (McGonigel et al., 1991, p. 48). Needs, issues, and problems are best understood if we look at the impact, feelings, and issues that contribute to the concerns of families with children with special needs. Family concerns were discussed earlier in this chapter under family impact. According to Trout and Foley (1990), many children with special needs live in a world where parents are disappointed, angry, confused, and lonely. And what is worse, they do not even know why they feel this way. They are struggling with a host of losses, including loss of self-esteem, control over their lives and the future of their child, an envisioned healthy infant, routine, or the delight of others when viewing or hearing about their new child (Trout & Foley, 1990). Trout and Foley (1990) also point out that in addition, families are dealing with informational overload and the manner in which information is interpreted and presented. And finally, these authors (Trout & Foley, 1990) discuss the impact of the child with disabilities on family dynamics, such as siblings resenting the attention and changes the new member of the family has caused, or feelings of parents who are denied the normal, happy social exchanges with their healthy children, other family members, and friends. As noted earlier in this chapter, Perske (1987) describes many of the feelings and concerns of families adjusting to children with special needs, including the drags, the blocks, the hurts, the guilts, the greats, the hates, and the escapes. He notes that these feelings can reoccur and are not sequential, and each family reacts differently. Perske (1987) also covers topics of concern, such as societal views, spiritual struggles, the future, survival, normalization, taking risks, financial concerns, family systems, sibling relations, peer relations, and parent/professional partnerships.

Similar concerns are noted by Peterson (1987). Parental comments refer to "enemies of fatigue and loneliness," "my ego had been wiped out," "my emotional battery is no longer rechargeable," "ambivalent feelings of detachment/attachment," and "our family life is nonexistent. Nothing we do is normal. Worse, nothing we do is happy." Although families of children with special needs share many general concerns, they are very individualized in situations and perceptions and also possess unique concerns for individual family members. Brinker's (1992) definition of family concerns is "a process of negotiating a collective concern from individual family members' concerns" (p. 307). There may be numerous concerns, some more important than others. Therefore, we must prioritize.

Family Priorities

According to McGonigel and associates (1991), family priorities are defined as "a family's agenda and choices for how early intervention will be involved in family life" (p. 48). After assessing family needs, individual families, as well as individual family members, have formed opinions as to services they and their child need and priorities they should adopt (Bailey, 1987). These priorities and values may differ from those of professionals, and thus respect, understanding, and negotiating of these priorities and values must occur. Equality is a high priority for parents of children with special needs (Biklen, 1985). Specifically, parents of children with special needs want the right to have their child educated at public expense; continuity in schooling; real integration (accepted as regular members of the school); parent integration; to have their child treated as individuals, not as stereotypes; their child to be regarded as assets not burdens; and open dialogue about their child's disability rather than holding them at arm's length or patronizing them (Biklen, 1985).

Family Resources

McGonigel and colleagues (1991) define family resources as "the strength, abilities, and formal and informal supports that can be mobilized to meet family concerns, needs or outcomes" (p. 48). Families, no matter how troubled, have strengths and resources they can call upon to help themselves, which may include professional support, spiritual belief systems, and informal supports found in friends and family.

Families can further develop coping strategies in order to build family resources and strengths. Many resources are within the family system or in other available system resources; however, the building of resources and strengths occurs when we recognize, utilize, and put it all together. Another concept you may encounter related to resources within a family is that of resiliency. Patterson (1992) has also stressed that the resilient family does not attempt to be a "super family," is flexible and realistic, incorporates the child's disability needs into the daily activities, establishes priorities based on shared values of family members, allows time for nurturing the marriage, protects themselves from too much outside intrusion, communicates, expresses emotions, learns about the disability, maintains professional relationships with service providers, and develops a positive attitude toward their child's condition. There are strategies to improve a family's resiliency factor. They include, for example, looking on the bright side, thinking family first, learning new ways to cope, making new friends and keeping the old, and sharing your knowledge (Rhinehart, 1992).

There are some factors that predict success regarding the resiliency of siblings of children who are chronically ill. These family factors include family size (more siblings enhance family life); attitudes (view as opportunity for enrichment and satisfaction; resources; if needs are met, family can focus on more conventional aspects of family life); stable marriage (better able to share challenges and satisfactions); communication; sharing information (and fears); two-way communication (feelings shared from child with chronic condition); coping (e.g., humor, family meetings); and similar beliefs (agreement on priorities regarding child rearing, and how these beliefs can be translated to the child with disabilities) (Leonard, 1992).

Response to Family Concerns, Priorities, and Resources

"At the heart of a family-centered approach to this part of the IFSP process is the recognition that only a family can determine for itself the concerns, priorities, and resources that it brings to early intervention" (Kaufman & McGonigel, 1991, p. 47). Briefly these include family input regarding needs and strengths, and family concerns as viewed by professionals as being important and valid.

A variety of informal and formal methods and measures are currently being used to assist families in identifying their concerns, priorities, and resources as part of the IFSP process (Kaufman & McGonigel, 1991). Whatever methods or measures used should be carefully screened by consulting family members," to ensure that it is respectful of families—non-intrusive, non-judgmental, and (if written) written in plain, jargon-free language" (Kaufman & McGonigel, 1991, p. 51). It is also important to ensure that there is a match between the areas addressed by any measure used and the prioritized areas that the family identifies. Methods include interview, conversations, chats, storytelling, brainstorming, and more formal measures such as checklists, inventories, surveys, and questionnaires (Kaufman & McGonigel, 1991). Recently the trend has been toward using semistructured interview formats rather than instruments because experience to date in Part C early intervention programs seems to be supportive of that approach. It is beyond our scope here to share specific approaches to family assessment, but you will find numerous references to them in the recent early childhood special education literature.

Some service programs may be detrimental for some children and families, in that they try to accomplish too much within the context of family-centeredness (LeLaurin, 1992). Certain essential features in programs have a beneficial impact on children, which include (within an ecological framework) a developmental approach, structure, organization, and home/school continuity.

Brinker (1992) suggests that the "resolution of conflict through negotiation of individually conflicting perceptions and needs will be the basis for the mobilization of team expertise to address family concerns" (p. 328). This negotiation will need to include family concerns, yet development of the child must constitute the majority of what the early intervention team does (Brinker, 1992). He cautions professionals about accepting "general templates" for the nature of families, use of standard methods for identifying family concerns, and simplistic criteria for evaluating how family-centered, child-centered, or professionally centered an early intervention program is.

Programs need to balance their mother-child focus with greater attention to fathers (Upshur, 1991). Both mothers and fathers rated home visits as most helpful, and parent groups and individual parent counseling as less helpful, thus indicating careful thinking about planning and delivering parent group services (Upshur, 1991). And finally, Slentz and Bricker (1992) determined that the approach to family assessment and intervention should be family-guided rather than family-focused with the primary focus of intervention and assessment on the child. With this approach, family outcomes would be included in the IFSP as they arise, rather than at entry to the program (Slentz & Bricker, 1992). They recommend an initial interview and a brief needs assessment as opposed to a comprehensive assessment of families (Slentz & Bricker, 1992). These researchers conclude with the notion that "family guided intervention practices can promote individualized plans of service that are appropriate and for the lifestyle, priorities, and context of each family. It is time to disembark the bandwagon of comprehensive family assessment and move toward a more carefully defined set of procedures appropriate for interventionists and respectful of families" (p. 18).

Professionals and early intervention programs must recognize and respect the fact that each family is individual in its concerns, priorities, needs, perceptions, and resources, as is each individual family member. Early intervention programs must be sensitive and embrace this unique and individual diversity of families of children with special needs. The needs of fathers, mothers, siblings, and other extended family members of the child with special needs must be considered when identifying concerns, priorities, and resources, and when planning and implementing family-centered services. However, this family-centeredness must be within the context of the child, with the child as the center of the process. That is, this process must not be at the expense of the child's developmental outcomes and early intervention goals.

With the 1997 Reauthorization of IDEA: PL 105-17 came the increased parental role in the IEP process. Advocating parents, who are IDEA-educated, are the key to the success of IDEA. With the 1997 Reauthorization of IDEA, there are many changes that involve parents. Most notably are the changes in mediation, discipline, IEPs, the role of parents on the placement team, inclusion of students with disabilities in statewide assessments, and inclusion of students with disabilities in standard curriculum. Parents who are well informed represent the best quality control that IDEA and the schools have available to them. Informed parents provide a "checks and balance" and can assist in directing IDEA resources for education of children with disabilities.

Recognizing Family-Centered Supports/Services and Collaboration as a Foundation for Positive Behavioral Supports and Activity-Based Intervention

Family-centeredness and collaboration are at the heart of positive behavioral supports and activity-based intervention. Implementation of positive behavioral supports ensures the "right fit" and is individualized to each child and family. The plan is custom-fit to the uniqueness of individual and family values. This process is proactive and promotes family empowerment. The collaboration with professionals, friends, and community members enhances positive behavioral supports and activity-based interventions. Those who are familiar with the child's and family's values, activities and routines, strengths, and culture can best support the child and family in ways that are functional and preferred. This approach promotes intervention in the child's natural environment, in daily routines, with respect for individual and family uniqueness.

Summary

Well, if this chapter has not exhausted the reader from its content, know that it has exhausted the author in the process of writing. It has been written with intensity, passion, and feeling for this topic. A most appropriate conclusion with a final thought follows. Jeff Moyer—singer, songwriter, and disability advocate—effectively expresses many of the emotions and feelings of parents of children with special needs in harmonious form. Someday technology may make it possible for you to press here > < in this book to hear this selection, but for now, the words alone must suffice. They are very meaningful words that definitely touch the heart. Please read the words with care . . . and try, if only for a moment, to "walk in our moccasins."

৯৯৯৯

The Long Haul
by Jeff Moyer

I was beside you
In the darkness of the cave when fires died,
Protecting and defending with fierce and pride.
Against my fear,
I held you near,
It's been a long haul.

The long haul—
I'm with you and beside you for the long haul.
One goal together—
Over the long haul.

Now when they told me
The challenges that blocked you on your way,
I knew that I had nothing more to say.
We have so much to do,
But we'll see it through—
Over the long haul.

I have the strength of a mountain
I'm as solid as a stone.
I'm as fierce as a tiger

For you're my child and you're my own.
You've been with me forever
I would lay down my soul.
Living waters together
As onward we flow—
Over the long haul.

We walk this path now
A road that leads you forward on your way.
You're moving down your path and on the way
I see you grow
And time will show
It's for the long haul.

The long haul—
I'm with you and beside you for the long haul
One goal together
It doesn't seem so far
For it's who you are
And it's for the long haul.

❧❧❧

Chapter 2 Suggested Activities and Resources

Activities

1. Spend an entire day (from dawn until bedtime) in a wheelchair or simulating another type of special need. Do all of the typical activities you do each day. Write down all of your thoughts and reflections throughout the day. Undoubtedly you will need to "cheat" from time to time, as your environment may not be very accessible, but try to keep this at a minimum. Record your "cheating" times and how you might need to adapt the environment. As you encounter others throughout your day, try to objectively determine if you are being treated any differently. Note attitudes of yourself and others. This experience can have a great impact and can help you to

have a tiny glimpse of what it might be like to experience such a need. If you have a special need, try to go to places you have never been to before. Note attitudes and accessibility concerns. Share reflections with classmates.

2. Build a rapport with a family with a young child (birth to eight years) with special needs. After spending time with the family, request to spend twenty-four hours or the weekend with them—not to do respite care (in absence of parents) but to join in with their typical activities. Note attitudes and accessibility concerns, if appropriate. Also note daily modifications, adaptations, assistive technology, and types of activities the family members share, or a need for any of the above. Share reflections with classmates. This experience, too, can have a great impact and can assist you in beginning to understand the impact of having a young family member with a disability. I would suggest that you might offer a few hours of respite care (if you have been trained and are comfortable and safe caring for the child independently, as well as the parents being comfortable with you caring for their child) to thank the family for allowing you to impose upon their lives.

3. As a class, visit a neonatal intensive care unit. Tour, if possible. Interview nurses/staff about their experiences with families (parents, siblings, extended families). Ask what they might feel to be key factors in family members adjusting to the impact of the birth of a child with a disability. Also tour the pediatric floor, if possible. Ask nurses and staff the same question. Also ask what they do to support family members during this time. What policies might they have that may promote or be barriers to family/child interactions and attachment? Make a list of other questions you might have.

4. Interview one family member and one professional about specific examples of ways to promote collaboration between professionals and family members. Also ask about times of disagreement when they may have needed to use negotiation techniques. What strategies have they used? What are some barriers to collaboration?

5. Invite a panel of family members of children with special needs to share their feelings about the impact of a child with special needs in the family. How have they adjusted? Discuss what supports, agencies, and individuals have been helpful. Share with them Perske's "Bewildering Times," as noted in this chapter. Ask them how they might relate to the different stages Perske has described. Make a list of additional interview questions. It would be most appropriate to share the list of questions and Perske's "Bewildering Times" with them prior to the visit, so they could be prepared to share only what they might be comfortable sharing.

6. View the video *When the Bough Breaks* (1991), available from the Wisconsin Department of Public Instruction. Stop the video after the dance, and as a class, discuss your interpretation of the dance. View the remainder of the video. Compare your interpretations with those of professionals and family members sharing in the last portion of the video.

7. Set aside at least an hour to take a look at two websites: Family Village: http://www.familyvillage.wisc.edu/ and Sibling Support Project: http://www.chmc.org/departmt/sibsupp. Family Village is unbelievable and

will lead you to a host of information about disabilities and families. The Sibling Support Project website will introduce you to SIBSHOPS, Sibnet, and Sibkids. It will be well worth your time. These are only two of many relevant resources you can find on the Internet.

Selected Resources

1. Try to locate a copy of Perske's *Hope for the Families*. Read each chapter (it is brief and very easy to read) and try some of the items under the "Consider these Options" sections. They are quite meaningful. Share these with a family with a child with special needs.

2. For more strategies, techniques, and examples of negotiation and mediation, refer to R. Fisher and M. Ury. (1981), *Getting to Yes: Negotiating Agreement without Giving In*, New York, Penguin Books.

3. *Exceptional Parent* includes many family stories, strategies, and resources in each issue. The parent and family perspectives are important for professionals to try to understand and be aware of.

4. For more information about SIBSHOPS, which are support programs for siblings of children with special needs, locate D. J. Meyer, and P. F. Vadasy (1994), *Sibshops: Workshops for Siblings of Children with Special Needs*, Baltimore, Brookes Publishing. This resource takes you through, step by step, how to implement SIBSHOPS. In addition, refer to the Sibling Support Project: http://www.chmc.org/departmt/sibsupp.

References

Anderson, M. A. (1985). Cooperative group tasks and their relationship to peer acceptance and cooperation. *Journal of Learning Disabilities, 18*(2), 83–86.

Bailey, D. B. (1987). Collaborative goal setting with families: Resolving differences in values and priorities for services. *Topics in Early Childhood Special Education, 7*(2), 59–71.

Bailey, D. B. (1991). Building positive relationships between professionals and families. In M. J. McGonigel, R. K. Kaufman, & B. H. Johnson (Eds.), *Guidelines and recommended practices for the individualized family service plan* (2nd ed). Bethesda, MD: Association for the Care of Children's Health.

Bailey, D. B., McWilliam, P. J., Winton, P. J., & Simeonsson, R. J. (1992). *Implementing family-centered services in early intervention: A team based model for change*. Cambridge: Brookline Books.

Barnard, W. S. (1985). A study of cooperation/collaboration among employment training systems. *Journal of Vocational Educational Research, 10*(3), 13–34.

Barry, E. (Ed.). (1977). *Early childhood education*. Wayne, NJ: Avery Publishing Group.

Bathshaw, M. L. (1991). *Your child has a disability: A complete sourcebook of daily and medical care*. Boston: Little Brown.

Biklin, D. (1985). *Achieving the complete school*. Columbia University: Teachers College Press.

Binkard, B. (1987). Brothers and sisters talk with PACER. Cited in D. J. Meyer & P. F. Vadasy (1994), *Sibshops: Workshops for siblings of children with special needs*. Baltimore: Paul H. Brookes Publishing Co.

Bishop, K. K., Woll, J., & Arrango, P. (1993). *Family/professional collaboration for children with special health needs and their families*. Burlington, VT: Family Professional Project.

Brinker, R. P. (1992). Family involvement in early intervention: Accepting the unchangeable, changing the changeable, and knowing the difference. *Topics in Early Childhood Special Education, 12*(3), 307–332.

Bronfenbrenner, U. (1995). The bioecological model from a life course perspective: Reflections of a participant observer. In P. Moen, G. H. Elder, Jr., & K. Luscher (Eds.), *Examining lives in context* (pp. 599–618). Washington, DC: American Psychological Association.

Bronfenbrenner, U. (1979). *The ecology of human development: Experiment by nature and design*. Cambridge: Harvard University Press.

Cleveland, D. W., & Miller, N. (1977). Attitudes and life commitments of older siblings of mentally retarded adults: An exploratory study. *Mental Retardation, 15*(3), 38–41.

Dunlap, L. L. (1997). *An introduction to early childhood special education*. Boston: Allyn and Bacon.

Dunst, C., Trivette, C., & Deal, A. (1988). *Enabling and empowering families: Principles and guidelines for practice*. Cambridge, MA: Brookline Books.

Dunst, C. J., Trivette, C. M., & Deal, A. (Eds.). (1994). *Supporting and strengthening family. Volume 1: Methods, strategies and practices*. Cambridge, MA: Brookline Books.

Families and Disability Newsletter. (1997). Vol. 8, No. 2. University of Kansas Beach Center on Families and Disability.

Farber, B. (1960). Family organization and crisis: Maintenance of integration in families with a severely mentally retarded child. *Monographs of the Society for Research in Child Development, 25*, (1, Serial No. 75).

Fisher, R., & Ury, M. (1981). *Getting to yes: Negotiating agreement without giving in*. New York: Penguin Books.

Fowle, C. (1973). The effect of a severely mentally retarded child on his family. *American Journal of Mental Deficiency, 73*, 468–473.

Gath, A. (1974). Sibling reactions to mental handicap: A comparison of brothers and sisters of mongol children. *Journal of Child Psychology and Psychiatry, 15*, 187–198.

Gordon, T. (1970). *Parent effectiveness training*. New York: Wyden.

Grossman, F. (1972). *Brothers and sisters of retarded children: An exploratory study*. Syracuse, NY: Syracuse University Press.

Kansas parent and professional resource manual: Active participation in the special education process. (1995). Kansas State Board of Education.

Kantos, S., & Dunham, J. (1987). *Neighbor care: Training manual for family day care*. (Grant No. 600840123).

Kaufman, R. K., & McGonigel, M. J. (1991). Identifying family concerns, priorities and resources. In B. H. Johnson, M. J. McGonigel, & R. K. Kaufman, *Guidelines and recommended practices for the IFSP*. Washington, DC: ACCH.

Labato, D., Barbour, L., Hall, L., & Miller, C.T. (1987). Psychosocial characteristics of preschool siblings of handicapped and nonhandicapped children. *Journal of Abnormal Child Psychology, 15*, 329–338.

LeLaurin, K. (1992). Infant and toddler models of service delivery: Are they detrimental for some children and families? *Topics in Early Childhood Special Education, 12*(1), 82–104.

Leonard, B. (1992). Sibling success: Needs more study. *Children's Health Issues, 1*(1), 9.

McCubbin, H. I., & Patterson, J. M. (1982). Family adaptation to crisis. In H. I. McCubbin, A. E. Cauble, & J. M. Patterson (Eds.), *Family stress, coping, and social support*. Springfield, IL: Charles C. Thomas.

McGonigel, M., Kaufman, R., & Johnson, B. (1991). *Guidelines and recommended practices for the IFSP* (pp. 47–55), 2nd ed., ACCH and NECTAS.

Meyer, D. J., & Vadasy, P. F. (1994). *Sibshops: Workshops for siblings of children with special needs*. Baltimore: Paul H. Brookes Publishing Co.

Patterson, J. (1992). Why us? How families develop resilience. *Children's Health Issues, 1*(1), 4–5.

Perske, R. (1987). *Hope for the families*. Nashville: Abingdon Press.

Peterson, N. L. (1987). *Early intervention for handicapped and at-risk children*. Denver: Love Publishing.

Rhinehart, P. M. (1992). The resiliency factor. *Children's Health Issues, 1*(1), 6–7.

Russell, C. L. (1997). We're special, too! Supporting siblings of children with special needs. *Disability Solutions, 2*(1), 1–7.

Sandler, A. (1997). *Living with spina bifida: A guide for families and professionals*. Chapel Hill: University of North Carolina.

Skirtic, T., Summers, J. A., Brotherson, M. J., & Turnbull, A. (1983). Severely handicapped children and their brothers and sisters. In J. Blacher (Ed.), *Severely handicapped young children and their families: Research in review* (pp. 215–246).

New York: Academic Press.

Slentz, K. L., & Bricker, D. (1992). Family-guided assessment for IFSP development: Jumping off the family assessment bandwagon. *Journal of Early Intervention, 16*(1), 11–19.

Summers, J. A., Dell-Oliver, C., Turnbull, A. P., Benson, H. A., Santelli, E., Campbell, M., & Siegel-Cansey, E. (1990). Examining the individualized family service plan process: What are families and practitioners preferences? *Topics in Early Childhood Special Education, 10*(1), 78–99.

Swan, W. W., & Morgan, J. L. (1993). *Collaborating for comprehensive services for young children and their families.* Baltimore: Paul H. Brookes Publishing Co.

Swartz, L. C. (1997). *Midland Mediation Service: Moving through conflict into resolution,* pamphlet.

Trout, M., & Foley, G. (1990). Working with families of handicapped infants and toddlers. *Infants and Young Children, 10*(1), 57–67.

Turnbull, A. P., & Turnbull, H. A. (1996). *Families, professionals, and exceptionality: A special partnership* (3rd ed.). Upper Saddle River, NJ: Merrill/Prentice-Hall.

Upshur, C. C. (1991). Mothers' and fathers' ratings of benefits of early intervention services. *Journal of Early Intervention, 15,* 345–357.

Wisconsin Department of Public Instruction (1991). *When the bough breaks.* Madison, WI: Author.

Internet resources:

Family Village: http://www.familyvillage.wisc.edu/

SIBSHOPS: http://www.chmc.org/departmt/sibsupp

IDEA (reauthorized) PL 105-17: Download the file from http://www.ed.gov/offices/OSERS/IDEA/the_law.html

National Parent Network on Disabilities: http://www.npnd.org/

Chapter

3

Principles of Positive Behavioral Supports (PBS)

INTRODUCTION

In this section of the text you will learn about the principles of positive behavioral supports, activity-based intervention, and developmentally appropriate practice. This chapter will provide an in-depth exploration of positive behavioral supports applied to young children within inclusive educational settings. Here are the objectives that the reader will address in Chapter 3. You should be able to:

- Understand the importance of examining children's behavior from an ecological perspective including familial, cultural, and community influences on social/emotional development.
- Recognize the relationship between developmental age and behavior.
- Identify the principles of positive behavioral supports and the application of these principles within inclusive early childhood education settings.
- Recognize the importance of merging positive behavioral supports, activity-based intervention, and developmentally appropriate practice within inclusive early childhood education settings.

A major goal for all early childhood education programs should be the design and delivery of a safe and nurturing environment that promotes learning, growth, and development for all children. The need for positive educational environments for young children is critical to the well-being of children in today's world given the ever increasing threats to the welfare of our nations young children. A growing number of social concerns such as violence, drug abuse, child abuse, and neglect are posing increased threats to the health and well-being of America's children as pointed out by the Children's Defense Fund 1998 report. Increased numbers of children face the threat of poverty and the risk factors associated with it.

Hanson and Carta (1995) reported that there were 14.6 million children living in poverty, and subsequently, those children were at greater risk for developmental delays, illness, lack of social/family supports, and increased levels of family stress. As a result of these changing demographic conditions and the enhanced risk factors associated with them, children served within early childhood educational settings represent a divergent group of youngsters in need of a variety of services and supports. The increased diversity among children in early childhood educational settings may pose new and unique challenges for the professionals working within these settings. This fact warrants that early childhood education professionals must remain cognizant of individual learning styles, temperament, and behavioral development of the children they serve in their quest to deliver child-centered educational services and supports.

Behavior management and/or discipline have been frequently cited as major concerns by teachers and related professionals in these and other educational settings given the range of diversity found in today's educational systems (Fantuzzo & Atkins, 1992). Early childhood education programs now find themselves in the position of serving a broader spectrum of children from diverse cultural, economic, community, and family settings. Many of these children bring into the educational setting an array of social/emotional issues that challenge the professional expertise and resources of teachers and programs alike. The forms of behavior displayed by some children are often considered to be incongruent with child care program expectations and judged intolerable by teachers and professionals within these settings. Therefore, professionals must be equipped with a conceptual basis for understanding adaptive and challenging forms of child behavior and the contributing factors that help to explain these responses.

Numerous factors influence the socioemotional development of children including ecological and developmental considerations. For purposes of this text, socioemotional development is defined best by Prizant and Weatherby (1990) as "a young child's development of capacities to experience and express a variety of emotional states, to regulate emotional arousal, to establish secure and positive relationships, and to develop a sense of self as distinct from others and as capable of achieving goals in interactions with the social and nonsocial world" (p. 1). These influencing factors comprise the context from which behavior originates and must be understood by professionals when attempting to design and deliver child-centered services and supports.

The basic premise of this chapter is not to imply that professionals or parents should control behavior in children, but rather that they should utilize approaches aimed at facilitating developmentally appropriate behavior in young children. The goal of positive behavioral supports is the attainment of meaningful outcomes for each child. Intervention efforts attempt to minimize and prevent the occurrence of challenging behavior in children through the management of antecedent conditions that occasion these behaviors and through the teaching of alternative behaviors and skills. These aims are best realized through the development of careful assessment and positive intervention practices.

Advocates for the use of positive behavioral supports are strongly opposed to the use of rapid suppression methods, which are aimed at the rapid reduction of behavior in children through punishment (Durand, 1990). An example of rapid suppression procedures would be spanking children as a form of punishment rather than utilizing positive supports aimed at identifying the purpose and cause of behavior, managing probable antecedents in the learning or home environment, and actively teaching positive alternative behaviors. The purpose of this chapter and text is to promote an understanding of children's behavior from a framework that acknowledges the developmental and environmental factors operating within each child's life that influence behavior.

Ecological Influences on Behavioral Development

The ecological perspective represents one among many models including behavioral, medical, cognitive, and social learning theories for understanding behavior in young children. For purposes of this text we will first examine the many ecological influences that shape behavioral development in children.

The ecological model acknowledges the relationship between behavior and environment and how environmental events and conditions influence behavioral development in children. The relationship between a child's behavior and various environmental events is termed the child's behavioral ecology (Thurman, 1977). The home, family, community, and key individuals within these environments in which the child interacts all constitute the child's ecology. Therefore, the influences that parents, family, culture, and community have in the formation of social/emotional skills are all critical components in the child's ecology. Researchers have long understood that optimal development in children is directly linked to the quality of the environments that they live and function in (Bradley & Brisby, 1993; Bronfenbrenner, 1977).

The ecological model stems from the field of eco-behavioral psychology and was originally implemented widely throughout Europe (Juul, 1977). Hobbs (1974) introduced the ecological model to special education and mental health professionals within the United States and elaborated on its use within France. The European service delivery system has traditionally utilized professionals known as "educateurs" to facilitate child-centered services within educational and mental health settings serving children. The "educateur" is a professional child care specialist who is cross-trained in the disciplines of education, child development, social work, and psychology and works directly with children and their families in coordinating activities between school and home (Juul, 1977). The professional role of the "educateur" is similar to that of the case coordinator professional working in early childhood programs in the United States.

The movement toward ecological models in early childhood education settings continues to be widely practiced within Scandinavian countries. Akesson and Granlund (1995) report that in Sweden early childhood educators (special and regular) have shifted their focus from exclusively the individual child toward a focus on the interaction between the child and their environment. The coordination of educational services and other supports to young children in Sweden are an example of the allied family approach whereby services and supports are family-centered (Akesson & Granlund, 1995; Dunst, Johansson, Trivette, & Hanby, 1991).

Currently, the ecological model is widespread in the United States as exemplified by the incorporation of the individualized family service plan (IFSP), a major component of PL 99-457 the Education of the Handicapped Act Amendment of 1986, in Part C of the 1997 reauthorization of IDEA. The IFSP promotes child and family-centered services and supports and requires a commitment to services in natural environments. As part of the interdisciplinary team process an IFSP is completed on all eligible infants and toddlers (birth to three years). The IFSP must include: (*a*) a statement of the child's present level of functioning in cognitive, speech and language, psychosocial, motor, and self-help skills; (*b*) a statement of the family's strengths and needs relating to the child's development; (*c*) a statement of the major outcomes expected to be achieved by the child and family; (*d*) the established criteria for determining progress; (*e*) the specific services needed to meet the unique needs of the child and family, including the method, frequency, and intensity of services; (*f*) the projected dates for initiation and anticipated duration of services and supports; (*g*) the name of the case manager from the profession most immediate to the needs of the child and family who will be the responsible party for implementation of the plan; (*h*) the procedural steps for the transition from early intervention services to the preschool program. The author's home state has recently revised the IFSP form to be consistent with the 1997 amendments to IDEA. A copy of this appears in Appendix A.

Turnbull and Turnbull (1997) have explored the family systems approach in providing early intervention services to children with disabilities and their families. The family systems approach is quite similar to the ecological model in that families are composed of a series of subsystems, which include husband-wife, parent-child, sibling, and family/extra-family (Turnbull & Turnbull, 1997). Each of these subsystems is important to the overall development of the child. In turn, each subsystem operates in a mutually synergistic role to influence the outcomes for members within the family. Stressors within these subsystems influence the degree of consistency or equilibrium within the child's life and other members of the family as well. When an imbalance occurs within one or more of these subsystems, the eco-system or family unit as a whole becomes subsequently stressed.

There are various stressors that could potentially impact on families. These include socioeconomic, marital, disability, or chronic health concerns. If one or more of these stressors become chronic and are not well managed because of either a lack of internal coping mechanisms on the part of the parent or as a direct result of inadequate levels of service and support, each member of the family becomes at risk for being negatively impacted. Although a precise relationship between the role of chronic stress and child development has not yet been empirically determined, the risk factors fostered by such chronic stress serve as just cause for concern (Bradley & Brisby, 1993). Research supports that children when confronted by chronic stress over time will often display challenging behavior in their attempts to understand their feelings and communicate their level of frustration and need for attention (Giddan, Bade, Rickenberg, & Ryley, 1995).

Bradshaw (1988) addressed the importance of children developing a healthy self-concept and how parents and families must provide the love and support for the child's developing self-concept. Some parents and families can detract from developing a healthy self-concept in their children through abandonment (Bradshaw, 1988). Bradshaw further asserts that "parents may abandon their children through the following ways: by physically leaving them alone; by ineffectively modeling their own emotions and feelings for their children; by not providing for their children's developmental dependency needs, by abusing them, by using their children to meet their own unmet dependency needs; by using children to heal their marriages; by living in denial of family issues; by not giving of themselves in terms of time, attention, and direction, and by acting shameless" (p. 3). Nurturing and consistent love and support from the family are essential to the development and psychosocial well-being of every child and are in fact their birthright. It is important that family stress be identified and minimized through the delivery of services and supports to reduce and minimize potential risk factors that could hinder the socioemotional development of the young child.

Children and adolescents identified with severe emotional and behavioral disorders can frequently trace the development of these problems back to their early childhood years. The emotional conflicts found within home and community settings have greatly influenced the lack of social/emotional development in many of these children and adolescents. Issues of concern that place children at risk for developing emotional and behavioral disorders include the absence of consistent cues from parents, parental-child abuse, insufficient bonding between parents and child, and general parental neglect. Research findings have indicated that parents within homes that are less than optimal in terms of functioning do not initiate quality contact with their children as frequently and play considerably less with their children (Giddan et al., 1995). Many of these behaviors if modeled within the home can negatively influence the child's own behavioral development and lead to subsequent behavior problems later on.

Children raised in stressful homes are also at a greater risk for abuse (Hanson & Carta, 1995). Straus (1980) reported that abusive parents had limited coping mechanisms and associated violence with stress, whereas Zirpoli (1986) in a review of the literature found that four major classes of variables were associated with parental child abuse. These categories were (*a*) parent factors, (*b*) sociocultural factors, (*c*) environmental factors, and (*d*) child factors. Parent factors included whether parents had been abused as children, exhibited poor parenting skills, suffered from low self-esteem, frequently used physical punishment to discipline their children, and infrequently used reinforcement to reward their children. Sociocultural factors included the acceptance of physical punishment by society, inadequate laws protecting the rights of children, limited child protection resources, and ambiguous child abuse laws. Environmental influences included marital conflicts between husband and wife, conflicts between parent and child, substance abuse, and unemployment. Finally, child factors that appeared to contribute to parental child abuse included the presence of disability or other risk factors such as prematurity and low birth weight.

Parental Influences

The significant role that parents and family have in the development of the child is obvious. Our intervention efforts must be inclusive of the parents and family whenever possible. Significant persons within these environments can often serve as agents of change provided that services and supports are sensitive to the strengths and needs found within these settings. Conversely, parents and other members of the family may serve as targets of our intervention efforts when the well-being of a child is in jeopardy. In cases where children are at risk for abuse and neglect at the hands of their parents or other family members, these individuals must certainly be considered targets for change to avoid undue harm to the child.

Parents shape the behavioral development of their children through modeling (see Figure 3–1). This concept has been considered a key element of social learning (Bandura & Walters, 1963). Bandura (1965) demonstrated the importance of modeling in the development of behavior through observational

Figure 3–1 Parents shape the behavioral development of their children through modeling.

learning. In other words, children imitate the behaviors they observe. This fact became more apparent in a recent study conducted by Hart and Risley (1995). They examined the importance of parent models in the language development of children. Hart and Risley (1995) studied forty-two children, ranging in age from six months to six years, all from Midwestern families of diverse socioeconomic backgrounds ranging from professionals (n = 13), working class (n = 23), and public welfare recipients (n = 6). Findings from the Hart and Risely (1995) study indicated that each of the participating families had a vested interest in the attainment of positive outcomes for their children; however, the limitations that were faced by children in the impoverished homes were noticeably different. All children who participated in their study developed acceptable language skills by age three despite the obvious economic voids felt by the lower income families.

The most important fact originating from the study that directly reinforced the importance of modeling in the developing child was that the affluent family participants were found to communicate more frequently with their children. The interactions between these sets of parents and their children were also found to be "richer" or more stimulating in terms of content than the interactions occurring between parents and children from lower socioeconomic conditions. The results from the Hart and Risley (1995) study support the importance of models in language development in the young child as well as the influence of socioeconomic status on cognitive development.

Language development influences social/emotional development in children as well (Giddan et al., 1995). Some theorists believe that social/emotional development begins at birth (Izard, 1991). Young children need exposure to models within home and educational environments that promote the use of language to express and communicate feelings from an early age. Giddan and colleagues

(1995) have described how this process occurs in the typically developing child and how atypical affective development occurs in young children who suffer from emotional and behavioral disabilities. The authors have indicated that the typically developing infant by nine months of age becomes aware of cause and effect through communication and the effect that their communicative attempts have on the environment around them (Giddan et al., 1995). By the age of twenty months children will use language to express their internal states (Giddan et al., 1995).

Martin and Pear (1996) have cited that parents often use modeling in an unsystematic manner to teach social amenities such as correct manners, saying please and thank you, and also for teaching language. Conversely, children who find themselves in home environments that are abusive and less than optimal in terms of functioning also learn negative social behaviors from the parental models they observe. As pointed out by Giddan and associates (1995), young children with emotional and behavioral disabilities frequently display an inability to use language to express their feelings, which is often evident by the time they enter elementary school. An ecological perspective is thus extremely useful in the assessment and intervention process to fully ascertain issues within the home, including parent-child interactions, or within educational settings between teacher and child. One myth that has been promoted within parts of our society has been the notion that "children are to be seen and not heard." This statement could not be further from the truth as far as social/emotional development is concerned and the relationship that communication and language have in the development of these skills in children. Suppression of language and communication only serves to suppress emotions and feelings, thus thwarting optimal behavioral development in children.

Other issues that must be considered when developing child and family-centered early childhood education and intervention include the sociocultural factors present in the child's and family's life. Cultural influences on development were first explored by Vygotsky, a Russian psychologist in the 1920s. Vygotsky (1978) maintained that behavioral development was significantly influenced by cultural expectations. These sociocultural influences on the development of social/emotional behavior in young children will now be explored in greater depth.

Sociocultural Influences

Sociocultural factors have an influential role in the social/emotional development of children. Given the changing demographics of our society and the projected increase of children from culturally and linguistically diverse backgrounds, cross-cultural awareness has become an essential professional competency for all early childhood educators (Barrara, 1993; Lynch & Hanson, 1992). Sociocultural factors associated with the child and family should be a primary consideration of educators as they attempt to effectively deliver services and supports to culturally and linguistically diverse children and their families. Professionals should strive to understand that child discipline is often varied within diverse sociocultural groups. For example, within traditional Native American families, it is common for children to be given the same degree of respect as adults, and this belief is reflected in the child discipline practices of the culture. Corporal punishment such as verbal and physical abuse is therefore not an accepted practice within traditional Native American families (Nelson et al., 1993).

Extended family members may also play a significant role in the child-rearing process within these families. Grandparents within traditional Native American families have an active role in the daily life of the child and family, including the provision of care, discipline, and guidance in the traditions of the family and culture. It is also a practice within Native American families to find value placed on group belonging rather than on individualism (Joe & Malach, 1992). Native American children have often been misunderstood by Anglo school settings where individual effort is praised and have instead been viewed as being too passive and unmotivated. This example illustrates a form of cultural incongruence where diverse cultural values have been misunderstood by professionals (from outside the culture) and therefore are incongruent with the beliefs held by the dominant culture (Nelson et al., 1993).

There are many other sociocultural influences that interact with the development of social/emotional skills in young children. These influences include demographic variables such as the location and size of the community, resources available to families and children including health services, socioeconomic conditions within a community or region, and degree of poverty and crime. Each of these factors may directly or indirectly influence the family system to some degree and subsequently affect young children within these families. Early childhood educators will be better able to provide meaningful services and supports to the children and families with whom they work if care and sensitivity are given toward understanding the sociocultural influences that are part of the child's life. The ecological perspective in service delivery accounts for the role that these influences have in the formation of behavioral development in the young child and provides a context from which to begin this process.

It is often difficult for professionals to reach a level of cross-cultural competence given cultural differences and a lack of experience and understanding. Lynch (1992) stated that "culture is akin to being observed through the one-way mirror; everything we see is from our own perspective" (p. 35). Developing cross-cultural competency can be very challenging because of our own bias, lack of self-understanding, and fear of the new and unfamiliar (Lynch, 1992).

Experts point out that cross-cultural competence can be enhanced through the development of self-awareness of one's own culture, through study of others' cultural heritage and traditions, through gathering information from cultural authorities, and through increased interactions with individuals who are linguistically and culturally diverse (Chan, 1990; Lynch, 1992). Professionals must remain sensitive to these influences on behavioral development in young children. Cross-cultural awareness is best obtained through gaining a thorough understanding of the characteristics of home and community environments that surround the child (Barrera, 1993; Nelson, Smith, & Dodd, 1993). Early childhood educators should explore questions aimed at gaining a better understanding about the language spoken in the home, cultural traditions practiced by the family, and the degree of involvement that extended family members may play in the child's life.

Developmental Age and Behavior

Educators and parents alike must consider the relationship between a child's developmental age and behavior when formulating performance expectations for the child. Frustration is often experienced by some caregivers and parents alike when children fail to live up to their expectations. Depending upon the level of understanding and tolerance exhibited by these individuals, some of them may externalize their frustration and intolerance and direct it toward the child in the form of anger. Such interactions often send a mixed message to the child resulting in feelings of guilt or shame. In reality, what has taken place is a failure to set developmentally appropriate expectations for the child given the child's age and developmental level. To aid in our understanding of what is developmentally appropriate for the young child in terms of behavior, we must first understand child development.

LeFrancois (1994) points out that the contextual or ecological model for understanding child development emphasizes the role of society, culture, and family in the process as we have discussed previously. This common theme is consistent with how services and supports are delivered to infants and young children and is especially evident in early childhood special education as has been noted. Given that the focus of this chapter is on understanding behavior in young children and the context in which it occurs, the ecological systems theory (Bronfenbrenner, 1979) is most appropriate as a beginning for examining child development and its relationship to behavior. As you progress through the book, you will encounter a number of additional references to the work of Une Bronfenbrenner as it relates to inclusive early childhood education.

Bronfenbrenner's ecological systems theory emphasizes the child's interaction with the environment as an active process in child development. This model has three basic elements: (*a*) the person, (*b*) the context (where the behavior occurs), and (*c*) the processes that produce the developmental change. This perspective is consistent with other ecological viewpoints as previously discussed in the chapter. The focus in Bronfenbrenner's model is on the developing child and the people, places, and things he/she interacts with. Bronfenbrenner (1979) points out that there is a strong relationship between a child's personality and the characteristics that compose the child's environments. The ecological systems theory serves as a foundation for early childhood educators in attempting to understand child development and behavior; however, the work of Erik Erikson (1968) and his theory of psychosocial development is critical to applying this understanding on a practical level. Erikson (1968) viewed psychosocial development as a series of eight stages, the first three of these being most relevant to this text. Erikson's first three stages of psychosocial development include the following:

Trust versus Mistrust (Ages Birth through Fifteen Months)

This stage occurs between birth and fifteen months in typically developing children. During this stage, the infant begins to develop increasing levels of trust in the world that he/she interacts with. The most significant individuals during this stage are, of course, the mother and father. It is therefore essential at this stage that the infant and mother establish a bond, and that the mother and father provide the infant with love and affection.

Autonomy versus Shame and Doubt (Ages Fifteen Months through Three Years)

This stage occurs between the ages of fifteen months and approximately three years. Children at this stage are faced with the urge to behave in their own way, yet are unwilling to accept full autonomy for their actions. It is important that parents and caregivers provide consistency and support as well as increasing opportunities over time for promoting independence. Erikson (1968) suggests a balance between firmness and flexibility on the part of parents. This holds true for educators as well.

Initiative versus Guilt (Ages Three through Seven Years)

This stage typically occurs between the ages of three and seven years and is centered on the child discovering his/her "self," just who they are as individuals. Children during this stage begin to explore more broadly the environment around them and in turn develop increased levels of independence. They become very inquisitive during this stage in their attempt to understand the world in which they live. When provided with consistency and support from parents and educators, children will begin to develop a sense of personal responsibility during this stage of development.

Erikson's theory provides us with a concrete means for understanding social/emotional development in children. As with any theory, no single viewpoint is complete. The landmark work of Erik Erikson, Albert Bandura, and Une Bronfenbrenner among others provides us with a conceptual framework from which to develop and evaluate our personal understanding of professional services and supports to young children. As you become a more seasoned professional, you will be better able to realize how best to draw from each as a resource in your own professional development. Some final suggestions on understanding behavior in the context of a child's developmental age are as follows:

- Have a reasonable expectation, given the child's age, development, previous learning, and presence of disability or other potential risk factors.
- Value each child as a special person with individual strengths, needs, and desires.
- View each child's behavior in a professional manner, being mindful to separate the child from the behavior.
- Attempt to understand the behavior from an ecological and developmental perspective taking into consideration these influences on the occurrence of the behavior.
- Remember that each child's behavior is often reflective of the presence or absence of structure in their environment, the quality of the structure, the presence or absence of clear and consistent instructional cues provided within the educational environment.
- Strive to maintain behavioral expectations for children that are developmentally appropriate and above all supported by a child-centered philosophy built on nurturing and unconditional respect for each child.

Principles of Positive Behavioral Supports

Positive behavioral supports (PBS), as stated in Chapter 1, consist of an underlying philosophy and set of strategies aimed at minimizing challenging forms of behavior and promoting positive alternative behaviors in all children. Some basic principles of PBS on which we as professionals must operate are as follows:

- Challenging behavior serves a need on the part of the child.
- Our responses to the behavior of young children are nonpunitive.
- Behavioral expectations are based on what is developmentally appropriate, thus lessening the likelihood of challenging forms of behavior.
- Play and learning environments should be physically designed and directed to each child's learning strengths as a means for preventing the occurrence of challenging forms of behavior (see Figure 3-2).
- Our instructional interactions with children who display challenging behavior are positive, directed toward redirecting inappropriate behavior, and the active teaching and nurturing of positive forms of behavior.

It is our view that these basic principles must underscore the services and supports provided to young children in all inclusive early childhood educational programs. The basis for positive behavioral supports stems from research conducted in the field of applied behavior analysis. Positive behavioral supports are basically concerned with the enhancement of the child's overall quality of life as the principle outcome measure of success. In order to obtain this outcome measure the challenging behavior displayed by a child must first be understood before an intervention can be designed and successfully implemented. Challenging behavior can be defined as a behavior that places the child or others at risk for harm, is frequently occurring, and impedes a child's ability to access positive outcomes such as successful peer interactions, school success, and other meaningful lifestyle outcomes. To understand the factors associated with challenging forms of behavior in young children a functional assessment must first be conducted.

Figure 3–2 Play and learning environments should be designed and directed to each child's learning strengths.

Functional Assessment and Positive Behavioral Supports

Functional assessment is a process aimed at identifying the specific causal factors that are associated with the occurrence of challenging behavior. It is a proactive and systematic approach used for first gaining an understanding of a child's behavior in terms of the function it serves, the context in which it occurs, and the factors that may be precipitating or maintaining this response in a child. In recent years this approach has been widely researched and has been successfully used within early childhood educational and home settings (Arndorfer, Miltenberger, Woster, Rortvedt, & Gaffaney, 1994; Lennox & Miltenberger, 1989).

Functional assessment has also been a method utilized by professionals in the design and delivery of positive behavioral supports as recommended in the 1997 amendments to IDEA. In fact, there is no better way to understand a child's behavior than in the context of the daily environments that he/she functions in. This form of behavioral assessment has been widely utilized by special educators specifically when attempting to understand and positively respond to challenging behavior experienced by some children. It is a widely accepted fact that at some point in time, all children will experience varying degrees of challenging behavior for various reasons. For some children with disabilities these behaviors can become more severe and challenging given the child's level of disability and degree of supports in the child's environment. Too often, the behavior of young children is either misinterpreted, or judged too harshly and out of context by adult caregivers, placing children at risk for punishment, neglect, and abuse.

A more objective and rational view to take concerning behavior of young children is that children behave out of need. The behavior they often exhibit is a function of their level of development, limited or emerging communication, and social/emotional skill levels, as well as the insensitivities and inconsistencies of the environments they live and function in (Durand, 1990; Hummel & Prizant, 1993). Challenging behavior for most children serves a functional purpose (Demchak & Bossert, 1996; Durand, 1990). In other words, the behavior serves a real purpose for the child.

The functions of behavior in children serve one or more of the following purposes: (*a*) social attention, (*b*) escape/avoidance, (*c*) sensory regulation. Behavioral excess can be the means a child uses to obtain attention from parents, teachers, or peers. Frequently the only time some children get attention is when they are behaving in a manner that an adult figure finds inappropriate. Other behaviors observed in children can be linked to escape or avoidance from a task or activity that the child deems to be unpleasant. In some instances, the child may be right: The task is unpleasant for one of many reasons, such as degree of difficulty; the task has little or no reinforcing qualities in the eyes of the child; and the child's desire to not engage in the activity can often be linked to poor instructional cues, thus performance of the task may bring about more pain and discomfort than satisfaction for the child. Escape behavior often serves a child's need to reduce the level of sensory input and stimulation that he/she may be experiencing, such as in a noisy classroom environment.

Typically developing children may have difficulty and experience a low tolerance level especially during periods of the day when they are overtired or hungry. Children with developmental disabilities such as autism or severe mental retardation and/or attention deficit disorders may have more concerns in this regard, therefore exhibiting these behaviors more frequently depending upon the lack of structure and level of environmental stimulation found in their classroom or home settings. They may also experience a need for increased sensory feedback and engage in stereotypical behaviors such as hand flapping, rocking, and occasionally self-aggression (self-hitting or self-biting) as a way of providing them with such sensory stimulation. The functions of such challenging behaviors are best identified through the functional assessment procedures.

Functional Assessment and Functional Analysis

Functional assessment of behavior is defined as a process that seeks to identify the specific variables or causal factors associated with the occurrence of challenging behavior and the modification of these variables to construct child-centered supports (Reichle & Wacker, 1993). The use of functional assessment for understanding difficult behavior in children is directed at providing the educator with useful information aimed at determining the causal factors that are related to such behaviors and events that may maintain these responses in children if they should persist. The functional assessment of behavior should determine the function(s) or cause(s) of problematic behavior. The information obtained from the functional assessment is vital to the development of positive child-centered interventions.

A distinction should be made between the terms *functional assessment* and *functional analysis*. The later term, functional analysis, is a process similar to functional assessment in that it attempts to identify variables associated with challenging behavior in children. However, functional analysis relies on experimental manipulations of the setting events or antecedents and consequence events that precipitate or maintain challenging behaviors. Gresham (1991) defined functional analysis as "the identification of important, controllable, and ideographic functional relationships for a target behavior" (p. 388). It is important to note these differences and to understand that functional analysis is a valuable tool in the assessment process where a child's behavior is of concern; it is, however, limited in its utility in classroom and child care settings. The drawbacks associated with functional analysis include the degree of professional expertise and training necessary to perform such procedures as well as the amount of time and logistical supports necessary to carry out these procedures with any degree of proficiency and integrity (Lerman & Iwata, 1993). Therefore it is recommended that teachers utilize functional assessment as their method of choice for understanding the behavior of children.

Conducting a Functional Assessment of Behavior

Functional assessment involves the use of many components to assess behavior. These components typically include (*a*) the use of structured interviews conducted with teachers, care providers, parents, and significant others who interact with the child on a frequent basis; (*b*) identifying the behavior(s) of concern, often referred to as the target behavior, and defining the behavior in measurable terms; (*c*) conducting direct observation and narrative recordings of the child within the classroom, at play, home, or other relevant settings; (*d*) determining the probable antecedent or consequence events that may be influencing the behavior; (*e*) scatter plot recording the frequency of the target behavior and the time frame in which the behavior occurred. A listing of the procedural steps used in conducting a functional assessment follows.

Structured Interview

The starting point for any functional assessment of behavior is the structured interview. The purpose of the structured interview is to identify and operationally define the target behavior. The structured interview is usually completed by the child's teacher and other instructional personnel who have frequent contact with the child. The input received from these individuals will lend a comparative perspective concerning the behavior of concern. Parents are also asked to complete the functional assessment interview. Parental input is highly regarded, given that parents know their children best. The information obtained from the parents will also indicate whether the target behavior also occurs at home. Put simply, the information obtained from parents and professionals is much like looking at a child's behavior through the eyes of many concerned and caring individuals in hopes that it will lend a context for understanding the behavioral patterns of the child. There are many variations of the structured interview that can be used. See O'Neill and colleagues (1990) for one of the more comprehensive forms available. An illustration of a generic structured interview form follows.

Components of a Functional Assessment of Behavior

Phase 1: Structured Interview

Complete a structured interview with teachers, other related educational personnel, and parents.

Phase 2: Identification of the Target Behavior

Upon completion of the structured interview process, the target behaviors that are the most pressing concerns are identified.

Phase 3: Defining the Target Behavior

The target behavior should be defined in measurable and observable terms that will facilitate observation and recording.

Phase 4: Conduct Observations of Behavior and Narrative Recording

Designate time periods in which the child's behavior will be observed within the natural context of the typical school day. Keep observation periods brief (approximate twenty minutes in length), and vary observations across morning, midday, and afternoons for a minimum of three to five days, noting the incidents of challenging behavior and the antecedent and consequence events.

Phase 5: Collection of Scatter Plot Data

Utilizing the scatter plot data form, collect data on the frequency of the target behavior and the times each day that the behavior occurs for a period of five to ten days. Evaluate the data to determine if the behavior has a pattern in which it occurs.

Structured Interview Format

Name of Child _____ Date _____

Completed By _____

Definition of the Target Behavior

1. Define the target behavior in observable and measurable terms.

Description of the Target Behavior

2. What are the events that typically happen prior to the occurrence of the behavior?

3. What are the events that typically occur following the behavior?

4. Does the target behavior occur at predictable times during the day?

5. If you answered yes to item 4, please indicate the time periods and activities that coincide with the target behavior.

6. What does the behavior accomplish for the child?

7. What is the communicative intent of the target behavior?

History

8. Are there any significant life events that could account for the behavior exhibited by the child?

9. Are there any medical/physical explanations that could explain the behavior displayed by the child?

10. Has this behavior been displayed by the child in the past? If so, what intervention methods have been used to address the behavior? Have these methods been successful?

Instructional

11. Is there a predictable schedule for the child each day?

12. If yes, what form does the schedule take (e.g., object, picture/symbol, written)?

13. Does the target behavior typically occur during group or individualized activities?

14. Does the behavior occur when the child is alone or engaged in solitary activities?

15. Does the behavior occur during play and/or unstructured times such as during transitions between activities?

16. What are the child's favorite activities, toys, preferences?

Operationally Defining the Behavior in Question

Once the functional assessment interview has been completed, the next step in the process is to glean from the interview if agreement can be reached as to whether or not there is a definitive behavior that is of most concern. If the process has reached this level, the answer is most likely yes. When attempting to define a target behavior, professionals and parents should attempt to reach agreement on the specifics of the behavior. Some points to consider are:

- Define the behavior in measurable and observable terms.
- Is everyone in agreement as to what the target behavior is and how it is operationally defined?

Some examples of ineffective operational definitions are as follows:

- Jim will comply with all teacher requests.
- Bob will wait quietly for his turn during snack time.
- Paul will behave during circle time.

Effective definitions emphasize the observable and measurable components of behavior and can be phrased in positive terms. Such examples are as follows:

- Paul will sign "finished" to his teacher when he has completed his snack.
- Joey when presented with a picture communication board will point with his finger to the desired activity when asked by his teacher "Which one would you like?"
- Susie when given the verbal cue "time to wash up for lunch" will proceed to the bathroom and wash and dry hands.

It is apparent from the list of examples that effective behavioral definitions are characterized by greater detail and are more explicitly stated. The operational definition should clearly pinpoint the behavior of the learner in terms that can be understood across all who work and interact with the child.

Methods of Recording Behavior

When confronted by a behavior that has become persistent or chronic, the educational team should conduct observations of the behavior within the child's environments while he/she is engaged in the typical daily routine. There are several observational recording methods that teachers can utilize in an effort to gain a better understanding of a child's behavior. These methods include anecdotal recording and scatter plot analysis.

Anecdotal Recording

Anecdotal or narrative recording is a method used for observing a child's behavior and recording in a narrative style the events that precede the behavior (antecedents), the behavior that occurs, and the events that follow a behavior (consequences). This method of observational recording has also been referred to as A-B-C recording (antecedents-behavior-consequences). The major objectives of anecdotal or narrative recording are to (*a*) observe the child in the natural setting and (*b*) observe the child throughout the day if possible, such as twenty minutes during the morning, twenty minutes during the midday, and twenty minutes during the late afternoon. Observation periods should be conducted during structured activity periods (such as circle time, activities, instructional periods) and also during unstructured activities (play) and if possible during transitions between activities. The observer should record a chronology of events during the observation period, labeling observed events as either antecedent, behavior, or consequences. Anecdotal recording can be quite helpful for determining how environmental events influence a child's behavior such as the presence or absence of clear instructional cues, inadequate levels of structure within the child's environment, hypothesized function of the behavior, and specific antecedent setting events or consequences that occasion and maintain the behavior. An example of anecdotal or narrative recording follows.

An Example of Anecdotal Recording

Name of Student: Kelly

Setting: Group Storytelling Time

Observer: Ms. Heitenger

Start Time: 1:00 p.m.   Stop Time: 1:20 p.m.

Antecedent	Behavior	Consequence	Perceived Function
1:02 Students enter room following lunch and begin to take their seats	Kelly slowly sits down and places his head on the desk	The teacher sits down and asks the children to listen to the story	Attention
1:04 The teacher begins to read from the book	Kelly sits up and listens to the story	The children listen attentively to the story	
1:10 The teacher continues to read the story and some of the children begin to get restless in their chairs	Kelly begins to squirm in his chair and begins to tap Billy on the shoulder and whispers to him	Billy tells Kelly to be quiet and pushes his hand away	Attention
1:11 The teacher asks Kelly to sit and listen and continues reading	Kelly leans on the table and gets out of his chair	The teacher ignores Kelly and continues reading	Escape/Adventure

Some key points to consider when conducting anecdotal or A-B-C recording are as follows:

- Designate time periods in which the child will be observed, preferably across structured and unstructured activities, times of day (morning, midday, afternoon), and three to five successive days across environments (educational and home settings).
- Attempt to observe in an unobtrusive manner by being as natural and unassuming as possible. Sit in an area of the room that will draw limited attention to you but will allow for clear observation.
- Keep observation intervals brief (ten to twenty minutes).
- Identify observed events as antecedents, behavior, or consequences.

Scatter Plot Analysis

Scatter plot analysis (Touchette, MacDonald, & Langer, 1985) is a method used to measure both the frequency of a target behavior and the time of day these responses occur. By charting both the frequency and time of day, the teacher can determine if a pattern exits. A problematic behavior can then be further analyzed to determine whether or not the behavior occurs during specific times of day, during specific activities, or when the child is with specific care-givers. As Touchette and colleagues (1985) have indicated "problem behavior may be correlated with a time of day, the presence or absence of certain people, a social setting, a class of activities, a contingency of reinforcement, a physical environment, and contributions of these and other variables" (p. 345).

Scatter plot analysis is very easy to implement within classroom or other applied settings and allows for easy interpretation of results. Touchette and associates (1985) recommend that when using scatter plot analysis, it is best to collect frequency data on the occurrence of a specific target behavior in fifteen-minute time intervals throughout the day. When utilizing this approach, the teacher would note the occurrence of the target behavior only when it occurs during the day. The data is then transferred to a scatter chart and a code is used to designate the frequency of the behavior within each time interval during the course of a day. It is most advisable when using scatter plot analysis to collect data on specific behaviors for a minimum of five days continuously. Upon determining if there is a pattern to explain the target behavior (i.e., when the target behavior occurs most/least frequently) the teacher then must determine from the data if there are specific instructional or environmental variables that could be related to the child's responses. If so, then specific instructional modifications can be made noting their effect on the behavior of concern. The following vignette illustrates how the scatter plot can be implemented within a classroom serving young children ages three to five.

VIGNETTE 3–1: USING SCATTER PLOT ANALYSIS WITHIN AN INCLUSIVE EARLY CHILDHOOD SETTING

Jonathan is a four-year-old boy who is a student enrolled in an inclusive preschool classroom. Jonathan has been evaluated and identified as PDD/NOS (pervasive developmental disorder/not otherwise specified). PDD/NOS is a clinical diagnostic term found within the *DSM IV Diagnostic and Statistical Manual* (4th edition). The term is used to refer to children who exhibit some but not all of the characteristics consistent with the diagnosis of autism. Jonathan has limited verbal communication skills. He prefers to rely on some gestural communication such as pointing to indicate some of his needs but is inconsistent in his communicative attempts. His attempts at verbal communication are limited to some echolalia (a repetition of a word or phrase that can be immediate or delayed), and he also experiences moderate receptive communication delays. There are eight other children in his classroom, six of whom are typically developing children, with the remaining child having attention deficit disorder.

The teacher, Mrs. Harmon, has become concerned in recent days that Jonathan has exhibited some physical aggression directed at her and also as self-aggression (hitting himself in the face) at different points during the day. She has asked for a behavioral consultant from the local educational agency to come and offer an opinion. She has also notified Jonathan's parents of her concerns and has asked them to be on the lookout at home for signs of these behaviors. The local consultant and Mrs. Harmon, with support from Jonathan's parents, develop a plan for gathering assessment information on his behavior at home and school. The consultant trained in the area of positive behavioral supports has recommended that a structured interview be conducted with Jonathan's parents and instructional personnel followed by a scatter plot using the following procedures:

Step 1: The team defines the behavior of concern as "physical aggression toward self or others" in the form of hitting self or others with closed hand and biting self or others.

Step 2: The team creates a chart for recording the occurrences of the target behaviors. The chart is divided into twenty-minute intervals throughout the school day beginning at 8:00 a.m. and finishing at 2:30 p.m. Intervals of twenty minutes are selected because they reflect the natural duration of many activities including the transitions between activities that the children engage in within their daily schedule.

Step 3: Data is to be collected for one week continuously, and the team meets to review the procedure and to ensure that all members of the team understand the process. The data collection procedure is as follows: Upon observing an occurrence of aggression within a designated time interval, a slash will be recorded within the corresponding time frame in which the behavior occurred.

Step 4: The team collects data throughout the week and inspects the results by week's end.

Step 5: The team generates plausible hypotheses to explain the pattern of Jonathan's behavior.

The data appears to indicate a trend. The team detects that Jonathan displays more frequent episodes of aggression (more than five occurrences in a given time interval) consistent with transitions between activities. These transitions occur between activities during lunch, nap, and play time. The behavioral consultant offers a hypothesis that may explain Jonathan's behavior during these periods: As previously noted, Jonathan experiences communication delays, and the teachers are reliant on verbal cues to provide directive feedback or reinforcement to the children. The consultant points out that this form of cue is not most conducive to Jonathan's learning style. Rather the teachers should be utilizing more visual cues such as objects or pictures and perhaps a visual schedule to pre-instruct Jonathan of impending changes in his routine. Jonathan's parents point out that they have been using a similar approach at home as was recommended to them by the Autism Society's Parent Support Group. Jonathan's educational team can now utilize this important information to formulate a set of instructional and environmental interventions that will hopefully reduce or eliminate the frequency of Jonathan's aggressive behavior.

The team will first begin by assessing Jonathan's ability to match objects to objects, objects to picture, and picture to pictures. Then a morning and afternoon schedule will be made utilizing the form most appropriate for Jonathan (in this case pictures will be used). In addition, the teacher will provide Jonathan with a picture during transitions between activities. This area will be explored in greater depth in Chapter 7. This case illustration provides a very good example of how pragmatic the scatter plot analysis method is in the assessment of behavior and in the development of informed hypotheses to explain problematic behavior in children.

Another useful assessment tool to be used with children with severe developmental disabilities who engage in severe and challenging forms of behavior such as Jonathan, is the Motivation Assessment Scale (MAS) developed by Durand and Crimmins (1993). The MAS is a sixteen-item questionnaire designed to assess the functions (or purpose) of challenging behavior. Before using the MAS, a target behavior should be predetermined. The MAS is a very useful assessment tool for understanding the behaviors of children with severe disabilities, such as in the case of children with severe mental retardation or in the case of children with autism or other pervasive developmental disorders who have limited communication systems. Often these children, given their communication challenges, will engage in perseverative self-stimulatory behaviors such as rocking, hand flapping, spinning

Scatter Plot Recording Form

Child's Name _____ Behavior Observed _____

Time	Monday	Tuesday	Wednesday	Thursday	Friday
8:00-8:15					
8:15-8:30					
8:30-8:45					
8:45-9:00					
9:00-9:15					
9:15-9:30					
9:30-9:45					
9:45-10:00					
10:00-10:15					
10:15-10:30					
10:30-10:45					
10:45-11:00					
11:00-11:15					
11:15-11:30					
11:30-11:45					
11:45-12:00					
12:00-12:15					
12:15-12:30					
12:30-12:45					
12:45-1:00					
1:00-1:15					
1:15-1:30					
1:30-1:45					
1:45-2:00					
2:00-2:15					
2:15-2:30					
2:30-2:45					
3:45-3:00					

Scatter Plot Recording Form

Child's Name ___Jonathan___ Behavior Observed____Aggression____

Time	Monday	Tuesday	Wednesday	Thursday	Friday
8:00-8:15	○	○	■	○	○
8:15-8:30	○	■	○	○	■
8:30-8:45	●	●	■	■	●
8:45-9:00	■	■	○	■	●
9:00-9:15	○	○	■	○	○
9:15-9:30	○	■	■	■	○
9:30-9:45	●	●	■	●	●
9:45-10:00	●	●	●	●	●
10:00-10:15	○	○	○	■	○
10:15-10:30	○	○	○	○	○
10:30-10:45	○	■	○	○	○
10:45-11:00	○	●	○	●	●
11:00-11:15	●	●	●	●	●
11:15-11:30	●	●	●	●	●
11:30-11:45 (Lunch)	■	■	○	■	■
11:45-12:00 (Lunch)	■	■	■	■	■
12:00-12:15 (Lunch)	○	○	■	○	○
12:15-12:30 (Nap)	●	●	■	●	●
12:30-12:45	●	●	●	●	●
12:45-1:00	●	■	■	●	●
1:00-1:15	○	○	○	○	○
1:15-1:30	■	■	○	■	○
1:30-1:45	■	●	■	○	○
1:45-2:00	○	○	■	○	■
2:00-2:15					
2:15-2:30					
2:30-2:45					
3:45-3:00					

○=no occurrences   ■=<5 occurrences   ●=>5 occurrences

of objects, or they may engage in self-injurious behaviors such as biting and head banging. Given the complexities of these behaviors and the challenging support needs posed by such a child's levels of disability, teachers and professionals should attempt to determine the perceived function(s) of the child's target behavior before commencing with an intervention program. In Jonathan's case, issues of communication would likely be related to aggression toward self or others. In such cases, the MAS represents a supportive assessment tool.

Challenges in Conducting Observational Recording of Children's Behavior

There are some confounding issues that can pose challenges to a teacher when conducting observational recording of children's behavior. Repp and colleagues, (1988) have identified these factors that may serve to threaten the accuracy and reliability of data collected through observation of children's behavior. These factors include reactivity, observer drift, location, and observer bias.

Reactivity refers to a change in a child's behavior in the presence of an observer. Reactivity can be controlled by allowing the child a period of acclimation whereby the child becomes comfortable with the presence of the observer. Observer drift occurs when the observer does not remain consistent with the behavioral definition, and thus occurrences of the target behavior may be missed or inconsistently recorded (Repp et al., 1988). This problem can be minimized by video recording a child's behavior and analyzing it later.

Interobserver Reliability

Interobserver reliability refers to the consistency between raters in measuring behavior (Kazdin, 1989). Kazdin (1989) has identified three major reasons that interobserver reliability is important. These include (*a*) it aids in consistency, (*b*) it controls for observer bias, and (*c*) it communicates how well the target behavior has been operationally defined. There are several reliability formulas that may be used for determining interobserver reliability based on the type of observational method used. The formula used for frequency recording is as follows:

$$\frac{\text{Smaller frequency}}{\text{Larger frequency}} \times 100 = \% \text{ interrater reliability}$$

As an example, two teachers record the number of times that Joseph shares toys during a twenty-minute play period. Their data looks like the following:

Observer 1 records 8 shares
Observer 2 records 10 shares

To calculate interobserver reliability they do the following:

$$\frac{\text{Smaller frequency (8)}}{\text{Larger frequency (10)}} \times 100 = 80\%$$

It is generally accepted among experts that interobserver agreement of 80 percent or better is acceptable and indicates consistency between raters. It is also recommended (Cooper, Heron, & Heward, 1987) that interobserver agreement be measured every third observation session. Often when teachers are attempting to assess behavior using observational methods reliability is a forgotten component. It is important to remember that the accuracy of the data collected is vital to the integrity of the assessment and intervention process. It is a given that time constraints and limited supports are a major reason that procedural detail is overlooked; however, as professionals we must stand accountable for the practices we employ with children. The children we teach are deserving of only the best professional practices that we can provide. Collecting reliability data serves as a checks and balances system for maintaining such necessary standards in our practice.

Developing a Hypothesis Statement

Upon concluding the functional assessment process, the data obtained concerning the child's behavior should be examined and the development of a hypothesis statement concerning the function of the child's behavior and the factors that may be associated with the behaviors should be considered at this point. Once the hypothesis has been completed, the development of a positive behavioral support plan can occur.

Positive Behavioral Support Plans

Following the completion of the functional assessment phase, the child's team (including parents and family) should commence to develop a positive behavioral support plan. Behavioral support plans are individualized around the strengths and challenges of the individual child and typically are designed to do one or more of the following:

- Modify setting events such as environmental, physical, or emotional challenges associated with high rates of challenging behavior.
- Modify and reduce the likelihood antecedents that are associated with setting events and that occur immediately prior to the challenging behavior.
- Teach positive alternative behaviors that serve the same function as the challenging behavior, thus allowing the child to get his/her needs met in an appropriate manner.
- Modify consequences to either avoid maintaining the challenging behavior or increase the positive alternative behavior.

As has been described in the previous example, functional assessment represents a major component of positive behavioral supports. To say that these procedures are foolproof would be absurd; however, they provide a systematic approach to understanding challenging behavior in young children that takes into consideration the developmental and ecological influences on the child and how these factors may be contributing to the presence of challenging behavior. It is therefore in the best interests of the child to give full attention to these influences through a proactive response rather than taking uninformed "guesses" as to the reason for challenging behavior in some children. It is the hope that these procedures will replace the use of negative consequences and punitive approaches often relied upon by some professionals and parents.

Merging PBS, ABI, and DAP

We the authors believe that the three roads must be merged in an effort to maximize the benefit to all young children. The roads to which we refer are of course positive behavioral supports, activity-based intervention, and developmentally appropriate practice in providing inclusive early childhood education. In the past, professionals who ascribed to a behavioral approach drew criticism about the limitations and pitfalls of such theoretical approaches in early childhood educational special education or regular education settings. Our focus is not to extend this argument for or against, but rather to demonstrate and detail how the merits of each can be converged. Strain and Hemmeter (1997) have provided a basis for understanding how behavioral approaches have positively influenced early intervention practices namely through understanding the functions of behavior in young children and the development of positive and proactive interventions.

Novick (1993) has described how developmentally appropriate practice and activity-based interventions can be integrated in applied practice with young children. We believe that positive behavioral supports are also a necessary part of this convergence that Novick (1993) has offered. The common thread of developmentally appropriate practice, activity-based intervention, and positive behavioral supports is that all three approaches, first, are centered on the child; second, value the child as an individual; and finally, as Novick (1993) writes, "emphasize choice and the development of problem-solving skills and curiosity" (p. 414). The authors believe that the integration of these approaches when carefully considered and understood can do more to benefit children than if they operate in isolation from one another. (See Figure 3–3).

Figure 3–3
The common thread of PBS, ABI, and DAP is that all three approaches value each child as an individual.

Summary

This chapter has focused on concepts central to socioemotional development in young children. The major goal of the chapter was to provide a rationale for the importance of understanding behavior in young children from an ecological context that would take into consideration developmental, environmental, familial, cultural, and other factors that influence the development of socioemotional skills. The chapter also introduced principles of positive behavioral supports and how these could be applied in an inclusive early childhood educational setting. An example was provided that highlighted each of these principles with respect to a young child who was experiencing some behavioral difficulty. Finally, the chapter addressed how positive behavioral supports could be successfully merged with more traditional developmentally appropriate practices and activity-based interventions to provide exemplary services and supports to young children.

Key points to consider from this chapter included the following:

- Development of an ecological perspective for understanding how familial, cultural, and community influences affect socioemotional development in young children.
- Maintaining behavioral expectations for young children that are developmentally appropriate given the child's age and developmental levels. The work of Bronfenbrenner and Erikson was cited and serves as a conceptual basis that must first be understood before working with young children.
- Principles of positive behavioral supports including the role of functional assessment in determining the context (events that occasion the behavior), the functions or purpose that the behavior serves for the child, and the importance of proactive, nonpunitive approaches in designing optimal educational services and supports for young children. Finally, the need for a systematic assessment of all factors that may be contributing to the occurrence of challenging behavior in the young child before attempting to develop an intervention was presented.
- The last portion of the chapter attempted to provide a rationale for the importance of merging best and effective practices in the areas of developmentally appropriate practice, activity-based intervention, and positive behavioral supports in the delivery of services and supports to young children. We learned that each of these approaches is child/family-centered, values each child/family as individuals, and desires positive educational and lifestyle outcomes for children and families.

Chapter 3 Suggested Activities and Resources

Activities

1. Read one of the articles listed under Selected Resources and provide a written reaction to how you feel these procedures could be applied in an inclusive early childhood educational setting in which you have participated in a practicum or in which you have worked.

2. Conduct an in-class discussion/debate concerning how developmentally appropriate practice could be successfully merged with activity-based intervention and positive behavioral supports within inclusive early childhood educational settings.

3. Observe young children (infants, toddlers, and preschoolers) within an early childhood educational setting and note how their behaviors are similar and different given various developmental levels.

4. Observe young children in an early childhood educational setting and note the effects that environment, instruction, and structure have on their behavior in both instructional and play settings.

5. Observe a young child in both home and educational settings during demand and free play times and note the effects that each of these settings has on the behavior of the young child. What factors may account for any similarities and/or differences in behavior across each of these settings?

6. Contact a local early childhood educational setting and ask to visit. While there learn about the structure within the program, how the schedule for each day is arranged given the differing age and developmental levels. Note the presence or absence of structure within the setting. Identify key features that promoted structure within the setting such as a predictable schedule, neat and organized classroom, structured transitions, staff-to-child ratios, and adequate space.

7. Conduct a functional assessment of a young child with challenges utilizing the methods outlined in the chapter. After completing the functional assessment, discuss your hypothesis concerning the function of the challenging behavior and then strategize positive approaches for minimizing the occurrence of the behavior and the teaching of alternative skills.

Selected Resources

1. Resources related to understanding the ecological influences on behavior in young children are as follows:

   Bandura, A., & Walters, R. H. (1963). *Social learning and personality development*. New York: Holt, Rinehart, & Winston.

   Bradshaw, J. (1988). *Bradshaw on: The family*. Deerfield Beach, FL: Health Communications Inc.

   Bronfenbrenner, U. (1979). *The ecology of human development*. Cambridge, MA: Harvard University Press.

   Lynch, E. W., & Hanson, M. (1992). *Developing cross-cultural competence*. Baltimore: Paul H. Brookes Publishing Co.

2. For gaining a better understanding of the relationship between developmental age and behavior, consult the following sources:

   Erikson, E. (1968). *Identity, youth, and crisis*. New York: W. W. Norton.

Giddan, J. J., Bade, K. M., Rickenberg, D., & Ryley, A. T. (1995). Teaching the language of feelings to students with severe emotional and behavioral handicaps. *Language, Speech, and Hearing Services in Schools, 26,* 3–10.

Izard, C. (1991). *The psychology of emotions.* New York: Plenum.

Prizant, B. M., & Weatherby, A. M. (1990). Toward an integrated view of early language and communication development and socioemotional development. *Topics in Language Disorders, 10,* 1–16.

3. For information about child-centered behavioral supports within inclusive early childhood educational settings, consult one or more of the following:

Arndorfer, R. E., Miltenberger, R. G., Woster, S., Rortvedt, A., & Gaffaney, T. (1994). Home-based descriptive and experimental analysis of problem behaviors in children. *Topics in Early Childhood Special Education, 14,* 64–87.

Durand, V. M. (1990). *Severe behavior problems: A functional communication training approach.* New York: Guilford Press.

Foster-Johnson, L., & Dunlap, G. (1993). Using functional assessment to develop effective individualized interventions for challenging behaviors. *Teaching Exceptional Children, 24,* 44–50.

4. For specific information on how developmental and activity-based child-centered behavioral supports can be effectively combined within inclusive early childhood educational settings, consult the following:

Novick, R. (1993). Appropriate practice: Points of convergence. *Topics in Early Childhood Special Education, 13,* 403–417.

Strain, P. S., McConnell, S. R., Carta, J. J., Fowler, S. A., Neisworth, J. T., & Wolery, M. (1992). Behaviorism in early intervention. *Topics in Early Childhood Special Education, 12,* 121–141.

References

Akesson, E. B., & Granlund, M. (1995). Family involvement in assessment and intervention: Perceptions of professionals and parents in Sweden. *Exceptional Children, 61,* 520–535.

Arndorfer, R. E., Miltenberger, R. G., Woster, S., Rortvedt, A., & Gaffaney, T. (1994). Home-based descriptive and experimental analysis of problem behaviors in children. *Topics in Early Childhood Special Education, 14,* 64–87.

Bandura, A. (1965). Influence of models' reinforcement contingencies in the acquisition of imitative responses. *Journal of Personality and Social Psychology, 1,* 589–595.

Bandura, A., & Walters, R. H. (1963). *Social learning and personality development.* New York: Holt, Rinehart, & Winston.

Barrara, I. (1993). Effective and appropriate instruction for all children: The challenge of cultural/linguistic diversity and young children with special needs. *Topics in Early Childhood Special Education, 13,* 461–487.

Bradley, R. H., & Brisby, J. A. (1993). Assessment of the home environment. In J. L. Culbertson & D. J. Willis (Eds.), *Testing young children* (pp. 128–166). Austin, TX: PRO-ED.

Bradshaw, J. (1988). *Bradshaw on: The family.* Deerfield Beach, FL: Health Communications, Inc.

Bronfenbrenner, U. (1977). Toward an experimental ecology of human behavior. *American Psychologist, 52,* 513–530.

Bronfenbrenner, U. (1979). *The ecology of human development.* Cambridge, MA: Harvard University Press.

Chan, S. Q. (1990). Early intervention with culturally diverse families of infants and toddlers with disabilities. *Infants and Young Children, 3,* 78–87.

Cooper, J. O., Heron, T. E., & Heward, W. (1987). *Applied behavior analysis.* New York: MacMillan Publishing Company.

Demchak, M., & Bossert, K. W. (1996). Assessing problem behaviors. *Innovations,* (4), 1–44.

Dunst, C. J., Johannson, C., Trivette, C. M., & Hamby, D. (1991). Family-oriented early intervention policies and practices: Family-centered or not? *Exceptional Children, 58,* 115–126.

Durand, V. M., & Crimmins, D. B. (1993). *The Motivation Assessment Scale.* Topeka, KS: Monaco & Associates.

Durand, V. M. (1990). *Severe behavior problems: A functional communication training approach.* New York: Guilford Press.

Erikson, E. (1968). *Identity, youth, and crisis.* New York: W. W. Norton.

Fantuzzo, J., & Atkins, M. (1992). Applied behavior analysis for educators: Teacher centered and classroom based. *Journal of Applied Behavior Analysis, 25,* 37–42.

Foster-Johnson, L., & Dunlap, G. (1993). Using functional assessment to develop effective individualized interventions for challenging behaviors. *Teaching Exceptional Children, 24,* 44–50.

Giddan, J. J., Bade, K. M., Rickenberg, D., & Ryley, A. T. (1995). Teaching the language of feelings to students with severe emotional and behavioral handicaps. *Language, Speech, and Hearing Services in Schools, 26,* 3–10.

Gresham, F. M. (1991). Whatever happened to functional analysis in behavioral consultation? *Journal of Educational and Psychological Consultation, 2,* 387–393.

Hanson, M. J., & Carta, J. J. (1995). Addressing the challenges of families with multiple risks. *Exceptional Children, 62,* 201–212.

Hanson, M. J., Lynch, E. W., & Wayman, K. I. (1990). Honoring the cultural diversity of families when gathering data. *Topics in Early Childhood Special Education, 10,* (1), 112–131.

Hart, B., & Risely, T. (1995). *Meaningful differences in the everyday experience of young American children.* Baltimore: Paul H. Brookes Publishing Co.

Hobbs, N. (1974). A natural history of Project Re-ED. In J. M. Kauffman & C. Lewis (Eds.), *Teaching children with behavior disorders: Personal perspectives.* Columbus, OH: Charles E. Merrill Publishing Company.

Hummel, L. J., & Prizant, B. M. (1993). A socioemotional perspective for understanding social difficulties of school-age children with language disorders. *Language, Speech, and Hearing Services in Schools, 24,* 216–224.

Izard, C. (1991). *The psychology of emotions.* New York: Plenum.

Joe, J. R., & Malach, R. S. (1992). Families with Native American roots. In E. W. Lynch & M. Hanson (Eds.), *Developing cross-cultural competence* (pp. 89–119). Baltimore: Paul H. Brookes Publishing Co.

Juul, K. D. (1977). Models of remediation for behavior disordered children. *Educational and Psychological Interactions* (Rep. No. 62). Malmo, Sweden: School of Education.

Kazdin, A. E. (1989). *Behavior modification in applied settings* (4th ed.). Brooks/Cole Publishing Company.

LeFrancois, G. R. (1994). *Of children: An introduction to child development* (8th ed.). Belmont, CA: Wadsworth Publishing Company.

Lennox, D., & Miltenberger, R. G. (1989). Conducting a functional assessment of problem behavior in applied settings. *Journal of the Association for Persons with Severe Handicaps, 14,* 304–311.

Lerman, D. C., & Iwata, B. A. (1993). Descriptive and experimental analyses of variables maintaining self-injurious behavior. *Journal of Applied Behavior Analysis, 26,* 293–319.

Lynch, E. W. (1992). Developing cross-cultural competence. In E. W. Lynch & M. Hanson (Eds.), *Developing cross-cultural competence* (pp. 35–61). Baltimore: Paul H. Brookes Publishing Co.

Martin, G., & Pear, J. (1996). *Behavior modification: What is it and how to do it* (5th ed.). Upper Saddle River, NJ: Prentice-Hall.

Nelson, J. R., Smith, D. J., & Dodd, J. M. (1993). Understanding the cultural characteristics of American Indian families: Effective partnerships under the Individualized Family Service Plan (IFSP). *Rural Special Education Quarterly, 11,* 33–36.

O'Neill, R. E., Horner, R. H., Albin, R. W., Storey, K., & Sprague, J. R. (1990). *Functional analysis: A practical assessment guide.* Sycamore, IL: Sycamore Publishing Co.

Prizant, B. M., & Weatherby, A. M. (1990). Toward an integrated view of early language and communication development and socioemotional development. *Topics in Language Disorders, 10,* 1–16.

Reichle, J., & Wacker, D. P. (1993). *Communicative alternatives to challenging behavior.* Baltimore: Paul H. Brookes Publishing Co.

Repp, A. C., Nieminen, G. S., Olinger, E., & Burusca, R. (1988). Direct observation: Factors affecting the accuracy of observers. *Exceptional Children, 55,* 29–37.

Strain, P. S., & Hemmeter, M. L. (1997). Keys to being successful when confronted with challenging behaviors. *Young Exceptional Children, 1,* 2–8.

Straus, M. A. (1980). Stress and physical child abuse. *Child Abuse and Neglect,* 4, 75–88.

Thurman, S. K. (1977). Congruence of behavioral ecologies: A model for special education programming. *The Journal of Special Education, 11,* 329–333.

Touchette, P. E., MacDonald, R. F., & Langer, S. M. (1985). A scatter plot for identifying stimulus control of problem behaviors. *Journal of Applied Behavior Analysis, 18,* 343–351.

Turnbull, A. P., & Turnbull, H. R. (1997). *Families, professionals, and exceptionality: A special partnership* (3rd ed.). Englewood Cliffs, NJ: Merrill/Prentice-Hall.

Vygotsky, L. (1978). *Mind in society: The development of higher psychological processes.* Cambridge, MA: Harvard University Press.

Zirpoli, T. J. (1986). Child abuse and children with handicaps. *Remedial and Special Education, 7,* 39–48.

Principles of Activity-Based Intervention (ABI)

INTRODUCTION

In Chapter 1 the rationale for understanding why positive behavioral supports, developmentally appropriate practices, and activity-based intervention are the foundation for successful inclusion of young children with disabilities in early childhood settings was introduced. In Chapter 4 we will examine in more detail the principles of activity-based intervention and consider why as an intervention approach it will help us in planning and implementing inclusion of infants, toddlers, preschoolers, and young children in the various early childhood settings. Here are the objectives that the reader will address in Chapter 4. You should be able to:

- Articulate in general the theoretical bases for ABI.
- Define activity-based intervention.
- Explain how it is important for inclusion and how it fits with positive behavioral supports and developmentally appropriate practice.
- Describe each of the components of activity-based intervention.
- Give one example of how activity-based intervention might be applied to address one goal of a child with a disability, given each of the six settings included in the chapter.
- Discuss some of the perceived drawbacks and concerns of early childhood educators and early childhood special educators about activity-based intervention.

Theoretical Foundations of Activity-Based Intervention

Bricker and Cripe (1992) have noted that ABI is "a synthesis of philosophies, curricular approaches, and instructional methodologies of special education, regular early childhood education, applied behavior analysis, developmental psychology, and speech-language pathology." While it is beyond the scope of what we need to address here, it will be helpful for you to have a brief introduction to some of the primary theories that are the underpinnings for these disciplines and for ABI. Maybe these theories will be familiar to you from your previous study and course work. In an article describing the relationship between activity-based intervention and developmentally appropriate practice, Novick (1993) summarizes the philosophical bases for ABI as drawing largely on the work of Piaget, Dewey, and Vygotsy, as does developmentally appropriate practice (DAP) in early childhood education.

All three of these philosophical perspectives, while having significant points of departure, stress the central importance of the relationship between the nature and quality of environments and the development of the child. The theory of constructivism developed by Jean Piaget requires that teaching "must match the child's developmental level to the types of knowledge being taught, promote autonomous thinking, actively involve the learner, and lead to the development of increasingly more sophisticated levels of understanding and reasoning" (Waite-Stupiansky, 1997). Lev Semenovich Vygotsky's notions about child development and early childhood education included the concepts of zone of proximal development, or ZPD, and scaffolding of children's learning (Berk & Winsler, 1995). ZPD refers to the place (setting/environment) in which development occurs as a result of the relationship between a child or children and adults or more capable peers. Scaffolding, while it is not a term coined by Vygotsky, has emerged from his work. It refers to effective interactions in the ZPD that build on the child's development by accomplishing the goals of joint problem solving, arriving at a shared understanding (intersubjectivity), having a positive emotional tone in interactions, keeping children engaged, and promoting self-regulation. Finally, John Dewey emphasized the importance of continuity and meaningfulness in the learning activities of children and the necessity of education nourishing the normally occurring interactions of the child with her environments.

The disciplines of early childhood special education and early intervention have comparatively brief histories, given that substantive attention to early identification and intervention for young children and their families really had its beginnings in the 1960s. Much of the early work with this population was dominated by the principles associated with behavioral theory and behaviorism. As Bricker and Cripe (1992) have noted, service delivery models and approaches for young children with disabilities were borrowed largely from the behavior analytic approaches used previously with adult populations and with school-aged children. Primarily over the past decade—and to a great deal in response to the need to merge professional philosophies, practices, and expertise to address mandates for least restrictive environment, natural settings, and inclusion—activity-based intervention has emerged as a useful foundation for integrating these different perspectives. Many prominent professionals and nationally influential leaders in early childhood special education, among them Diane Bricker, have moved away from the traditional application of behavioral principles and toward the use of naturally occurring antecedents and consequences in natural environments—such as the home, child care center, or kindergarten—to meet specialized needs of young children with disabilities.

Defining Activity-Based Intervention

You may recall from Chapter 1 that activity-based early intervention is an approach that comes from the landmark work of Diane Bricker and Juliann J. Cripe (1992) in their book entitled *An Activity-Based Approach to Early Intervention* and in the recently published second edition of that text. They have defined this approach as "a child-directed, transactional approach that embeds intervention on children's individual goals and objectives in routine, planned, or child-initiated activities and uses logically occurring antecedents and consequences to develop functional and generalizable skills." Let's break down this definition into four elements. The first is a child-directed transactional approach. In quality early childhood settings, young children are given many opportunities each day to initiate activities, based on their own interests and motivations. When young children initiate actions, whether they are verbal or physical, the people (children and adults) and the environment (for example, a toy that has been activated) respond or reciprocate. That constitutes transaction, and it is critical that young children learn that their actions bring about reactions—that they can make things happen. It is especially important that young children with disabilities have these opportunities, since for a variety of reasons they may be less likely to have occasion to initiate. The second element of the definition is the embedding of specialized goals and objectives in routine, planned, or child-initiated activities. Bricker and Cripe (1992) have defined these three types of activities as follows and have noted that they are of course often combined. (See Figure 4–1.)

Routine Activities

"Routine activities refer to events that occur on a predictable or regular basis, such as meals, diapering, and dressing at home; and snacks, clean-up, and preparation for departure at center-based programs. Often, with thought, these activities can be used or refocused to provide children opportunities to learn new skills or practice skills being acquired" (p. 44).

Figure 4–1 The classroom is an excellent place for teacher directed or child initiated situations that can address specialized goals.

Planned Activities

"Planned activities refer to designed events that ordinarily do not happen without adult organization. Planned activities should interest children and be developed in ways that children find appealing, as opposed to being designed exclusively to practice a target skill. Examples included activities such as planting seeds, acting out a song, or playing circus" (p. 44).

Child-Initiated Activities

"Activities initiated by the child are referred to as child-initiated activities. If children introduce and persist in an activity, the actions and events associated with the activity are probably appealing to them. Activities that are inherently interesting to children require little external support or reward" (pp. 44–45).

Young children with disabilities—if they have been identified, evaluated, and determined to be eligible for special education services—will have a plan (either an IEP or an IFSP) that spells out the specialized goals and objectives that should be addressed to advance their development and learning. Historically in special education we have to some extent come to believe that the specialized goals and objectives established as a part of that planning process would have to be addressed by highly specialized activities, often delivered in one-on-one sessions with teachers or interventionists specially trained in special education. What we now know is that these goals and objectives can frequently be effectively addressed in the routines, child-initiated activities, or planned group activities of an inclusive early childhood setting. This is not to say that sometimes more highly structured and intensive intervention will not be necessary to assist some young children with disabilities in making progress toward their objectives.

The third element of the definition of activity-based intervention is the use of logically occurring antecedents and consequences. Zirpoli (1995) has defined antecedents as "the events occurring before a child exhibits the target behavior." Consequences are the "events occurring after the target behavior." Target behavior refers to the desired behavior or behavior of interest engaged in by the child. Antecedents might include such things as the actions of other children or adults, toys and other learning materials, aspects of the environment, schedules, or even more difficult to observe things such as internal states like sleepiness. Consequences might include such things as the activation of a toy, laughing or crying, positive or negative attention from others, or a tangible reward. Observing individual or groups of young children in various settings, it is possible to distinguish among antecedents, behaviors, and consequences and to see patterns specific to particular children, times of the day, and antecedent-consequent connections that foster both desired and undesired behaviors. In other words, we can systematically look for what precedes a child's behavior, we can understand aspects of the behavior itself—for example, its intensity, duration, and frequency—and we can look at what happens after the behavior occurs—the consequences.

Activity-based intervention tells us that we can often use the antecedents and consequences that are typically occurring in inclusive settings for young children to foster behaviors that address the specialized goals and objectives of children with disabilities. For example, Emily is a twenty-four-month-old child with Down's syndrome. She is enrolled in an inclusive toddler child care center. One of Emily's specialized goals, which came from the assessment of the occupational therapist, is to increase her wrist flexibility and rotation. She loves to play in water, and one of the regular activities of the center is playing at the water table. One of the caregivers saw this as an excellent opportunity to help address this specialized objective for Emily. The antecedents (events occurring before the behavior) were having Emily and another child come to the water play table, giving her a small plastic container from which to pour water, and modeling for her how to scoop and pour the water. In order to get the desired behavior related to Emily's goal, the caregiver assisted her in holding her container with water up higher to require the need for greater wrist rotation to do the pouring. The consequences (events occurring after the behavior) were that Emily obviously enjoyed seeing the water pour and splash, her attention and effort were extended, and she was playing cooperatively next to another child. Here is another example provided by the mother (Melinda) in one of the families with whom the authors have been privileged to partner in early childhood special education service and training.

> As a family we look back on the integrated preschool experience for Megan with fond memories (see Figure 4–2). Through this experience Megan had opportunities that other children with disabilities did not have. The other children at the preschool program also gained from their exposure to Megan. I especially like the way Megan's individual goals were integrated into the daily activities, for example—the prone stander. Megan and a friend would work together at the sand table, participate in free play, and do art activities, all while Megan was in her prone stander. Also each child would be allowed to try Megan's walker. This taught them about sharing, taking turns, and it let them ask questions and understand something about Megan's walker and her special needs. Megan would imitate the actions of the other children in the program. Megan would not wear a hat, head band, or Halloween facemask. However, during a skit at a reading conference on the university campus, Megan was up on stage with the other children wearing a paper bag (with a teddy bear face) over her head! All of the children were holding hands and singing "The Teddy Bear Picnic" song. I was so happy to see her participating with the group and amazed at the fact she was wearing a bag over her head. She was loving every minute of it.

One of Megan's specialized objectives was related to mobility. The antecedents in her inclusive preschool related to this objective were her walker, the main motivating and interesting activities around the room, and the encouragement and involvement of the other children. Megan's behavior (using her walker) resulted in her gaining access to these activities. The consequences were that she received positive comments from others, but also that she was able to control her own access to interesting and fun play activities. A second objective for Megan was to increase the amount of time that she was actively engaged in play and other activities with her peers. The skit in which she participated with

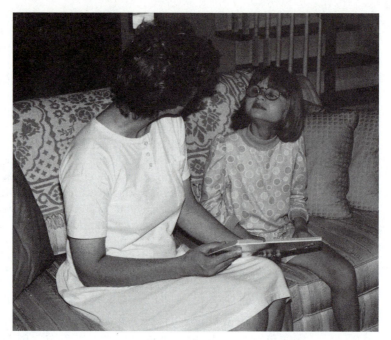

Figure 4–2 This is Meggan and her mom.

her classmates was an important activity in working toward this goal. She was part of the fun of making the masks, practicing singing the song, and watching the fun that the other children were having. These were all antecedent events before the behavior of wearing the mask, holding hands, and singing the song on stage before an audience at the reading conference. The consequence was that all of the children were excited, the activity was fun, and they were treated to refreshments.

The fourth and final element of the definition of activity-based intervention is the focus on functional and generative skills. The intervention done with a young child with a disability should be relevant and practical to them now and in the future, and the skills that they learn should be usable in a variety of settings, not just the environment in which the skill is learned. Bricker and Cripe (1992) have described functional skills as those "that permit children to negotiate their physical and social environment in an independent and satisfying manner to themselves and others in their social milieu." Generative skills are those that generalize to other settings. If a child learns to tie her shoes, that skill can be used in other settings, so it is generalizable.

We have briefly described the four elements, or components, of the definition of activity-based intervention. They include (1) child-directed transactions; (2) embedding of specialized goals and objectives in routine, planned, or child-initiated activities; (3) use of logically occurring antecedents and consequences; and (4) focus on functional and generative skills. Put together with the principles of positive behavioral supports and developmentally appropriate practice, the foundation for successful inclusion is established. You will find these four elements useful in making judgments about the extent to which particular activities with young children are truly activity-based. Now we will examine how principles of activity-based intervention, in general terms, fit and have relevance for various typical inclusive settings for young children. This is intended to introduce you to some of the issues, challenges, special considerations, and attributes of these six settings as they relate to ABI and to set the stage for more in-depth consideration of applications of the process of inclusion in these early childhood settings.

Considerations for Activity-Based Intervention in Various Early Childhood Settings

Home-Based Services

For our purposes home-based intervention services will refer to the specialized service delivery provided primarily to infants and toddlers aged birth to thirty-six months with disabilities and their families, rather than services for preschoolers and older children. Why should we have early intervention services in home settings? The question may seem simple but in fact can become quite complicated and controversial. Before we detail the rationale for activity-based intervention in home settings, it will be useful to introduce some of the factors that have been and continue to be potential roadblocks to this form of early intervention. While the dates may be arguable, up until the mid-1980s, and with the passage of Part H (now Part C) of PL 99-457 (Education of the Handicapped Act Amendments of 1986), family-centered early intervention delivered in natural settings (including homes) was the exception. For one thing, professionals were more likely to speak of *parents* rather than *family* as a unit. While parent involvement and parent training were typically espoused as important goals and program components, too often that translated into parents being expected to learn intervention techniques, then generalize what they learned to the home in order to be extensions of the professionals. Parents were often expected to be compliant, appreciative learners, not *collaborators and partners*.

Furthermore, intervention delivered in homes has historically tended to be viewed by many professionals as troublesome and messy. A common source of frustration for a home interventionist was that parents didn't seem committed to or willing to participate in intervention activities that were intended to help their child. Professionals—sometimes with little knowledge of or interest in the family's situation, concerns, needs, or stresses—expected cooperation in achieving the goals and objectives that they (the professionals) had established for the child. Home-based early intervention was and still is uncomfortable to many early interventionists and other professionals because their training and experience often tells them they must be experts in a setting (maybe a center, classroom, or clinic) over which they have more control. Another roadblock to home-based early intervention is the now refuted notion that family members (parents especially) are uniformly not objective or reliable in determining the needs of their young children with disabilities, or realistic in their expectations. The author suggests that yet another roadblock to home-based early intervention has to do with economics and administrative convenience. Home-based programs tend to be more difficult to monitor and to quantify the amount of service provided. Home-based programs can be more costly because travel and extra time may be involved, the family's schedules may change, and so forth. Home-based programs tend to be more difficult to research and evaluate, and that affects the ability of program developers to secure federal, state, and local funding. Home-based programs are difficult to "show off."

Certainly, however, over the past two decades there have been a number of successful home-based early intervention models that have been adopted and funded as ongoing programs in states and local communities. Some examples of such programs are the Portage Project (Shearer & Shearer, 1976), the SKI*HI Institute (1989), the UCLA Infant Studies Project (Bromwich, 1981), Project LIFT (Sampon, 1988), the ETIPS model (Folio & Richey, 1990), and Project ECHO (Kaiser, 1988). There are, of course, many other models and established programs for home-based early intervention reflecting a wide array of philosophies, target groups, types of disabilities, and age groups.

The reader interested in more detail about the historical development of home-based early intervention is referred to the sources noted above as a sampling of program models and to a book chapter authored by Bailey and Simeonsson (1988). For an understanding of the current status and application of home-base services, the reader may wish to see the book by Carol S. Klass (1996) entitled *Home Visiting: Promoting Healthy Parent and Child Development.* Two of the central themes advanced by Klass and particularly relevant to our consideration of ABI in home settings are her focus on parent as the expert and their partnership with professionals, and her emphasis on the routines, rituals, and celebrations of home as the basis for home visitor interventions. Despite progress in the development of home as a component of the continuum of early intervention service settings, the author suggests that these roadblocks are continuing concerns.

To summarize, the roadblocks are specific to (1) the ways in which professionals have traditionally viewed best practices in early intervention (parent as an extension of the professional rather than partner); (2) the tendency to artificially separate all needs and goals/objectives for (especially) infants and toddlers from needs/goals/objectives relevant to the family as a unit; (3) preservice training programs, in special education and related disciplines, which have not adequately prepared individuals for delivery of services in home settings; and (4) economic and administrative difficulties associated with home-based early intervention. With the full implementation of PL 99-457 and its reauthorization in PL 101-476 (IDEA) we now have a clear mandate to include home-based service as a part of a comprehensive system of service delivery.

There are at least two fundamental reasons why home-based services for young children with disabilities are justifiable. The first is that it may be the preferred form of service from the family's point of view. There are many logical and understandable reasons why professionals may not be welcome in a family's home. But there are also many instances where families will welcome and prefer this form of service. An obvious example is that their child may be medically fragile and confined to the home. Also it may be more convenient for the family, they may be more comfortable, or travel may be too demanding or too expensive. Bailey and Simeonsson (1988) has noted that family members may prefer home-based services for these practical considerations as well as because their family is viewed as a unit (system) and they receive personalized attention. A second reason for home-based services is that it is recommended practice. Actions taken by the Division of Early Childhood (DEC) of the Council for Exceptional Children (CEC) have underscored the need for quality home-based early intervention. The Report of the DEC Task Force on Recommended Practices (1993) has underscored the need for quality home-based early intervention. The report includes the following four recommendations specific to home-based services. Note that especially the first recommendation stated (SDM 11) has a focus on activity-based intervention (ABI).

SDM 11. Staff base the nature, delivery, and scope of intervention upon activities of daily living (e.g., bathing, feeding, play, bedtime, etc.).
SDM 12. Intervention includes all family members (family members being defined by the family) who wish to be involved.
SDM 13. The level of intensity and range of services match the level of need identified by the family.
SDM 14. Staff base their communication with family members upon principles of mutual respect, caring, and sensitivity.

Additionally, the DEC has adopted a position statement on inclusion, stating that all children have the right to participate in "natural settings within their communities" (DEC, April 1993). It is noted in the statement that a family's home is one such setting.

We have addressed in general what home-based intervention is, why it is justified, and some of the roadblocks to its implementation. We now turn our attention to what the "fit" is between home-based service and activity-based intervention (ABI). Activity-based intervention includes having major outcomes and objectives for young children and, to a large degree, following children's leads in reaching them. Families at home have goals (and objectives, though they may not be so named), and their children are engaged in activities and routines substantially dominated by child choice (play). They want and need to initiate, choose, and play. So if we are to follow their lead, we will play.

Frost (1992) has pointed out that perhaps the best thing that we as adults can do to discover the meaning of play for young children is to go out and play, to reflect upon our own childhood play and to once again look at play through the eyes of the child. This is to take the lead of the child. Bricker and Cripe (1992) note that early intervention, specifically ABI, should use authentic activities, and most certainly homes and the happenings therein meet these criteria. They also have described the factors necessary for successful application of ABI in home-based programs. Attributes of the staff include skill in observation of children and planning; ability to recognize and capitalize on child initiations, routines, and planned activities as they relate to specialized needs of children; and the ability and willingness to assist others, for example, family members. Structure is another factor needed for success. The structure must allow adequate time for intervention to occur in the home setting as well as a means of systematically monitoring the child's progress. Because ABI includes planned activities and use of routines, as well as taking advantage of child initiations, home visitor staff must have both the philosophy and the associated skills. Identifying routines with families and jointly planning with the family regarding how their routines will be used to address goals and objectives is very important. (See Figure 4–3.)

Figure 4–3 Emily enjoys looking at books with her brothers.

Family Day Care Homes

The second setting that we will introduce regarding its potential as the location of activity-based intervention for young children with disabilities is the family day care home. Family day care homes have been discussed by Alston (1992) as the oldest, most common, and most popular form of day care provided in the United States. Hofferth and Kisker (1992) have described this form of service as a home setting generally located in neighborhoods, serving at least one nonrelated child, sometimes licensed or regulated but often nonregulated, and including children from infants through adolescence. Typically no more than five are enrolled. It is reasonable to assume that parents/families of children with a variety of disabilities may choose to enroll them in family day care homes for much the same reasons that parents of children without disabilities do. Those reasons include the following: (1) Family day care homes are located in close proximity to the home of the families served so that transportation and access are easier, (2) it is often possible for the communication and team partnership between family members and the provider to be established and nurtured because they have more time and access to each other, and (3) the family day care home is likely to be more personal and "home-like" and to reflect the neighborhood and community of the children's home. Certainly it is important to add to this list that parents would tend to choose a family day care home setting for their child because they felt that the provider would recognize and accommodate the uniqueness and special strengths and developmental needs of their child.

Not a great deal has been written about the inclusion of young children with disabilities in family day care homes, and even less information is found specific to the application of activity-based intervention in these settings.

However Deiner (1992) points out that the inclusion of children with disabilities is not a new idea. Family day care arrangements possibly serve more children with disabilities than any other. With the increased attention on family-centered approaches and natural settings, the usefulness of family day care for young children with disabilities could be assumed to continue to increase. Alston (1992) has emphasized in her text on family day care that it is important for the provider of family day care to recognize developmental problems and to seek the guidance and expertise of specialists in better serving children with special needs.

Infant and Toddler Nursery and Child Care Settings

The third type of setting that we will consider with regard to its role in the provision of activity-based intervention for very young children with disabilities is the group setting, either full day or partial day, in which infants and toddlers receive care. For our purposes we will include children from birth to three years. Certainly the issues and practices related to the provision of care in these day care and larger group settings also apply in large measure to the previous settings in which infants and toddlers are frequently cared for—homes and family day care homes. In Chapter 10 we will look in some detail at ways in which you might apply activity-based intervention and positive behavioral supports to facilitate inclusion in the various infant and toddler settings. With regard to characterizing developmentally appropriate care for infants and toddlers, it is important not to think of programs for them as scaled-down versions of preschool programs. Having warm and patient adults is possibly the most important factor. This would seem to apply whether the infant or toddler has special needs or is typically developing, and this notion is certainly consistent with our previous consideration of the need to provide positive behavioral supports.

Lally, Torres, and Phelps (1994) have identified two main sources of problems related to current practices in providing group care to infants and toddlers. One is that our society appears unwilling to take the profession of infant and toddler child care seriously, to accept evidence that quality group care is not harmful to children and families, and to prepare and pay caregivers adequately. Second, we have tended to put people who may be familiar with preschool aged children or older children but not with younger children in positions of responsibility, and the results are often that the environments are too large and too impersonal and may have unnecessary structure and emphasis on learning and education rather than development and nurturing. These authors note that "a preschooler has already formed a pretty solid sense of identity, with definite likes, dislikes, inclinations and attitudes, but an infant or toddler is *forming* his or her sense of identity." An article written by a former preschool educator who changed professional roles to work with infants and toddlers (Keenan, 1998) makes some interesting points regarding the differences. Keenan concludes that the most salient differences are that in working with infants and toddlers nonverbal communication with children and coworkers and communication daily with parents is more important, the intensity of relationships is greater, there is greater emphasis on the individual child rather than the curriculum, there is the necessity of careful observation in creating curriculum, and it is particularly important to use routines as nurturing times.

Central to the reauthorization of IDEA is the requirement that, in the delivery of early intervention services, families must be provided service settings that constitute natural environments for infants and toddlers. Certainly infant and toddler group care settings have become and will continue to be one of the primary places for carrying out the mandate of the law under Part C to give preference to natural environments.

So what are some of the issues, challenges, and considerations associated with using activity-based intervention in group care settings for infants and toddlers with a variety of types and severity of special needs? One is that in these settings we depend in large measure on the initiations of the infant or toddler (child-directed) to guide us in terms of care, play, socializing, and the like, rather than on caregiver or teacher-directed activities. Very young children with disabilities may be less capable of providing these initiations that afford us the situation and milieu for addressing their specialized needs. For example, a toddler with severe cerebral palsy may not have the mobility skills necessary to move around the room or playground and get to equipment, objects, toys, or other children's activities as readily as other children, thus limiting our opportunities to take advantage of the child's movement initiations to intervene. It is important, however, to note that most infants or toddlers with disabilities will be very capable of providing us much direction for what interests them. It is up to us as caregivers, interventionists, and infant educators to learn to recognize what are sometimes subtle cues and to provide the right opportunities and supports needed for self-directedness.

Consider for a moment the relationship between ABI and the usual routines that occur in infant/toddler group care settings. The developmentally appropriate practices for infants and toddlers provided by the National Association for the Education of Young Children (Bredekamp & Copple, 1997) state that it is inappropriate to move swiftly through routines with little communication or warm interactions. Rather it is appropriate during routines such as diapering, feeding, and changing clothes to be especially attentive and communicative, with regard to both initiating and responding to the actions of the child (transactional). The routines carried out in infant and toddler child care settings are natural opportunities for embedding intervention on specialized goals and objectives. As noted earlier, we will take up in some detail in Chapter 10 the applications of ABI, as well as positive behavioral supports and developmentally appropriate practice, in infant and toddler group care settings as inclusionary environments for very young children with special needs.

Head Start Programs

The fourth general category of settings that we will consider with regard to how the principles of activity-based intervention have relevance is Head Start. It will serve to introduce this section by relating the story of a mother with whom the author has been privileged to work.

On October 11, 1990, my son Brandon Dewayne Campbell was born. He had to have breathing tubes once a month. In that time they found out that he had only nine ribs on one side, only one kidney, six fingers, half a bone missing, and a club foot all connected to the left side. On April 4, 1992, Brandon had his spine fused and left leg amputated above the knee. I was confused whether or not to have it done and right now I know that I did the right thing. He goes everywhere on his artificial leg and I am so proud of him. Brandon goes to Head Start when he turns three. I believe that he will like it. I feel like it will help him a lot. I feel really good about him going. On September 22, 1993, Brandon had another surgery to have his fingers separated. It took three hours and fifteen minutes to complete it. When I got to go back in the recovery room to see him, I could see that he was in a lot of pain. It hurt me to see him in so much pain, but I know he will get through this because my Brandon is a tough fighter. He's got to be as much as he's been through. Brandon also has a feeding button in his stomach to be fed his milk every four hours. He could never take a bottle; he would gag every time you tried to stick a bottle in his mouth. Brandon has had a tough time. I hope this is the last major surgery, and that getting used to Head Start will be his next challenge. I want him to go to Head Start because he can be with other children his age. I think Head Start will help him a lot to get along and get ready for school. And he needs to spend time with other children and not so much with me. (*Note:* As of this writing, Brandon has completed first grade and is doing very well.)

This heartfelt story from a mother about her child's experience helps illustrate for us the place of activity-based intervention in the Head Start setting. In his first three years of life Brandon and his family have been through a great deal. He still has significant need for specialized goals, objectives, and activities to address his special needs, but he is ready to have those addressed in a natural setting around other children who do not have disabilities, and that is what his family wants for him. Much of the time that would have otherwise gone to the typical growth and development, play, and other activities of an infant and toddler has been consumed by visits to doctors, surgeries, and attending to Brandon's special physical and medical needs. Barbara (Brandon's mom) wants him to be around other children his age and to learn the social and preacademic skills that will pave the way for him when he enters school. Brandon is being transitioned into the Head Start classroom from a home-based early intervention service. Like many families with young children with disabilities, Brandon's family sees Head Start as a means of making his life more like that of other children his age—for him to be in a natural setting. Barbara also hopes that she will continue to have support, a central role, and the opportunity to help teachers and others better understand and serve Brandon through Head Start's parent involvement component.

Head Start programs are certainly viewed as natural settings and have a history of more than twenty-five years of serving children with disabilities and typically developing children in the same classrooms. The Head Start mandate for serving children with special needs is well established. Since 1972 Head Start has operated under a congressional mandate requiring that a minimum of ten percent of the children served by a grantee have a diagnosed disability. In their extensive historical review of Head Start, Zigler and Muenchow (1992) note that the services provided to children with disabilities have become one of Head Start's most commendable features. It is one thing to place children together in time and space, but it is quite another to have the child with a disability as an active participant. If, for example, Brandon, because of his health and physical limitations, were to sit with the teachers and watch the other children at play on the playground, or if he were to be excluded from an art activity because he couldn't hold the brush like other children, the fact that he is in a natural setting may be of little or very limited value. Activity-based intervention requires that professionals (in this instance Head Start teachers), family members, and others look very carefully at how the specialized needs (goals and objectives) of a child with a disability can be addressed in the context of active participation in the routine curriculum and activities of natural settings, such as Head Start classrooms.

Head Start classrooms are certainly not uniform, so each one will vary somewhat with regard to schedule of routines and activities and the curriculum and assessment guides followed. However, Head Start programs are committed to making and following a plan for their children with disabilities that will afford them opportunities "to be included in the full range of activities and services normally provided to all Head Start children" (Head Start Performance Standards on Children with Disabilities, 1993). We also know that by law children with disabilities enrolled in Head Start aged three to five must have an individual education program (IEP) stating that Head Start is an appropriate setting and spelling out the special needs of the child in terms of goals and objectives. The specialized interventions necessary to accomplish a child's goals and objectives can be undertaken as a part of the typical routines and activities of a Head Start classroom. You will recall that ABI includes activities planned by the teacher as well as child-initiated activities and activities normally occurring as a part of routines. All of these elements of ABI are available in the natural setting of a Head Start classroom.

For readers interested in a comprehensive review of the development of Head Start from its beginning in the mid-1960s up until 1990, you are referred to the source noted above, a book by Edward Zigler and Susan Muenchow (1992) entitled *Head Start: The Inside Story of America's Most Successful Educational Experiment*. It is a fascinating description of the origins of Head Start and the political, economic, and other factors that have influenced it over the years. The book also addresses the evidence regarding Head Start's effectiveness as well as the authors' views of the program's future. Despite its successes and history of political support across different administrations, Head Start continues to be challenged regarding its quality and the extent to which benefits to children and their parents are maintained over time (Kanthorwitz & Wingert, 1993).

Preschool/Kindergarten Settings

The fifth category of setting we need to overview as it relates to activity-based intervention is the preschool environment. Of course the nature of a setting for three- to five-year-old children varies significantly, and we have already addressed one of the primary settings, Head Start. Where else are preschoolers to be found and in what kinds of activities are they engaged? This is a question that you will be able at least to some extent to answer for yourself based on your personal and/or professional experiences. Preschoolers may be in partial day or full day public or private child care or prekindergarten settings, or more frequently they may be in public schools in which services for typically developing children along with services for young children who are at risk and/or have special needs have been combined.

Finally, in response to the question of where preschoolers may be found, we must add kindergarten. Berk (1996) has highlighted that with regard to their developmental status and needs, five-year-olds have much more in common with three- and four-year-old children than they do with six-, seven-, and eight-year-olds. The leadership provided to educators, interventionists, and other child care professionals from the National Association for the Education of Young Children regarding professional standards and developmentally appropriate practices reinforces very clearly the view that kindergartens should look more like, and operate more like, preschool environments. In explaining this perspective NAEYC has emphasized that most five-year-old children have not made the cognitive shift to more logical thinking, reasoning, and self-directedness that has been found and assumed to be occurring between ages five and seven (Bredekamp & Copple, 1997).

The answer to the question about what preschoolers are doing in these varied settings is a complicated one. It depends upon the philosophy and practice of the program and will vary from highly structured settings in which specific curricula are followed, to address primarily through teacher-directed activities preacademic and academic areas, to highly unstructured settings in which the emphasis is almost exclusively on child-directed play. There are of course numerous books and resource guides that provide curricula for use with preschool-aged children. The features that these curricula tend to have in common are that they emphasize opportunities for creativity and self-expression of children, they focus on activities that require integration across developmental domains (such as motor and language), they employ a unit-based approach to learning and play activities (for example, units related to seasons, holidays, community helpers, etc.), they follow a logical developmental sequence, and they are facilitated by the preschool environment being divided into learning and play centers (such as dramatic play, blocks, dress up, etc.). Overriding all of the models for how to deliver preschool education services and the different approaches to curriculum design and emphases are the principles of developmental appropriateness provided by NAEYC. You are referred to the 1997 revised edition of *Developmentally Appropriate Practice in Early Childhood Programs* edited by Sue Bredekamp and Carol Copple for a complete listing and description of appropriate and inappropriate practices for three- through five-year-olds. Figure 4–4 below restates and summarizes a few of these practices.

Given this brief introduction to the nature of preschool environments, we can now relate them to the principle of ABI and discuss in general how it might be used to facilitate inclusion of children with a variety of special needs. It is important in the beginning to note that ABI is applicable to any of the approaches and curricular models applied to preschool education, since specialized goals, objectives, and intervention strategies are embodied in whatever routines, activities, and classroom arrangements are being used. Traditionally you might note that in preschool curriculum guides the authors tended to either add a chapter or section focusing on children with special needs or have emphasized at the end of an activity description how it might be adapted to be used with children with particular disabilities. More recently the emphasis has been on assuming that in

Appropriate	Inappropriate
experiences insure success most of the time and yet are challenging	expectations and teacher requirements typically beyond child's ability
schedule of the day has a variety of active and quiet times	overdependence on teacher-directed and led activities
goals of the curriculum cover all developmental domains	goals over emphasize a few dimensions of development
various means are used to assess progress, including observation, work samples, and more formal procedures	overdependence on standardized tests
partnerships with parents/families are established and nurtured	parents are communicated with primarily to talk about problems
teachers are qualified through college-level preparation in child development and early childhood and they have ongoing professional development	teachers lack specific training and experience with young children and do not engage in ongoing professional development

Figure 4–4
Appropriate and inappropriate practices for three-through-five year-olds.

large measure the regular routines and activities of the classroom are the starting point for all children, including those with special needs, and that specialized goals and objectives (from the child's IEP or IFSP) can be addressed across the various routines, activities, and play associated with the type of preschool setting. This is not to say that carrying out an effective inclusive preschool does not require additional time and more systematic planning and a closer partnering with parents. Van den Pol, Guidry, and Keeley (1995) have summarized the issues about how to create an inclusive preschool in this way:

> Creating an effective environment for an inclusive preschool classroom requires much thought and planning. It is important to consider the individual needs and goals of each child, as well as those of the class as a whole. Even before the first child sets foot in the classroom, gather materials that are safe as well as developmentally appropriate, develop strategies to ensure the free and effective flow of communication needed for a smoothly running classroom, arrange the physical setting of the classroom to ensure safety and encourage independence, and develop rules for the classroom that consider the needs of the children as well as the adults. With careful attention to planning and classroom arrangement, you will create a dynamic and exciting environment where learning is not only encouraged but also fun. (p. 19)

In Chapter 11 you will be provided with five vignettes, or short teacher/child/family descriptions, that will illustrate specifically for you how ABI is applied in inclusive preschool environments to address the specialized goals for young children with varying degrees and types of special needs. For now we will complete our consideration of ABI and preschool with an abbreviated example. David is a four-year-old who was diagnosed at age three as having a moderate to severe speech articulation disability. His speech is largely understood by his parents, who have learned to interpret his words and meaning, but it is about 50 percent unintelligible to other people. David omits many initial consonant sounds that typically children by age three are able to consistently produce. For example, he might say "aby" for "baby" or "ater" for "water." David's speech difficulties are more and more affecting his interactions and communication, especially with friends. He has been certified by the school system and has been receiving speech therapy once a week for thirty minutes in a clinical setting. He is in a preschool classroom, and it is desirable to address some of his objectives related to articulation in the natural environment using what has been referred to (Umansky & Hooper, 1998) as "natural situations" and applying a "collaborative consultation" model (coordination and teamwork among parents, preschool teacher, and speech therapist). The parents are very interested in improving the consistency between home and preschool with regard to helping David, and the speech therapist has agreed to come into the classroom to work with David in the context of the ongoing activities and to consult with the teacher and other adults working in the classroom.

In this example, David's normal day in the preschool is rich with opportunities to use activity-based intervention to work on the goals of improving his articulation, decreasing his omissions, and increasing his ability and willingness to communicate with other children. One of the *routines* of the classroom is putting on coats, hat, gloves, and the like, in preparation for going outside in cold weather. This is a good opportunity for the teacher or other adult to talk with David ("We are putting on your *h*at, can you say *h*at?"). Among the *planned activities* of the classroom is circle time when the teacher reads a book to all of the children. David might have next to him the speech therapist (who has arranged to be there during this period in the morning) or another adult who helps David to say some of the words taken from the story, when the teacher invites response from the children. The book has been selected to include some of the words on which David is currently working.

There are of course many opportunities for *child-initiated* activities in the classroom, and David especially likes to play at the block table with a particular friend. This is a good opportunity for David to practice his speech in a circumstance where he is very motivated to communicate with his friend and where there are *logically occurring antecedents and consequences*. The blocks and block play table (antecedents) are natural and logical for preschool classrooms, and the outcomes of the activity (consequences) are naturally rewarding to David, that is, having fun with and talking to and being understood by a friend and constructing something from the blocks. You can see how all of these activities are *transactional* in that they facilitate give and take between David and other children or adults, and you can conclude that the activities are *functional* and will *generalize* to other times and places in David's life. Finally, we have not in this example dealt with how to collect information in a systematic manner to provide evidence for how much progress David is making toward his goals and objectives. Ongoing assessment, evaluation, and data

Figure 4–5
Conversations between children in the regular routines and activities of the day are part of addressing specialized language and speech development goals.

collection are very necessary, however, and we will take up the matter of how to do it further into the book. (See Figure 4–5).

Early Elementary Grades

The sixth and last general category of setting with which we need to establish a connection with activity-based intervention is that of the early elementary grades 1 through 3. The inclusion process and related practices at elementary grade levels have recently received a great deal of attention in most regular as well as special education literature. Invariably you will find at least one article in many of the journals that you would most frequently use that directly or indirectly addresses inclusion. Karagiannis, Stainback, and Stainback (1996) have discussed the increasing trend toward inclusion in schools and have highlighted the clear evidence of its growing benefits for teachers, students, and society. It has been suggested (O'Brien & O'Brien, 1996) that inclusion is a strong and positive force for renewal in our public schools.

Despite the fact that for elementary schools and early elementary grades the issues are no longer whether to include but rather how to carry out a successful process, there has been very minimal upward extension of the principles of ABI from the infant, toddler, and preschool period to the first three grades of school. Given the fact that the nature of education and learning is significantly different between preschool and school-aged settings, this is not surprising. Grades 1 to 3 may frequently be organized in a manner that gives majority time to teacher-directed activities. This reality affects the balance that is assumed in ABI among teacher-directed and child-initiated transactional activities and routines. However, it is our belief that ABI, with some "fine-tuning," has equal relevance for academic settings such as grades 1 through 3. You will see that we have elaborated on this relevance and detailed applications of ABI, along with DAP and PBS, in the last chapter (Chapter 12) of this book.

In its description of developmentally appropriate practices, the National Association for the Education of Young Children (Bredekamp & Copple, 1997) has emphasized that for six- through eight-year-olds in primary grades the curriculum should be integrated across subjects and developmental domains and that the content of the curriculum should be relevant, engaging, and meaningful to the children themselves. Moreover, in the NAEYC practice statements there is indication that "pull-out" programs are fragmenting and often undermining, that children with disabilities should be included in all aspects of the classroom environment, and that teaching strategies should facilitate active involvement and address individual developmental levels of students. These indicators and recommended effective practice in primary grades are very compatible with the tenets of ABI. For example, children should have opportunities for exploration (child-directedness), and teachers should strive to plan and carry out learning activities that have relevance and meaning to the children (functional and generative skills).

Some Concerns Regarding Activity-Based Intervention

Concerns about the use of activity-based intervention principles as a foundation for facilitating inclusion of young children from birth to age eight in natural preschool environments and regular classrooms can be viewed from the perspectives of parent/family members, early childhood educators and caregivers, early interventionists and special educators, or professionals in related disciplines such as physical therapy, occupational therapy, speech and language pathology, nursing, and psychology or social work. Maybe you currently hold one of these roles, or you are preparing yourself to assume one of them. You might think especially of these concerns as they relate to your discipline (or parent and family role) and to your obligation to collaborate and work as part of a team with other disciplines and points of view. Remember that we have discussed in Chapter 1 some of the concerns and reservations that both professionals and consumers (families and children) might have about inclusion. The issues summarized below and those specific to activity-based intervention are closely tied to concerns about inclusion, even though ABI does not always necessitate an inclusive setting.

Family members of young children with disabilities may have concerns that activity-based intervention is not precise, systematic, or controlled enough to ensure that their child will make good progress toward achieving her/his specialized objectives. Bricker and Cripe (1992) have described how much of what we have done historically in early childhood special education was adapted from behavioral models applied to older populations of individuals with disabilities. They note that intervention was delivered in a "fashion that employed one-to-one, highly structured, adult-directed, massed-trial training approaches." Maybe in a rather significant way professionals in special education and related disciplines have established an expectation in parents that this approach was the only way to be sure that progress was being made.

Tied to this traditional approach was the necessity to develop objectives that were very precise, measurable, and highly observable in controlled circumstances but often not very functional, generalizable, family or teacher friendly.

So one primary concern that parents/families might have is that their child's specialized needs are in a sense left to chance to be addressed in ABI, and they may lack evidence (frequencies, percentages, etc.) of objectives being met. Families may also have concerns that their child with special needs will not be given their fair share of the adults' attention in the context of inclusive classroom activities, or that their child's health and/or safety may be at risk, especially for children who may be medically fragile, who have comprehensive or orthopedic disabilities, or who have limited expressive language abilities.

Professionals in special education, including early intervention and early childhood special education, may have some of the same concerns described above related to the differences between ABI and the traditional ways of delivering educational services to children with disabilities. Frequently their preparation has not included much if any emphasis on the philosophy and rationale for ABI, collaborative and teaming skills in working in natural and inclusive settings, family-centered approaches, or creative ways of assessing and measuring progress across varied settings and activities. So for many of these professionals ABI is somewhat foreign and incompatible with the ways in which they have been trained and the ways in which they have carried out (and been rewarded for and successful in) their professional responsibilities. There may be to some extent a "don't fix it if it isn't broken" point of view and a cherished and somewhat supportable belief held historically by many special educators that children with special needs, left to the devices or "regular" educators, will not be adequately served. Also special educators may agree with the principles and approach of ABI but simply feel ill-prepared with regard to their skills or their personal and professional style to carry it out.

Hesitancy and resistance from early childhood educators and caregivers about ABI tend to center around (1) their lack of awareness and knowledge of and experience with disabilities, (2) their concern that planning for and attending to the specialized needs and goals of children with disabilities will take away from other children, (3) the historical lack of substantive emphasis on and commitment to inclusionary practices in their disciplines of early childhood education and child and family science, and (4) the time constraints and complexities associated with merging in their lesson and daily plans and routines attention to how those teacher-directed activities, routines, and opportunities for child-directed play will include adaptations to meet the goals and objectives for children with special needs. Parents of typically developing children in settings where ABI is being applied may also have concerns. In particular they may feel that their child is not receiving the quality of attention and/or instruction that they as parents expect either because children with disabilities require an inordinate amount of the teacher/caregivers time and energy or because the content and delivery of the activities and curriculum are "watered down." Parents may also have concerns for the safety of their children, especially if the nature of the disability includes overly aggressive or very unacceptable social behavior, such as repetitive actions, verbal outbursts, tantrums, or self-injurious behavior.

In a recent journal article by Rule, Losardo, Dinnebeil, Kaiser, and Rowland (1998), the authors address the status of translating naturalistic intervention/instruction (including activity-based intervention procedures) research into practice. The authors point out that while naturalistic instruction has broad philosophical appeal and a number of empirically supported naturalistic procedures have been identified, there remains a significant need to find ways to help practitioners (such as early childhood educators or caregivers) apply the results of research in their service delivery settings. They suggest guidelines for the organizing and reporting of research in ways that will facilitate translating research to practice.

Finally, we should acknowledge that to some extent the manner in which professionals are prepared and deliver services to young children with disabilities and their families by the related disciplines listed above sometimes relates to concerns specific to ABI. At the risk of oversimplifying, it is fair to say that a significant number of professionals in related disciplines—for example, physical therapy—are not comfortable with the bulk of a prescribed therapy being delivered in a nonclinical setting and in the context of normally occurring routines, teacher-directed activities, and child-initiations. And they may not, as we noted above with regard to special educators, feel that their training has prepared them to view regular educators and families as collaborators and members of a team on which they serve. There are also issues of professional standards and credentialing as well as economic and political influences that impact related disciplines' view of inclusion in general and ABI in particular. Our intention here is not to agree or disagree with or to address the issues and concerns introduced in this section of the chapter. You will find that as a part of the process of reading and studying this book, and engaging in some of the suggested activities, you will formulate your own professional positions about the efficacy and relevance of both professional and consumer misgivings about ABI.

Summary

The activity-based intervention approach to the planning and delivering of services to young children with disabilities and their families has over the last ten years become prominent. ABI provides an excellent framework for meeting the specialized needs of children in natural environments and through inclusive processes. One way to think about ABI is that it represents a blend of what have historically been successful elements of both special education and early childhood education. Activity-based intervention guides educators, interventionists, child care providers, and others to embed intervention activities aimed at addressing specialized objectives into the typical routines and experiences that might be a part of the day for children of comparable chronological and developmental ages.

As you have learned from this chapter, ABI emphasizes the importance of taking advantage of children's interests and initiatives and the use of logically and naturally occurring antecedents (the circumstances that precede a behavior) and consequences (the actions/feelings resultant from the behavior). Activity-based intervention principles and practices are applicable to the various settings in which young children with special needs are most often served, including home, family day care, nursery schools and child care, Head Start, preschool, kindergarten, and the early elementary grades. However, it is useful to think of ABI as having relevance for the broader context of a child's experience, for example, going out to a restaurant, visiting friends or relatives, attending church, or going shopping. Activity-based intervention continues to be "work in progress," but it holds great promise as the approach—in tandem with DAP and PBS—through which we further the cause of inclusion for young children with various types and levels of disability.

Chapter 4 Suggested Activities and Resources

Activities

1. Interview professionals from different disciplines—for example, early childhood educator, early interventionist/early childhood special educator, physical or speech therapist, nurse, school psychologist, social worker—and compare their varying perspectives on the pros and cons of ABI. Relate their opinions and experiences to the chapter content, including the section on concerns.

2. Conduct a library literature search on the topic of ABI and develop a short position paper to share with the class. You might do this as part of a small group or team effort.

3. Search websites of various parent/family advocacy and support organizations as well as professional associations and synthesize their stated positions on inclusion. Relate this to the principles of ABI.

4. Ask to make an informal talk, maybe with a partner from class, to a parent/family advocacy or support group—making clear that it is an assignment for class—about ABI and ask them for feedback about your presentation and about their experiences with ABI.

5. Select one of the six settings detailed in the chapter and draw a picture of what you would like your inclusion classroom (or maybe the living room, if it is home-based) to look like and how its organization and contents might foster ABI.

Selected Resources

Curriculum and intervention guides: Activity-Based Intervention Guide by Marcia Cain Coling and Judith Nealer Garrett (1995) and published by Therapy Skill Builders; *Family-Centered Intervention Planning: A Routines-Based Approach* by R. A. McWilliam (1992) and published by Communication Skill Builders.

Videos: Activity-Based Intervention by Diane Bricker, Peggy Veltman, and Arden Munkers; and *Family-Guided Activity-Based Intervention for Infants and Toddlers* by Julian J. Woods Cripe, both published by Paul H. Brookes Publishing Co.

Book: An Activity-Based Approach to Early Intervention by Diane Bricker and Julian J. Woods Cripe (1992) and published by Paul H. Brookes Publishing Co.

References

Alston, F. K. (1992). *Caring for Other People's Children: A Complete Guide to Family Day Care.* New York: Teachers College Press.

Bailey, D. B., & Simeonsson, R. J. (1988). Home-Based Early Interventions. In S. L. Odom & M. B. Karnes (Eds.), *Early Intervention for Infants and Children with Handicaps* (pp. 199–216). Baltimore: Paul H. Brookes Publishing Co.

Berk, L. E. (1996). *Infants and Children: Prenatal through Middle Childhood.* (2nd ed.). Boston: Allyn & Bacon.

Berk, L. E., & Winsler, A. (l995). *Scaffolding Children's Learning: Vygotsky and Early Childhood Education.* Washington, DC: National Association for the Education of Young Children.

Bredekamp, S., & Copple, C. (Eds.) (1997). *Developmentally Appropriate Practice in Early Childhood Programs: Revised Edition.* Washington, DC: National Association for the Education of Young Children.

Bricker, D., & Woods Cripe, J. J. (1992). *An Activity-Based Approach to Early Intervention.* Baltimore: Paul H. Brookes Publishing Co.

Bromwich, R. M. (1981). *Working with Parents and Infants: An Interactional Approach.* Baltimore: University Park Press.

DEC Executive Committee (1993). *Position Statement on Inclusion.* Adopted at the CEC Convention Annual Business Meeting, San Antonio, April 7.

DEC Task Force on Recommended Practice (1993). *DEC Recommended Practices: Indication of Quality in Programs for Infants and Young Children with Special Needs and Their Families.* Council for Exceptional Children. Reston, VA.

Deiner, P. L. (1992). Family Day Care and Children with Disabilities. In D. L. Peters & A. L. Pence (Eds.), *Family Day Care: Current Research for Informed Public Policy* (pp. 129–145). New York: Teachers College Press.

Folio, R., & Richey, D. (1990). Public Television and Video Technology for Rural Families with Special Needs Young Children: The ETIPS Model. *Topics in Early Childhood Special Education, 10*(4), 45–55.

Frost, J. E. (1992). *Play and Playscapes.* Albany, NY: Delmar Publishers, Inc.

Hofferth, S. L., & Kisker, E. E. (1992). The Changing Demographics of Family Day Care in the United States. In D. L. Peters & A. L. Pence (Eds.), *Family Day Care: Current Research for Informed Public Policy* (pp. 28–57). New York: Teachers College Press.

Kaiser, C. (1988). *Project Echo.* A Presentation at the Division of Early Childhood Conference of the Council for Exceptional Children, Nashville, TN.

Kanthorwitz, B., & Wingert, P. (April 12, 1993). No Longer a Sacred Cow: Head Start Has Become a Free-Fire Zone. *Newsweek.*

Karagiannis, A., Stainback, W., & Stainback, S. (1996). Rationale for Inclusive Schooling. In W. Stainback & S. Stainback (Eds.), *Inclusion: A Guide for Educators* (pp. 3–15). Baltimore: Paul H. Brookes Publishing Co.

Keenan, M. (1998). Making the Transition from Preschool to Infant/Toddler Teacher. *Young Children, 53*(2), 5–11.

Klass, S. (1996). *Home Visiting: Promoting Healthy Parent and Child Development.* Baltimore: Paul H. Brookes Publishing Co.

Lally, R. J., Torres, Y. L., & Phelps, P. C. (1994). Caring for Infants and Toddlers in Groups: Necessary Considerations for Emotional, Social, and Cognitive Development. *Zero to Three: National Center for Clinical Infant Programs, 14*(5), 1–8.

Novick, R. (1993). Activity-Based Intervention and Developmentally Appropriate Practice: Points of Convergence. *Topics in Early Childhood Special Education, 13*(4), 403–417.

O'Brien, J., & O'Brien, C. L. (1996). Inclusion as a Force for School Renewal. In W. Stainback & S. Stainback (Eds.), *Inclusion: A Guide for Educators* (pp. 29–45). Baltimore: Paul H. Brookes Publishing Co.

Rule, S., Losardo, A., Dinnebeil, L., Kaiser, A., & Rowland, C. (1998). Translating Research on Naturalistic Instruction into Practice. *Journal of Early Intervention. 21*(4), 283–293.

Sampon, M. A. (1988). Project LIFT: A Rural Family-Focused Early Intervention Model. In *Alternative Futures for Rural Special Education*. Proceedings of the Annual ACRES Conference. (ERIC Document Reproduction Service No. EC 211 005).

Shearer, D. E., & Shearer, M. S. (1976). The Portage Project: A Model for Early Intervention. In T. D. Tjossem (Ed.), *Intervention Strategies for High Risk Infants and Young Children* (pp. 335–350). Baltimore: University Park Press.

SKI*HI Institute (1989). *Home-Based Programming for Families of Handicapped Infants and Young Children: A Manual for Parent Advisors and Other Home Interveners*. Department of Communicative Disorders, Utah State University, Logan.

Umansky, W., & Hooper, S. R. (1998). *Young Children with Special Needs*. Columbus, OH: Merrill Prentice Hall.

U.S. Department of Health and Human Services (1993). Head Start program performance standards on services to children with disabilities. Washington, DC.: U.S. Government Printing Office.

Van den Pol, R., Guidry, J., & Keeley, B. (1995). *Creating the Inclusive Preschool: Strategies for a Successful Program*. Tucson, AZ: Therapy Skill Builders.

Waite-Stupiansky, S. (1997). *Building Understanding Together: A Constructivist Approach to Early Childhood Education*. Albany, NY: Delmar Publishers.

Zigler, E., & Muenchow, S. (1992). *Head Start: The Inside Story of America's Most Successful Educational Experiment*. NY: Basic Books.

Zirpoli, T. J. (1995). *Understanding and Affecting the Behavior of Young Children*. Englewood Cliffs, NJ: Prentice-Hall, Inc.

Principles of Developmentally Appropriate Practice (DAP)*

INTRODUCTION

According to the National Association for the Education of Young Children (NAEYC), it is important to have knowledge about children's development and learning; specific knowledge about the unique, individual children we serve; and current information and understanding of the social and cultural contexts in which our children grow and develop. This information is necessary if we are to make decisions that are developmentally appropriate for children. The underlying assumption of developmentally appropriate practice (DAP) is that we, as adults and as children's caregivers and teachers, have children's best interests at heart. We care about their well-being, and we want to make the best decisions possible regarding their care and education.

As simple as that may seem, it is not. Our perspectives of what DAP is and for what it is useful may vary. For example, DAP may be the basis for curricular decisions or it may be a philosophy we use for all decisions we make for children's lives. What is developmentally appropriate for one child may not be appropriate for another because of the differences in children and the differences in their social and cultural contexts. Our common goal is for every child to reach his or her full potential within the context of care in which we are responsible—realizing that all contexts affect and are affected by each other (Bronfenbrenner, 1979). With this in mind and as students and practitioners of developmentally appropriate practice, it is important that we make a closer examination of DAP. Here are the objectives the reader will address in Chapter 5:

- Review the definition of DAP.
- Understand a theoretical basis for DAP.
- Understand the similar philosophies of NAEYC and the Division for Early Childhood of the Council for Exceptional Children (DEC/CEC) with regard to DAP.

---

*Written by Dr. Linda H. Richey, Ph.D., Associate Professor of Child and Family Studies in the Department of Curriculum and Instruction at Tennessee Technological University.

- Describe the connection between and among DAP, PBS, and ABI.
- Examine DAP with regard to its applications in activities and lesson plans including all domains of children's development, that is, cognitive, language, social, emotional, motor, and physical.

Developmentally Appropriate Practice

It may help the reader at this point to specifically examine the term *developmentally appropriate practice*. It would be easy to state that when referring to DAP, professionals are referring to those decisions made for children—for example, curricular, assessment, activity, environmental planning, and the like—that will enhance a child's growth and development. As a means to a deeper understanding of the term, and ultimately what the term means when it is manifested into practice, it would be beneficial to look at each aspect of the term. To that end, the terms *development, appropriate,* and *practice* will be discussed within the context of DAP and with the overriding goal of understanding what DAP means to professionals and to children.

Development

The Goal 1 Early Childhood Assessments Resource Group submitted the following definition of development to the National Education Goals Panel (Shepard, Kagan, & Wurtz, 1998):

> Growth or maturation that occurs primarily because of the emergence of underlying biological patterns or preconditions. The terms *development* and *learning* are distinguished by the presumption that one is caused by genetics and the other by experience. However, it is known that development can be profoundly affected by environmental conditions. (p. 37)

An ideal way to observe growth and development in children is to observe their play. Play is functional for children: children learn through play. Through play children learn about their world and the people in it. As professionals we must pay attention to play and how important it is to the whole child.

It is important to note that children develop in different contexts. Homes, preschools, grandparents' houses, churches, public schools, playgrounds, and neighborhoods are all contexts for children to learn and grow. Also, the interaction of these contexts affects children's development, for example, the partnership between school and home. We must consider the effect our laws, values, and belief systems have on children's development. Religious beliefs, materialistic-centered or person-centered values, and federal government legislation—such as welfare reform, funding of Head Start, and the Individuals with Disabilities Education Act—affect families' and children's well-being and, specifically, children's development. The controversies over the media's influence on children's development—for example, televised sexual situations and violence, and the covert advertisement of tobacco products to children—are two ongoing debates that reflect the concerns and beliefs that many citizens of the United States have about child development and the decisions and choices we make as a country for our children (Noah, 1997; Potter, 1996; Sarracino, 1995).

The Industrial Revolution, the Great Depression, the Vietnam War era are all periods of time that have had a major impact on children and families, including the development of children. Bronfenbrenner (1979) has detailed this best in his ecological systems theory of development, recently referred to as bioecological systems theory. According to Bronfenbrenner children's development is impacted by five systems. As introduced in Chapters 1 and 2, these five systems are the microsystem, mesosystem, exosystem, macrosystem, and chronosystem.

Theories of Development.

Theories of Development.   Theories have been developed over a period of time to help explain the many observations and beliefs various scholars have had about human and child development. Within these theories are definitions of the process of development and explanations of how development occurs. These theories are grounded in the experiences and perspectives of the theorists shaped in the time period in which he or she lived. Also, these theories, viewed as important explanations for the process of human development and change over time, are accepted by the disciplines of psychology and developmental psychology, child development, and education as a means to study and make decisions about and for children.

For the purpose of understanding the contribution these perspectives have with regard to studying and understanding child development, it is helpful to group the major theories of development and learning. Five groupings to consider are the following: maturational, psychodynamic, behavioral, cognitive developmental, and environmental. No perspective can explain every aspect of development; therefore, it is important to examine each theoretical perspective for what it can teach us about development or how the perspective can help us understand the developmental process.

From each theory of child development we can extract key ideas to help us define developmentally appropriate practice, our ultimate goal in this section of the chapter. Although the student of child development may align herself or himself with a particular theory, it is still advantageous to examine all theories for information or ideas to help us formulate this definition. Therefore, each theory or, if necessary, group of theories will be examined for this information.

The maturational theories of Hall, Havighurst, and Gesell have provided many scholars a foundation from which to work and complete research. Through the collection of *normative data* about all developmental domains, these scholars have provided a wealth of descriptive information about children's development. Although this perspective has not explained how a child develops, it has provided support for the necessity of *nurturing adults* who are *responsive* to children's needs.

Freud and Erikson are well known for their psychosexual and psychosocial perspectives, both psychodynamic theories of development. Although Freud's perspective is less useful in explaining the process of child development, it does advise us to learn about individual children from *various sources* and to pay attention to the *early years.* Both Freud and Erikson valued the examination of the mind and mental constructs of individuals. Erikson, a student of Freud, chose to look at the social aspects of development and the *importance of society's expectations* for people and its effects on children's development. Erikson did make an important connection of developmental stages and specific cultural values.

The classic behavioral theories of Watson, Skinner, and Bandura have been helpful because of their application value in educational environments and in research. In education, especially, a proliferation of work has resulted from the application of the principles from this perspective. Skinner's use of *reinforcement* and *punishment* to manipulate behavior was tempered by Bandura's added perspective of the importance of *active learning* for children. Most important was Bandura's concern for the development of *self-efficacy* in children and the means for children's learning, that is, *modeling and observational learning.*

Piaget is the most prominent cognitive developmental theorist. According to Piaget, children *construct their knowledge by exploring their environment.* Similar to Bandura, *active learning* is important, that is, learning that occurs naturally when children are allowed the freedom to *explore* and to *discover.* In addition to Piaget, information-processing theory is a new addition to this category. In this perspective, children are also viewed as active learners where their environment has a direct impact on what and how they learn. It is important to note that information-processing theory includes *practice* as a means for children to learn, for example, memory rehearsing.

More recent theoretical perspectives examine the contexts of development. Bronfenbrenner's bioecological systems theory, Vgotsky's sociocultural theory, and Lorenz and Tinbergen's ethological perspective focus on the environments in which children grow and develop. Bronfenbrenner's bioecological model examines the influence of a variety of environments or *contexts* in which children are present (for example, home and school); environments that affect children's development but they are not present (such as the parents' workplace); and the interactions of those environments. It is noted in this perspective that other contexts have a tremendous effect on children's development but are more intangible, such as societal values, beliefs, culture, and the effects of major historical periods.

Similar to Bronfenbrenner's perspective, Vgotsky, Lorenz, and Tinbergen also believed that culture and development are connected. Vgotsky believed children acquire knowledge from *their interactions with others,* specifically other people who have had more experience or have more knowledge, such as older siblings, parents, and teachers. Children's development is affected by their interaction with these important people in their lives. The ethological perspective also supports the importance of children's environments, including their social, cultural, and physical environments. This evolutionary perspective has introduced the idea of the *sensitive period* of development in children, that is, an important period of time in a child's life when they are more receptive to learning specific skills or concepts.

In reviewing the more established theories and the newer perspectives, it is important to also include the humanistic perspective best represented by Rogers. From it comes the concept of the *uniqueness of the individual* and the importance of *meeting individuals' basic needs* before other development can occur. As a student of human development and specifically child development, the reader may find it helpful to have an eclectic approach to child development. Detailed reviews of these theories can be found in Thomas (1996) or in other scholarly works (Berk, 1997; Papalia, Olds, & Feldman, 1998).

Basic Principles of Child Development.
Using the various theories of child development and decades of research, current scholars have agreed on

the basic principles of child development. Gestwicki (1995) summarizes them as follows:

- There is a predictable sequence in development.
- Development at one stage lays the base for later development.
- There are optimal periods in development.
- Development results from the interaction of biological factors (maturation) and environmental factors (learning).
- Development proceeds as an interrelated whole, with all aspects (physical, cognitive, emotional, social) influencing the others.
- Each individual develops according to a particular timetable and pace.
- Development proceeds from simple to complex and from general to specific. (pp. 8–9)

Bredekamp and Copple (1997) included and expanded upon these principles in their "principles of child development and learning that inform developmentally appropriate practice" (pp. 9–15). These principles also have a direct correlation to the theoretical concepts of child development. A brief discussion of these expanded principles follows.

The sequence of development has been documented. Although development occurs in a predictable sequence, individual variation occurs across the different developmental domains. For example, a child may be at an eighteen-month developmental level in gross motor skills and be at a twelve-month level in expressive language ability. Children cannot be labeled with a specific chronological age and be expected to perform at a normative level.

Sensitive or optimal periods for learning do occur for young children, and early experiences can positively or negatively affect children's development. For example, a toddler who needs to explore her environment, but cannot because of being in a body cast as a result of hip surgery, will miss the many rich opportunities to discover her world. Therefore, her world will need to be brought to her or structured for her in such a way that she may investigate it.

Social and cultural contexts and experiences are critical in children's development and learning. Children's developmental potential is influenced by heredity (biological factors) interacting with children's environments (both social and physical). As active, observational learners children will learn and formulate their perceptions of the world from their daily lives and using their own knowledge and skills. It is imperative that the teachers in children's lives meet them at their developmental level and abilities and be prepared to expand on those abilities. For example, a six-year-old boy who has a specific speech disability and cannot learn to read phonetically will not find success in a first grade classroom where the teacher will use only a phonetic approach to reading, including a daily read-aloud session in the reading group. For this child to find success, methods matched to his or her current ability with the goal of building on strengths will enable the child to be successful and to progress academically with self-esteem intact.

Children's experiences and learning must be supported by skillful teachers who know when to challenge children to take the "next step." Teachers should know children well enough to provide experiences that will not frustrate them, but that will challenge them. This includes being aware of individual learning styles, special needs or talents, or special circumstances that may impact a

Figure 5–1 Teachers and caregivers must know all of the children in their care well enough to provide experiences that will not frustrate them, but will challenge them.

child's learning. It involves giving young children many chances to discover and practice new skills in the context of play. Play is the medium. Play *is* children's work. Even in the early elementary years play should be considered *the* major method of fostering children's development in all developmental domains. Peck, McCaig, and Sapp (1988) state that "learning cannot be rushed, but it can be stimulated through the provision, extension, and expansion of play and projects children find meaningful, thus motivating" (p. 68).

Children will benefit from being cared for by adults who are sensitive, nurturing, and responsive. Fearful and stressed children cannot develop optimally, whether their fear stems from outside the classroom (for example, violence on the streets or in the home) or inside the classroom (such as a punitive, verbally abusive teacher). Children's basic needs, for instance, proper nutrition, must be met for them to reach their full potential. Children who are fed, who get adequate rest and active play, and who have a healthy self-esteem have a better chance at developing optimally in all developmental domains (see Figure 5-1).

Appropriate

What educational and nurturing practices are appropriate and best for children? What discipline or guidance strategies should we use with children? What type of schedules and routines are best for a two-year-old or an eight-year-old child? The new father questions picking up his crying infant. Will it spoil her? The new mother questions returning to work. The preschool teacher cannot decide if the use of time-out is the best method for the children in her care. The kindergarten teacher wants to do what's best for his group of children. Should he set up learning centers? The grandfather wants to attend all of his granddaughter's soccer games, but is that in the best interest of the child? Should his granddaughter even be playing soccer at age six? How are decisions made about what is right for children—what are the best practices in the classroom, best guidance strategies at home and at school?

Using basic principles of child development, guidelines have been established for what constitutes appropriate practices for children. As professionals, we have decided what is appropriate practice for children in group care settings and in more formal educational settings. As professionals we have adopted an ethical code of conduct to help us define what is appropriate practice with regard to our own professional behavior. Laws have been established to guide our society in what is considered right and wrong when relating to and caring for children. The principles of development guide us. They give teachers, caregivers, and parents a list of guidelines to help us make the best decisions regarding the care and education of young children. These principles help us to determine what is appropriate practice in caring for young children in their natural environments, but are we talking about age appropriateness, individual appropriateness, or developmental appropriateness? How do we discern the three concepts?

As stated by Bredekamp and Copple (1997) age and individual appropriateness must be considered when defining "developmental appropriateness." Age appropriateness includes an understanding of the typical sequence of development in all developmental domains. This sequence is predictable, although there will be individual variance in the rate of acquisition of skills in each domain. This leads us to the second concept of individual appropriateness. Individuals are unique with different strengths and needs.

Both of these concepts must be considered when determining appropriate learning experiences for young children. For example, a seven-year-old child with spina bifida who walks with the assistance of crutches may not have the gross motor skills of most children her age. Is it appropriate to deny her the experience of being included in group games because she needs to "run" with crutches? Is it age appropriate to give her the opportunity to play in these group games? Is it individually appropriate to allow her the chance for this social interaction that is experienced in group games? Another example is a child who has a significant cognitive delay. Although the child is chronologically five years old, he is operating cognitively at the level of a two-year-old. What are the age appropriate experiences and toys for him? How does a teacher determine what is individually appropriate for him? Only through an understanding of typical development and then an understanding of the individual child can developmentally appropriate experiences be planned for that child (see Figure 5-2).

Practice

According to Bredekamp and Copple (1997) we must consider major areas of concern related to our practices with children. It is suggested that the reader refer to Bredekamp and Copple (1997) for a discussion of the specific practices related to each area. Areas of concern for each age group are included, that is, there are areas of concern for infants, toddlers, three through five-year-olds, and six through eight-year-olds. Also refer to Appendix A for NAEYC's Position Statement, "Guidelines for Decisions about Developmentally Appropriate Practice." It may serve the reader to visualize the guidelines as organized by the five areas of concern, using examples of a child in natural settings. The areas of concern for five-year-olds are "creating a caring community of learners, teaching

Figure 5–2
Appropriateness requires
an understanding of
typical developmental
milestones and individual
appropriateness.

Major Categories of Appropriate and Inappropriate Practices for Infants

Playing	Reciprocal relationships with families
Eating	Policies
Sleeping	Staff qualifications and development
Diapering	Staffing patterns
Health and safety	

Note: From Developmentally Appropriate Practice in Early Childhood Programs (rev. ed.) (pp. 72–80), by S. Bredekamp and C. Copple (Eds.), 1997, Washington, DC: NAEYC. Copyright 1997 by the National Association for the Education of Young Children. Adapted with permission.

Major Categories of Appropriate and Inappropriate Practices for Toddlers

Relationships among caregivers and children	Reciprocal relationships with families
Living and learning with toddlers	Policies
Environment	Staff qualifications and development
Health and safety	Staffing patterns

Note: From Developmentally Appropriate Practice in Early Childhood Programs (rev. ed.) (pp. 81–91), by S. Bredekamp and C. Copple (Eds.), 1997, Washington, DC: NAEYC. Copyright 1997 by the National Association for the Education of Young Children. Adapted with permission.

Major Categories of Appropriate and Inappropriate Practices for Three- through Five-Year-Olds

Creating a caring community of learners
Promoting a positive climate for learning
Fostering a cohesive group and meeting
   individual needs
Teaching to enhance development and learning
Environment and schedule
Learning experiences
Language and communication
Teaching strategies

Motivation and guidance
Constructing appropriate curriculum
Integrated curriculum
The continuum of development and learning
Coherent, effective curriculum
Curriculum content and approaches
Assessing children's learning and development
Reciprocal relationships with parents
Program policies

Note: From Developmentally Appropriate Practice in Early Childhood Programs (rev. ed.) (pp. 123–135), by S. Bredekamp and C. Copple (Eds.), 1997, Washington, DC: NAEYC. Copyright 1997 by the National Association for the Education of Young Children. Adapted with permission.

Major Categories of Appropriate and Inappropriate Practices for Six- through Eight-Year-Olds in the Primary Grades

Creating a caring community of learners
Promoting a positive climate for learning
Building a democratic community
Teaching to enhance development and learning
Environment and schedule
Teaching strategies
Motivation and guidance
Constructing appropriate curriculum
Integrated curriculum
The continuum of development and learning

Coherent, effective curriculum
Curriculum content: language literacy;
   mathematics; social studies; science; health
   and safety; art, music, drama, dance;
   physical education; outdoor activity
Assessing children's learning and development
Establishing reciprocal relationships with parents
Policies
Staffing, grouping, and environment
Staff qualifications and development

Note: From Developmentally Appropriate Practice in Early Childhood Programs (rev. ed.) (pp. 161–179), by S. Bredekamp and C. Copple (Eds.), 1997, Washington, DC: NAEYC. Copyright 1997 by the National Association for the Education of Young Children. Adapted with permission.

---

to enhance development and learning, constructing appropriate curriculum, assessing children's learning and development, and establishing reciprocal relationships with families." A brief summary of Josh, a five-year-old in kindergarten, and his teacher Mr. Thomas follows.

Caring Community of Learners.

Josh is a five-year-old boy who is in the middle of his kindergarten year. He attended Head Start the year before. His kindergarten teacher, Mr. Thomas, knew him before the first day of school because of the transition planning that occurred in the community between Head Start and the public elementary schools. Mr. Thomas also made a home visit before the beginning of school. He has continued regular communication with Josh's mother and grandmother with whom Josh lives. Fortunately, the school administration provides a staggered kindergarten admission program that allows the teacher more individual time with each new child.

Mr. Thomas values the uniqueness of each child. This is obvious even to the casual observer. The classroom reflects children's art and other creations. During story time children hear the stories they had dictated to Mr. Thomas the day before. The children enjoy their time with their teacher, as evidenced by the lively discussions on the playground and at the lunch table. Mr. Thomas encourages his children's prosocial behaviors and is honest and informative with them when they ask about Josh's wheelchair. Josh has blossomed with Mr. Thomas' guidance and care. The learning environment is child friendly with work tables, learning centers, quiet and active centers, and opportunities for children to work in small groups and with friends. Sometimes the classroom is humming with children at work, and other times laughing and talking accompany the children's classroom activities. Josh especially enjoys recess when Mr. Thomas plays catch with him, an activity he used to enjoy with his father before he was incarcerated. Josh feels accepted and safe in Mr. Thomas' care.

Teaching to Enhance Development and Learning.

Occasionally Josh comes to school wearing dirty clothes. Mr. Thomas understands how important it is for Josh to feel accepted by the other children. Staying in touch with Josh's family has helped Mr. Thomas to understand some of their needs. At times Josh's mother is overwhelmed with the workload of caring for her family, including caring for her mother, working a variable second and third shift job, and continuing to provide love and support to her husband. There are times when Josh's clothes do not get washed. Mr. Thomas plans for those times with an extra change of clothes and a quick cleanup.

Josh's mom appreciated the concern Mr. Thomas gave the family when Josh's father was undergoing the process of trial and his transition to prison. Josh had reacted negatively to this traumatic period in his family's life, for example, he exhibited withdrawn behavior and lack of motivation or eagerness to participate in any of the activities he had previously enjoyed. Mr. Thomas gradually reached Josh with patience, kindness, and a keen eye for Josh's reactions to the many school activities. It seems that Josh responded very positively during "pet week." Mr. Thomas made a point to allow Josh the responsibility for the classroom's pets—the feeding and care of Wiggles (the snake) and Ben and Jerry (the gerbils). During the animal care routines Mr. Thomas used the situation for them to have private time together where they talked about some of the issues bothering Josh.

Mr. Thomas has been very successful in getting Josh and his peers to work together on an art project. Puppet shows have been a favorite activity for most of the class. Josh has been working with friends to make puppets using a variety of materials and methods. Stick puppets, sock puppets, and cloth puppets have been some of the favorites. Finding books in the library about puppets has been especially productive. Also, Josh and his friends have been paired with second graders to help with this project. The "big guys" have helped in some of the measuring and assembling of the puppets. A field trip to a puppet show at the public library was a special treat for the entire class. It has been especially enlightening for Mr. Thomas to engage in discussions on the different types of puppets, especially after a representative from the local university's drama department brought her personal collection of marionettes. Needless to say Big Bird and Cookie Monster, along with the Count, were part of Puppet Day, a day when families were invited to view the creations and productions of the class and their second grade friends.

Constructing Appropriate Curriculum.
It has been a challenge for Mr. Thomas to plan and provide a developmentally appropriate curriculum for his children given the state-mandated kindergarten curriculum. Also, the past year has seen a noticeable increase in students who do not use English as their primary language in the home. Mr. Thomas spent many summer days preparing for the current year. It was important that the children's goals and objectives were attainable. It was Mr. Thomas' professional philosophy that all children should start at their developmental level and should have success in the classroom. Mr. Thomas rejected the ideas of dittos and worksheets and supported a hands-on approach to learning, a developmentally appropriate practice. There was some concern from the administration, although it was obvious that Mr. Thomas' curriculum plans were more in line with appropriate practices for children, especially given the inclusionary nature of his classroom. Josh and other children in the class had various needs. Morgan had been diagnosed with juvenile diabetes. Ali used a hearing aid. Given that he had children of differing abilities, it made sense to build upon their strengths.

Assessing Children's Learning and Development.
As Mr. Thomas prepared for his year with the children, it was necessary to get a realistic picture of what his children's strengths and needs were. The traditional kindergarten readiness test had to be used, but Mr. Thomas wanted information that would help him plan appropriate experiences for his children. He enlisted the help of the children's families by having them complete a questionnaire about the child and his or her family. Also, during the staggered admission times, Mr. Thomas closely observed his children's interactions with their peers and siblings. Realizing that the environment was new to these children, Mr. Thomas systematically made further observational notes. He chose to keep a portfolio on each child, a very personal record of each child's work, anecdotal notes, and reports of observations. Developmental assessments and/or screenings were also used to gain information about individual children (see Figure 5-3).

Relationships among Caregivers and Children

Establishing Reciprocal Relationships with Families.
Josh's mother liked Mr. Thomas from the first introduction at the Head Start transition planning meeting. At first she had felt a little awkward during the home visit, but she quickly overcame the feeling. It had been obvious to her that Mr. Thomas took his teaching responsibilities seriously. The great expectations for the year that he verbalized for Josh helped her. She cared deeply for her family and appreciated an ally for Josh. She appreciated Mr. Thomas listening to her talk about Josh—her concerns and worries *and* her joys. She had so many plans for Josh. She felt reassured that she and Mr. Thomas would be working together for Josh's benefit.

This partnership grew during the first two months of school. When Mr. Thomas realized that the family was experiencing a major trauma at home, an experience Josh's mother really did not want to talk about much, he offered a

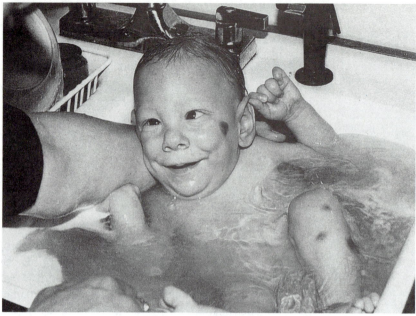

Figure 5–3 There are many useful ways to assess the developmental and educational status of young children, including the valuable information and insight provided by their families.

sympathetic ear. When Josh started showing signs of problems at school, Mr. Thomas immediately consulted with Josh's mother. A home and school team approach helped Josh through the rough spots and made the partnership stronger because of the growing trust. The use of a three-ring communication notebook was especially beneficial in the many communications between Mr. Thomas and Josh's mother and grandmother. It provided a very satisfactory way to keep current information about Josh's progress and challenges in the classroom. It also provided an easy way for Josh's mom to communicate with the school. A quick written note in the morning gave Mr. Thomas information about Josh's experiences at home.

Josh's mother really wanted to volunteer in the classroom but could not because of her work schedule. She appreciated it when Mr. Thomas suggested that she send materials for the puppets. She knew that would be a real contribution to the class. Also, when books about pets were sent home, she or Josh's grandmother eagerly read them to Josh. As difficult as it was to get off from work, Josh's mother managed to negotiate with her supervisor a time replacement plan that enabled her to go to Josh's puppet show.

In summary, Josh is valued for the unique individual that he is. His teacher observes him in the classroom and also views him within the context of his family and home. Many different methods are used to learn about Josh and his classmates—their strengths, needs, talents, and interests. As Mr. Thomas makes plans for Josh and his classmates, he has the expertise to know the range of developmental levels that will be found in his classroom. He is aware of and values the diversity in his classroom—children with special needs and cultural variety. Mr. Thomas implements developmentally appropriate practice in all aspects of his position as kindergarten teacher. See page 135 for a summary of the major categories of appropriate and inappropriate practices to consider for five-year-olds.

Developmentally Appropriate Programs

Bredekamp (1997) states that "developmentally appropriate programs are ones that not only reflect what is known about children's development and learning but also contribute to the overall development of the children who participate" (p. 36). Early childhood professionals note that decisions must be made for the care and education of children in children's programs, whether a day care center, a public school classroom, or activities used for early intervention. The revised position statement of the NAEYC regarding DAP states that professionals must acknowledge three "dynamic and changing" areas of understanding related to making those decisions for children. Those areas include what is known about child development and learning; what is known about the strengths, interests, and needs of the individual children in the group; and knowledge of the social and cultural contexts in which children live (NAEYC, 1997).

A Shared Philosophy Results in Similar Recommended Practices

Professionals in the fields of early childhood education and early childhood special education have agreed upon recommended practices in their respective fields. These practices are considered best practice when providing care and education for young children. Increasingly in the literature one may find resources on curricular approaches to applying developmentally appropriate practice in inclusive early childhood classrooms for the benefit of all children (Miller, 1996). Documents have been published outlining these practices and their rationale. The major documents in early childhood education are Bredekamp and Copple's (1997) *Developmentally Appropriate Practice* and Bredekamp and Rosegrant's (1992) *Reaching Potentials: Appropriate Curriculum and Assessment for Young Children, Volume 1*. The document supporting the best practices for early childhood special education including the conceptual base upon which it is written can be found in the NAEYC publication (1996) *Guidelines for Preparation of Early Childhood Professionals*. In this book the personnel standards for early education and early intervention can be found. Common strands reflecting accepted philosophical beliefs about early childhood education and early childhood special education are found in both sets of recommended practices. These strands include the following:

- The importance of early childhood as a period of development.
- The importance of families in the optimal development of children and the need for partnership with those families.
- A holistic perspective of child development, including all developmental domains (cognitive, physical, language, and social) of children and the use of that perspective in planning learning experiences and the learning environment.
- The need for appropriate and ethical assessments of young children's strengths and needs.

- Recognizing the diversity of children and families and that cultural context is a significant force to consider when working with children and families.
- The need to collaborate and communicate with various professionals representing different disciplines.
- The importance of developmentally appropriate practice.

As stated earlier, Bredekamp emphasized five major areas to consider when planning programs for young children. Those same areas are reflected in DEC/CEC best practices for planning intervention for children with special needs. As a reminder, these areas are "creating a caring community of learners, teaching to enhance development and learning, constructing appropriate curriculum, assessing children's learning and development, and establishing reciprocal relationships with families" (Bredekamp, 1997).

The last strand, the importance of developmentally appropriate practice, can be functionally applied to the practices of positive behavioral supports (PBS) and activity-based intervention (ABI). As plans and activities are developed for children, with consideration of their individual goals and objectives, the principles of these techniques (PBS and ABI) are very useful for children with and without disabilities. These principles reflect the underlying philosophy of the strands and areas previously mentioned.

For example, Shari is a four-year-old little girl with cerebral palsy. Her goals and objectives include a focus on gross and fine motor skills, and speech and language development. She is an outgoing, determined child and a hard worker. In a regular preschool classroom she has made friends and many gains in her specific objectives. Because the teachers implement a developmentally appropriate program, Shari is finding success in this learning environment. The curriculum is child-centered and play-based. It is structured so that children can work in small groups or can work individually. Children are challenged, yet find success on a regular basis. The physical and social environments are structured for every child's success. The teachers collaborate with Shari's occupational, physical, and speech/language therapists to not only develop teacher-directed activities for Shari but also set up the room so that child-initiated activities can occur that will support Shari's objectives. The atmosphere in the classroom is child friendly and not punitive. Shari knows the developmentally appropriate rules of the classroom and is secure in the predictability of the routines and schedules. When inappropriate behavior does occur, whether Shari's or another child's, the consequences are appropriate for the child, predictable, natural, and logical. Parents and other family members plus volunteers from the community are regularly seen and used in the classroom. The family's input on programming decisions for Shari is valued and encouraged. A truly trusting and empowering relationship for both the family and the preschool staff is developed through consistent, honest communication.

Shari's objectives include working on fine motor skills and self-help skills, such as feeding herself. Also, at the art center, her fine motor skills are targeted when she uses the stubby crayons and other materials that are regularly supplied for Shari and the other children. During free play Shari joins in dramatic play at the housekeeping and dress-up center. Props are provided that will encourage her use of language and interaction among her peers. Circle time finds Shari singing with her friends and her teacher. Songs are chosen with children's interests and objectives in mind. Conversations at lunch may, at times, focus on topics that have selected words.

Environment and Experiences

DAP, Developmental Stages, and the Learning Environment

Using the principles of child development we are aware of the different stages of development as defined by chronological age—infants, toddlers, preschoolers/kindergartners, and children of middle childhood. We may continue to use these categories to plan for children, but we cannot ignore the need for observing children individually, especially if we are considering the needs of a child with a developmental delay. The value of DAP is that the concept of individuality is built into the definition and used in practice. Children may develop following a predetermined sequence of domain-specific skills, but there will be variations. The skilled practitioner will expect this.

Activities and lesson plans may be developed for groups of children with adaptations for individual children or for home experiences where siblings can be considered. Integration of developmental domains and integration of children's goals and objectives can be accomplished through play in children's natural environments whether at home, in the day care center, in preschool, or in an elementary school classroom.

Summary

Children are children first! They are children before they are students. They are just *children* before they are considered children with disabilities. They are children before they are the objects of our intervention, strategies, policies, or targets for screening and assessing. As professionals we must remember that. We must remember that children are members of families, diversified families that function at a variety of levels, but families nonetheless. As professionals we have quite a responsibility and the potential for great satisfaction with our work with children and families. Developmentally appropriate practice, with its grounding in basic child development principles and recognition of the importance of families in children's lives, provides us a means to accomplish our shared goals and objectives for children's overall development in natural settings.

Chapter 5 Suggested Activities and Resources

Activities

1. List activities or practices you think would be developmentally appropriate for children of various age groups (infant, toddler, preschooler, kindergarten, first through third grades). As you decide about these activities and practices, make a note of the context (social and cultural) in which these activities and practices will occur. For example, what would be an appropriate practice for a crying infant? Define the contexts both socially and culturally. Compare your lists with your peers. Discuss how the contexts may affect the practices implemented. Are there some practices or activities that are never considered developmentally appropriate, regardless of contexts?

2. In the example using Shari, a four-year-old with cerebral palsy, the following statement is made: "The physical and social environments are structured for every child's success." Specifically, what does that mean for a preschool classroom?

3. How might a program that is developmentally inappropriate affect a child's success at achieving specific goals and objectives? Develop goals and objectives for an imaginary child or for one with whom you have worked. Determine how inappropriate practices would negatively impact the child's success or, at least, not support attainment of goals and objectives.

4. Some educators emphasize that children in first grade must focus on academics—reading, mathematics, and writing—at the expense of implementing practices that are more developmentally appropriate. How would you defend the position that children can, indeed, focus on academics, but can do it in a developmentally appropriate way.

5. Research definitions of "developmentally appropriate practice" in professional journals, textbooks, curriculum guides, and the like. Analyze the definitions with regard to basic child development principles.

6. Review and discuss with your class colleagues the joint position statement of the International Reading Association (IRA) and the National Association for the Education of Young Children (NAEYC) published in May 1998 and entitled *Learning to Read and Write: Developmentally Appropriate Practices for Young Children*. Consider how this position statement relates to the needs of young children with disabilities and the goal of inclusion in early childhood education and child care settings.

Selected Resources

1. *Books*

Bredekamp, S., & Copple, C. (Eds.). (1997). *Developmentally Appropriate Practice in Early Childhood Programs* (rev. ed.). Washington, DC: NAEYC.

Bredekamp, S., & Rosegrant, T. (1995). *Reaching Potentials: Transforming Early Childhood Curriculum and Assessment—Volume 2*. Washington, DC: NAEYC.

Bredekamp, S., & Rosegrant, T. (1992). *Reaching Potentials: Appropriate Curriculum and Assessment for Young Children—Volume 1*. Washington, DC: NAEYC.

Bronson, M. B. (1995). *The Right Stuff for Children Birth to 8: Selecting Play Materials to Support Development*. Washington, DC: NAEYC.

Goffin, S. G., Stegelin, D. A. (Eds.). (1992). *Changing Kindergartens: Four Success Stories*. Washington, DC: NAEYC.

Schickendanz, J. (1998). *Much More Than the ABCs: The Early Stages of Reading and Writing*. Washington, DC: NAEYC.

2. *Journal articles*

Burchfield, D. W. (1996). Teaching All Children: Four Developmentally Appropriate Curricular and Instructional Strategies in Primary-Grade Classrooms. *Young Children, 52,* 4–10.

Dunn, L., & Kontos, S. (1997). Research in Review. What Have We Learned about Developmentally Appropriate Practice? *Young Children, 52,* 4–13.

Kostelnik, M. J. (1992). Myths Associated with Developmentally Appropriate Programs. *Young Children, 47,* 17–23.

Kuball, Y. E. (1995). Goodbye Dittos: A Journey from Skill-Based Teaching to Developmentally Appropriate Language Education in a Bilingual Kindergarten. *Young Children, 50,* 6–14.

Pelander, J. (1997). My Transition from Conventional to More Developmentally Appropriate Practices in the Primary Grades. *Young Children, 52,* 19–25.

Vander Wilt, J. L., & Monroe, V. (1998). Successfully Moving toward Developmentally Appropriate Practice: It Takes Time and Effort. *Young Children, 53,* 17–24.

3. *Videos*

NAEYC. (1991). *Teaching the Whole Child in the Kindergarten* (video). Washingon, DC: NAEYC.

NAEYC. (1993). *Developmentally Appropriate First Grade: A Community of Learners* (video). Washington, DC: NAEYC.

NAEYC. (1994). *Designing Developmentally Appropriate Days* (video). Washington, DC: NAEYC.

NAEYC. (1998). *Tools for Teaching Developmentally Appropriate Practice: The Leading Edge in Early Childhood Education* (video series). Washington, DC: NAEYC.

4. *Booklet*

NAEYC and IRA. (1999). *Learning to Read and Write: Developmentally Appropriate Practices for Young Children.* A joint position statement of the International Reading Association (IRA) and the National Association for the Education of Young Children (NAEYC). Washington, DC: NAEYC.

5. *Brochures*

NAEYC. 1998. *A Caring Place for Your Infant.* Washington, DC: NAEYC.

NAEYC. 1997. *A Caring Place for Your Toddler.* Washington, DC: NAEYC.

NAEYC. 1997. *A Good Kindergarten for Your Child.* Washington, DC: NAEYC.

NAEYC. 1997. *A Good Preschool for Your Child.* Washington, DC: NAEYC.

NAEYC. 1997. *A Good Primary School for Your Child.* Washington, DC: NAEYC.

NAEYC. 1998. *Code of Ethical Conduct and Statement of Commitment-Revised 1997.* Washington, DC: NAEYC.

6. *Websites*

www.naeyc.org National Association for the Education of Young Children

http://www.udel.edu/bateman/acei/ Association for Childhood Education International

http://www.childrensdefense.org/ Children's Defense Fund

http://www.ed.gov/offices/OERI/ECI/ National Institute on Early Childhood Development and Education

References

Berk, L. (1997). *Child Development* (4th ed.). Boston: Allyn and Bacon.

Bredekamp, S. (1997). NAEYC Issues Revised Position Statement on Developmentally Appropriate Practice in Early Childhood Programs. *Young Children, 52,* 34–40.

Bredekamp, S., & Copple, C. (Eds.). (1997). *Developmentally Appropriate Practice in Early Childhood Programs Serving Children from Birth through Age 8* (rev. ed.). Washington, DC: National Association for the Education of Young Children.

Bredekamp, S., & Rosegrant, T. (Eds.). (1992). *Reaching Potentials: Appropriate Curriculum and Assessment for Young Children,* Volume 1. Washington, DC: NAEYC.

Bronfenbrenner, U. (1979). *The Ecology of Human Development: Experiments by Nature and Design.* Cambridge, MA: Harvard University Press.

Gestwicki, C. (1995). *Developmentally Appropriate Practice: Curriculum and Development in Early Education.* Albany, NY: Delmar.

Miller, R. (1996). *The Developmentally Appropriate Inclusive Classroom in Early Education.* Albany, NY: Delmar.

National Association for the Education of Young Children. (1996). *Guidelines for Preparation of Early Childhood Professionals.* Washington, DC: Author.

National Association for the Education of Young Children. (1997). NAEYC Position Statement. Developmentally Appropriate Practice in Early Childhood Programs Serving Children from Birth through Age 8. In S. Bredekamp & C. Copple (Eds.), *Developmentally Appropriate Practice in Early Childhood Programs* (rev. ed.), (pp. 3–30). Washington, DC: Author.

Noah, T. (1997, June 9). Joe Camel Is FTC Quarry—Again. *U.S. News & World Report, 122, 58.*

Papalia, D. E., Olds, S. W., & Feldman, R. D. (1998). *Human Development* (7th ed.). Boston: McGraw-Hill.

Peck, J. T., McCaig, G., & Sapp, M. E. (1988). *Kindergarten Policies: What Is Best for Children?* Washington, DC: National Association for the Education of Young Children.

Potter, W. J. (1996). Considering Policies to Protect Children from TV Violence. *Journal of Communication, 46,* 116–123.

Sarracino, C. (1995, November 27). Where Have All the Children Gone? *Insight on the News, 11,* 22.

Shepard, L., Kagan, S. L., & Wurtz, E. (Eds.). (1998, February). *Principles and Recommendations for Early Childhood Assessments.* Goal 1 Early Childhood Assessments Resource Group Report. Washington, DC: National Education Goals Panel.

Thomas, R. M. (1996). *Comparing Theories of Child Development.* Pacific Grove, CA: Brooks/Cole.

Section II
Procedures

OVERVIEW

Section II: provides an overview of procedures. The topics of assessment, effective teaching, and intervention are addressed in Chapters 6 and 7, respectively. Every attempt has been made within these chapters to demonstrate a link between the assessment process and planning and delivering instruction and intervention. This link has also been illustrated throughout the text, most especially in Section IV: Applications. It is critical that professionals in the disciplines of early childhood education, early childhood special education, and child and family studies understand this important linkage and learn to apply it in their work. The assessment process should provide us with an understanding of the child and family in a functionally relevant context. As a set of procedures, it is designed to seek answers to relevant questions about the child and family. The information gathered from this process should then lead us to develop effective interventions aimed at the provision of relevant services and supports that are child- and family-centered.

Readers will note that in Chapter 6, the topic of assessment is addressed from a developmental progression. The initial section of the chapter addresses how infants and toddlers with disabilities have been and continue to be identified and diagnosed and the response of their parents and families upon learning such news. The chapter next introduces the role of traditional clinic-based assessment and explores both the benefits and limitations of such a model.

One aspect of traditional assessment that is addressed in this section is the emotional and psychological impact that such a process can have on the child and parents. Oftentimes, evaluation clinics can be so sterile and impersonal that the children and families who are consumers of these professional services are minimized. In addition, the assessment tools and procedures used do not provide the contextual clarity that is most relevant to the child and family in their typical environments. This is not to say that this approach is completely negative. There are many positive aspects of such professional services for children and families affected by disability. In the case of children born with multiple disabilities who

145

also experience health impairments, the presence of a well-trained team consisting of medical personnel, educators, and related professionals sensitive to the needs of children and families can be viewed as not only a comfort but vital to sustaining the quality of life for a child and family.

Transdisciplinary play-based approaches and functional assessment as they relate to identifying functional and behavioral concerns of assessment are next introduced. Two very important areas are also examined. These include the role of parents and families in the assessment process and utilizing assessment information to construct meaningful educational programs for young children and families. Too often, parents are not given an active role in the assessment process. Oftentimes, with traditional forms of assessment, they are placed in observation rooms where they observe a professional, who has barely been introduced to their child, as he or she attempts a variety of tasks, many of which are often nonfunctional. As the process unfolds, the child is then introduced to a series of other professionals, who delve into their "specialized" bag of tricks in search of "an answer." This may occur five or six times over the course of a day. At the close of an exhausting day for both the child and his/her parents, the team of professionals will share their findings, which typically are accompanied by a label that describes their child. Afterward, the parents—who are somewhat dismayed, fearful, and exhausted from the expenditure of emotional and physical energy—are faced with terms they do not understand, procedures they were not necessarily preinformed about, and a label that now defines their child. They must now wait a period of two to four weeks for the written results that will contain a summary of conclusions and recommendations typically without follow-up with regard to implementation of these recommendations. The parents must now hope that their local team of educational professionals can take this body of information and help them digest it and develop a program that will enhance the life of their child and family.

A contrast to this approach are transdisciplinary play-based and functional assessment that maximize the input of parents and families and attempts to involve them as partners in the process. Parents know their children much better than any professional, and therefore their input and active role is not only encouraged but essential to the process.

Finally, pertaining to the issue of assessment, the chapter demonstrates how transdisciplinary play-based assessment and functional assessment have greater utility in the development of meaningful interventions because they are conducted within the context of the natural environments that constitute the child's life. These environments may include home, infant/toddler program, early childhood special education classroom, preschool, kindergarten, and early elementary settings. The information obtained through the process of assessment should serve to develop meaningful services for children and families. Interpretation of this information and practical applications serve as a measure of success where the process of assessment is concerned.

Chapter 7, Effective Teaching and Intervention Practices, begins by stating the importance of selecting socially valid intervention goals. Here again is another major instance where the input of parents and families is not only helpful but in many ways the yardstick by which the acceptability of our intervention plan is measured. Early childhood education and interventions should seek to develop meaningful skills and abilities in children and families by expanding on the strengths and understanding the concerns of each instead of highlighting their limitations and "deficits." Individualized family service plans (IFSPs) and individualized educational programs (IEPs) should focus on the development of skills that are relevant in current and future environments, inclusive of transition and life span needs, and that promote enhanced quality of life outcomes for children and families.

Methods are provided in the areas of positive behavioral supports, activity-based intervention, and developmentally appropriate practices relevant to intervention. These do go into some depth and in some ways are a departure in terms of presentation from traditional texts in the area of early childhood education. Many are written in reference to their use with young children with disabilities and their families, but this does not preclude them from being applied to typical children as well. Emphasis is placed on the rationale and development of these procedures and their application across a variety of children, differing in age and development, and across a continuum of settings with the convergence of PBS, ABI, and DAP within inclusive settings in mind.

Chapter

6

Assessment

INTRODUCTION

This chapter will discuss the assessment of young children with developmental delays and/or disabilities in the context of the inclusion process. Here are the objectives the reader will address in Chapter 6. You should be able to:

- Describe how disabilities are identified in infants and toddlers and the response of parents and families in first learning of their child's disability.
- Describe the importance of the assessment process for determining the strengths and support needs of an individual child.
- Compare and contrast the role of traditional, clinic-based assessment for young children with developmental delays, including the strengths and limitations of such a model, to other assessment approaches.
- Understand team-based assessment approaches including multidisciplinary, transdisciplinary, interdisciplinary, and functional assessment models.
- Understand and describe functional assessment.
- Provide a rationale for parental partnership throughout the assessment process.
- Utilize assessment information to construct meaningful child-centered programming within inclusive early childhood educational settings.

The Diagnosis of a Developmental Disability

Parents of young children are often first informed by medical personnel such as their pediatrician or developmental pediatrician that their child has a developmental delay or disability.

> *Developmental Delay:* A developmental delay refers to a measured delay or "lag" in development in one or more of the following areas: cognitive, physical, communication, social/emotional, or adaptive behavior. A developmental delay does not necessarily indicate a permanent condition.

The identification of a developmental delay or disability may occur before birth (prenatally), at birth (perinatally), or shortly after the birth of a newborn (postnatally). For children born with multiple or severe disabilities, their disability is typically diagnosed early in life.

Examples of Severe Disabilities Affecting Infants and Toddlers

Cerebral Palsy: Cerebral palsy is a condition caused by damage to the central nervous system either prenatally (before birth), perinatally (during birth), or postnatally (after birth). Cerebral palsy is not a disease and is not curable; although with appropriate education and therapy persons with cerebral palsy can lead very productive and meaningful lives. Causes of cerebral palsy include lack of oxygen, trauma, illness to the mother during pregnancy, poisoning, and other factors. Unified Cerebral Palsy, (1999), NICHCY (1993)

Down Syndrome: Down's syndrome represents a chromosomal condition that results in mental retardation. It is caused by an extra chromosome (forty-seven) instead of the typical forty-six. The incidence rate is approximately 1 in every 1,000 births resulting in approximately 4,000 children born with Down's syndrome each year in the United States. The condition is characterized by low muscle tone; slanted eyes with epicanthal folds (folds of skin at the inner eyes); short broad hands; broad feet; flattened bridge on the nose; short neck; small head; small oral cavity; short, low-set ears; and high-pitched, shortened cries during infancy. Often children born with Down's syndrome suffer from respiratory problems, gastrointestinal disorders, and heart defects. Many of these medical problems can now be surgically corrected resulting in a lengthier and more enjoyable life. Children born with Down's syndrome now have greater possibilities for the future due to early intervention and improved educational and medical interventions. Many children with Down's syndrome, if provided with appropriate services and supports during the early stages of development, can achieve levels of educational success leading to meaningful employment as adults and independent living. (National Information Center for Children and Youth with Disabilities [NICHCY, 1993])

Fetal Alcohol Syndrome (FAS): Fetal alcohol syndrome (FAS), the leading cause of mental retardation and the second most common birth defect, is a condition resulting in physical and behavioral disabilities because of a child's exposure to heavy amounts of alcohol in utero. Children born with FAS often exhibit failure to thrive; distinct facial and physical abnormalities including microcephalus, eye abnormalities, fattened nasal bridge, and indistinct philtrum (area between nose and lip); and central nervous system dysfunction resulting in mental retardation, developmental delays, diminished sucking reflex, hyperactivity, impulsivity, and specific learning disabilities. (South Dakota University Affiliated Program, School of Medicine, University of South Dakota, 1994)

continued on page 150

Multiple Disabilities: This term refers to children born with simultaneous impairments (mental retardation, ortho/motor disabilities, sensory impairments, medical health concerns) often caused by syndromes or unknown causes. The combined effect of these disabilities necessitates medical, educational, and habilitative services and supports immediately following detection.

Other Health Impairments: This category refers to children having limited strength, vitality, or alertness due to chronic or acute health problems—such as heart conditions, tuberculosis, rheumatic fever, nephritis, asthma, sickle cell anemia, hemophilia, epilepsy, lead poisoning, leukemia, or diabetes — that adversely affect a child's educational performance. (National Information Center for Children and Youth with Disabilities, [NICHCY], 1993)

Spina Bifida: Spina bifida is a condition that occurs during the developmental process and refers to a cleft spine or failure for the spinal column to appropriately fuse leaving an opening in the vertebrae (spina bifida occulta), or a condition where the meninges or protective covering around the spinal cord has pushed through an opening in the vertebrae (meningocele), or the most severe form of this condition in which the spinal cord protrudes through the back (myelomeningocele). Many children born with myelomeningocele also have a co-occurrence of hydrocephalus (an accumulation of cerebral spinal fluid in the brain) necessitating insertion of a shunt to relieve the fluid buildup. Medical advances now permit many children born with these conditions to live as a result of pediatric surgical techniques allowing medical teams to conduct surgery within the first forty-eight hours of life. Many children with spina bifida will be challenged by bladder and bowel control, and many may need catheterization (insertion of a tube in the bladder) to manage bladder functions. (National Information Center for Children and Youth with Disabilities, [NICHCY], 1993)

Many children may also be identified as having a disability later in their development such as during their preschool years or while in early elementary school. Parents and families, as you learned in Chapter 2, frequently experience a range of emotions upon first being told that their child has been affected by a disability or a medical/health condition that impacts the development and well-being of their child. These emotions can range from anger, denial, depression, and eventual acceptance (Turnbull & Turnbull, 1997). However, remember that each family and person within a family is unique, thus influencing the intensity and time needed to progress through the cycle of emotions. The level of emotional support that can be provided by family, friends, and professionals is critical during this period in assisting parents and their child. However, emotional strength and support are attributes that parents of all children, including parents of children with disabilities, will need throughout life as they meet with each challenge. As Akesson and Granlund (1995) state: "Parents are the most important people in the lives of their children, giving love, care, and continuity" (p. 520). With this in mind, we must encourage and support parental involvement at all service and support levels. Most often, parents and family will remain constant in the lives of their children, unlike the countless numbers of professionals who will be ever changing throughout a single child's life span. The supports and skills we offer to dedicated parents and families will hopefully serve them well as they move through the myriad of medical, educational, and related service programs seeking what most families want for their children, including safety, health, happiness, success, and independence.

As previously stated, the challenges faced by parents and children with disabilities at the earliest stages of a child's life are often pervasive throughout their life span. This point is well illustrated by Michael Bērubē, a writer and professor of English at the University of Illinois at Urbana-Champaign and also the father of a child with Down syndrome. He writes in his book, entitled *Life As We Know It: A Father, a Family, and an Exceptional Child* (1996):

> when I am wounded by matters of the heart, my grief tends to take root in rage and stay there; when I am saddened that all is not and will not be well with Jamie, my grief bypasses anger at agentless entities like chromosomes and quickly defaults into fear for his future (p. 134).

The feelings that Bērubē (1996) has described about his own young child diagnosed with Down syndrome mirror the reality that is shared by many parents and families of children with disabilities (see Figure 6–1). The fear and uncertainty described are present for most parents and families at each stage of their child's development from infancy into adulthood. These fears may be made worse as parents attempt to access quality services and supports across the life span for their child—supports that are often not present or so poorly funded and staffed that quality assurance is not a reality. This cycle often begins in the early (preschool) years before a child enters formal schooling.

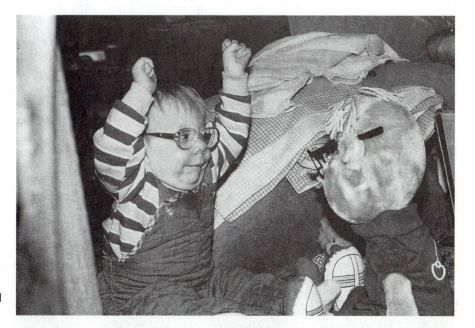

Figure 6–1 Parents are confronted with a wide array of emotions after the birth of a child with special needs,

Upon first learning that their young child has a developmental delay or disability, parents and families must then prepare for the assessment process in which their child's strengths and support and education/intervention needs will be determined. The prospects of such a task can serve to generate more anxiety and concern on the part of parents and family and cause significant emotional duress. Yet the assessment process is crucial to the development of meaningful supports and services for a child. The emotional investment of the parents, child, and family throughout this process cannot be overstated, thus necessitating that professionals be both empathetic and sensitive when participating in the assessment process. In an effort to identify the abilities needed by early childhood professionals, the National Association for the Education of Young Children (1996) collaborated with the Division of Early Childhood of the Council for Exceptional Children. In that work is a statement of the attributes desired in an early childhood special educator specific to assessment and evaluation.

Assessment Competencies

Programs prepare early childhood special educators to:

A. Assess children's cognitive, social/emotional, communication, motor, adaptive, and aesthetic development by the following means.
1. Select and use a variety of informal and formal assessment instruments and procedures, including observational methods, to make decisions about children's learning and development.
2. Select and administer assessment instruments and procedures based on the purpose of the assessment being conducted and in compliance with established criteria and standards.
3. Develop and use authentic, performance-based assessments of children's learning to assist in planning, to communicate with children and parents, and to engage children in self-assessment.
4. Involve families as active participants in the assessment process.
5. Participate and collaborate as a team member with other professionals in conducting family-centered assessments.
6. Communicate assessment results from others as an active team participant in the development and implementation of the IEP and IFSP.
7. Monitor, summarize, and evaluate the acquisition of child and family outcomes as outlined on the IFSP or IEP.
8. Select, adapt, and administer assessment instruments and procedures for specific sensory and motor disabilities.
9. Communicate options for programs and services at the next level and assist the family in planning for transition.
10. Implement culturally unbiased assessment instruments and procedures.

B. Develop and use formative and summative program evaluation to ensure comprehensive quality of the total environment for children, families, and the community.

From Guidelines for Preparation of Early Childhood Professionals, 1996.

Importance of the Assessment Process

The assessment process is essential for the development of child- and family-centered supports and is also mandated under the IDEA (Individuals with Disabilities Education Act). Under Part H of the 1986 amendments to IDEA and what is now Part C of the 1997 reauthorization, infants and young children from birth through two years of age are eligible for early intervention services if they meet eligibility requirements. To be eligible, children must have a measured developmental delay, as defined by each state, in one or more of the following five areas: cognitive development, physical development, communication development, social/emotional development, and/or adaptive behavior; or the child must have a diagnosed condition that will likely result in a developmental delay; or the child is at risk for a developmental delay if services are not provided (IDEA, Section 632 [1]). Children who are between the ages of three and five years or school-aged are eligible to receive services under Part B if they experience a disability that may include mental retardation, hearing impairments including deafness, speech or language impairments, visual impairments including blindness, serious emotional disturbance, orthopedic impairments, autism, traumatic brain injury, other health impairments, or specific learning disabilities; are in need of special education and related services, and at the State's discretion include children experiencing developmental delays, as defined by the State and measured by appropriate diagnostic instruments and procedures, in one or more of the following areas: physical development, cognitive development, communication development, social or emotional development, or adaptive development, and who by reason thereof, need special education and related services (IDEA, Section 611).

Both Part C and Part B of IDEA maintain regulations that pertain to the evaluation and assessment of children birth through age two years, and children ages three to five years, respectively.

Definitions of Evaluation and Assessment under Part H

Evaluation refers to the use of testing (typically standardized) to determine eligibility for services.

Assessment refers to the process of information used to ascertain a child's current levels of functioning in the areas of cognitive development, motor development, psychosocial development, communication development, and adaptive development.

Typical evaluation tools would be standardized tests that provide a standard score and percentile ranks as well as an age equivalent to help determine a percentage of delay and therefore determine eligibility. Some states require a 40 percent delay in one area or a 25 percent delay in two areas of development before eligibility criteria are met and services and supports can be provided.

Under the law, Part C mandates for each infant and toddler with a disability and their family the development of an individualized family service plan. This includes:

A. Assessment and program development
  1. A multidisciplinary assessment of the unique strengths and needs of the infant and toddler and the identification of services appropriate to meet such needs.
  2. A family-directed assessment of the resources, priorities, and concerns of the family and the identification of the supports and services necessary to enhance the family's capacity to meet the developmental needs of their infant or toddler with a disability.
  3. A written individualized family service plan developed by a multidisciplinary team, including the parent or guardian, as required by subsection (D) of this section.
B. Periodic review
  After eligibility is determined assessment must take place to assist in development of goals and curriculum. The individualized family service plan shall be evaluated once a year and the family shall be provided with a review of the plan at six-month intervals (or more often when appropriate based on infant or toddler or family needs).
C. Promptness after assessment
  The individualized family service plan shall be developed within a reasonable time after the assessment. With the parent's consent, early intervention services may commence prior to the completion of such assessment.
D. Content of plan
  The IFSP shall be in writing and contain the following:
  1. A statement of the infant's or toddler's present levels of physical development, cognitive development, communication development, social or emotional development, and adaptive development, based on acceptable objective criteria.
  2. A statement of the family's resources, priorities, and concerns relating to enhancing the development of the family's infant or toddler with a disability.
  3. A statement of the major outcomes expected to be achieved for the infant or toddler and the family, and the criteria, procedures, and time lines used to determine the degree to which progress toward achieving the outcomes is being made and whether modifications or revisions of the outcomes or services are necessary.
  4. A statement of specific early intervention services necessary to meet the unique needs of the infant or toddler and the family, including the frequency, intensity, and the method of delivering the services.
  5. A statement of the natural environment in which early intervention services shall appropriately be provided.
  6. The projected dates for initiation of services and the anticipated duration of such services.

7. The identification of the service coordinator from the profession most immediately relevant to the infant's or toddler's or family needs (or who is otherwise qualified to carry out all applicable responsibilities under this subchapter) who will be responsible for the implementation of the plan and coordination with other agencies and persons.

8. The steps to be taken supporting the transition of the toddler with a disability to preschool or other appropriate services.

E. Parental consent

The contents of the individualized family service plan shall be fully explained to the parents or guardian and informed written consent from such parents or guardian shall be obtained prior to the provision of early intervention services described in such plan. If such parents or guardian do not provide such consent with respect to a particular early intervention service, then early intervention services to which such consent is obtained shall be provided (IDEA, Sec. 636).

The educational rights of children who are school-aged or ages three to five years with disabilities are protected by IDEA under Part B. Children who are eligible under this part of the law are afforded a free and appropriate public education, the right to nondiscriminatory assessment by a multidisciplinary team including parents as part of the team, confidentiality, and the right to due process. These rights and freedoms are the same rights and freedoms as afforded all school-aged children with disabilities.

In summary, we have described how evaluation and assessment are mandated under the IDEA. The distinction between these two terms is that evaluation is for the expressed purpose of determining eligibility, and assessment is used for the development of educational and related services given the child's strengths and areas of need. The following sections will examine the methods of assessment most typically used with young children who experience disabilities, including some of the strengths and limitations of each approach in terms of their ability to contribute to meaningful child-centered services and supports as well as their usefulness related to facilitating the inclusion process.

Models of Assessment

Traditional Assessment

The traditional assessment model has typically utilized a team of professionals within a clinical setting most often affiliated with a medical school, hospital, university, or public school district. The clinical assessment process usually involves the child and parents being referred to a clinic or evaluation center by a physician or school district. Upon receiving a referral, the parents will be asked by the evaluation team to complete a packet of prereferral forms that ask relevant information about their child, their child's family history, developmental history, and presenting concerns. Valuable information can be derived from the child's developmental history, including information about the mother's pregnancy, presence or absence of complications during pregnancy or birth, the child's delivery and early months following birth, including relevant medical and health information.

After completing the prereferral information the family is then scheduled for an evaluation to be conducted by a team of professionals, which may often include psychologists, early childhood special educators, speech/language pathologists, occupational therapists, physical therapists, nurse (practitioners), nutritionists, audiologists, physicians, and social workers. Each of these professionals contributes their own unique set of specialized skills to the assessment process. More specifically, the contributions offered by these professionals in the assessment of young children includes the following:

Developmental Psychologist: The psychologist is most often the professional who will conduct the assessment of the child's cognitive and adaptive behavior skills. They will also provide consultation in the development of programming resulting from assessment data and offer parent and family training and counseling services, if needed.

Early Childhood Special Educator: The early childhood special educator will typically provide support in the administration of criterion-referenced assessment tools and some standardized assessment instruments aimed at identifying the child's developmental levels. The early childhood special educator also plays a key role in the development of child-centered programming and will likely be the individual who oversees the implementation and coordination of educational and related services programming in the educational and home settings.

Early Childhood Educator: The early childhood educator's role on the team is to ensure developmentally appropriate practices, to facilitate inclusion as part of the child's team, and to provide direct instruction and support to the child and their family. The early childhood educator is also skilled in the area of authentic assessment.

Speech/Language Pathologist (SLP): The speech/language pathologist is responsible for the assessment of both receptive and expressive communication skills. The SLP will also provide suggestions in the design of communication programs for children who are delayed, disordered in development, or nonverbal, and who are in need of augmentative communication devices to assist them in communicating with others. Oral motor issues that may interfere with feeding may also be addressed.

Occupational Therapist: The occupational therapist's role is to offer expertise in enabling the child to maximize existing sensory/motor functions and to assist with optimizing levels of independent performance or greater approximations at independence. They will also utilize adaptive equipment and prosthetics if necessary to assist in these aims. The occupational therapist may team with the speech/language therapist, nutritionist, and physical therapist in the assessment of a child's feeding skills. These professionals will also make recommendations for programming in the areas of feeding and swallowing if this is an area of need.

Physical Therapist: The physical therapist assesses the child's motor skills and other special concerns relating to the child's positioning and handling if the child experiences orthopedic and/or motor dysfunction. The therapist can also assess motor function as it relates to central nervous system development (e.g., presence or absence of reflexes).

Nurse (Practitioner): A nurse (practitioner) may also serve on the child's evaluation team if the child experiences special health concerns such as medication use, tube feeding, and catheterization and other relevant medical, physical, and health concerns (Orelove & Sobsey, 1996).

Audiologist: The audiologist is charged with the assessment of audiological function and hearing loss. The audiologist will provide recommendations concerning the use of amplification or assistive hearing devices for children with hearing losses.

Physician: There may be a variety of general physicians and specialists who participate in the assessment process depending upon the child's presenting medical/health needs. Most commonly, the child's pediatrician will provide access to other medical specialists through referral. A developmental pediatrician may also be involved. The developmental pediatrician is a specialist trained in the medical/health concerns of young children with atypical development. A pediatric neurologist is another medical specialist who may provide assessment and consultation if neurological concerns are present such as in the case of seizure disorders, cerebral palsy, and autism, just to name a few examples. A pediatric geneticist can assist families with the identification of genetic disorders and reoccurrence rates for the family in future children.

Many children and their families may experience limited access to highly trained early child specialists if they reside in rural or underserved areas. Regional child clinics such as those we have described may provide such services; however, within rural areas families must sometimes travel great distances to access such a clinic.

A Typical Evaluation

Upon arriving at the clinic, the parents and their child are typically welcomed by the clinic team and staff before commencing with the assessment process. The welcoming time is deemed essential to the process and is aimed at reducing anxiety on the part of the child and his/her parents and is also for establishing a rapport from which all future interactions will stem. As described by Linder (1990) the fear and anxiety provoked by such a process can be overwhelming for both the child and parents.

The welcoming usually consists of brief introductions by the team of professionals, interaction with the child and his/her family, and an explanation of the schedule of activities for the entire day. After the initial greetings and introductions are completed, the child will then be evaluated by individual professionals with time built in for breaks and lunch. It is common for a comprehensive assessment to include a broad array of evaluations individually or team administered in each of the following areas: cognitive, educational, physical, social/emotional, and speech/

language (Culbertson & Willis, 1993). As Culbertson and Willis (1993) have indicated, the comprehensive evaluation or clinical assessment process has many steps. These include gathering relevant information about a child's strengths and areas of need and developing informed hypotheses. The clinic team attempts to test the hypotheses through the gathering of data, observing the child in various situations, and interacting with the child's parents and family. The assessment data is evaluated by each team member, conclusions are drawn, and a preliminary report of the findings is prepared and shared with the child's parents at the parent interpretive at the close of the day. The parent interpretive is designed to share the findings of the evaluation process with the child's parents, including findings related to the child's strengths and areas of need and recommendations for educational programming.

The entire evaluation process is usually completed immediately following lunch, with members from the child's team and parents meeting for the parent interpretive where test results, diagnosis, and recommendations are then provided. The process is not over at this point for either the parents or the child. In rural areas, it is common for families to drive for several hours to procure the services of such a clinic, and thus the trip home following the assessment process can be even more devastating, leaving the parents and child drained of all physical and emotional energy reserves.

Following the clinical assessment, parents must absorb the new information learned from the process concerning their child and come to terms with the assessment outcomes. The postevaluation period for both parents and other family members such as siblings often involves learning the complexities of professional jargon and labels that have been attached to their child or unique acronyms associated with various services and supports that they will now be linked with. They must also attempt to internalize the recommendations made by professionals into their family system.

In the following vignette Dr. Carol Russell, Assistant Professor of Child and Family Studies at Emporia State University and the mother of a child with comprehensive special needs, offers a better understanding of how families and professionals engage in the assessment and program planning process within the context of an IEP conference.

VIGNETTE 6-1: CASE ILLUSTRATION: THE PARENT/PROFESSIONAL CONFERENCE

A pair of striking dark brown eyes with long lashes met mine. My eyes were drawn to a contagious bright smile and a halo of curls surrounding a sweet face. After a quick, "Hi," and without a chance for my reply, all I could see was a whirl of purple, a brown curly ponytail, and a small wheelchair whizzing down the hallway.

This was my first encounter with Angie, a seven-year-old girl with spina bifida. It was my second year of teaching. Angie and her family had just moved to our district, and Angie was to be in my first grade class. I had received a "pile" of information to read, and I was on my way to her IEP meeting when I "sort of" met her. I was a bit nervous. I had classes on inclusion in college. Last year, my first year of teaching, I had a child who received speech therapy and another with diabetes. But Angie's situation was a bit more complicated. I learned that spina bifida results from the failure of the spine to close during the first month of pregnancy. For Angie this also resulted in paralysis from the waist down; bowel and bladder incontinence, requiring catheterization at school; shunted hydrocephalus, with shunt malfunctions possible; and possible seizures. The information I received also stated that Angie was diagnosed with ADHD, an anxiety disorder, and a visual-perceptual learning disability.

I knew there was to be a large group at this meeting, but it wasn't until I walked into the room that I realized just how many professionals were involved in this little girl's life. There was the special education director, the OT, PT, PT assistant, PE teacher, adaptive PE teacher, the principal, the school psychologist, the school counselor, a family counselor, the special education teacher, three special education paraprofessionals, one student teacher, the music teacher, the art teacher, an inclusion specialist, the school nurse, a respite care provider, Angie, her two older sisters and parents. I was overwhelmed. I can't imagine how Angie and her family must have felt.

We proceeded with the introductions. Then Angie and her two sisters, Cindy and Mandy, chose to go to the computer corner of the classroom to play some computer games. The special education director who was facilitating the meeting turned to Angie's parents, Lynn and Spencer. "Please tell us about your family."

Lynn began with a family history that made me want to cry and applaud for this family at the same time. "The first week of Angie's life she had three surgeries, one to close the lesion (opening) on her spine, one for her colostomy, and another for her shunt. It was touch and go that first week. We were in shock while trying to survive and explain what we could to our older daughters. Angie was in the hospital for a month before she could go home. She was in and out of the hospital that first year, with a total of nine surgeries by the end of that year. Angie has received early intervention services since infancy and had been fully integrated in a preschool program from ages two to five years. She was fully included in a regular kindergarten class last year. She's had a wheelchair since she was two, and she now uses a reciprocating gate orthosis (RGO) for walking about an hour a day."

Spencer continued, "Angie is quite a talker. Sometimes her verbal strengths mask her challenges. You assume because she can talk about something that she understands it. She can talk her way around several things. She works hard for the therapists . . . goodness knows she's had a few. She loves school and also does her best for teachers. Although she tries to be as independent as she can, the environment is often a barrier, as is her dependency on adults for much of her self-care needs. "One major medical concern is prevention of bladder infections. Angie has only one kidney and we must protect it. She has also had two femur fractures in the past three years. Right now we're dealing with some of Angie's fears and behaviors we don't quite understand. She fears big things (like large buildings/monuments) and thunderstorms . . . to the point of gagging and throwing up. We have been told by a neurologist that this could be emotionally triggered, but neurologically based."

The special education director added, "We just received the report from the neuropsychologist with the results of evaluations and recommendations for all of us to try."

Lynn continued, "We have a lot going on. We had a difficult time locating support services here. We hear that respite care is difficult to find. We have kind of had the "run around" when it comes to transitioning services . . . medical, educational, and community supports. And the girls are having a difficult time dealing with the move. They want us to move "back home" to our "old house.""

The special education director stated that he had made copies of Angie's IEP from her old school district for all of the team. He then went around the room asking for specifics from each professional regarding the goals relating to them and scheduling times for therapy and interventions.

Lynn continued, "We feel very strongly about inclusion. Angie has been in an inclusionary setting since age two. We do not want her "pulled out." If a one-on-one is required that cannot occur in the regular classroom, then we'd like to request an extended school day."

The P.T. replied, "Well, I am so booked that I don't see how I could see Angie if I couldn't see her during the school day. I work with children every morning before school and after school already."

The school nurse also replied, "I'm only here on Mondays and Wednesdays. I'm not sure how we're going to schedule her catheterization times."

The PE instructor questioned, "Well I just need to know what she can and can't do."

The O.T. stated, "I can see Angie on Thursdays after school for forty-five minutes to work on fine motor. I've never worked with dressing or computer skills, so I'm not too sure about that."

Then it was my turn to talk. I had never worked with a child with spina bifida before. Other than the information I received before the meeting, I had no idea what to expect. I honestly had many fears at this point. What is my role? What do I need to learn to do? What if I hurt her? How do I work with all of these professionals? And how do I live up to the expectations of Angie's parents? Do I really want to do this???

Just then, I felt a tap on my shoulder. Angie was handing me a piece of paper. I smiled and accepted it. As I unfolded it I saw a penciled drawing of a little smiling girl in a wheelchair and a taller smiling woman. At the top of the page was written, with some letters reversed and no spaces between the words, "IWANTTOBEINYOURCLASS." I turned to Angie to thank her and her arms flew open to give me a hug. After accepting the hug, I turned to the team and said, "I'll learn a lot, but it's going to be a great year!"

No one assessment model is complete nor always appropriate. This is certainly the case in point where traditional, clinic-based assessment of young children is concerned. However, the traditional, clinic-based assessment model, when correctly implemented and utilized, can provide us with valuable information concerning the individual strengths and support needs of the child. Some of the strengths of this model of assessment include:

- Provision of services by a multidisciplinary team of well-trained professionals such as early childhood educators, psychologists, speech/language therapists, occupational and physical therapists, special educators, child and family specialists, and medical staff including developmental pediatricians, geneticists, child psychiatrists, registered dietitians, and nurse practitioners.
- Access to diagnostic and evaluative technology often used by medical and health professionals, speech/language therapists, and audiologists.
- The compilation of relevant performance information about a child's individual strengths and support needs.
- The development of carefully derived recommendations intended to be utilized in the development of child- and family-centered interventions.
- An ongoing resource for the child and family across time, including reevaluation and follow-along.

Conversely, proponents of play-based assessment, one-form of functional assessment, believe that traditional, clinic-based assessment cannot provide the optimal picture of a child (Linder, 1990). Linder (1990) and others believe that traditional assessment does not allow for observation and interaction with the child and his/her natural environment, thus not necessarily providing us with the most accurate view of the child. Second, the child evaluated within these settings is placed at a disadvantage because of their lack of familiarity and comfort with the new surroundings and different people with whom they will work during the course of a day. (See Figure 6–2.)

The tests that are used to evaluate the child may also be biased especially in the case of children with severe disabilities who have severe communication,

Figure 6–2 Play-based assessment provides a clearer picture of a child.

sensory, physical, or emotional challenges. Another criticism is that traditional assessment does not provide us with information concerning the child's ability to perform functional skills that are useful in the child's daily life. Traditional forms of assessment are not often as flexible given the reliance on standardized assessment instruments which require that the examiner follow a standardized format for test administration.

One of the major limitations of standardized test instruments is that they are not often appropriate for children with severe disabilities who may experience physical and communication impairments that limit their full participation. Also, standardized tools have not been normed for children with disabilities. These instruments usually provide age equivalents that compare children with disabilities tested against same-aged children who are not disabled. Finally, one major criticism leveled against traditional assessment within school programs by educators is that the use of these instruments does not necessarily result in effective interventions. The relationship between assessment results and recommendations is not always clear for the teacher or direct care staff faced with the responsibility of program implementation.

Team-Based Assessment Approaches

There are a variety of team-based assessment approaches that have been used to assess young children. These approaches include the multidisciplinary, transdisciplinary, interdisciplinary, and functional assessment models. For more in-depth reading on this topic, see Orelove and Sobsey (1996), *Educating Children with Multiple Disabilities: A Transdisciplinary Approach* (3rd ed.). It provides an excellent in-depth analysis of each of these models.

Multidisciplinary Assessment

The multidisciplinary approach represents one form of a team-based model most commonly used. Basically, the multidisciplinary model allows for individual team members to independently assess a child, but does not provide for integration of professional services in that individual professionals work separate from one another in the assessment process and the reporting of results.

Interdisciplinary Assessment

The interdisciplinary assessment approach provides for more interaction between professionals. It allows for independent assessment and evaluation by each professional on the team; however, the interdisciplinary model allows for the integration of assessment findings among team members and also in the provision of team-based recommendations.

Transdisciplinary Assessment

Transdisciplinary assessment differs greatly from the previous models in that individual team members are predesignated as team facilitators during the assessment process with remaining team members serving in consultative roles (Orelove & Sobsey, 1996). The transdisciplinary approach is characterized by high levels of team involvement and mutual goals (Giangreco, 1986). The transdisciplinary assessment approach views parents as full members of the team and encourages their full involvement at all levels in the team process including assessment, development of interventions, and implementation of intervention approaches.

One of the major ingredients inherent to the success of this approach is the level of trust and mutual support that must be present within the team and its members. Professionals must be less territorial and willing to share their expertise among all members and allow for the designated facilitators to serve as case coordinators in the delivery of services to individual children and families. Team members provide both direct and consultative roles in the delivery of these services. In rural or underserved areas the transdisciplinary approach has been utilized by therapists training parents and teachers to perform therapeutic techniques in areas such as speech/language, occupational therapy, or physical therapy. In turn, parents have assisted educators in the integration of these specialized approaches into the day-to-day educational and habilitative programming for their child.

Functional Assessment

Functional assessment has traditionally focused on the child's strengths relative to their natural environments and demands found within those settings. Emphasis is typically given to determining the child's ability to perform functional tasks within these settings. Examples of functional tasks include communicating needs and wants, playing with objects or toys, feeding, drinking from a cup, and dressing. Functional assessment for infants and young children typically includes components such as direct observation of behavior within the natural environments the child regularly functions in, use of play-based assessment techniques utilizing toys within natural play contexts, and the direct involvement of the child's mother and father in the play-based assessment. (See Figure 6–3.)

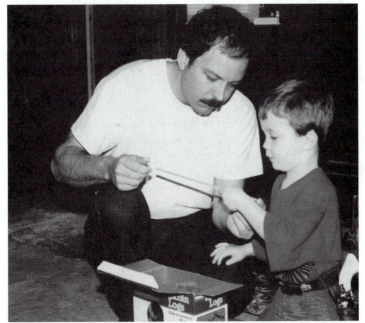

Figure 6–3 Functional assessment of young children encourages the direct involvement of the child's family.

Functional assessment offers many advantages when testing young children. Several experts (Bailey & Wolery, 1989; Linder, 1990) have indicated the strengths of this model, which include (*a*) flexibility—the degree of flexibility afforded by these procedures during the assessment process offers children more freedom during testing; (*b*) validity—the validity of functional assessment procedures is more ecologically valid or functionally relevant to the child, mother, and father, maximum parental involvement and input; and (*c*) relevance—information obtained through the functional assessment process is most relevant to planning intervention. An additional strength of this model is its applicability for assessing children with severe disabilities. Traditionally, children with severe disabilities have been labeled untestable, when in reality the standardized assessment instruments used to assess these children have not been designed for children who experience multiple disabilities such as limited communication skills and motor disabilities. Given the flexibility of functional assessment methodologies and the emphasis on direct observation and assessment of functional skill levels within relevant environments, these methods are better suited for determining the strengths and support needs of young children with severe disabilities.

Functional and Transdisciplinary Assessment

There is a strong relationship between functional and transdisciplinary assessment approaches. Each of these approaches is child- and setting-specific, and the procedures they each utilize are transdisciplinary in design. The true strength of these combined approaches is the degree of flexibility they allow for in terms of professional expertise employed during the assessment process. As Linder (1990) has indicated, the convergence of these components within a model "is holistic and dynamic and allows for change in terms of participants, content, and sequences given the individual needs of the child" (p. 1). As is the case with any quality assessment, the assessment process should be designed around the presenting strengths and support needs of an individual child and their family. Similarly, the professionals who constitute the team should also be selected with these factors in mind.

However, some limitations do exist with these approaches, depending on the purpose of the process. Is the child being assessed for evaluation purposes? If so, the child most likely will have to undergo standardized testing of one variety or another for the purpose of determining cognitive functioning. The confirmation of the child's level of functioning is relevant for determining eligibility for services within most states and territories, although the functional and transdisciplinary assessment model provides flexibility so that adaptations can be made during the evaluation process. These limitations can be overcome with a careful understanding of each child and the family's needs, the purposes of the assessment process, and the team members' roles prior to the actual evaluation.

Assessment Associated with Activity-Based Intervention

There are many commonly used assessment tools that are associated with activity-based intervention. These approaches to assessment have many strengths associated with them. Some of these include the manner in which information obtained through the assessment converts easily into the child's program plan. Second, all of the materials mentioned here have curriculum and/or evaluation components that accompany them as part of a total package. Finally, none of the tools cited here require specialized materials or test kits in order to utilize them. Rather, they assess a child's strengths and areas of need within the context of authentic activities found within the child's natural environments, thus producing a more realistic and naturalistic view of the child and family.

One of the most commonly used approaches for assessment and program planning is: *The Carolina Curriculum for Infants and Toddlers with Special Needs* (2nd ed.) (Johnson-Martin, Jens, Attermeier, & Hacker, 1991). The *CCITSN* is intended to be used with young children with disabilities who are functioning in the birth to twenty-four-month developmental range. The curriculum was built on normal sequences of development; however, it is adaptable to needs of individual children with varying degrees of atypical development, including children with developmental lags and children with more comprehensive needs as the result of severe disabilities. The *CCITSN* includes an assessment component to aid in program planning or "curriculum entry" (Johnson-Martin et al., 1991). The preassessment stage includes the assembling of materials commonly found within the child's environments, including toys, textured materials, bells, rattles, mirror, play-doh, and small jars with lids, among others. The assessment incorporates the principles of activity-based intervention by allowing the child and parent to interact with the various materials in a relaxed manner while the early childhood educator observes and records the child's preferred activities and the manner in which the child and parent interact. The early childhood educator may also instruct the parent to attempt specific activities. Items on the *CCITSN* are scored as a pass, emerge, or fail. This information is then converted to the child's program plan by developing curricular objectives from the items scored as either emerging or failed. An additional version is appropriate for preschoolers with special needs and is entitled *The Carolina Curriculum for Preschoolers with Special Needs* (Johnson-Martin, Attermeier, & Hacker, 1990).

One useful assessment and curriculum planning tool is the *Assessment, Evaluation, and Programming System for Infants and Children (AEPS)* developed by Diane Bricker. There are several versions of the *AEPS* that include the *AEPS Measurement for Birth to Three Years* (Bricker, 1993), the *AEPS Curriculum for Birth to Three Years* (Cripe, Slentz, & Bricker, 1993), the *AEPS Measurement for Three to Six Years* (Bricker & Pretti-Frontczak, 1996), and the *AEPS Curriculum for Three to Six Years* (Bricker & Waddell, 1996). Basically, the *AEPS* represents an assessment and evaluation system that also has an associated curriculum. Bricker (1993) makes the distinction between the terms *evaluation* and *assessment* by stating that "evaluation is concerned with comparing performance results over time, whereas assessment determines the current performance status" (1993, p. 236). Thus, the *AEPS* is a curriculum-based assessment tool that links assessment to meaningful intervention.

The *AEPS* can be used by early childhood special educators and other interventionists including speech/language therapists, physical therapists, occupational therapists, and psychologists (Bricker, 1993) for children from birth to three years of age, and another version of the instrument is available for children three to six years of age. The *AEPS* measures specific skill areas in the following domains: fine motor, gross motor, adaptive, cognitive, social communication, and social. Specific skills within these domains are judged to be necessary and relevant for young children to function in their environments.

The *AEPS* is administered while the child engages in typically occurring activities as part of their daily routines, and items are selected for assessment based on the child's developmental level. Scenarios may also be created such as during play or other activities to facilitate assessment on more specific terms. Scoring of the *AEPS* is either a 2, for items passed consistently, a 1, for inconsistent performance, or a 0, for items not passed. A child's performance on the *AEPS* is totaled and compared to the total score possible for a specific domain and then converted to a percentage score for that domain. Quarterly administration of the *AEPS* is recommended to maintain ongoing evaluation of performance (Bricker, 1993).

Another criterion-referenced assessment tool that ties in assessment with activity-based intervention is the *Infant-Preschool Assessment Scale (IPAS)* (Flagler, 1996). The *IPAS* allows educators and other related professionals to observe children within play and other routines within natural environments to identify a child's level of developmental functioning; to identify areas of strength, emerging skills, and areas of need; and to evaluate child progress and program effectiveness (Flagler, 1996). The *IPAS* is intended for children ages birth to sixty months. Items from the *IPAS* are scored as either pass, emerge, or fail. Parent and family participation in the assessment process is encouraged as part of the *IPAS*. Results from the *IPAS* can be utilized by educational professionals in the design of developmentally appropriate curriculum activities for a child and to monitor ongoing progress. The *IPAS* can be used in isolation for the purposes previously described or as part of a more comprehensive team evaluation (Flagler, 1996).

A most widely used curriculum-based assessment tool for typical preschoolers or those with developmental delays is the *Hawaii Early Learning Profile (HELP)*. The *HELP* (VORT, 1995) addresses the areas of (*a*) assessment and early identification, (*b*) intervention and instructional planning, (*c*) parent/family involvement, and (*d*) teaming and training of personnel. The *HELP* utilizes a curriculum-based approach to assessment, including direct observation in natural settings and attempts to link assessment to program planning. An appealing aspect of the *HELP* is that it can be modified and adapted to meet the needs of children with various developmental delays.

A very useful tool that has been developed to assist with monitoring children suspected of being at risk for developmental delay is the *Ages and Stages Questionnaires: A Parent Completed, Child Monitoring System* (Bricker, Squires, & Mounts, 1995). The *ASQ* was designed to monitor potential developmental problems in young children through the use of a series of questionnaires designed to be completed by parents. The questionnaires are to be completed by the child's parents in four-month intervals beginning at age four months and proceeding through age forty-eight months. One of the major benefits of the monitoring system is that it permits parents to systematically monitor their child's progress on a more regular basis in a cost-efficient manner. This represents a positive departure from the traditional model of having children reevaluated and maximizes on the need to observe and monitor child progress in shorter intervals, which is deemed necessary in the case of infants and young children.

As we conclude this section on assessment related to activity-based intervention, it is important to understand the many potential benefits of this method of assessment and program planning for children and their families. The merits of such an approach are that they provide teachers and related professionals with meaningful methods for obtaining assessment information and the conversion of this information into useful intervention programs. They are child and family friendly and are portable approaches that take into account the value of observing children and their families within natural contexts engaged in typical activities.

Authentic Assessment

Authentic assessment represents another form of assessment appropriate for use in early childhood educational settings in which a child's progress is measured through the compilation of student work samples over time on developmentally appropriate activities. One form of authentic assessment that has gained much notoriety in recent years is portfolio assessment, which has been widely used with children in preschool and early elementary grades. Another name that can be given to this form of assessment is permanent product assessment, since a documented account of a child's progress is maintained through the collection of work samples over time. As pointed out by Gronlund (1998), there are three basic forms the portfolios can take. These are display portfolios, which document the variety of activities that children perform in the context of their classroom; showcase portfolios, which highlight a child's best work in a given area; and finally, the working portfolio, which illustrates a sampling of the child's work over time related to specific learning objectives.

Experts agree that teachers utilizing the portfolio method should plan and organize the portfolio collection, designating the frequency in which they will collect material, how the material relates to stated goals and objectives, and teacher commentary attached to work samples to provide additional information concerning a child's performance (Gronlund, 1998). Portfolio assessment represents a useful and ongoing form of assessment that is classroom-based and will not only serve to document a child's progress toward stated learning objectives but also serve as a means for teachers to evaluate their performance in facilitating learning in children.

Family Participation in the Assessment Process

One of the major themes that will be reinforced throughout this text is that parents and families are equal partners in the process at all levels from assessment to intervention. Without question parents entrust the care and well-being of their child to "professionals" in the child care and educational fields for a major portion of their child's life. As professionals we must not take such responsibility lightly. It is essential that we maintain the highest standards of quality assurance in all aspects involved with the care and education of young children. Parents can offer us as professionals much in the way of relevant information pertaining to their child, and through effective partnerships we can utilize the knowledge of parents to the fullest extent to our benefit and more importantly for the benefit of the child.

Information obtained from parents during the assessment process beyond the information gathered through formal assessment can pertain to such things as their child's likes and dislikes, methods of responding, levels of tolerability, preferred and nonpreferred tasks, sleep patterns, typical behavioral patterns, response to novel situations, fears, and developmental and medical histories. More important, parents can be assistive during the actual assessment process during activity-based assessment sessions such as play and snack times and in the presentation of more difficult tasks in ways that may encourage their child to respond. In short, we as professionals have much to learn from our parental counterparts in terms of understanding their child. We should then accept this role as partner with an attitude of respect and consider it our honor to serve a parent's most precious gift, their child.

Translating Assessment Information into Meaningful Educational and Intervention Programs

The link between assessment and practice that is evident in the curriculum-based assessments introduced above is sometimes missing. Early childhood teachers may complain that much of the assessment information contained in a child's file is either too clinical or meaningless in explaining "what to do in terms of activities." A good evaluation should define a child's strengths and challenges in terms of learning. Information gathered during the assessment process should specifically identify developmentally appropriate skills specific to the child's strengths as well as emerging skill areas. The child's primary mode of learning should be identified and recommendations provided for establishing learning tasks and activities. Generally speaking, skills should be targeted within each of the domains assessed including cognitive, motor, communication, adaptive behavior, and social/emotional skill areas. Specific skill areas targeted for instruction include development of gross and fine motor skills; development of language and communication, including selection of communication form (object, picture, gestures, signs, verbal) or augmentative communication forms if necessary; development of play skills and self-help skills such as feeding, dressing, and other self-care skills such as toileting, washing hands, and brushing teeth. Of course, the selection of skills should be based on what is developmentally appropriate for the child, fully taking into consideration results obtained from the assessment battery and input from parents.

One important consideration to bear in mind for children with disabilities, when developing the child's individualized education program, is that priority should be given to teaching skills and addressing specialized objectives in multiple settings that embody developmental appropriateness. Selection of goals and objectives for the child and family should consider current and future environments in which the child functions and the demands and skills necessary for those settings. Attempts should be made to make activities developmentally appropriate, inclusive, and child-centered. Instructional and environmental supports should be provided that facilitate successful approximations and promote partial or full participation to the greatest extent possible. Examples of instructional modifications to consider follow. Are there any preinstructional considerations such as:

- What is the child's learning style? Previous learning history?
- What is the child's primary communication mode?
- What methods have been used successfully to teach new skills to this child in the past?
- Do you have a full understanding of the child's cognitive and other developmental skill levels?
- What are the preferred or favorite activities of the child?
- What methods do the child's mother and father recommend in terms of structuring activities?
- How does the child respond to choice-making opportunities?
- What type of instructional cues does the child respond to best? Object, picture, gestural, verbal, and combinations thereof?

Ideally, these questions can be addressed and answers identified during the assessment process through analyzing the child's performance during activity-based assessment such as play-based or curriculum-based assessment. It is important to remember that the assessment process should be centered on answering questions related to how a child learns, the level of supports necessary to facilitate optimal learning outcomes, and the individual strengths of the child and family that can be enhanced through the development of appropriate instructional supports.

Summary

This chapter has introduced and discussed assessment in terms of process and outcomes for young children with disabilities. Several terms were introduced related to assessment. These included *developmental delay,* a term used to refer to children who present a measured delay or "lag" in their development in one or more areas such as cognitive, physical, communication, social/emotional, or adaptive behavior. We also learned that a developmental delay does not necessarily indicate a permanent condition. The term *developmental disability* was also introduced, which by definition is illustrative of a severe or chronic disability that affects persons between the ages of five and twenty-one years. Developmental disability is attributable to a cognitive or physical impairment or combination of these, necessitating services and supports to assist with education and habilitation. This definition extends to infants and toddlers under age five, if they have a substantial developmental delay or specific congenital or acquired condition(s) with high probability of resulting in a developmental disability if these services and supports are not provided. A distinction was also made between the terms *evaluation* and *assessment.* Evaluation refers to the use of testing to determine whether or not a child is eligible to receive special services, whereas assessment refers to the process of gathering relevant information to determine at what level a child is functioning in key development areas (cognitive, motor, psychosocial, communication, and adaptive behavior).

The identification and diagnosis of developmental disabilities in children was discussed in terms of the procedural components and also from the perspective of the family in terms of their acceptance, interaction, and participation in the process. The *parent/professional partnership* pertaining to assessment and the development of the IFSP or IEP was also examined in the vignette. This vignette provided realistic examples of professional behaviors that are conducive and not so conducive to successful parent/professional interactions.

The major portion of the chapter dealt with the examination of assessment models including traditional *clinic-based assessment* and *activity-based assessment*. The strengths and contributions of each model were described as were the limitations of each approach. Clearly, the activity-based model of assessment for young children with developmental delays or disabilities has more strengths in terms of promoting parental involvement and also in the development of meaningful, child-centered, positive behavioral supports and activity-based interventions. Team-based assessment models such as the *multidisciplinary, transdisciplinary,* and *interdisciplinary* approaches were examined in terms of strengths, limitations, and applications in the assessment of young children. Finally, *functional assessment* tied to activity-based interventions was explored at great length.

This chapter has attempted to provide a rationale for the importance of child- and family-centered as well as developmentally appropriate approaches to assessment. It also explained how vital quality assessment procedures are in understanding a child's disability, learning strengths, and areas of support need leading to the development of effective interventions in school and home settings.

Chapter 6 Suggested Activities and Resources

Activities

1. Review the vignette that described the interaction between parents and school officials at the IEP meeting for Angie. What were some of the positive behaviors displayed by the teacher concerning Angie's educational service and support needs? Identify some aspects of the interaction that were less than positive, and discuss how these could be improved upon in future meetings.

2. Select and review sample assessment tools used in the evaluation of young children. Examine several of these instruments and determine if they are examples of standardized or functional assessment tools. Also, determine their role and function in the assessment process, the target population in terms of age and disability levels for which they are intended, and administration protocol.

3. Interview a parent or family of a young child with a disability concerning their viewpoints on the assessment and program planning process. Attempt to sensitize yourself to the concerns voiced by the parents and family members during the interview.

4. If possible, sit in and observe an IFSP or IEP meeting for an infant, toddler, or young child with a disability. Take note of who is in attendance; the input of each professional, parent, and family member who is present; and the group dynamics experienced by participants during the meeting. In general, was the meeting positive? Did participants have the best needs of

the child and family in mind? Did the meeting result in positive action taken to procure meaningful learning outcomes for the child and family?

5. View the videotape entitled *Activity-Based Intervention* (1995) by Bricker, Veltman, and Munkres, published and distributed by Paul H. Brookes Publishing Company, to gain additional insight into activity-based assessment and intervention.

6. Consult the text entitled *Transdisciplinary Play-Based Assessment* by Linder (1990) for additional information on the merits of play-based assessment for young children.

Selected Resources

1. *Textbooks on assessment*

McLean, M. E., Bailey, D. B., & Wolery, M. (1996). *Assessing Infants and Preschoolers with Special Needs* (2nd ed.). Upper Saddle River, NJ: Prentice-Hall.

Sattler, J. M. (1993). *Assessment of Children* (3rd ed.). San Diego: Sattler.

Wodrich, D. L. (1997). *Children's Psychological Testing: A Guide for NonPsychologists*. (3rd ed.). Baltimore: Paul H. Brookes.

2. *Websites*

Division for Early Childhood (DEC) of the Council for Exceptional Children (CEC): http://www.dec-sped.org

National Information Center for Children and Youth with Disabilities: http://www.kidsource.com/NICHCY/index.html

3. *Journal articles*

McLean, M. (1998). Assessing Young Children for Whom English Is a Second Language. *Young Exceptional Children, 1,* 20–26.

Rous, B., & Hallam, R. A. (1998). Easing the Transition to Kindergarten: Assessment of Social, Behavioral, and Functional Skills in Young Children with Disabilities. *Young Exceptional Children, 1,* 17–27.

References

Akesson, E. B., & Granlund, M. (1995). Family Involvement in Assessment and Intervention: Perceptions of Professionals in Sweden. *Exceptional Children, 61,* 520–535.

Amendments to the Individuals with Disabilities Education Act of 1997. H.R. 5, 105th Cong., 18-*1* Sess. (1997).

Bailey, D. B., & Wolery, M. (1989). *Assessing Infants and Preschoolers with Handicaps*. Columbus, OH: Merrill.

Bérubé, M. (1996). *Life as We Know It: A Father, a Family, and an Exceptional Child*. New York: Pantheon Books.

Bricker, D. (1993). *AEPS Measurement for Birth to Three Years*. Baltimore: Paul H. Brookes Publishing Co.

Bricker, D., & Pretti-Frontczak, K. (1996). *AEPS Measurement for Three to Six Years*. Baltimore: Paul H. Brookes Publishing Co.

Bricker, D., Veltman, P., & Munkres, A. (1995). Activity-Based Intervention. Baltimore: Paul H. Brookes Publishing Co.

Bricker, D., & Waddell, M. (1996). *AEPS Curriculum for Three to Six Years*. Baltimore: Paul H. Brookes Publishing Co.

Cripe, J., Slentz, K., & Bricker, D. (1993). *AEPS Curriculum for Birth to Three Years*. Baltimore: Paul H. Brookes Publishing Co.

Culbertson, J. L., & Willis, D. J. (1993). *Testing Young Children: A Reference Guide for Developmental, Psychoeducational, and Psychosocial Assessments*. Austin, TX: PRO-ED.

Flagler, S. L. (1996). *Infant-Preschool Play Assessment Scale*. Chapel Hill: Chapel Hill Training Outreach Project.

Giangreco, M. F. (1986). Delivery of Therapeutic Services in Special Education Programs for Learners with Severe Handicaps. *Physical and Occupational Therapy in Pediatrics, 6* (2), 5–15.

Gronlund, G. (1998). Portfolios as an Assessment Tool: Is Collection of Work Enough? *Young Children, 53,* 4–10.

Johnson-Martin, N., Jens, K. G., Attermeier, S. M., & Hacker, B. J. (1991). *The Carolina Curriculum for Infants and Toddlers with Special Needs* (2nd ed.). Baltimore: Paul H. Brookes Publishing Co.

Johnson-Martin, N. M., Attermeier, S. M., & Hacker, B. (1990). *The Carolina Curriculum for Preschoolers with Special Needs*. Baltimore: Paul H. Brookes Publishing Co.

Linder, T. W. (1990). *Transdisciplinary Play-Based Assessment: A Functional Approach to Working with Young Children*. Baltimore, MD: Paul H. Brookes Publishing Co.

McClean, M., Bailey, D. B., & Wolery, M. (1996). *Assessing Infants and Preschoolers with Special Needs* (2nd ed). Columbus, OH: Merrill.

NAEYC. (1996). DEC/CEC Personnel Standards for Early Education and Early Intervention: Guidelines for Licensure in Early Childhood Special Education. In NAEYC *Guidelines for Preparation of Early Childhood Professionals*. Washington, DC: Author.

Orelove, F. P., & Sobsey, D. (1996). *Educating Children with Multiple Disabilities: A Transdisciplinary Approach* (3rd ed.). Baltimore: Paul H. Brookes Publishing Co.

Squires, I., Potter, L., & Bricker, D. (1995). *The ASQ User's Guide*. Baltimore: Paul H. Brookes Publishing Co.

Turnbull, A. P., & Turnbull, H. R. (1997). *Families, Professionals, and Exceptionality: A Special Partnership* (3rd ed.). Englewood Cliffs, NJ: Merrill/Prentice-Hall.

VORT Cooperation. (1995). *HELP for Preschoolers: Assessment and Curriculum Guide*. Palo Alto, CA: Author.

Chapter

Effective Teaching and Intervention Practices

INTRODUCTION

The purpose of this chapter will be to examine and describe effective teaching and intervention practices for young children and their families. The National Association for the Education of Young Children (NAEYC) and the Division of Early Childhood Special Education (DEC/CEC) have developed a comprehensive set of performance-based competencies needed by all educators in the field of early childhood education. These standards have been taken into consideration in the preparation of this chapter. Here are the objectives that the reader will address in Chapter 7. You should be able to:

• Understand the process of identifying and selecting socially valid intervention goals and objectives in the areas of PBS (positive behavioral supports), ABI (activity-based intervention), and DAP (developmentally appropriate practice).
• Recognize child/family-centered longitudinal educational and family service plans that promote meaningful educational and quality-of-life outcomes.
• Become familiar with positive behavioral supports, activity-based intervention, and developmentally appropriate practice methods.
• Understand how to develop goals and objectives that reflect the principles of PBS, ABI, and DAP.
• Know how to design child-centered learning environments.
• Describe methods for promoting successful inclusion.
• Describe methods of evaluating intervention effectiveness/outcomes.

Your readings thus far have described the fundamental knowledge and skills needed among professionals in the field of early childhood education. We have eluded briefly to the topic of intervention in previous chapters, but not in sufficient depth. This chapter will explore this important topic in greater detail, while building on the information presented up to this point. Further application of these principles of intervention across developmental levels will be described in Section III of the text.

Selection of Socially Valid Goals and Objectives

Oftentimes, educators create educational objectives aimed toward developing a skill that a child cannot perform, rather than placing their emphasis during intervention on expanding skills that the child can perform. Too often this scenario takes place resulting in an educational objective that may never be attained by a child, high levels of frustration on the part of the teachers who fail to understand the child's lack of progress, and an inefficient use of instructional time. Also, missing in such cases is the genuinely solicited input of the parent(s) and families in the development of a child's individualized educational program (Wheeler, 1996). Parental input is critical as a genuine measure of social validity regarding the goals and objectives that are developed for their child. (See Figure 7–1.)

As described in the previous chapter (Chapter 6), the assessment and evaluation process should not lead to intervention goals and objectives referenced around the "needs" or "limitations" of a child and family. Rather, interventions should be built on skills that the child currently has in his/her repertoire and/or emerging skills. This approach, also referred to as a "strengths model," is designed to place emphasis on developing interventions that expand on existing skills by teaching and promoting generalization of these skills across time, settings, and teachers, and also by building fluency and maintenance of emerging skills.

Vygotsky referred to this as the "zone of proximal developments" (Vygotsky, 1978). Basically Vygotsky believed that instruction should promote independence in children, and thus in order to accomplish this aim, instructional expectations should be consistent with an individual child's developmental capabilities.

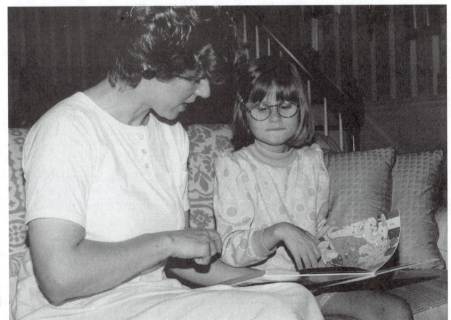

Figure 7–1 Parental input is essential to the selection of socially valid goals and objectives.

An illustration of this is as follows: Consider Brittany, a five-year-old child with significant delays in cognitive and language skill areas. Brittany has been utilizing gestures consistently in her communication and is now beginning to use echolalic speech in context. Rather than build on these existing skills (gestures) and emerging skills (echolalic speech), her teacher has failed to build these strengths into her individual educational plan (IEP) and has focused on a more nonfunctional goal that will be taught in isolation. In this instance, she has recommended to the speech/language pathologist (SLP) that she should possibly work on Brittany's ability to verbally pronounce isolated speech sounds, rather than developing Brittany's skills in a more functional communication system that would pair gestures with simple words. Hopefully, the SLP in such a case would view this as an opportunity to redirect the classroom teacher, providing her with a rationale for teaching the functional use of communication to Brittany because these skills are present and emerging (even though delayed) and need to be reinforced through a plan of systematic intervention.

Given the importance of selecting intervention goals, some guidelines should be considered when formulating intervention goals for children and families. Intervention goals and objectives should be developed that are socially relevant for both the child and family. This process is referred to as social validation (Kazdin, 1989). Social validation is a process used to evaluate the acceptability of intervention prior to its implementation or to evaluate the outcomes of an intervention. This process is best utilized when maximum input is obtained from parents and family members as well as other team members. Ultimately, the input obtained from parents and family should be the decisive element in the development of an intervention with additional constructive input provided by early childhood education professionals and other members of the child's team. Consider the following vignette.

VIGNETTE 7-1: SELECTING SOCIALLY VALID INTERVENTION GOALS

Consider the following example: You have been called in as the early childhood special education consultant to provide consultative services and supports to your school system with respect to Emily, a five-year-old child. Emily's family consists of her mother, father, and brother, who is eight years of age. Emily and her family live in a rural area that has been traditionally underserved due to location and limited resources.

There are numerous strengths where Emily and her family are concerned. These include a loving and supportive family whose mission statement is "finding solutions to life's challenges." Emily's family is fervent in their desire to help Emily attain the very best in terms of quality-of-life outcomes. Emily also has a very good classroom teacher, who is eager to assist Emily in learning, and a dedicated mother, who is well-educated with respect to Emily's educational rights and freedoms and who also happens to be a strong advocate on behalf of Emily and her family. The challenges that Emily and her family are confronting are somewhat serious, but certainly do not constitute obstacles that are insurmountable. Emily is visually impaired, can distinguish light and images when in close range (two to three feet), but is considered legally blind (visual acuity of 20/200 or less in the better eye after the best possible correction with glasses or contact lenses) (Heward, 1996). Emily is also challenged by delays in expressive language and has been diagnosed with severe mental retardation. Emily will also engage in severe and challenging forms of behavior that includes head hitting (hitting herself in the head with a closed fist) and screaming.

Emily's family is concerned that the window of opportunity for teaching alternative skills is rapidly narrowing unless intensive educational and related services are provided that directly address these issues. The rural location in which Emily and her family live provides limited access to vision specialists, therefore prompting the local educational team to recommend that Emily's family consider placing her at the state residential school for the blind. Emily's family has vehemently opposed such an option and had requested that an educational evaluation be conducted to focus on Emily's educational needs, especially in the areas of behavior and communication. This evaluation was conducted by a technical assistance team from the nearby state university consisting of professionals trained in the area of positive behavioral supports and early childhood special education.

Results from the functional analysis of behavior indicated that Emily's behavior is linked to her communication needs and serves the function of gaining attention from teachers and caregivers. Emily's language delay has resulted in her having minimal verbal communication abilities. She has never been taught any form of functional communication (sign or augmentative) and therefore relies on her behavior to gain access to attention from those around her. Emily's teachers and family have been unaware of the function that these behaviors serve for her and have continued over time to consistently provide Emily with attention during these time periods, thus serving to reinforce or strengthen this pattern. The technical assistance team also determined that Emily works best when she is provided with choice of two items, given access to attention from the teacher, and presented with a high degree of structure during instructional periods. This high degree of structure consists of hand-over-hand prompts when she is taught a new task and frequent verbal and tactile cues to initiate and continue working on a task or activity.

The M-team has been called at the request of Emily's mother, who wants to speak about the design of Emily's IEP. As the meeting unfolds, some of the team members express concern over Emily's inability to communicate and whether her current placement, a classroom for young children with severe disabilities, is most appropriate given the intensity of Emily's needs. Some members of the team suggest a more specialized environment such as the state school for the blind.

Emily's mother addresses the educational team with the following issues:

1. Provision of education for Emily within her community school so that she may continue to enjoy the full benefits of childhood, which for her include the benefits of a stable and supportive home and family, a connection with her community, and access to family and friends.

2. A revised educational program emphasizing more collaborative efforts in the design of a comprehensive intervention plan designed to assist Emily in the development of communication skills and self-help skills such as toileting, as well as increased accountability through better documentation of Emily's performance through the daily collection of performance data.

3. Increased access for Emily to related services in the areas of speech/language therapy (currently Emily receives one hour per week in isolation) and occupational therapy (currently consultation occurs at a minimum of three times per year); and finally, more frequent access to the vision specialist in her role as a consultant to Emily's teacher.

4. Respectful inclusion of parental input. Your task as early childhood special education consultant is to oversee the development of Emily's IEP and to coordinate the professionals assigned to assist with the implementation and delivery of educational and related services and supports to Emily.

Given that social validation plays such a key role in the development of interventions:

- How would you as the consultant in this case take into consideration the input from Emily's parents and family with respect to her educational goals and objectives?
- Second, how could you educate your colleagues to be more sensitive and in tune with the strengths of Emily and her family rather than the challenges they face?
- What are some fundamental philosophical issues of team members that must be addressed before Emily can receive the quality of services and supports needed by her?
- Finally, what other issues related to the principle of social validation should be considered by you the consultant as you attempt to promote a win-win on behalf of Emily and her family?

Analysis and Summary

In response to the task that you were given as a consultant concerning Emily's educational program, you should have considered the following:

1. The input of Emily's mother should have served as the guidepost in the development of a positive behavioral support and an activities-based intervention plan for Emily. The concerns raised by Emily's mother included inclusive community schooling for Emily; development of a comprehensive intervention plan in the areas of communication and self-help skills; access to consultative services and supports from trained specialists in the areas of speech/language, occupational therapy, and vision; and greater family input into Emily's educational program with respect to quality assurance and content.

2. In your role as consultant, you must serve in a dual capacity: as educator/advocate for Emily and her family and also as an agent of change

dedicated to informing your colleagues about what constitutes best and effective practice in terms of providing an appropriate education to Emily.

3. From the applied example, some members of Emily's team are generally opposed to Emily receiving her education within an inclusive community school setting. Some beliefs held by these opposing professionals could originate out of self-doubt that they have the capabilities and resources to offer the best possible education as far as Emily is concerned. Also, their feelings of self-doubt could be related to the minimal level of interaction with students having diverse learning needs such as in Emily's case. Finally, they may also believe that Emily would benefit more and it would be easier if Emily were taught at a "specialized school" with other children having similar conditions.

As a consultant trained in the area of early childhood special education, you realize that based on the literature, you must try and dispel such attitudes and beliefs held by your colleagues through information and sharing of your expertise. Several approaches have been advocated to confront and modify these attitudes and beliefs. Bricker (1995) states that the successful inclusion of young children is influenced by three major factors: attitudes, resources, and curricula. With regard to the attitudes displayed by your colleagues, training and attitude awareness concerning the capabilities of persons with disabilities would be strongly encouraged. As Bricker (1995) points out, adults in care giving roles must be made aware of how influential their words and attitudes can be to young children. The negative attitudes displayed by teachers toward a child with disabilities can significantly impact the attitudes of peers as well and have a detrimental effect on all levels.

Another issue for team members to consider in Emily's case is that successful inclusion is more than having a specialist trained in the area of vision to work with her. Rather, it is about all persons working together for the good of each child and dedicating themselves as a team to the pursuit of a total quality approach in the design and delivery of educational services to Emily (including attitudes and beliefs). Successful inclusion can be a reality for Emily, and this scenario reminds us of the goal of ecologically based interventions. Not only is an ecological intervention aimed at teaching new behavior and skills to a child, but it is also about changing elements in the child's environment including the behavior of those persons with whom the child interacts (Wheeler, 1991).

One method that has been demonstrated to be successful in facilitating a change in attitude toward inclusion of children with severe disabilities into the general education setting is the MAPS Process. MAPS is an acronym for the McGill Action Planning System (Forest & Lusthaus, 1990), which was developed in Canada and is a systems approach dedicated to fostering the successful inclusion of children with severe disabilities. The MAPS Process is built on the fundamental beliefs that all children can learn, that systems disable people by placing limitations and labels onto them, that educators need to support and nurture *every* child, and that labels should not be a part of the planning process—that a child should be valued for simply being a child. Finally, the MAPS Process is dedicated to simple and practical approaches that everyone can assist in implementing. The MAPS Process is basically a collaborative problem-solving session(s) similar to a focus group whereby participants are led by a facilitator who generates images on a chart that becomes the plan of action for the child and her/his team. These visual images are intended to assist the participants in understanding relationships that will be turned into active problem-solving strategies.

Parents and family members are key participants in the MAPS Process and assist in understanding who their child is from a family's perspective. The MAPS Process also attempts to derive the plan of action from a series of guided questions led by the facilitator that examine the dreams, hopes, and expectations for the child; the fears associated with the worst case scenario or outcomes that the parents fear for their child; descriptors about who the child is, including likes/dislikes, strengths, and abilities; and the needs of the child. Finally the information is synthesized and the planning team develops the plan of action that will be implemented (Forest & Lusthaus, 1990). (See Figure 7–2.)

Having considered these many factors with regard to Emily, you by now have become aware of the job ahead for you as "consulting teacher." You must try your best to facilitate the development of optimal educational services and supports as deemed important and necessary for a quality educational program for her. In doing so, you will need to serve as team leader, consultant, advocate, resource specialist, and cheerleader to accommodate the many roles and responsibilities that exist. This by no means implies that you are a "one-person show" or that you carry the weight of the world alone. You must therefore be willing to release some of these roles, delegate, and recruit others from the team to assist you in overseeing the implementation of Emily's educational plan. The willingness to do this will hopefully result in a more positive outcome for not only Emily but also Emily's team.

Longitudinal Educational Planning

Longitudinal educational planning (LEP) is a process aimed at the identification of educational objectives that are referenced from current and future educational

Figure 7–2 Teaming and collaboration are essential to the program planning process.

settings. It represents a plan for linking current developmental and learning experiences and teaching strategies with those required in the next or future educational settings (NAEYC, 1996). One of the many benefits of this process is facilitating successful transitions for children as they progress from one educational level to the next. But LEP is more than simply ensuring a smooth transition. Rather, it is a process aimed at delivering educational and related services and supports to children and their families with emphasis on quality, continuity, and viable outcomes. Related to this is quality assurance. Quality assurance is a process which influences best and effective practice. Quality assurance places an emphasis on program quality, child- and family-centered services, and the attainment of valued outcomes.

Continuity as part of the LEP process attempts to ensure that critical components of programming are present across age and grade levels for young children. As indicated by Lombardi (1992) there are three key elements related to LEP that are needed to provide effective early childhood educational services. These are developmentally appropriate practice, parent involvement, and supportive services.

Developmentally appropriate practice (DAP) is concerned with whether activities and expectations coincide with what is developmentally appropriate given a child's age and development. DAP also believes in the positive affirmation of children and in promoting active learning and exploration through creative experiences for young children. Parental involvement as we have previously discussed is an essential ingredient in the attainment of longitudinal educational outcomes for all children. Parents should be actively encouraged to participate in the education of their children.

Families have become a changing dynamic and are more diverse than ever in terms of their composition. Children originate from a variety of home and living situations. These include single-parent families, blended families, families impacted by poverty, and multicultural families. Educators must remain aware and sensitive to these diversities so that they may be more responsive to the inclusion of all families throughout the educational life of their child. Finally, longitudinal educational program planning is also largely influenced by the degree in which the lifestyle support needs of the child and family are attended to. This is especially true in the case of children and families impacted by poverty, disability, or catastrophic conditions. Children and family needs are compounded by these conditions and are reflected in the level of support service needs in the areas of health care, child care, and family counseling. Longitudinal educational planning seeks to identify the needs of each child and family with respect to these support needs and develop comprehensive interagency plans and formal agreements that will ensure that services are provided to those in need.

PBS, ABI, and DAP Teaching and Intervention Methods

When developing effective teaching intervention methods for young children, one must be mindful of the standards set forth by the profession as to what constitutes best and effective practice. There has been some debate on this matter among professionals in the field especially when considering the diversity of learning needs among young children. Generally speaking, professional early childhood educators have ascribed to the following basic principles as set forth by NAEYC (1996) where effective intervention is concerned. These have included the use of developmentally appropriate practice such as the use of play, small group activities, open-ended questioning, group discussion, cooperative learning, inquiry experiences, integrated learning experiences, and scheduling, which are focused on the child's needs and interests with adaptations for children with disabilities. These components have been generally agreed upon by special educators working in the field of early childhood special education but have nevertheless been expanded on, given the diversity encountered in children with special learning and behavioral needs.

The standards put forth by the Council for Exceptional Children's Division for Early Childhood (CEC/DEC) also stress the importance of developmentally appropriate practice, specific adaptations given individual children's needs, development of the IEP/IFSP in partnership with families, use of assistive/adaptive technology when appropriate, team-based assessment and intervention, and, finally, the use of systematic planning in linking instructional goals and learning experiences (DEC/CEC, 1996).

With these competencies in mind, the purpose of this chapter is to provide early childhood educators with a basis for developing a theoretical construct that can be readily applied in educational settings serving young children and families. The text incorporates the philosophies of positive behavioral supports and activities-based interventions as the platform from which to operate. The obvious reasons for this merger of approaches is their focus on children and families and also because of their general applicability across the range of early childhood educational settings. The partnership of these approaches only serves to strengthen and complement each, and together they provide educators with a cadre of meaningful instructional approaches for teaching young children.

Positive behavioral support is congruent with activity-based intervention (Horner et al., 1990). This method of providing behavioral supports to enhance learning and lifestyle options has been successfully employed with a variety of learners, including children with severe disabilities and autism (Dunlap & Fox, 1996; Turnbull & Ruef, 1996). More recently these approaches have been employed with young children with severe disabilities and their families (Fox, Dunlap, & Philbrick, 1997; Turnbull & Turnbull, 1996). Positive behavioral supports are characterized by a values-based philosophy that promotes the well-being and dignity of each individual. Positive behavioral supports represents an embracing of approaches from areas such as augmentative/alternative communication, inclusion, self-determination, and behavioral supports designed to develop a program of individualized lifestyle supports for the individual (Turnbull & Ruef, 1996). Positive behavioral supports seeks to modify environmental events that precipitate challenging behaviors, called setting events, to minimize the occurrences of such behaviors as well as actively teach positive alternative skills. Proponents of positive behavioral supports do not support the use of punitive procedures of any kind. (See Figure 7–3.)

Positive behavioral supports should be viewed as first a philosophy that shapes practice. Second, they also represent a set of strategies aimed at the prevention of challenging behavior in young children. Finally, they embody a set of positive teaching and intervention tools when coupled with a structured and nurturing environment to promote positive behaviors in children.

Figure 7–3 Positive behavioral supports attempt to modify environmental events which coincide with challenging behavior.

An essential ingredient needed to successfully support these approaches in early childhood educational settings is a philosophical and applied commitment to the active use of these procedures within early childhood educational settings among all team members. A philosophical statement is helpful and can serve as a guidepost to team members in their efforts to deliver services and supports. But a philosophy cannot stand alone, and therefore, team members must be equipped with the skills necessary to implement these levels of support specific to the individual needs of children on a daily basis. As pointed out by Strain and Hemmeter (1997), early childhood educators must become more comfortable with challenging behaviors in children if they are to become agents of change.

Specific methods utilized in positive behavioral supports include the following:

1. Functional assessment of behavior.
2. Development of behavioral support plans.
3. Intervention.
4. Evaluation of intervention progress and outcomes.

Typically when children "misbehave," as it is sometimes referred, they are responding out of unmet need. When one considers the developmental limitations of many children with respect to communication coupled with insensitive caregivers, these responses seem very reasonable. However, many educators, caregivers, and often parents respond in a negative fashion toward behavior in children that is the slightest bit out of the ordinary. Educators may not view behavior in children from an objective viewpoint. Instead, they may use their own point of reference or values system to place judgment on the child's behavior. Adult caregivers and teachers may often fail to realize their own contribution toward these behaviors and place the burden onto the child.

Strain and Hemmeter (1997) offer two extremely valuable points along these lines. They recommend, first, that educators stop placing the blame on the child and, second, that educators stop blaming challenging behavior on extraneous events, such as failure to take medication on time, and stop saying that the child simply is like he/she is for no explainable reason. Finally, another issue that is typically encountered where children's behavior is concerned is that each of us has our own degree of tolerability for diverse behavior and learning styles in children. Our tolerability may be influenced by the degree of training and or exposure we have had to diverse learning and behavior and by our personality makeup in that some of us may be more relaxed than others in such situations. Our response to these patterns in children can be influenced by how we perceive these responses of children as positive or negative and our role as educators in helping to teach children prosocial behaviors.

Finally, challenging behavior can be defined as behavior that limits the learning potential, social inclusion, and quality of life for a child. Teachers and parents alike should be mindful that behaviors which cause them concern given this definition are potential targets for change. One important point to remember is that these targeted behaviors should be socially relevant and not insignificant behaviors that are minor in nature, such as a failure to pay attention, daydreaming, talking out of turn, or failing to sing with the class during circle time. Often, children are labeled for such insignificant behaviors and singled out in front of their peers and made an example of because the teacher may be having a bad day and is low on the threshold of tolerabilty.

So the next question would be: What would positive behavioral supports in the classroom look like for an individual child? Well, after carefully conducting the functional assessment of behavior and taking into account the factors or setting events that influence the child's behavior and the function(s) that these behaviors serve for the child, the next step would be to develop a behavioral support plan. These factors were discussed in the applied example provided in Chapter 5. Behavioral support plans can be inclusive of many things depending on the support needs of a particular child. For example, behavioral support plans can include environmental supports as well as instructional supports that include the development of programs to teach new skills, promote social inclusion, or teach generalization of skills already learned.

Examples of specific behavioral supports include the following:

I. Introduce an Individual Schedule

Some children may need individual schedules to help them maintain their behaviors, such as task engagement, or to aid them in communicating. Hogdon (1995) illustrated the utility of visual cues (individualized schedules) for young children. Children with communication disabilities may process visual cues much faster. They assist in maintaining task engagement, clarify information for the child, provide structure, and facilitate smooth and effective transitions between activities, thus minimizing the occurrence of challenging behavior. Depending on the developmental levels of each child, the schedule may consist of an object board, a photo activity schedule, picture/symbol activity schedule, or photos or picture/symbols paired with words.

II. Maintain a Classroom Schedule That Indicates Activities and Time Frames for the Entire Class Day

Another recommended practice for teachers is to employ a classroom schedule that is displayed within the classroom to indicate the time frames and types of activities for the entire class each day as illustrated in the following:

Classroom Schedule Inclusive Kindergarten

8:00–8:10	Transition into classroom
8:10–8:30	Circle time (greetings, calendar, singing)
8:30–8:45	Individual seat work
8:45–9:20	Literacy
9:20–10:00	Music or physical education, integrated physical therapy on P.E. days
10:00–10:30	Small group instruction (preacademics), individual work with modifications
10:30–10:50	Individual play time plus transition
10:50–11:20	Lunch
11:20–11:30	Transition/restroom/toileting/hand washing programs
11:30–11:50	Story time
11:50–12:15	Language activity
12:20–12:50	Recess
12:50–1:20	Cooperative learning group activities
1:30–2:00	Learning centers
2:00–2:30	Art
2:30–2:45	Transition/cleanup
2:50	Exit school

Source: Adapted from J. J. Wheeler (1998). Reducing Challenging Behavior in Learners with Developmental Disabilities through the Modification of Instructional Practices. In A. Hilton & R. Ringlaben (Eds.), *Best and Promising Practices in Developmental Disabilities*, (263–272). Austin, TX: Pro-Ed.

III. Match Level of Instruction to Child's Abilities

Instructional demands may be much greater than what is developmentally appropriate for a child. This is often observed in the area of communication. For children who experience communication delays (expressive or receptive) such auditory processing disorders make it difficult for them to process verbal information. Frequently, children who experience these learning challenges become easily frustrated and develop challenging behaviors in their attempt to communicate their needs. Teachers respond in a reactive manner by scolding, placing the child in time-out, and subsequently labeling the child. An example of a positive behavioral support plan would be to assess whether the child can use gestures to communicate or respond to gestures paired with verbalizations, and utilize such forms of communication during instruction, gradually building the child's communication repertoire by the use of reinforcement both social and tangible for their efforts.

IV. Use Clear and Consistent Instructional Cues

Often teachers and classrooms lack the degree of structure needed for some children. Teachers must be mindful to identify the instructional cues needed by children in their classrooms and maintain consistency in using these cues.

V. Determine Developmentally Appropriate Length of Activities

Behavior problems often develop because the demands associated with an activity do not correspond to the child's developmental need. Activities may be too long, may lack stimulation, and are often just too demanding for a child. Teachers should attempt to match the length of an activity to the child's developmental level. For very young children activities should be approximately ten minutes in length progressing to fifteen to twenty minutes for older preschoolers. Some variation may occur with regard to these time limits depending upon the nature of the activity and whether the activity is child-directed or teacher-directed, and individual- or group-oriented. As children move into lower elementary levels, activities may range from fifteen to thirty minutes depending on the nature of the activity. Variations on these would, of course, be recommended around the individual needs of every child. Additional considerations must be given for children with disabilities and necessary modifications made.

VI. Vary Activities by Alternating Low Demand with High Demand Activities

One method used to facilitate positive behavior in young children is to alternate low demand activities (activities preferred by a child) with high demand activities (activities that are not as preferred by the child). It is recommended that teachers begin each day with a low demand activity and end each day with a low demand activity. This promotes a positive association for the child as they begin and end each day with a pleasant and fun activity that is hopefully low in stress. Another benefit from this teaching approach is that the low demand activities serve as a naturally occurring reinforcer for a child after they complete a task that is not as pleasant for them.

VII. Provide Children with Choice-Making Opportunities

Providing children with choice-making opportunities within their daily schedule is critical. There are many benefits associated with the ability to make choices. Children are affirmed and feel important and valued when they are provided with choice-making opportunities. This leads to a sense of personal satisfaction and an improved quality of life; it also promotes independence and increases a child's motivation to learn and actively participate in their learning. Finally, choice often serves to prevent challenging behaviors from occurring (Bamberra & Koger, 1996).

Figure 7–4 Permit children access to preferred activities.

As pointed out by Bamberra and Koger (1996) teachers should allow children to select choices from a list of options (activities), present the child with real objects (toys, food, refreshments), and allow the child to choose. (See Figure 7–4.)

These strategies represent a sampling of the most commonly used positive behavioral support practices that are advocated for teachers and families to employ with young children. They do not differ from what we consider to be best and effective practice in teaching all children, yet provide us with a systematic approach to proactively support optimal learning, positive behavior, and overall development in children.

Another intervention approach most commonly used in early childhood settings is activity-based intervention (Bricker & Cripe, 1995). Activity-based intervention as defined by Bricker and Cripe (1995) contains four elements: "Child-directed transactional approach, goals and objectives embedded in daily routines, uses logically occurring antecedents and consequences, and develops functional and generative skills" (p. 40). Basically, these elements can be broken down and operationalized as follows:

I. Activity-Based Intervention Believes in Facilitating a Child's Interests and Encouraging Them to Make Choices and Initiate Activities

II. Activity-Based Intervention Targets Intervention Goals within the Context of Naturally Occurring Routines for the Child Rather Than Providing Intervention within an Artificial Context

III. Activity-Based Intervention Utilizes Three Main Types of Activities: Routine Activities Such as Those That Occur on a Daily Basis at Home and Within Early Childhood Settings

These include meal time, dressing, snack, and transitions. The second type is planned activities that are basically directed by the teacher, parent, or another adult. Last, there are child-initiated activities that consist of activities chosen and initiated by the child during planned or unplanned contexts. See Figure 7–5.

IV. Finally, Activity-Based Intervention Seeks to Develop Functional Skills in Children That Will Not Only Be Useful during the Course of Their Day but Also Generalize to New Settings

The natural relationship between positive behavioral supports and activity-based intervention is quite obvious. Both approaches are child- and family-centered, provide structure for the child that still allows for child-initiated activities and choice-making opportunities, teach functional and meaningful skills to the child that will also generalize, structure the environment for the child's success, utilize proactive teaching strategies aimed at minimizing the occurrence of challenging behavior, and, finally, provide a learning environment that values children, families, and the importance of a safe and nurturing learning environment.

Figure 7–5 An example of routine activities.

Developing Goals and Objectives

Goals and objectives are essential elements of an effective intervention plan. Goals are simply statements on the IEP or IFSP that are long term in nature and state directionality. A goal statement will typically be written to reflect an increase in a behavior or skill. There are, however, instances when goals are written to decrease a behavior, such as in the case of severe and challenging behaviors. There are also occasions when a goal statement is written with the intent to maintain a skill at current levels.

Objectives, on the other hand, are substeps that constitute a goal. It is easy to think of objectives being much like the stairs on a staircase leading upward to where the goal statement can be found. Well-written objectives should have three major components: conditions, performance, and criteria.

I. Conditions

What is needed for the child to perform the behavior? Example: "Upon being seated at the table and given a cup full of water, John will drink from the cup unassisted across five independent trials."

The conditions in this example are as follows: "upon being seated at the table and given a cup full of water." Conditions are those things that are essential for performing the behavior or skill by the child or the circumstances in which the behavior will occur.

II. Performance

What will the child do? Example: "John will drink from the cup unassisted."

The performance component of an objective is simply the skill or behavior that the child is being asked to perform. What is it that you the teacher expect the child to do?

III. Criteria

What are the performance expectations? How will you determine whether or not a child has correctly performed the task, and how will you determine when a child has mastered the objective? In this case, "John will drink unassisted from the cup across five independent trials."

Performance criteria statements can be written to reflect speed in performing a task, accuracy, or quality. The important point to remember is that teachers must have an established criteria from which they evaluate students if they are to demonstrate measurable success on the part of the learner.

How are goals and objectives derived for a child? As was discussed in Chapter 6 on assessment, the information obtained from the assessment process should translate into the formation of instructional goals and objectives as illustrated in the following:

Development of Instructional Goals and Objectives

Stage 1: Assessment
Standardized instruments, ecological assessments, direct observation, and parent/family input.

Stage 2: Development of Instructional Program
Process data from assessment; identify strengths and areas of concern; prioritize goals/objectives; define instructional procedures; design positive behavioral support plan, instructional activities, and evaluation procedures.

Stage 3: Implementation of Instructional Program
Provide daily instruction on stated goals and objectives, collect performance data, and evaluate student progress toward attainment of objectives.

State 4: Evaluation of Progress and Outcomes
Utilizing a process evaluation system, evaluate the child's performance daily and weekly as stated in the instructional program based on stated goals and objectives or (desired outcomes). Modify instructional procedures if warranted based on evaluation data.

When designing instructional goals for a child, there are some other considerations we must attend to as we translate the assessment information into workable goals and objectives. If based on the assessment a child demonstrates in a set of skills, we can then determine that the child has acquired the skills, provided they are developmentally and age appropriate. With further assessment we can determine if the child is fluent in these skills (fluency can be defined by how consistent the child can perform the skills). If the child has fluency, we then can establish goals and objectives that will work toward the maintenance of the skills as well as their generalization or transfer to new and different conditions. These are examples of skills that a child could work on semi-independently or independently. Second, if a child displays the beginnings of a skill or behavior, then we can say the child is beginning to display emergence in these areas. These skills should then be targeted for instruction either individually or in groups. This is a strategy that is often employed with learners who have developmental delays or disabilities. This approach also integrates nicely into the NAEYC guidelines and does not seek in any way to violate those developmental principles of learning, yet seeks only to support individual children as needed in the area of instruction. Instruction may be direct or indirect, such as through the use of incidental teaching approaches. Vignette 7-2 provides a good illustration of teaching an emerging skill.

VIGNETTE 7-2: INSTRUCTIONAL PROGRAM FOR TEACHING HOW TO USE A SPOON

Consider the following example of teaching a young child aged twenty-four months to learn how to eat with a spoon. Generally in designing such a program several considerations must first be addressed. Is this an appropriate goal for a child of twenty-four months? Yes. It depends on the individual child, of course, but generally speaking this is a skill that could first emerge between fourteen and eighteen months in many children. However, special considerations should be given to children with oral/motor issues, such as in the areas of chewing and swallowing food. Cognition and motivation also play a role because often many children, including typically developing children, will show little or no interest in using a spoon to eat but will continue to use their hands.

In the example provided, let us consider Josh. Josh has been using his hands to accommodate his feeding until recently. His parents have encouraged Josh to eat with a spoon, but at this point Josh has not maintained his interest in doing so. Josh enjoys eating and feeding himself with his hands. He experiences no difficulty in chewing or swallowing, but does demonstrate a cognitive delay though no signs of motor delay. He also experiences a delay in the area of language. Given that Josh's parents want him to eat with a spoon, we have developed a program for teaching Josh this skill.

I. Objectives/Outcomes.
  A. Provided with the opportunity at regularly scheduled meal times, Josh will use his spoon to eat 100 percent of the time for five consecutive sessions. (This is consistent with the routines-based component of activities-based intervention.)
  B. Provided with the opportunity Josh will:
    1. Pick up and grasp the spoon.
    2. Scoop the food.
    3. Raise the spoon to his mouth.
    4. Remove food from the spoon, chew, and swallow the food.
    5. Repeat steps (1) through (5) until finished eating.

Each of these steps is a component on the task analysis associated with teaching Josh to eat independently with his spoon.

II. Assessment.
  A. Measurement of performance—percentage of steps performed to criteria based on the task analysis.
III. Teaching Environments.
  A. Teaching will be conducted at the center-based program with follow-up of procedures within the home setting.

IV. Task Structure/Action Steps.
   A. Backward chaining.
      1. One step of the task analysis will be taught at a time beginning with step (4):
         "Removing food from his spoon, chewing, and swallowing the food." The rationale for this approach is that this is the most naturally reinforcing step of the sequence, thus serving as a motivator for Josh to learn the task.
      2. The teacher will assist Josh through the remainder of the steps proceeding in a backward fashion moving from the last step to the first step.
      3. Performance criteria—completion of each step independently at 100 percent for three consecutive trials before introducing the next step in the sequence.
V. Instructional Prompts.
   A. System of most-to-least prompts.
      1. The teacher will pair verbal cues with physical prompts to assist Josh in grasping, scooping, and guiding food to his mouth.
      2. The teacher will fade physical prompts as Josh displays increased competence in his abilities to master each of these substeps.
      3. The teacher will fade prompts to include shadowing, light touches to Josh's hands when needed to steady or prompt.
      4. Prompts will gradually fade to verbal cues.
   B. Consequences.
      1. Verbal praise will be provided as reinforcement.
      2. Eating the food will serve as a naturally occurring reinforcer.
      3. Schedule of reinforcement: Praise will be provided frequently during this initial stage of implementation, gradually moving to intermittent reinforcement as a means of promoting increasing levels of independence.
VI. Maintenance and Generalization.
   A. Josh's parents will assist with the implementation of the same procedures at home as a means of promoting generalization.

With the applied example of Josh, we see the level of detail required in developing an instructional program that merges best and effective practices in PBS, ABI, and DAP for a child. The general components of an instructional program, goals, and objectives will remain the same, but the level of supports provided will be more intense as the child's level of needs intensifies. For a child with significant developmental delays or disabilities the level of supports would be much more in depth than in the example of Josh. In order to successfully support children in educational environments we must remain sensitive at all times to their individual support needs.

Generally, goals and objectives should be written in each of the major areas: cognitive, social, self-help, gross motor, fine motor, and communication.

There are several valuable resources to consult in the area of curriculum development. These will be presented at the conclusion of the chapter. Prepublished curricula can be extremely helpful in developing an instructional program for a child. They may be adapted to be more child- and setting-specific and serve as a tool for teachers in curriculum development for individual learners and/or classwide with multiple learners.

Designing Child-Centered Learning Environments

Child-centered learning environments are necessary in order to ensure the maximal growth and development in children. Environments that educate young children should provide organization and structure within the confines of a safe and nurturing environment. The level of structure provided within the physical setting can do so much to promote positive behavior and learning on the part of the child. There are, of course, state standards that govern the environments that serve to educate young children with respect to density (the number of children present in a given setting) and also for issues concerning the safety, health, and well-being of children in these environments. Zirpoli (1995) has indicated that classrooms serving large groups of children pose many problems. Some of these problems—including lack of caring on the part of caregivers and limited access to care providers—result in greater degrees of stress among children as evidenced by degrees of challenging behavior. Other factors with regard to the classroom can positively or negatively impact the learning and general social/emotional well-being of a child. Given these considerations some general guidelines are necessary with regard to structuring child-centered learning environments.

The NAEYC recommends that learning environments for children should protect their health and well-being and be supportive of their physiological needs for activity, stimulation, fresh air, rest, and nourishment. Effective programs provide a balance of rest and active movement for children throughout the course of the day. Also provided is the opportunity for outdoor experiences. Finally, a program must protect the child's psychological safety and promote a feeling of relaxation and comfort rather than an environment full of emotional stress (Bredekemp & Copple, 1997).

The physical structure of the classroom should have predesignated areas specific to types of activities. These include areas for individual work, group work, circle time, learning centers, play and leisure areas, snack, storage areas for toys and materials, and a sink for cleanup. Individual areas can be identified by carpet squares, colored wall areas, or small area rugs.

A plan should be developed to allow for maximum movement within the classroom, as well as adaptations for children in wheelchairs. A classroom schedule, aside from individual schedules for each child, should be developed that will designate the flow of the classroom to accommodate for all children's needs and to minimize the number of children in the same area at different times of the day. A plan for easing children to and from transitions throughout the day is also an essential part of providing a supportive learning environment. It is important that procedures for diapering, assisting with toileting, hand washing, and other such procedures are well defined as part of the classroom routine for both caregivers and children.

A detailed list of appropriate practices related to providing an appropriate environment for children has been developed by Bredekamp and Copple (1997) as part of the NAEYC's "developmentally appropriate practice in early childhood education." Examples of these include:

Infants

- Walls are painted with lead-free, easy-to-clean paint.
- Soft carpeting and flooring are easy to clean and neutral in color.
- The materials have bright colors that infants enjoy.
- Pictures of infants and their family members are hung on walls at heights that infants can see.
- Auditory stimulation in the form of music is provided.
- Play areas are comfortable with pillows, foam rubber mats, and soft carpeting where babies can lie on their stomachs or backs and be held and read to.
- Space is arranged so that children can enjoy moments of quiet play by themselves, have ample space to roll over and move freely, and can crawl toward interesting objects.
- Toys provided are responsive to the child's actions.
- High chairs are used only when needed.
- The infant sleeping area is away from active play and eating areas.
- Infants have their own diapering supplies and extra clothes within easy reach of the changing table.
- Storage for disinfectants, gloves, and plastic bags is clearly labeled.
- Adults follow health and safety procedures including proper hand washing methods and the "universal precautions" to limit the spread of infectious disease.
- The diapering and food storage areas are separate, and caregivers do not move from one to the other without careful hand washing and other necessary procedures.

Toddlers

- Adults warmly greet toddlers and their parents by name when they arrive.
- Children are acknowledged for their accomplishments and helped to feel increasingly competent and in control of themselves.
- Adults respond quickly to toddlers' cries or other signs of distress, recognizing that toddlers have limited language with which to communicate their needs.
- Adults respect children's developing preferences for familiar objects, foods, and people.
- Adults model the type of interactions with others that they want children to develop.
- Adults patiently redirect toddlers to help guide children toward controlling their own impulses and behavior.
- Children have daily opportunities for exploratory activity, such as water and sand play, painting, and playing with clay or play dough.
- Adults respect children's schedules with regard to eating and sleeping.

- Caregivers plan a transition into naptime with a predictable sequence of events.
- Caregivers organize classroom space into interest or activity areas, including areas for concentrated small group play, being alone, art/water/sand and other messy activities, dramatic play, and construction.
- The environment contains private spaces, with room for no more than two children, that are easily supervised by adults.
- Emergency evacuation plans are posted on the wall near the daily record charts; a bag of emergency supplies and child emergency forms are immediately accessible.
- The group size and the ratio of adults to children are limited to allow for the intimate, interpersonal atmosphere and high level of supervision that toddlers require. Maximum group size is twelve, with one adult for no more than six toddlers, preferably fewer. Staffing patterns limit the number of different adults toddlers relate to each day.

Promoting Successful Inclusion

As we know, successful inclusion consists of a number of elements. Among these elements is how open and accepting the teacher is to the idea of inclusion. Attitude is a central feature in the success of inclusion no matter what the age group of the children (Smith, Polloway, Patton, & Dowdy, 1998). Another element is the professional skill necessary to work with children who experience diverse learning needs. The key is that children are children and that learning falls within a continuum. The degree to which a teacher values all children and accepts and embraces diversity is central to the success of inclusion.

Teachers within inclusive settings are also in need of administrative support that embraces the philosophy of inclusion in both theory and practice. Children educated within these settings need to feel a sense of connection and belonging. These elements are transcended within the environment and in how the teacher functions and serves the educational needs of all children as well as in how children are valued within the school setting on the whole. All children are to be valued and accepted for who they are, the gifts they bring, and the needs they place before us. Educational settings reflect a small microcosm of society in terms of diversity, and through such diversity learning is enhanced.

With respect to inclusion of young children in early childhood settings there is some concern, however, given that NAEYC's standards of developmentally appropriate practice recommend that teachers not conduct formal instruction at the preschool level as indicated by Udell, Peters, and Piazza (1998). As pointed out by Udell and associates (1998) early childhood special education is founded on the premise that intense early intervention maximizes the learning potential of young children with disabilities and minimizes the impact of disability on the quality of life of the child. So the obvious question becomes: "How does one merge these differing philosophies within an inclusive early childhood setting?" Rather than view one approach as correct and the other as incorrect, it would be far better to look at how one can strengthen the other. Positive behavioral supports, activities-based intervention, and developmentally appropriate practices attempt to do this by embedding their philosophies within the context of naturally occurring sequences within an educational setting. As the authors point out, the convergence of these philosophies builds a model of support depending on the individual needs of a child, and through the use of these strategies within a classroom all children benefit in both a direct and indirect manner.

Bricker (1995) stated that there are three elements that directly influence successful inclusion of young children. These are attitudes, resources, and curricula. Bricker also points out that each of these elements is necessary to make inclusion a reality and that they cannot stand alone in isolation and produce the desired effect. Bricker (1995) elaborates on this by stating that "successful inclusion is a multidimensional and complex process worthy of more study than it has received" (p. 188). We have discussed the importance of attitude, but how these attitudes and beliefs are shaped is worth exploring. Attitudes toward successful inclusion are built on the foundation that persons involved in the delivery of educational services and supports to young children have a positive regard for all children—an acceptance of children for who they are as individuals. These individuals must be committed to supporting children in inclusive environments, and their beliefs must translate into actions that support these efforts toward inclusive education (Bricker, 1995).

In the model provided by Bricker (1995) resources are equally as important. As she has indicated, access to specialists is vital. This is especially true in rural and underserved areas of the country where early intervention specialists are not easily found. Thus attitude without resources in the form of technical assistance is not enough to produce the changes needed to promote successful inclusion. Many programs need the assistance of a cadre of professionals trained in working with young children with disabilities to provide educational and related services and supports needed for successful inclusion. Educators not having experience in working with children with disabilities will be in need of technical assistance and training to support the educational needs of the child. Bricker (1995) also adds the importance of collaboration in the planning and decision-making process when facilitating inclusion of young children, as well as the need for appropriate environments and equipment to accommodate children with disabilities. Basically this process involves a joint effort between administrators, teachers, parents, and all direct care staff in planning and decision-making efforts.

Finally, the third component of Bricker's (1995) model is the curriculum. She asserts that successful inclusion of young children with disabilities hinges on curricular content that provides consistency and support centered on naturalistic approaches, relevant activities, and interactions among children. (See Figure 7–6.)

Specific inclusionary practices are individual- and setting-specific, but one example of successful strategies for promoting the inclusion of young children with autism is described by Schwartz, Billingsley, and McBride (1998). Autism is a pervasive developmental disorder characterized by the presence of markedly atypical or impaired development in social interaction and communication and a markedly restricted repertoire of activity and interests (DSM IV, 1994). Schwartz and colleagues (1998) describe strategies that have been effective in the Alice H. Hayden Preschool at the University of Washington. They recommend the following for promoting positive learning outcomes for children

Figure 7–6 Successful inclusion promotes inter-action among children.

with autism, including the development of relationships and participation as members of the class. These include:

1. *Teaching communicative and social competence.* Functional communication skills are taught to children with autism using gestures, pictures, and symbols as a means for promoting communication and understanding, precisely the areas of learning most affected by autism. They also teach functional speech skills such as social interaction and imitation.
2. *Using instructional approaches within the natural context.* The program reinforces the importance of teaching skills within the context of developmentally appropriate activities and typical classroom routines.
3. *Teaching and providing opportunities for independence.* This goal is accomplished through building in opportunities for choice within a child's daily routine, the use of individualized photo activity schedules, regularly scheduled routines, and freedom to interact with peers and participate in classroom activities throughout the day.
4. *Proactively building a classroom community.* Individual supports are provided to all children so that they might more fully participate and succeed in their attempts at learning. Activities are planned that will promote active engagement of all children; planning is conducted to promote group interaction such as large and small group activities. Large group activities include circle time, singing, and story time. Small group activities involve children in cooperative games, projects, and preacademic activities.
5. *Promoting generalization and maintenance of skills.* Planned generalization and maintenance of skills is an important component of any program. As pointed out by Schwartz and associates (1998), this is best accomplished through targeting skills for instruction that are meaningful in the life of the child, using instructional prompts sparingly and gradually fading them over time as the child becomes proficient in a skill, using

naturally distributed trials consisting of direct instruction and naturally occurring opportunities for incidental teaching and learning, and, finally, using common materials for teaching that the child has ready and frequent access to over time.

Many of these strategies have been previously elaborated on in the chapter, but here we witness the incorporation of these approaches within a broad programmatic context. The authors cite some of the conclusions from utilizing these methods to promote successful inclusion of children with autism and offer these insights:

> View children holistically . . . , view the outcomes of inclusion broadly rather than as simply the attainment of discrete and isolated skills. In other words, what are the global outcomes for the child as a result of inclusion such as greater participation as a member of the class, greater degrees of independence, and greater lifestyle outcomes. (Shwartz et al., 1998)

Inclusion has been the center of debate among general education and special education professionals since its inception. Clearly, there is a value to the concept if it is done and done well. Rather than focus on the arguments that divide us as professionals, it would be far more advantageous to recognize the value of all children, their need for love and support, the rights and freedoms they are entitled to, and the role we as educators play in facilitating enhanced learning and lifestyle outcomes for them and their families. Our energies should be devoted to the study and refinement of support models that will accommodate the range of diversity encountered in our society with emphasis on total quality for all. As pointed out by Bricker (1995), research into how to promote successful inclusion of children and the critical elements associated with this process that will foster the growth and development of every child is desperately needed.

Methods of Evaluating Intervention Effectiveness and Outcomes

Program evaluation is a necessary ingredient of any successful early childhood educational program in order to ensure the attainment of measured outcomes, identify areas in need of improvement, and affirm or establish program priorities. Evaluation can be done at the macro (programmatic) level or at the micro (individual child) level.

There are basically two models most commonly used in program evaluation. These include formative evaluation, in which the program utilizes best and effective practice in the development of educational services and supports for young children. Summative evaluation examines the program after implementation with respect to the degree in which the program meets its stated goals and objectives.

Evaluation must also be conducted at the individual level with regard to the IEP or IFSP. Basically this involves a management by objective approach that is child and family friendly in that the services and supports provided to the child and family meet or exceed those as written in the individualized education program or the individualized family service plan. The IEP/IFSP serves as a benchmark against which to measure our performance in the delivery of educational services and supports.

A framework for evaluating the IEP/IFSP for infants, toddlers, and preschoolers with disabilities was recommended by Notari-Syverson and Shuster (1995). They developed five basic criteria for examining the quality of IEP/IFSP objectives. These were functionality (how useful is the skill for the child in his/her daily environment?); generality (can the skill be generalized across a variety of environments, materials, and people?); instructional context (can the skill be taught within the context of naturally occurring routines?); measurability (the extent to which the skill can be measured for evaluation purposes); and hierarchical relation between long-range goal and short-term objective (is the short-term objective a substep critical to the achievement of the long range goal?).

In short, program evaluation is needed at all levels to ensure quality assurance in the delivery of best and effective practices to young children and their families. Program evaluation is intended to develop and maintain the highest level of standards in the development and delivery of services and supports. For teachers, it enables us to accurately measure the progress of a young child toward the attainment of educational goals and objectives that will hopefully lead to increased quality-of-life outcomes.

Summary

The purpose of this chapter was to familiarize you with best and effective intervention practices used in the delivery of educational services and supports to young children and their families. A key element in the design of child- and family-centered intervention is the social validity of goals and objectives. In working with young children and families, practitioners must learn to value and rely on the input of parents and family members as it pertains to the development of intervention goals. Aside from their role as team members, parents and families know their children and the needs of their children and families firsthand. Our role as intervention agents is to build and provide a model of support around each child and family's individual strengths and areas of challenge and to serve in the role as facilitator of shared and valued outcomes for both child and family. The importance of goals and objectives examined from a longitudinal focus was also explored as was their relevance with respect to the overall quality-of-life enhancement for children and families. Often, teachers and programs are concerned about only one year at a time in the life of the child, but in the case of all children long-range planning is considered important for preparing for transitions and for securing desired outcomes that contribute to the growth and development of the child and the support of family goals.

Innovative practices such as positive behavioral supports, activity-based intervention, and developmentally appropriate practices were described in depth as well as their value for all children across learning environments. The merger of these approaches was explored with applied examples provided throughout the chapter that referenced these principles in action. The role of these approaches in the design of educational goals and objectives and how these principles can be embedded in the design of learning environments for young children was also provided from both a philosophical and applied programmatic perspective.

Specific strategies for designing programs to promote successful inclusion were described including the importance of developing a program committed to the ideals in terms of both philosophy and how this influences practice. Critical elements of inclusion were described from the work of Bricker (1995), which identified the importance of three components in facilitating successful inclusion. These were attitude, resources, and curricula. In addition, examples of implementing inclusionary practices in preschool environments were examined.

Finally, program evaluation was explored at both the programmatic and individual child levels. The importance of program evaluation in the measurement of stated goals and objectives is critical in the development and delivery of quality services and supports to children and families.

Chapter 7 Suggested Activities and Resources

Activities

1. Have the class examine and critique a series of IEP/IFSPs with respect to how closely they adhere to best and effective practice in the areas of positive behavioral supports and activity-based intervention. Have the students reflect on how these documents could be enhanced and prepared in a manner that better reflects these ideals.

2. Arrange for students to individually meet with parents and families and interview them about their perspectives on planning educational programs for their children. Stress the importance of really listening and being in sync with parent and family perspectives as they complete this activity.

3. Present the class with applied examples of young children and families, and develop a MAPS session for these children and families. Follow up this activity with a session devoted to reflecting on the experience and have students self-evaluate related to how closely the session met with the goals of the MAPS process.

4. Have students generate a list of program quality indicators with respect to intervention practices and discuss them in class related to current practicum experiences.

5. Provide students with copies of curricula such as the *Carolina Curriculum for Infants and Toddlers with Special Needs* (2nd ed.), developed by N. Johnson-Martin, K. G. Jens, S. M. Attermeier, and B. J. Hacker, and published by Paul H. Brookes; the *Carolina Curriculum for Preschoolers with Special Needs,* developed by N. Johnson-Martin, S. M. Attermeier, and B. J. Hacker, also published by Paul H. Brookes; *Assessment, Evaluation, and Programming System (AEPS) for Infants and Children,* edited by D. Bricker, and published by Paul H. Brookes; and *Transdisciplinary Play-Based Intervention Guidelines for Developing a Meaningful Curriculum for Young Children,* by T. W. Linder, and published by Paul H. Brookes. Discuss how these curricula have been developed and how they might be applied in educational settings serving young children. Also provide students with applied examples and have them utilize and adapt these curricula for individual children.

Selected Resources

The following resources will provide the reader with a more in-depth understanding of effective intervention.

1. *Books/curricula*

Bricker, D., & Cripe, T. W. (1993). *An Activity-Based Approach to Early Intervention*. Baltimore: Paul H. Brookes Publishing Co.

Bricker, D., & Waddell, M. (1996). *AEPS Curriculum for Three to Six Years*. Baltimore: Paul H. Brookes Publishing Co.

Linder, T. W. (1993). *Transdisciplinary Play-Based Intervention: Guidelines for Developing a Meaningful Curriculum for Young Children*. Baltimore: Paul H. Brookes Publishing Co.

2. *Videos*

Bricker, D., Veltman, P., & Munkres, A. (1995). *Activity-Based Intervention*. Baltimore: Paul H. Brookes Publishing Co.

Reif, S. (1995). *ADHD: Inclusive Instruction and Collaborative Practices*. Port Chester, NY: National Professional Resources Inc.

3. *Articles*

Division for Early Childhood (1998). Division for Early Childhood (DEC) Position Statement on Interventions for Challenging Behavior. *Young Exceptional Children, 1,* 11.

Fox, L., Dunlap, G., & Philbrick, L. A. (1997). Providing Individual Supports to Young Children with Autism and Their Families. *Journal of Early Intervention, 21,* 1–14.

Grisham-Brown, J., & Hemmeter, M. L. (1998). Writing IEP Goals and Objectives: Reflecting an Activity-Based Approach to Instruction for Young Children with Disabilities. *Young Exceptional Children, 1,* 2–10.

Horner, R. H., & Carr, E. G. (1997). Behavioral Support for Students with Severe Disabilities: Functional Assessment and Comprehensive Intervention. *Journal of Special Education, 31,* 84–104.

References

American Psychiatric Association (1994). *Diagnostic and Statistical Manual of Mental Disorders* (4th ed.). Washington, DC: Author.

Bamberra, L. M., & Koger, F. (1996). Opportunities for Daily Choice Making. *Innovations: AAMR's Research to Practice Series*. Washington, DC: American Association on Mental Retardation.

Bredekamp, S., & Copple, C. (1997). *Developmentally Appropriate Practice in Early Childhood Programs*. Washington, DC: National Association for the Education of Young Children.

Bricker, D. (1993). *Volume 1—AEPS Measurement for Birth to Three Years*. Baltimore: Paul H. Brookes Publishing Co.

Bricker, D. (1995). The Challenge of Inclusion. *Journal of Early Intervention, 19,* 179–194.

Bricker, D., & Cripe, J. W. (1995). *An Activity-Based Approach to Early Intervention.* Baltimore: Paul H. Brookes Publishing Co.

Bricker, D., & Pretti-Frontczak, K. (1996). *Volume 3—AEPS Measurement for Three to Six Years.* Baltimore: Paul H. Brookes Publishing Co.

Bricker, D., & Waddell, M. (1996). *AEPS Curriculum for Three to Six Years.* Baltimore: Paul H. Brookes Publishing Co.

Cripe, J., Slentz, K., & Bricker, D. (1993). *AEPS Curriculum for Birth to Three Years.* Baltimore: Paul H. Brookes Publishing Co.

Division for Early Childhood/Council for Exceptional Children (1996). DEC/CEC Personnel Standards for Early Education and Early Intervention: Guidelines for Licensure in Early Childhood Special Education. In NAEYC (Eds.), *Guidelines for Preparation of Early Childhood Professionals* (pp. 29–43). Washington, DC: NAEYC.

Dunlap, G., & Fox, L. (1996). Early Intervention and Serious Problem Behavior: A Comprehensive Approach. In L. K. Koegal, R. L. Koegal, & G. Dunlap (Eds.), *Positive Behavioral Support: Including People with Difficult Behavior in the Community* (pp. 31–50). Baltimore: Paul H. Brookes Publishing Co.

Forest, M., & Lusthaus, E. (1990). Everyone Belongs with the MAPS Action Planning System. *Teaching Exceptional Children, 22,* 36–39.

Fox, L., Dunlap, G., & Philbrick, L. A. (1997). Providing Individual Supports to Young Children and Their Families. *Journal of Early Intervention, 21,* 1–14.

Heward, W. L. (1996). *Exceptional Children: An Introduction to Special Education* (5th ed.). Englewood Cliffs, NJ: Merrill/Prentice-Hall.

Hogdon, L. (1995). *Visual Strategies for Improving Communication.* Troy, MI: Quirk Roberts Publishing.

Horner, R. H., Dunlap, G., Koegal, R. L., Carr, E. G., Sailor, W., Anderson, J., Albin, R. W., & O'Neill, R. E. (1990). Toward a Technology of Nonaversive Behavioral Support. *Journal of the Association for Persons with Severe Handicaps, 15,* 125–132.

Kazdin, A. E. (1989). *Behavior Modification in Applied Settings* (4th ed.). Pacific Grove: CA: Brooks/Cole.

Linder, T. W. (1993). *Transdisciplinary Play-Based Intervention: Guidelines for Developing a Meaningful Curriculum for Young Children.* Baltimore: Paul H. Brookes Publishing Co.

Lombardi, J. (1992). *Beyond Transition: Ensuring Continuity in Early Childhood Services.* University of Illinois at Urbana-Champaign, Children's Research Center.

(ERIC Document Reproduction Service No. EDO-PS-92-3)

National Association for the Education of Young Children (1996). *Guidelines for Preparation of Early Childhood Education Professionals.* Washington, DC: Author.

Notari-Syverson, A. R., & Shuster, S. L. (1995). Putting Real Life Skills into IEP/IFSP's for Infants and Young Children. *Teaching Exceptional Children, 27,* 29–32.

Smith, T. E. C., Polloway, E. A., Patton, J. R., & Dowdy, C. A. (1998). *Teaching Students with Special Needs in Inclusive Settings* (2nd ed.). Boston: Allyn & Bacon.

Schwartz, I. S., Billingsley, F. F., & McBride, B. M. (1998). Including Children with Autism in Inclusive Preschools: Strategies That Work. *Young Exceptional Children, 2,* 19–26.

Strain, P. S., & Hemmeter, M. L. (1997). Keys to Being Successful When Confronted with Challenging Behavior. *Young Exceptional Children, 1,* 2–8.

Turnbull, A. P., & Ruef, M. (1996). Family Perspectives on Inclusive Lifestyle Issues for People with Problem Behavior. *Exceptional Children, 63,* 211–227.

Turnbull, A. P., & Turnbull, H. R. (1996). Group Action Planning as a Strategy for Providing Comprehensive Family Support. In L. K. Koegal, R. L. Koegal, & G. Dunlap (Eds.), *Positive Behavioral Support: Including People with Difficult Behavior in the Community* (pp. 99–114). Baltimore: Paul H. Brookes Publishing Co.

Udell, T., Peters, J., & Piazza, T. P. (1998). From Philosophy to Practice in Inclusive Early Childhood Programs. *Teaching Exceptional Children, 30,* 44–49.

Vygotsky, L. S. (1978). *Mind in Society: The Development of Higher Psychological Functions.* Cambridge, MA: Harvard University Press.

Wheeler, J. J. (1991). Educating Students with Severe Disabilities in General Education Settings: A Resource Manual. *ERIC Clearinghouse on Disabilities and Gifted Education,* Document Number ED 336 899.

Wheeler, J. J. (1996). The Use of Interactive Focus Groups to Aid in the Identification of Perceived Service and Support Delivery Needs of Persons with Developmental Disabilities and Their Families. *Education and Training in Mental Retardation and Developmental Disabilities, 31,* 294–303.

Wheeler, J. J. (1998). Reducing Challenging Behaviors in Learners with Developmental Disabilities through the Modification of Instructional Practices. In A. Hilton & R. Ringlaben (Eds.), *Best and Promising Practices in Developmental Disabilities* (pp. 263–272). Austin, TX: Pro-Ed.

Zirpoli, S. B. (1995). Designing Environments for Optimal Behavior. In T. J. Zirpoli (1995), *Understanding and Affecting the Behavior of Young Children* (pp. 122–150). Englewood Cliffs, NJ: Merrill/Prentice-Hall.

Section III
Issues

OVERVIEW

Section III: of the text deals with the topic of issues in inclusive early childhood education. Chapter 8 of this section addresses the issue of cultural diversity. Today's society is reflective of a level of diversity never before experienced in our country. A little more than twenty years ago, young children with disabilities and their families were not afforded the same degree of access as they experience today with regard to specialized educational services and supports. Other underrepresented groups including non-English speaking cultures have grown considerably and are reflected in today's early childhood settings. Professionals must be provided with training that places emphasis on developing cultural competency including an ability to respect all diversity and to embrace children and families for simply who they are—children and families. Educators must be made aware of and sensitive to the challenges that children and families of underrepresented groups confront in dealing with professionals who may represent the "dominant culture."

Educators must also view the diversity that children present not as an issue but rather as an enrichment and a contribution. This philosophy and practice must also extend to children with disabilities. We are of a culturally diverse society, and our educational programs and services to young children and families simply mirror this fact. We the authors believe that all children should and can be educated within inclusive educational settings provided that responsible inclusion is practiced. Such a model reflects an embracing and acceptance of diversity and the richness it has to offer us all.

Chapter 9, entitled Future Directions in Inclusive Early Childhood Education, is a collection of topics related to future directions, including consumer and professional advocacy, research, public policy, technology and the advances of medical science (such as recent research on early brain development), diversity, families, the processes and practices associated with the field, and, finally, personnel preparation. The chapter represents a compilation of empirically and socially relevant findings expressed by each of the authors. Specific areas have been designated for each of the contributors given their area of professional expertise. It is the intention of the authors that this chapter will make a contribution not only to the text but more importantly to the professional development of you the student and consumer of this text.

As a developing professional each of you must be alert to and cognizant of the trends and directions that your field will take over the years. This practice not only will keep you employable but will sharpen your skills as a professional so that you might be a better advocate for your profession, a better service/support provider to the children and families with whom you work, and a better voter, able to influence public policy as it applies to your professional interests and able to make a difference in the policies and laws that are enacted and influence the lives of children and families. Finally, the purpose of this chapter is to help you envision the possibilities that exist and to aid you in reflecting on the past, present, and future factors that influence the delivery of services and supports to children and families and the professionals who serve them.

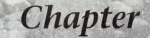

*Respecting Cultural Diversity**

Chapter

8

INTRODUCTION

Four major divisions characterize this chapter. First, the concept of cultural diversity is examined. To that end, a definition of the term is provided. Looking at the broader aspects of the term, elements and components that constitute it are established. One of the main reasons for including the present chapter in the text is the ever changing demographics that show the growing presence of ethnic and racial groups as the majority populations in the United States. Hence, this factor, too, will be addressed.

Second, the topic of responding to cultural diversity in early childhood education will be observed in relation to multicultural education in order to establish the focus of the chapter text. Third, the three issues of positive behavioral supports, activity-based intervention, and developmentally appropriate practices are explored with regard to cultural diversity. In particular, the author looks at how these concepts acknowledge cultural diversity. The chapter concludes by providing direction on meeting the challenge of diversity in inclusive early childhood education. The teacher, the curriculum, and the partnership between education and the home are discussed.

Here are the objectives that the reader will address in Chapter 8. You should be able to:

- Understand the terms *culture, cultural diversity, cultural differences, ethnic groups, values,* and *value systems.*
- Demonstrate an awareness of the changing demographics of the population of the United States.
- Distinguish between cultural diversity in schools, often referred to as multicultural education, and cultural diversity in early childhood education.
- Examine cultural diversity with regard to the contemporary issues of positive behavioral supports, activity-based intervention, and developmentally appropriate practices.
- Demonstrate an awareness of resources available to address the challenge of structuring general education to facilitate the success of diverse learners.

---

*Written by Dr. Elouise Jackson, PhD., Associate Professor of Special Education in the Department of Curriculum and Instruction at Tennessee Technological University.

What Is Cultural Diversity?

As we begin the discussion, explanation of a series of terms will be helpful. Descriptors outlined by Lockwood, Allen, Ford, and Sparks (1991) follow and are modified in order to set the stage for establishing common understandings.

- *Culture* is represented by the traditions, customs, values, belief systems, and social habits of a particular group.
- *Cultural differences* are those qualities and practices that people exercise to define themselves as a cultural group. These can be cultural groups or subgroups existing within the larger cultural group. Cultural group/subgroup differences can coexist with and within the larger cultures, but are often misunderstood.
- *Cultural diversity* is a conglomeration of the multiple cultures and languages introduced by people of different races and lifestyles that contribute to the enrichment of society. This definition is enhanced by the one put forth by NAEYC (1996).
- *Linguistically and culturally diverse* is an educational term used by the U.S. Department of Education to define children enrolled in educational programs who are either non-English-proficient (NEP) or limited-English-proficient (LEP). Educators use this phrase, linguistically and culturally diverse, to identify children from homes and communities where English is not the primary language of communication (Garcia, 1991).
- Language is seen as playing a significant role in ethnic and cultural identity (Corderio, Reagan, & Martinez, 1994).

Yet another aspect of the definition must be included in order to obtain a more comprehensive description of the term *cultural diversity.* Cushner, McClelland, and Stafford (1992) not only identify children of multiple cultures but recognize children and youth who may have special educational and other needs (the hearing impaired, the visually impaired).

- *Ethnic groups* have several distinguishing characteristics. They share a common ancestry, history, tradition, and community. Identification with ethnic groups may be involuntary, although individual identification with a group may be voluntary (Lockwood et al., 1991).
- *Values* represent the major influences in a person's life. They are the highest priorities and guide cultural decision making.
- *Value systems* also vary among individuals and are diversified among subcultural groups within ethnic populations (Brito, 1980).

The United States is becoming a multicultural society (Holden, 1990; Riche, 1991; *U.S. News and World Report,* 1991). The 1990s witnessed continued growth of Hispanic, black, and Asian peoples while the still significant white majority continued to decline. Rapid growth among racial and ethnic groups remains high, particularly in the younger age groups (Holden, 1990). Holden reports that, according to the Population Resource Center, by 2030 one-third of the population will be Hispanic, black, and Asian. By 2000, one-third of school-aged children will represent diverse ethnic and racial groups. The United States is expected to become a nation with no racial or ethnic majority during the twenty-first century (Riche, 1991). With this background in mind, let us proceed to look at the difference between the concept of responding to cultural diversity in early childhood education and that of multicultural education. This step will further set the stage for exploring and understanding the case for respecting cultural diversity in early childhood education.

Cultural Diversity: In Schools and in Early Childhood Education

Multicultural Education in Schools

In short, multicultural education in the United States is a concept or idea that all students—regardless of gender, social class, ethnic, racial, or cultural characteristics—should have an equal opportunity to learn in school (Banks, 1997; Miller-Lachmann & Taylor, 1995). A key impetus for its momentum was the issues resulting from the civil rights movement of the 1960s. Ethnic groups, specifically African Americans, followed by other groups, demanded that the schools and other educational institutions reform their curricula to reflect their experiences, histories, cultures, and perspectives. Banks describes four levels of integration of multicultural content that have evolved. Level 1, the contributions approach, focuses on heroes, holidays, and discrete cultural elements. Level 2, the additive approach, blends content concepts, themes, and perspectives into the curriculum without changing its structure. The transformation approach, Level 3, modifies the structure of the curriculum in order for students to view concepts, issues, events, and themes from the perspectives of diverse ethnic and cultural groups. At Level 4, the social action approach, students make decisions on important social issues and take action to solve them. Banks notes that the four approaches are often mixed and blended in actual teaching situations. Other scholars have also classified multicultural education approaches (Gibson, 1984; Lynch, 1989).

The task of structuring general education environments to facilitate the success of learners with special needs is an important challenge confronting educators today (Voltz, 1995). In their discussion of school inclusion and multicultural issues in special education, Meyer, Harry, and Sapon-Shevin (1997) use the term *inclusive curricula* as they address ways ability-disability can be incorporated into the practices of teaching and learning. Their examples are exemplified through the four levels of integration of multicultural content presented by Banks (1997).

As part of a national effort to influence the delivery of comprehensive and meaningful educational and related services to children with disabilities, gifts, and/or talents, the Division for Culturally and Linguistically Diverse Exceptional Learners (DDEL) of the Council for Exceptional Children has started a publication series entitled *Multiple Voices for Ethnically Diverse Exceptional Learners*. The primary purpose of DDEL is to provide the forum for understanding and addressing the needs of exceptional learners from diverse ethnic, linguistic, and cultural heritages (Ford, 1995).

Multicultural education is also a process. As a process, it seeks to accept and affirm the pluralism that students, communities, and teachers represent (Nieto, 1992). Bennett (1995) further describes the process as one whereby a person becomes multicultural or develops competencies in multiple ways of perceiving, evaluating, believing, and doing. Fostering understanding and acceptance is both a domestic and international concern given the interdependence among all nations of the world. Strategic vehicles of the process are the curriculum, instructional procedures, and interaction among the school, students, and home. A major outcome is the change of instruction and learning approaches so that all students have equal opportunities to learn in educational institutions (Banks, 1997). The reader is encouraged to pursue more in-depth reading on multicultural education in schools for a broader base of knowledge.

Cultural Diversity and Early Childhood Education

The United States is expected to become a nation with no racial or ethnic majority during the twenty-first century (Riche, 1991). Today, the population of children below the age of six years is becoming increasingly diverse (Clark, 1995). Very young children come to know that color, language, gender, and physical ability differences are connected to privilege and power. Therefore, we must not underestimate the ability of children to comprehend what they see and hear. Very young children can be taught anti-bias identity and attitude (Derman-Sparks and the A.B.C. Task Force, 1989). (See Figure 8-1.)

Second, young children must know that their culture and language, integral parts of self-identity, are accepted and respected (Clark, 1995). NAEYC's position statement (1996) on responding to linguistic and cultural diversity specifies that educators must accept the legitimacy of children's home language, re-

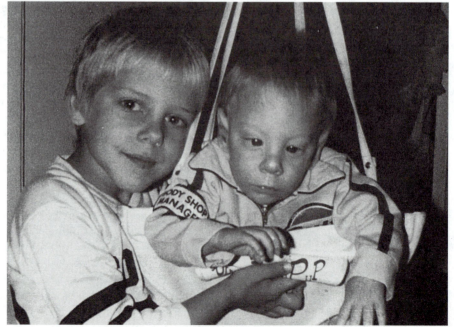

Figure 8–1 Young children are instinctively accepting of one another.

spect (hold in high regard) and value (esteem, appreciate) the home culture, and promote and encourage the active involvement and support of all families. Early childhood educators must remember that education settings can be unpleasant if cultural influence is not acknowledged, valued, and acted upon in curricular decisions. What is needed is culturally responsive education practices programs that actively engage youngsters and help them build upon their own sense of identity (Rodd, 1996). (See Figure 8-2.)

Two resources bear mentioning in the effort to respond to the ever increasing diversity of children enrolled in early childhood programs. One is a document developed by the Division for Early Childhood (DEC) of the Council for Exceptional Children. The *Recommended Practices: Indicators of Quality in Programs for Infants and Young Children with Special Needs and Their Families* (DEC Task Force on Recommended Practices, 1993) calls attention to culture as well as curriculum content. A second resource is the *Anti-Bias Curriculum: Tools for Empowering Young Children,* published by the National Association for the Education of Young Children. The book provides information helpful in dealing with issues of race, ethnicity, and disabilities.

Kendall (1996) outlines five primary goals of multicultural education in preschool classrooms:

1. To teach children to respect others' cultures and values as well as their own.
2. To help all children learn to function successfully in a multicultural, multiracial society.
3. To develop a positive self-concept in those children who are most affected by racism—children of color.
4. To help all children experience in positive ways both their differences as culturally diverse people and their similarities as human beings.
5. To allow children to experience people of diverse cultures working together as unique parts of a whole community (p. 10).

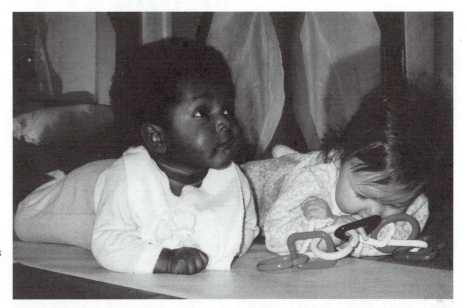

Figure 8–2 Children's cultural origins should be respected and acknowledged.

Cultural Diversity and Contemporary Issues

This section will look at cultural diversity in relation to three current trends that are receiving much attention in early childhood education. These trends are positive behavioral supports (PBS), activity-based intervention (ABI), and developmentally appropriate practices (DAP).

Cultural Diversity and PBS

Four descriptors summarize the essence of the PBS approach:

1. Nonpunitive responses to children's behavior.
2. Understanding what is developmentally appropriate for the child and having behavioral requirements that match the child's developmental abilities.
3. Providing a learning environment that is designed and managed to facilitate the desired behaviors.
4. Ensuring that responses to undesired behavior are positive, specific to the behavior, and intended to teach and nurture.

Respecting cultural diversity in light of applying positive behavioral supports in the guidance of child behavior entails observing two key factors concerning the teachers. One factor is an established level of self-awareness; the second is a consideration of particular aspects of culture in working with diverse families. Harry (1997), in relating personal experiences working with families, suggests that at the outset we rethink the meaning of the word *values*. She subscribes to an understanding of our values as "belief systems—not facts." She also says we should keep in mind that values represent the major influences in a person's life. They are the highest priorities and guide cultural decision making. Value systems vary among individuals and are diversified among subcultural groups within ethnic populations (Brito, 1980). Harry (1997) reminds us of the relativity of our own perspectives. By remembering this it will be much easier to respect beliefs and practices that seem very different from our own.

Two controversial issues commonly exist regarding parenting styles. One is the issue of whether parenting should reflect authoritarian or democratic relationships between adults and children. A second is the use of corporal punishment. Considering these two issues and the attributes of the PBS approach, contrasting views automatically arise. At this point the question is: How can professionals assist parents in situations where our help is desired? Here is where the factors of self-awareness and consideration of aspects of culture come into play. When there is obvious difference in belief systems, Harry (1997) suggests we seek ways to add to, rather than try to change, the parents' repertoire of disciplinary methods by offering alternatives in areas where parents express a need. For example, if there are occasions where the parent thinks that a particular kind of disciplinary procedure is not working, the professional can suggest alternatives.

Family functioning, an element or aspect of culture, might be considered here. One can observe the roles of family members, the focus of decision making, rules of interaction, and cooperation and sharing. Standards for children's independence and the way in which a family relates to others outside the family context are additional variables. What actually occurs within a family, that is, in its manner of functioning, exemplifies its own specific culture. The professional might also consider that external relationships may be affected by religious beliefs, health practices, child-rearing patterns and expectations, the family's perceptions of outside assistance and intervention, and their view of the role of educators and education (Lockwood et al., 1991; Wayman et al., 1991).

Harry (1997) presents five steps (or ways of thinking) toward cultural reciprocity that professionals can develop through practice:

1. Identify the issues that divide you and the family you're working with.
2. Identify the underlying beliefs/values that underlie the family's practices.
3. Ask about the beliefs and values that underlie the family's practices.
4. Lay out both sets of beliefs explicitly for discussion, taking care to present them as two different but equally valuable points of view.
5. Begin your process of collaboration by seeking a point in the family's value system that you share.

A key to successful collaboration in family/professional relationships is the professional's understanding of the complexities of their own values, beliefs, and attitudes about working with families, different ethnic/racial groups, and particular issues. Such understanding enables one to perceive a child and family more accurately. A well-established self-awareness helps one to be open and honest. Initial interactions with families should convey a message of reciprocity on the part of the professional (Kendall, 1996; Harry, 1997). Time and work spent at the onset, building relationships, will be time spent wisely. (See Figure 8-3.)

Figure 8–3
Parent/Professional relationships should be centered on building a relationship.

Cultural Diversity and ABI

A review of the distinctive features of activity-based intervention will be helpful as the following discussion deals with particular aspects of the approach. According to Bricker and Cripe (1992), ABI is a child-centered, transactional approach that embeds intervention on children's individual goals and objectives in routines as well as planned or child-initiated activities. ABI uses logically occurring antecedents and consequences to develop functional and generalizable skills. The approach allows the teacher, caregiver, or interventionist to address the special needs of a child with a disability in the context of regular routines, activities, and materials in an inclusive setting. Features of the ABI concept of concern here are the embedding of intervention in routines and activities and the use of naturally occurring antecedents and consequences in inclusive settings. Linking cultural diversity to ABI can be accomplished by grasping a better understanding of child development in a cultural context.

Although children acquire developmental milestones, their growth and development are influenced by the culture in which they are reared. Bowman and Stott (1994) state that developmental milestones take on meaning only in the context of a child's social life. The meaning of behavior is derived from the values and expectations of members of a culture. That is, the source of meaning for the child would be the family context. It is here that children learn to balance their needs and wishes with the constraints and freedoms of the social world in which they live. It is in the context of the family that children learn to express the developmental predispositions in ways that are consistent with their family's and culture's practices. Culture also influences how and what children learn.

When professionals make decisions about intervention and observe naturally occurring antecedents and consequences, their decisions should be made from a knowledge of what children know, what they need, their interests, family culture, and the local community and its concerns (Rodd, 1996). Children are socialized by their teachers also. Instead of a possible clash between the education environment and the home, the child should make an easy transition between home and school. Professionals should develop sensitivity to and insight about the children's backgrounds. Such knowledge helps establish respect for cultural beliefs and practices and increases the potential for their incorporation into intervention and programs (Rodd, 1996).

Bowman and Stott (1994) provide insight into how teachers (or other professionals) might gain a better understanding of the behavior of young children in order to make sense of what is happening in their lives. As they indicate, their approach is based on questions posed by Florio-Ruane (1995).

1. Ask: What is the "context" (interpersonal, personal, physical, and material) of the settings where interactions are occurring? Such information tells about other settings in which children live, in comparison to the school environment.
2. Ask: What do specific actions mean to teachers (professionals), to children, and to parents? Different behaviors can have similar meanings; similar behaviors can have different meanings.
3. Ask: How do teachers (professionals), children, and families interpret each other as individuals and as members of social systems? Honest, objective informants may be helpful in interpreting perceptions.

It should be noted that although Bowman and Stott's point of reference is teachers, the author perceives the approach relevant to other professionals as well. Personnel who serve young children with disabilities and their families consist of a cadre of individuals as members of multidisciplinary teams.

Clark (1995), in her article on culturally appropriate practices, states that the best way to learn about children's cultural backgrounds is to rely on the families. First admit to having very little knowledge; then exhibit a willingness to learn. Too, it is well to remember that children's play is a source of insight. Among other characteristics, children's play is symbolic and meaningful (Jalongo, 1992). Jalongo indicates that it represents reality with an "as if" or "what if" attitude and reveals experience with those representations of reality. Such representations are a reflection of the child's culture (Vold, 1985). Vold sees those symbols and values attributed to them as a reflection of the child's culture. To be sure, this author recommends that parent verification may be necessary.

Cultural Diversity and DAP

Bredekamp and Rosegrant (1992) describe the original intent of DAP as a framework, philosophy, or approach to working with young children that requires adults to pay attention to what we know about how children develop and learn, and what we learn about the individual needs and interest of each child in the group. Since publication of the document, several scholars have essentially concluded that the framework is not for all children, specifically children of culturally diverse backgrounds (Atwater, Carta, Schwartz, & McConnell, 1994; Jipson, 1991; Lubeck, 1994; New & Mallory, 1994; Powell, 1994; Rodd, 1996; Williams, 1994).

Following the discussions put forth in NAEYC publications subsequent to release of the DAP guidelines, debate surged on conceptual and methodological issues. New and Mallory (1994) argue that the grounds upon which the guidelines were designed have long been recognized as exclusionary. Included here are such situations as segregated neighborhoods, where segregated early childhood programs exist, and the physical exclusion of young children with disabilities. According to New and Mallory:

> The implementation of several decades' worth of policies and programs have not been sufficient to overcome traditional practices and basic social attitudes regarding the inclusion of culturally and developmentally diverse children. It would seem to be the case that any guidelines purporting to describe developmentally appropriate practices for all children would therefore need to make explicit attempts to reverse this long-established national trend. (p. 5)

Clark (1995) concurs with the narrow nature of the document, specifically with regard to the role of the teacher in addressing the variations associated with culture and developmental diversity.

A second issue regarding the limitations of the developmentally appropriate guidelines is that of curriculum content. Rodd (1996) states that many early childhood educators do not really know what is meant by "developmentally appropriate practices." Nor do they know how to implement them. Both Rodd and

Spodek (1986) say that the content of the early childhood curriculum should reflect the pluralist community's diverse perspectives, experiences, and values. Children and family beliefs and practices should be acknowledged and respected, to the point of becoming a part of the education setting and program.

In a study conducted by Jipson (1991), the use of developmentally appropriate practice was examined as a curricular base for early childhood programs. Selections from teachers' classroom journals and personal narratives provided the context for the study. Jipson analyzed the information to determine the capability of developmentally appropriate practice to respond to cultural diversity. Analysis revealed that teachers perceived DAP as often failing to acknowledge the roles of culture, care taking, interconnectedness, and multiple ways of knowing in the teaching-learning experiences of young children. Jipson concluded that further examination of the cultural appropriateness of early childhood education models and curriculum is necessary. Specifically, she recommends that the status of the DAP document be questioned in its perceived role as the standardized teacher's guide for early childhood education and a major element in the socialization of young children to monocultural norms. Any document of such limitations should not occupy a leadership position.

Williams (1994) presents a description worthy of observation. Acknowledging the circumstance of values that underlie the preparation of any document, Williams looks at those underlying DAP in light of traditional values affecting teaching and learning behaviors still retained in some Native American communities. Factors considered the value set regarding DAP, including the child-centered perspective, experiential/constructive orientations, interactive priorities, and family emphasis, as these represent the directives across the eight-year age span of the document. Values identified by Williams as salient in the guidelines are the prominence of the individual (versus the family), independence in the construction/acquisition of knowledge, and the prominent tendency in the valuing of overt expression of language.

In contrast, there is variation in belief and practice prominent enough among the Native American nations to be recognizable by many Native American people. Williams identifies four tendencies and dispositions nurtured in many Native American communities: the group as center, interdependence and knowledge, interactive rule structures (speaking, listening behavior), and the importance of the extended family. In concluding, the author sees several points of "clash" in expectations between teachers and children when applying the DAP guidelines without awareness of possible differences in value systems. A rethinking of the guidelines is recommended.

Powell (1994) views the guidelines in terms of parents and pluralism. The focus is the inclusion of parent perspectives in decisions about quality programs for young children. The role of parents in the DAP statement centers on two aspects: the parent as consumer in the selection of an early childhood program and the parent's contribution to the relationship with a program. Powell draws three conclusions following discussion of the two aspects and the DAP document. One, it is unlikely that parents will be effective agents for promoting the profession's ideas about program quality as the child-centered approach espoused in the DAP statement runs contrary to didactic program preferences of many lower-income parents of diverse backgrounds and some middle- and upper-income parents as well. Second, the DAP document challenges the pluralistic character of the early childhood field by recommending practices that some populations are unlikely to value. Third, the DAP document needs clear statements about equality in the parent-provider relationship. Such clarity would improve the inclusiveness of the guidelines for accommodating diversity in early childhood programs. Powell, too, recommends a rethinking of the model of professionalism presented in the document.

Although the DAP guidelines were developed as a framework, a philosophy, or an approach, the standards have become widely adopted as an index of quality for early childhood programs, birth to age eight. Atwater, Carta, Schwartz, and McConnell (1994) review the applicability of the model to programs for young children with special needs. Their premise is that the guidelines as they currently exist are not sufficient as a guide for planning and evaluating the effectiveness of programs for young children with special needs. Thus, they offer a framework for expanding the concept and application of the model. The authors identify common goals and assumptions of DAP and early childhood special education (ECSE), describe key features of ECSE that are vital to support the inclusion of children with special needs, and provide strategies for blending DAP and ECSE to obtain a set of best practices that meet the needs of all children. Common goals of DAP and ECSE are individualization, de-emphasis of standardized assessment, curriculum-linked assessment, child-initiated activities, active child engagement, social interaction, and cultural diversity (an emerging recognition).

Key to ECSE is flexibility in instructional strategies, criterion of the next environment, and outcomes-based assessment and monitoring. Suggested areas of integration of DAP and ECSE in practice include strategies to facilitate the engagement of children with diverse abilities in typical early childhood activities. These strategies allow individually focused intervention within the context of inclusive classroom activities—embedding interventions in classroom activities and routines, arranging the ecology to promote active engagement, and employing "least to most intrusive" intervention strategies. The expansion of the DAP model in the area of inclusion deserves commendation and shows a step forward in making the model more applicable. Professional collaboration is a must, as Atwater and associates (1994) urge.

Pronounced scholarly attention continues to be given to the prominent role afforded the DAP document in guiding program quality. Sufficient question continues to arise concerning the sufficiency of the statement, particularly in addressing cultural diversity and issues surrounding programs for young children with special needs. The model has serious limitations. Much more discretion should be exercised in its use as a resource. With the aforementioned discussion of the nature of the DAP statement in mind, the next section will describe recommendations for meeting the challenges of diversity in inclusive early childhood programs.

Meeting the Challenges of Diversity in Inclusive Early Childhood Education

The term *cultural diversity* is defined at the beginning of this chapter as a conglomeration of the multiple cultures and languages introduced by people of different races and lifestyles that contribute to the enrichment of society. Cushner and colleagues (1992) provide a more comprehensive description by recognizing children and youth who may have special educational and other needs (the hearing impaired, the visually impaired).

It is necessary to remember that today's trend is toward inclusion, an approach in which children with disabilities are placed in education settings with, and receive services side by side with, children who have no disabilities.

Voltz (1995) tells us that the task of structuring general education to facilitate the success of diverse learners is an important challenge facing educators. The text that follows in this section relates some of the resources designed to help meet the challenge. The presentation is in no way an evaluative review. It simply makes the reader aware of available resources.

Reaching Potentials: Appropriate Curriculum and Assessment for Young Children, Volume 1 (Bredekamp & Rosegrant) is a book representative of references focused on establishing quality early childhood programs. According to its editors, the purpose of the book is to operationalize—that is, make meaningful—the *Guidelines for Appropriate Curriculum Content and Assessment,* developed jointly by the National Association for the Education of Young Children and the National Association of Early Childhood Specialist in State Departments of Education. The four sections address curriculum content and assessment in programs serving children ages three through eight. Multicultural curriculum, developmentally and culturally appropriate programs, reaching potentials of linguistically diverse children, and reaching potentials of children with disabilities are some of the topics for which guidelines are presented.

The Anti-Bias Curriculum: Tools for Empowering Young Children (Derman-Sparks and the A.B.C. Task Force, 1989) is a product that embraces an educational philosophy that differences are valued. It offers specific techniques and content that allow teachers to establish the curriculum for their setting in relation to specific groups of children and families. This document as well as the preceding one both address the topic of disabilities.

Diversity in the Classroom by Francis Kendall (1996) is written as a journey through various points toward genuine multiculturalism. The journey involves visiting child development (including racial awareness and racial attitudes), self-examination, talking with parents, and so on, until the final chapter, developing the multicultural classroom environment.

Several books on multicultural education and cultural diversity in education are noteworthy: Banks and Banks (1997); Bennett (1995); Corderio, Reagan, and Martinez (1994); Cushner, McClelland, and Stafford (1992); DeVillar, Faltis, and Cummins (1994); Miller-Lachmann and Taylor (1995); and Nieto (1992). Some of these resources provide detailed descriptive information on the characteristics and goals of multicultural education, revamping the curriculum, teaching practices, learning styles, inclusion, students with special needs, enhancing the staff, garnering support for changes, family and community involvement strategies, and other related issues. A repeated topic of discussion is parent-community involvement. Banks (1997) applauds its importance because it acknowledges the importance of parents in the lives of their children, it recognizes the diversity of values and perspectives within the school community, it provides a vehicle for building a collaborative problem-solving structure, and it increases the opportunity for all students to learn in schools.

Those who avail themselves of the resources cited will likely encounter content that differs significantly from personal value systems. It is recommended that deep reflective thought be given to such issues, as those beliefs that we hold passionately are the ones most likely to be shared with others, especially our children.

A final noteworthy resource is a series entitled *Multiple Voices for Ethnically Diverse, Exceptional Learners,* produced by the Division for Culturally and Linguistically Diverse Exceptional Learners, and published by the Council for Exceptional Children. Volume 1, Number 1 (1995) contains research and teacher articles. Among the research are articles that look at learning and cultural diversities in general, special education classes, and issues in the implementation of innovative instructional strategies. Teacher articles include information on bilingual literature, curriculum guidelines from a Navajo teacher's perspective, and using instructional games to explore African culture.

Summary

The influence of culture and values on family identity cannot be overstated, whether children are typically developing or exceptional learners. Recognizing, acknowledging, and better understanding the concept of culture in relation to a given family will increase the likelihood that education and services will be appropriate and effective (Wayman, Lynch, & Hanson, 1991). Our nation is confronting two obvious realities. One, education and services to children and families must reflect practices that are culturally relevant to the given family. Two, the trends toward a multicultural society continue to materialize. It is hoped that this chapter serves to further heighten awareness of the necessity of meeting the challenges of diversity in a pluralistic nation.

Chapter 8 Suggested Activities and Resources

Activities

1. Interview individuals representing various cultural and linguistically diverse backgrounds to compare group traditions, customs, values, and belief systems. Consider individuals who are first generation American-born versus those who are immigrants to America.

2. Reflect on ways you promote respect for cultural diversity in daily life. Identify other opportunities whereby you might support and encourage cultural sensitivity. Compare your lists.

3. Read Banks (1997) to get an in-depth understanding of the four levels of integrating multicultural content into the curriculum. List advantages and disadvantages of each approach.

4. Use the five steps toward cultural reciprocity outlined by Harry (1997) as the basis of an interview with a professional or parent to examine a successful collaborative parent-professional partnership.

5. Observe an early childhood setting known to demonstrate culturally responsive education practices, and identify ways that the program engages and helps children build upon their own sense of identity.

6. Select one of Kendall's primary goals of multicultural education in preschool classrooms and observe how a teacher addresses it in the curriculum.

7. Considering the term *values* as "belief systems—not facts," examine some of the ways your own perspectives differ from those of a subculture group within the ethnic population with which you identify.

8. Review the DAP approach to working with young children, and write a statement describing your position concerning the sufficiency of the guidelines as a tool for planning and evaluating the effectiveness of programs for young children with special needs.

Selected Resources

1. Catlett, C. (Ed.). (1993). *A Compendium of Early Intervention Training Activities.* Rockville, MD: American Speech-Language-Hearing Association.

2. Ford, B. A. (Ed.). (1997). *Multiple Voices for Ethnically Diverse Exceptional Learners.* Reston, VA: The Division for Culturally and Linguistically Diverse Exceptional Learners.

3. Garcia, S. B. (Ed.). (1994). *Addressing Cultural and Linguistic Diversity in Special Education: Issues and Trends.* Reston, VA: The Division for Culturally and Linguistically Diverse Exceptional Learners.

4. Hanson, M. J., Lynch, E. W., & Wayman, K. I. (1990). Honoring the Cultural Diversity of Families When Gathering Information. *Topics in Early Childhood Special Education, 10* (1), 112–131.

5. Lindgren, J. (Ed.). (1991). *A Bibliography of Selected Resources on Cultural Diversity.* Minneapolis, MN: PACER Center & National Early Childhood Technical Assistance System, Frank Porter Graham Child Development Center, The University of North Carolina.

6. Lynch, E. W., & Hanson, M. J. (1993). *Developing Cross-Cultural Competence: A Guide for Working With Young Children and Their Families.* Baltimore: Paul H. Brookes Publishing Co.

7. Nieto, S. (1995). *Affirming Diversity: The Sociopolitical Context of Multicultural Education* (2nd ed.). New York: Longman.

8. *Our Children, Our Hopes: Empowering African-American Families of Children with Disabilities* (videocassette). (1993). Minneapolis, MN: PACER Center.

9. Roberts, R. N. (1990). *Developing Cultural Competent Programs for Families of Children with Special Needs.* Washington, DC: Georgetown University Child Development Center.

References

Atwater, J. B., Carta, J. J., Schwartz, I. S., & McConnell, S. R. (1994). Early Educational Practices: Problems and Promises. In B. L. Mallory & R. S. New (Eds.), *Diversity and Developmentally Appropriate Practices: Challenges for Early Childhood Education* (pp. 183–200). New York: Teachers College Press.

Banks, J. A. (1997). Approaches to Multicultural Reform. In J. A. Banks & C. A. Banks (Eds.), *Multicultural Education: Issues and Perspectives.* (3rd ed.). (pp. 229–250). Boston: Allyn and Bacon.

Banks, J. A., & Banks, C. A. (Eds.) (1997). *Multicultural Education: Issues and Perspectives.* (3rd ed.). Boston: Allyn and Bacon.

Bennett, C. (1995). *Comprehensive Multicultural Education: Theory and Practice* (3rd ed.). Boston: Allyn and Bacon.

Bowman, T., & Stott, F. M. (1994). Understanding Development in a Cultural Context: The Challenge for Teachers. In B. L. Mallory & R. S. New (Eds.), *Diversity and Developmentally Appropriate Practices: Challenges for Early Childhood Education* (pp. 119–133). New York: Teachers College Press.

Bredekamp, S., & Rosegrant, T. (Eds.) (1992). *Reaching Potentials: Appropriate Curriculum and Assessment for Young Children.* (Vol. 1). Washington DC: National Association for the Education of Young Children.

Bricker, D., & Woods-Cripe, J. J. (1992). *An Activity-Based Approach to Early Intervention.* Baltimore: Paul H. Brookes Publishing Co.

Brito, T. (1980). Cultural Awareness: Working with Parents of Handicapped Children. In E. Jackson & J. Karp (Eds.), *Program Strategies for Cultural Diversity* (pp. 37–39). University of Washington, Seattle: Western States Technical Assistance Resource.

Clark, P. (1995). Culturally Appropriate Practices in Early Childhood Education: Families as the Resource. *Contemporary Education, 3* (66), 154–157.

Corderio, P., Reagan, T., & Martinez, L. (1994). *Multiculturalism and TQE: Addressing Cultural Diversity in Schools.* Thousand Oaks, CA: Corwin Press Inc.

Cushner, K., McClelland, A., & Stafford, P. (1992). *Human Diversity in Education: An Integrative Approach.* New York: McGraw-Hill.

DEC Task Force on Recommended Practices (1993). *Division for Early Childhood Recommended Practices: Indicators of Quality in Programs for Infants and Young Children with Special Needs and Their Families.* Reston, VA: The Council for Exceptional Children.

Derman-Sparks, L. (1989). *The Anti-Bias Curriculum: Tools for Empowering Young Children.* Washington, DC: National Association for the Education of Young Children.

DeVillar, R., Fallis, C., & Cummins, J. (Eds.) (1994). *Cultural Diversity in Schools: From Rhetoric to Practice.* New York: State University of New York Press.

Florio-Ruane, S. (1995). Sociolinguistics for Educational Researchers. *American Educational Research Journal, 24* (2), 185–197.

Ford, B. A. (1995). *Multiple Voices for Ethnically Diverse Exceptional Learners.* Reston, VA: The Division for Culturally and Linguistically Diverse Exceptional Learners.

Garcia, E. (1991). *The Education of Linguistically and Culturally Diverse Students: Effective Instructional Practices.* Santa Cruz, National Center of Research on Cultural Diversity and Second Language Learning: University of California. (ERIC Document Reproduction Service No. ED 338 099)

Gibson, M. (1984). Approaches to Multicultural Education in the United States: Some Concepts and Assumptions. *Anthropology and Education Quarterly, 15* (1), 99–120.

Harry, B. (1997). Leaning Forward or Bending over Backwards: Cultural Reciprocity in Working with Families. *Journal of Early Intervention, 21*(1), 62–72.

Holden, C. (1990). Changing U.S. Demography. *Science, 248,* 307.

Jalongo, M. R. (1992). Children's Play: A Resource for Multicultural Education. In E. B. Vold, *Multicultural Education in Early Childhood Classrooms.* NEA Early Childhood Education Series. Monograph from NEA Professional Library. (ERIC Document Reproduction Service No. ED 345 865)

Jipson, J. (1991). Developmentally Appropriate Practices: Culture, Curriculum, Connections. *Early Childhood and Development, 2* (2), 120–136.

Kendall, F. (1996). *Diversity in the Classroom* (2nd ed.). New York: Teachers College Press.

Lockwood, R., Allen, A., Ford, B., & Sparks, S. (1991). *Culture, Differences? Diversity!* Wilmington, OH: Department of Education: Division of Special Education.

Lubeck, S. (1994). The Politics of Developmentally Appropriate Practice. In B. L. Mallory & R. S. New (Eds.) (1994), *Diversity and Developmentally Appropriate Practices: Challenges for Early Childhood Education* (pp. 17–43). New York: Teachers College Press.

Lynch, J. (1989). *Multicultural Education in a Global Society.* London: Palmer Press.

Mallory, B. L., & New, R. S. (Eds.) (1994). *Diversity and Developmentally Appropriate Practices: Challenges for Early Childhood Education.* New York: Teachers College Press.

Meyer, L. H., Harry, B., & Sapon-Sevin, M. (1997). School Inclusion and Multicultural Issues in Special Education. In J. A. Banks & C. A. Banks (Eds.), *Multicultural Education: Issues and Perspectives* (3rd ed.). Boston: Allyn and Bacon.

Miller-Lachman, L., & Taylor, C. (1995). *Schools for All: Educating Children in a Diverse Society.* New York: Delmar Publishers.

NAEYC Position Statement. Responding to Linguistic and Cultural Diversity—Recommendations for Effective Early Childhood Education (1996). *Young Children, 2* (51), 4–12.

New, R. S., & Mallory, B. L. (Eds.) (1994). Introduction: The Ethic for Inclusion. In B. L. Mallory & R. S. New (Eds.), *Diversity and Developmentally Appropriate Practices: Challenges For Early Childhood Education* (pp. 1–13). New York: Teachers College Press.

Nieto, S. (1992). *Affirming Diversity: The Sociopolitical Context of Multicultural Education*. New York: Longman.

Powell, D. R. (1994). Parents, Pluralism, and the NAEYC Statement on Developmentally Appropriate Practice. In B. L. Mallory & R. S. New (Eds.), *Diversity and Developmentally Appropriate Practices: Challenges for Early Childhood Education* (pp. 166–182). New York: Teachers College Press.

Riche, M. F. (1991). We're All Minorities Now. *American Demographics, 13,* 26–34.

Rodd, J. C. (1996). Children, Culture, and Education. *Childhood Education, 72* (6), 325–329.

Staff. (1991). Counting Heads. *U.S. News and World Report, 110,* 16.

Spodek, B. (1986). Development, Values, and Knowledge in the Kindergarten Curriculum. In B. Spodek (Ed.), *Today's Kindergarten: Exploring the Knowledge Base, Expanding the Curriculum* (pp. 32–47). New York: Teachers College Press.

Vold, E. B. (1985). Understanding America and Its Peoples. *Dimensions, 13,* 4–6.

Voltz, D. L. (1995). Learning and Cultural Diversities in General and Special Education Classes: Framework for Success. In B. A. Ford (Ed.), *Multiple Voices for Ethnically Diverse Exceptional Learners* (pp. 1–11). Reston, VA: The Division for Culturally and Linguistically Diverse Exceptional Learners.

Wayman, K. I., Lynch, E. W., & Hanson, M. J. (1991). Home-Based Early Childhood Services: Cultural Sensitivity in a Family Systems Approach. *Topics in Early Childhood Special Education, 10,* 56–75.

Williams, L. R. (1994). Developmentally Appropriate Practice and Cultural Values: A Case in Point. In B. L. Mallory & R. S. New (Eds.), *Diversity and Developmentally Appropriate Practices: Challenges for Early Childhood Education* (pp. 155–165). New York: Teachers College Press.

Chapter 9

Future Directions in Inclusive Early Childhood Education

INTRODUCTION

The following chapter is concerned with selected future directions in the field of inclusive early childhood education. In many ways, this chapter is about you. As an entry level professional moving toward the completion of your degree and licensure, you will be an agent of change and will help in shaping the direction of the field and the delivery of educational services and supports to children and families. The topics to be explored in this chapter center around the future as it pertains to policy, research, practice, and families in the area of inclusive early childhood education. Here are the objectives that the reader will address in Chapter 9. You should be able to:

- Become familiar with the foundations for future directions including the areas of policy, research, practice, and families.
- Understand the role of public policy and society's support for children and families.
- Understand the part that research has in shaping the practices of the future, including the advances of medical technology and early brain research in the prevention of disabilities, and the contribution of emerging technologies toward enhancing the quality of life for children and families affected by disabilities.
- Identify future perspectives in the delivery of practices in early childhood special education, which include assessment, evaluation, intervention, and related therapies. Topical areas such as transition, teaming and collaboration, inclusion, seamless systems, and planning will also be examined.
- Recognize the importance of personnel preparation and the training and development of future professionals.

Foundations for Future Directions

As you may know or will come to learn in your professional development, there are many factors that influence our disciplines and the children and families whom we serve. A mix of political, social, economic, and other variables influences the field of early childhood education and subsequently affects the needs of children and families. When one considers the well-being of children in America, the data is revealing about the overwhelming needs of America's children and families and the risks they encounter. In a recent report entitled *The State of America's Children Yearbook 1998,* published by the Children's Defense Fund, the following data speaks to the needs of our children and families:

- Thirty-two states require no prior training for child care teachers, who also rank as some of the lowest paid workers in America, earning on average $12,058 per year and receiving no benefits or leave.
- In 1996, 3.1 million children were reported abused or neglected.
- Significant numbers of American families have lost welfare benefits since 1993, with former welfare recipients earning less than $10,000 per year.

These statistics are examples of general indicators that America's children and families are facing increasing risks in greater numbers. Educational programs serving children and families are becoming increasingly challenged by the growing numbers of children affected by poverty; working poor families, many of whom originate from diverse cultural backgrounds; increased rates of child abuse and neglect; children born to teenaged mothers, which is now estimated to be approximately 56 percent of all children born in the United States (CDF, 1998); and the list goes on and on.

Sadly, American policy makers and the society at large have sent a mixed message to children and families. Many children are currently placed in inadequate child care facilities or in private care settings because of economic factors that force both parents to work. In single-parent families, the economic burden can be more overwhelming. In response to the question that you by now are asking—Why are our children and families in such a plight and what can be done to improve the situation?—Hart and Risely (1995) in their book entitled *Meaningful Differences in the Everyday Experience of Young American Children* respond that "inertia, divided opinion, and uncertainty about outcomes virtually assure that what is being done will continue to be done—a bit of prevention and a lot of repair" (p. 208). Needless to say the problems are many for children and families today. The need for improved and enhanced programs to provide educational and other support services to these individuals is apparent given the data. However, societal support is needed for the creation and maintenance of these programs.

The efficacy of early intervention has been established despite the challenges to the contrary offered by its critics; however, as pointed out by Hart and Risely (1995), the long-range benefits over successive generations will not be realized immediately. Hart and Risely (1995) state that "present intervention programs are familiar; their cost and relative effectiveness are known. There are questions, though, concerning their long-term effectiveness. Intergenerational transmission of enriched experience takes years, and whether this process will keep up pace with the increasing demands of a technological society and the growing numbers of families raising children in poverty remains uncertain" (p. 209). Given these factors, the need for future policies that directly address the needs of children and families must be enacted: Advocacy organizations should

Figure 9–1 Action research conducted by applied practitioners is a means by which teachers can systematically evaluate their words and modify their practices.

continue to lead the good fight in insuring that the needs and rights of children and families are protected through legislation. The National Association for the Education of Young Children (NAEYC), has emphasized this by stating that "the current political climate underscores the need for early childhood professionals to take further responsibility in educating the public and the private sector on the importance of early learning"(p. 2).

Second, continued research efforts are needed to document the broad-scale benefits of early childhood education not only in general terms but also at the classroom level as well. Action research conducted by applied practitioners is a means by which teachers can systematically evaluate their work and modify their practices. Borgia and Schuler (1996) cite the benefits of action research not only in terms of improved practice but also as a powerful vehicle to promote school reform and improved practices. (See Figure 9–1.)

Next, improved practices in early childhood education must be a future priority. State standards for licensing and credentialing need to become more uniform and rigorous to ensure the development of high-quality professionals. University training programs should aim to develop more action-oriented personnel preparation programs that are based in applied research, enabling student trainees to develop demonstrated competencies under the watchful eye of university mentors and master teachers. University programs must also strive within such programs to connect student trainees with families and children to better understand their role as educators in the lives of these individuals. Exposure to inclusive educational settings while in training needs to become more common practice within university-based programs. The integration of programs serving children and families within interdisciplinary training programs at both undergraduate and graduate levels is a positive step toward the development of professionals trained to work with *all* children and families. (See Figure 9–2.)

Figure 9–2 University preparation programs must strive to connect students with children and families.

Research

It is possible that you may not fully understand and/or appreciate the relevance of research as it relates early childhood education and early childhood special education. Before we launch into a brief consideration of future directions in research, it is probably useful to say a few words in general about research and its place in determining why and how we carry out our responsibilities in educational settings and other service programs for young children and their families. Webster defines research as "careful, systematic, patient study and investigation in some field of knowledge undertaken to discover or establish facts or principles." The choices that we make about why and how to do early childhood education and special education and specifically inclusion are taken in part from the facts and principles derived from research. That is, the findings of research are applied to our practice (teaching or intervening). One of the central questions asked of a researcher who seeks funding or support for her/his study is: What is the relevance and meaningfulness of your research? How will it make a difference in what we do and contribute to what we know is best?

Central to this text is the theme that in order to achieve early and responsible inclusion, we must merge ideas, methods, and resources and collaborate across disciplines in service delivery settings for young children. The reality is that research has historically been unidisciplinary, just like the provision of services and the preparation of personnel. Another reality is that many professionals who work on behalf of young children and their families, whether they are, for example, early elementary grade teachers or home-based infant interventionists, frequently lack familiarity with empirical evidence to support or refute their practices.

This lack of knowledge regarding research may come from a belief that research is not relevant, important, or even necessary. It may also come from simply a lack of time or lack of access to reports on research. Or it may be that practitioners find the journals in which research is detailed confusing and hard to understand! However, though you may or may not be directly involved in the conduct of research as a part of your career, it behooves you as a professional to stay abreast of research evidence and consider how it fits with your practice as an educator. In order to accomplish this, it is desirable to maintain an affiliation with professional organizations, to digest the articles found in the journals and newsletters of those organizations, to participate in local and statewide chapters, to attend professional conferences, and to expect the leaders in your professional setting to support and assist you in utilizing research findings to better serve young children and their families.

Michael J. Guralnick (1997) points out in *The Effectiveness of Intervention* that while there have been methodological problems in research, the twenty-five-year period from 1970 to 1995 has resulted in establishing in general the efficacy, or the effectiveness, of early intervention. He refers to the twenty-five-year period as first-generation research and advocates that what remains to be done in a second generation of research is to more precisely identify the variables associated with successful intervention in three domains, including program features, child and family characteristics, and outcomes of early intervention. With regard to program features, the research questions center around what aspects of a program—for example, the curricular content and application—are associated with success.

The next domain for second-generation research is the examination of the relationships between characteristics of the child and family and successful intervention. Think of characteristics of the child as including the type and severity of the disability and characteristics of the family as including things like diversity, poverty, or attributes considered to place families at risk, such as the age of one or both parents. The third domain of need for future research has to do with the effectiveness of research as it relates to outcomes. Historically early intervention programs have looked at outcomes that were domain-specific, for example, how much gain did a child make in gross motor development. Future research might focus on more comprehensive outcomes, such as the effect of intervention on social competence. You can relate these three areas of research to the future of inclusion or natural environments as central features of intervention.

We have concluded that responsible and systemically planned inclusion (see Chapter 1) is desirable, and we believe in and are mandated under federal law to apply least restrictive environments and natural settings. An example of a related research question might be: How effective are activity-based intervention and specific strategies of positive behavioral support in a kindergarten (program features) for children with comprehensive disabilities (child and family characteristics), given the desired result of significant child progress across all developmental domains (outcomes of intervention)? Kontos, Moore, and Giorgetti (1998) in a study of the ecology of inclusion point out that as there is an expansion of opportunities for early childhood special education services to be provided in inclusive settings, research investigations of inclusion will correspondingly increase. They stress the importance, for future research on early inclusion, of linking together the inclusive experiences of children with the outcomes.

To summarize our brief consideration of research, we conclude that the efficacy of early intervention and early childhood special education, including the practice of inclusion, is reasonably well established in research. What remains for future research is to more precisely identify the attributes of inclusive programs and to understand the relationships among those settings and their practices, the needs of children and families (given their uniqueness), and the outcomes that are identified for young children and families through planning processes like the IFSP and IEP. Perhaps you will be a participant, either as a researcher or through a study done in your setting, in carrying out this research in the years to come. It is likely that as a professional who serves young children and their families, you will be the beneficiary of this research. And in consort with what we already know about the most effective practices to achieve inclusion, you will use applied research to improve the lives of young children and their families. (See Figure 9–3.)

Public Policy

The role of public policy will be central to the support of children and families in the future to maintain current programs and to assist in the development of new and improved service and support delivery systems. The allocation of funds has become increasingly more competitive as resources and allocations have lessened. This trend will call upon educational and social service and delivery systems to maintain higher degrees of accountability with measurable outcomes being the yardstick of program success. There is both good and bad with this approach. When policies lose sight of the human factor and programs are merely evaluated in terms of quantifiable results, there should be concern. Second, we as educators must turn our concern toward quality assurance, in

Figure 9–3
Future research is needed to understand the relationship between the inclusive experiences of children and outcomes.

other words, how services and supports are delivered to young children and families. Quality assurance involves a values base that serves as the foundation for program delivery. Early childhood education programs that maintain a focus on quality assurance typically place value on the quality of their programs, including maintaining a child- and family-centered focus, and the attainment of valued outcomes. The movement toward quality assurance within early childhood education programs will continue to grow as more families become self-empowered. Families have grown more involved over time in the development of programs, and through their self-advocacy efforts, programs have become more accountable and sensitive to the individual needs and capacities of children and families.

The recent research evidence we have gained about brain development in the very young child can be expected to impact more significantly our public policy regarding how and when we provide a variety of services to babies and toddlers and their families, including those who have disabilities and those who do not. In a special edition of *Newsweek* magazine published in the spring/summer of 1997, a variety of articles about infant and toddler development, targeting an increased understanding by the general public, are offered. Here are some of the highlights. One can readily see how these facts might influence how we serve very young children and their families.

Selected Highlights of Research on Early Brain Development

- Babies are "learning machines" and need lots of time and attention from significant adults who will foster their natural curiosity.
- Young children's achievement of developmental milestones should be used only as very broad guidelines, since each baby's brain forms the connections required for sensory and motor abilities in a unique way.
- The structure of babies' brains is not genetically determined and set at birth. Rather, early experiences and infant stimulation determine the actual "wiring" of the brain.
- By twelve months an infant's "auditory map" is formed, and she/he will be unable to pick out phonemes that have not been heard numerous times. For learning language, an infant's brain is "neuroplastic," but that plasticity lessens with age.
- While traumatic events may significantly influence the behavior of adults, they actually change the "organizational framework" for the brain of a young child.
- Preschool education should be about exploration, play, and listening to, guiding, and helping your children make sense of the world rather than strict schedules, formal teaching, and adult dominated direction.
- Neural connections that are reinforced by a baby's exposure to language and other experiences become permanent; if not reinforced, they are eliminated.
- While three out of 100 newborns will have a birth defect, more and more of these children, because of early intervention, will lead "normal" lives of independence and self-determination.
- Genetics is estimated to determine about 50 percent of a child's personality.

Parents and families will continue to be major role players in the formation of public policies pertaining to young children and families. Programs such as "Partners in Policymaking" (Zirpoli, Weick, Hancox, & Skarnella, 1994) exist in most states. Such programs were designed to assist parents and families of children with disabilities in the development of self-advocacy skills. Such programs have produced several positive outcomes such as increased social support networks for families, the development of self-determination skills in families, and influence on policy makers as to the importance of meaningful policies that positively impact the lives of children with disabilities and their families.

In conclusion, what can be done to positively impact on the development of policy in the future? Policy makers should be encouraged by professionals to link funding allocations to valued outcomes as perceived by the consumers of the services and supports, the parents and families. Second, policy makers should become familiar with programs and visit them on a regular basis and interact with the people whose lives are impacted by such programs. Policy makers should also seek to increase the incentives and recognize programs for their quality. As professionals we can further assist policy makers by supporting our various professional organizations, serving as advocates for all children and families, assisting with public awareness campaigns to ensure that members of the community at large understand the importance of early childhood education and real services and supports to young children and families, and insisting on high degrees of professional competencies for professionals in the field.

Future Directions in Service Delivery Practices

The following section will address future directives as they pertain to service delivery machines. Service delivery practices include such areas as assessment, program planning, program implementation, and administrative supports, among others.

Early Identification/Child Find and the Future

As we continue to find and identify children with special needs, we must remember the importance of *early* identification. The recent brain research demonstrates the windows of opportunity and the importance of providing very young children with opportunities and intervention. The primary means of identifying young children who may require intervention will likely continue to be the use of a variety of screening procedures. Many assessment instruments intended for use with very young children include a screening component. Our approaches to screening can be expected to become more diverse and systematic in the future, including both formal and informal methods, greater use of parent questionnaires, more reliance on neonatal screening and early diagnosis, and emphasis on periodic and ongoing screenings. Blackman (1995) has suggested that having a systematic approach in a community in which duplication is avoided is as important as the techniques of screening. As your professional development proceeds, you will learn how to use various educational and developmental screening instruments and procedures as well as gain some understanding of the contributions of other disciplines to the process.

Assessment

With regard to the area of assessment and the future, we will continue to focus on a developmentally appropriate process of assessment, planning, and implementation, as well as early identification and child find processes that are child and family friendly. The portfolio and authentic assessment processes are still fairly new to the field and have great potential for documenting progress. This has been illustrated by the Reggio Emilia philosophy that has taken the early childhood movement in the United States "by storm." In brief, Reggio Emilia (as originated and practiced by parents and teachers in Reggio Emilia, Italy, for the past thirty years) focuses on a child-initiated, teacher- and parent-supported curriculum with strong hands-on and culturally enriched experiences. The integration of the arts in an aesthetically pleasing environment and artistic expression and appreciation are primary to children's learning. As stated, this philosophy emphasizes the utilization of documentation as a primary means of assessment, reflective learning, parental information, and teacher, curriculum, and program feedback. Portfolio assessments are very familiar to the Reggio Emilia philosophy. A collection of photos, videos, children's drawing, writing samples, audio recordings, and the like, are examples of the contents of a child's portfolio.

There is still debate about the "measurability" of this process. But this does not need to be an either/or issue. The more information that we can collect about children's development, the better view of the child we will have. As we become more skilled with portfolio collection and interpretation, we will recognize the value of this documented profile of children's developmental progress.

As we look into the future, another aspect of developmentally appropriate assessment of young children is the level by which this process is family friendly. One example of the first such tools is the Transdisciplinary Play-Based Assessment (TPBA), by Linder (1990). The TPBA has been very well received by families. Family members have a clear role in this process. They are directly involved. The importance of the partnership with families is illustrated by the appointment of a Parent Facilitator in the TPBA process. The entire process is explained to the parents as they view the assessment occurring. The stress is thus reduced for the parents and child as they are in a play-based environment such as typical preschool or infant educare setting. Whatever assessment tools are utilized, DAP and child/family friendliness must be respected and evident in the process. As you, in your professional role, make determinations about what instruments and approaches you will use or expect from others, you will want to keep in the forefront whether or not the assessment tool is family friendly. That is, does it respect and include information from families and does it treat parents/families as equal partners?

Planning and Implementation and the Future

Although there are a variety of theories, philosophies, and program models to choose from, in order to successfully include children with special needs we must effectively move from the assessment process to planning (IFSP/IEP and general curriculum) to implementation in the natural environment. The importance of both age and individual appropriateness must be the focus. We must draw from the various team disciplines and their expertise. We must continue to find effective ways to embed the child's individual goals into the daily routines, child-initiated activities, and teacher-directed experiences through ABI and PBS. This can happen only if we are competent in these practices. Continued in-service training on these techniques and practices, while individualizing to each child, will help its success. We have many teachers in the field who have not had the benefits of exposure to such successful ways of including children with special needs and promoting their developmental growth and independence.

But before applying strategies, caregivers, interventionists, teachers, and schools must be committed to understanding the child's disability and the impact on the child's education in order to successfully plan and implement goals. Adaptations according to the child's disability and the natural environment must be explored. Early childhood educators must continue to focus on play as the child's means of learning about his/her environment and developing cognitively, physically, and socioemotionally. Resources to learn about various disabilities and the impact on child and family must be utilized.

Positive Behavioral Supports

It is hoped that in the future, positive behavioral supports (PBS) will become a component of every teacher's repertoire of teaching skills. Sadly, teachers and some parents and families have been conditioned in the past through their training and exposure to view positive behavioral supports as an adjunct to their teaching or parenting, when in fact, these approaches have been designed to be efficiently integrated into the various natural environments for a child, such as school or home. To some degree, there has also been a bias toward the use of behavioral procedures in some areas of education. Too often this bias and lack of understanding toward positive behavioral support methods has been reflected in a child's educational program. Frequently, teachers rely on rapid suppression methods as a last resort or the use of punitive techniques in an attempt to extinguish a behavioral response from a child. Rather than resort to consequence-based approaches, positive behavioral supports seek to be a proactive set of interventions, grounded in a child- and family-centered philosophy that produces meaningful and lasting changes for a child and their family.

To combat some of these opposing professional attitudes, more awareness and knowledge are needed as to the virtues of PBS as an integrated tool for use with all children and families. The merits of PBS are many; the drawbacks few. Among the virtues, PBS is a philosophy that values children and families, it is longitudinal by design, it seeks meaningful outcomes for children and families, and it promotes durable and lasting change through understanding challenging behaviors in children and through the active teaching of positive, alternative behaviors. PBS is aimed at the prevention of challenging behaviors; it recognizes the limitations and challenges that such behaviors present not only to caregivers but more importantly to the children who engage in them.

More training is needed for practitioners, and it is hoped that this will become a component of every university personnel preparation program in the future. As we move toward the development of inclusive teacher preparation programs at the college level, student trainees must become more fluent in the use of positive behavioral support strategies. Teachers and administrators must also come to realize that all behavior has a meaningful purpose in the eyes of the individual. Often the form they employ to meet that need is not always the best option, but through the teaching of positive alternative skills and the development of a behavioral support plan, a child will be better capable of learning. It is also important in the future that we prepare parents and families in the use of PBS approaches within the home as well.

Finally, resources exist to familiarize students, parents, and families with the merits of PBS, and these resources will become more widely available to teachers and parents as they develop skills in this area. Hopefully, teachers and families will have the benefits of in-service training in the development of positive behavioral support plans. Positive behavioral supports should be incorporated within schools as a component of model school or program development. It is a philosophy that emphasizes a positive regard for children and families and their diversity, that complements activity-based intervention and developmentally appropriate practice, and that is supportive of the concept of responsible inclusion.

Assistive Technology

Most assuredly your professional responsibilities in working on behalf of young children and their families are going to require you to have a significant level of technological expertise. This is true whether you work with infants or children in the early elementary grades, and it seems clear that for the future the emphasis on technology applications will continue to increase. Hopefully, you are in preservice or in-service programs that prepare and support you in this regard. Haugland and Wright (1997) have pointed out that the question is not whether computers will be used with young children, but rather how they will be utilized and will it be in ways that support developmentally appropriate learning experiences.

Specific to assistive technologies, including computers and other applications, for young children with special needs and to support inclusion efforts, there is a growing trend and empirical support for their use. You can think of assistive technology as including anything from "low-tech" devices such as switches to operate toys to "high-tech" and more complex applications such as computers and software. Lesar (1998) studied the preparedness of early childhood special education professionals and found that while they recognized the importance of technology in serving their children and families, many of them felt inadequately prepared to do so. It is incumbent on early childhood educators and special educators, and those who are responsible for their preparation, to enhance their skills in this area.

There are a rapidly expanding number of resources to assist us in planning and carrying out effective assistive technologies with young children with disabilities (Blackman, 1995). As an example, Fallon and Wann (1995) describe how computers and software can play an important role in activity-based thematic instructional units to support inclusive early childhood education classrooms.

Administrative Supports

- Administrators must understand and recognize the importance of early intervention, as well as the concepts of person first, family-centeredness, transdisciplinary teaming and collaboration, ecological approach, responsible inclusion, independence/self-determination/self-advocacy, ABI, PBS, DAP, transitions, sensitivity to diversity, and assistive technology.

- Administrators must also be committed to best and effective practice regarding the above. They must be willing to commit to the time and money it takes to share philosophy, provide additional in-services to staff (and for themselves), and be committed to and accessible to families.
- Administrators must be good negotiators, collaborators, and mediators. They must be willing to deal with conflict and offer conflict resolution training to their staff.
- They must have an approachable style, an "open door policy." Communication skills must be strong and fostered, valued, and reinforced with staff.
- Service providers must be assured that they have administrative support to be family-centered, and a transdisciplinary team; to respect the ecological approach and serve children in their natural setting; to practice responsible inclusion; to promote independence/self-determination/self-advocacy, ABI, PBS, DAP, and transitions; to be sensitive to diversity; and to secure needed assistive technology for children with special needs.

Transitions/Seamless Systems

Transitions mean change, and change can be difficult for all of us. This change, if faced unprepared, can cause fear and stress. As we look to the future, we can predict transitions in our system that all children, families, schools, and agencies must deal with. We know if we plan ahead and prepare for these changes, we can experience this transition with less stress. For smoother, seamless transitions to occur, we must, as systems, think and plan proactively rather than reactively.

As stated in Chapter 1—and illustrated in Chapters 9, 10, and 11—several transitions exist for young children with special needs and their families, including hospital to home, home-based to center-based services and preschool programs, center-based and pre-K programs to kindergarten and public schools, kindergarten to primary grades, grade to grade, and school to school. Continuity is the key to seamless transitions. According to Lombardi (1993) three key elements to continuity are DAP, parent involvement, and supportive services to families.

Successful transitions do not occur naturally. As systems we must promote continuous services and continuity for young children with disabilities and their families. Hospitals, preschool programs, elementary schools, and agencies must advocate seamless transitions through procedures and policies with the key elements of continuity (DAP, parent involvement, and supportive services to families) as their foundation. Several checklists and steps are available. Two of the most frequently cited barriers to transition procedures are time and finances. Administrators must allow time and financial support for the possibility of success. Systems, as a whole, must be committed to the importance of this process.

Another tool to facilitate the networking of systems to develop continuity within their process is by formulating a transition policy of local agencies. Commitment by all would promote success of such a policy. Target areas for a transition policy include provision of services on a continuous basis without interruptions, procedures for timely transfer of records, acceptance of fiscal responsibility for certain transition activities, determination of the characteristics of children and families to be served by the agency/program, allotment of resources and personnel for certain transition activities, parental involvement in all aspects of transition, and assurance of confidentiality during transition.

Another perspective on the transition to school that is important to recall as we look to the future is the issue of readiness. Are we looking for child readiness or school readiness? In other words, is the focus on getting the child ready for the environment or the environment ready for the child? This is not a new issue to the field; it has been controversial for years. It was the first of the national education Goals of 2000 and the Educate America Act: "All children will start school ready to learn" (National Education Goals Panel, 1997). NAEYC's position statement emphasizes that discussions of school readiness must consider "the diversity of inequality of early life experiences of children; the wide range of variation of development and learning in young children; and the degree to which school expectations of children entering kindergarten are reasonable, appropriate and supportive of individual differences" (NAEYC Position Statement on School Readiness, 1990, p. 21). Furthermore, "NAEYC believes it is the responsibility of school to meet the needs of children as they enter, and to provide whatever services are needed in the least restrictive environment to help each child reach his or her potential" (NAEYC Position Statement on School Readiness, 1990, p. 21). With this perspective, how much preparation of the child and family should there be? Should the preschool child be subjected to a list of survival skills to learn before the first day of school? Or should the schools make a stronger effort to understand and meet the needs of the child? Should the stress and coping land on the child and family or on the teachers and schools?

Programs that are focused on the child, and committed to continuity and seamless transitions, must develop and maintain transition procedures and promote activities that support children with disabilities and their families. They must develop, agree to, and commit themselves to a transition policy for implementation of seamless services to young children with special needs. We must move beyond our concern for transition and bridge gaps to ensure effective and continuous services to young children with special needs and their families (Lombardi, 1993). To focus on the future, our primary emphasis must remain on the child and supporting the family.

Families

For the last twenty years an ecological perspective has helped our understanding of the functioning of children and families, that is, from the study of child development to decision making resulting in public policy (Bronfenbrenner, 1979). It continues to be a valuable perspective in the study of children growing up in families and communities and the functioning of those children, families, and communities. It is an important perspective as we consider the future and as we continue to explore what are best practices, effective programs, and family-friendly public policies. It is useful as an organizing perspective for research conducted in these areas. Within the social contexts and relationships of contexts, educational practices can be examined.

Quality of life and the families' well-being will be areas of focus to consider for future research. Collaborative decisions made by families and professionals versus our unilateral professional decisions for families may impact these two areas. McGregor and Goldsmith, (1998) in order to expand our understanding of families, review these two concepts and also include a third concept, standard of living. They suggest that as we study families and individuals in families, we must understand individuals' actual reality, their perception and satisfaction with that reality, and the indicators of that reality. As we implement specific processes—for instance, inclusion and strategies (such as positive behavioral supports or activity-based intervention)—with families who have young children with special needs, we must analyze how these practices support or inhibit their quality of life and well-being as individuals and as families.

Another area to consider is the community's responsibility for children and the families of those children. Where are the lines drawn for support, care, and education of young children, both with and without disabilities, within familial and community contexts? Granted, federal legislation is in place to provide for the educational needs of young children with special needs. This legislation includes a major family component. But when do concerns of all children become a "public matter," a term used by Garbarino and Kostelny (1995) in their discussion of public responsibility for children? How will implemented practices for young children with special needs, for example, inclusion, impact the implemented practices for young children *without* special needs? Will communities and, ultimately, the institutions of those communities respond to the parenting and education challenges that all families encounter? Will the process of inclusion impact decisions for the whole educational community?

An integrated, community-based service system has been viewed as a foundation for optimal outcomes for young children with disabilities and their families (Roberts, Rule, & Innocenti, 1998). As integrated, comprehensive services are offered to families, inclusionary educational settings will be a part of those services. Community agencies and health services will also be important components of these services. It will be important that families are an integral part of the service system, not only as consumers but also as policy makers and as monitors of service standards (Roberts et al., 1998). Researchers may be able to garner the components and supports necessary to achieve a community-based, integrative, and comprehensive service system. For example, what is necessary to introduce and support an inclusionary philosophy in educational settings and in other community settings? What is needed to implement and maintain inclusionary practices? Will inclusionary practices in educational settings generalize to community settings? Or is the reverse a more accurate picture?

Inclusion as a process can be very effective and help achieve optimal outcomes for young children with special needs and their families, as well as typically developing children. More information on the outcomes of inclusionary thinking and practices will, no doubt, be forthcoming. It will be useful to study the effects of inclusion in the educational and home environment, including family functioning and family interactions. Given a strong, effective family-professional partnership, will inclusionary practices create tension and more stress in families, or will it provide support and positively expand families' perspectives with regard to their fulfilling family responsibilities, especially those responsibilities related to meeting the needs of their children with special needs?

Do inclusionary practices in an educational setting affect general parental satisfaction? Research targeting the role satisfaction of parents, especially the component of role spillover, may be especially fruitful. As defined by Rogers and White (1998), role spillover has previously consisted of three major components: marital, parental, and labor-force participation. Relating role spillover to parenting, researchers may target how multiple roles affect the increase or decrease of family stress reactions, or the possible protective effects of having many roles. As children with special needs are included in settings for typically developing children, specific parental roles related to these settings may increase—for example, volunteers in the classroom, room mothers or fathers, or chaperones. How will these additional responsibilities affect the families involved? How will the interactions of families of children, both typically developing and with special needs, affect their own well-being and the inclusionary program?

Personnel Preparation

The manner in which we organize and implement preservice programs aimed at preparing professionals to work on behalf of young children and their families is most certainly in a period of significant reform and change. These changes are driven by mounting evidence specific to what constitutes best and effective practices in the delivery of services to young children with special needs (and all young children) and their families as well as by the guidelines and standards disseminated by professional organizations. An example of the latter is the *Guidelines for Preparation of Early Childhood Professionals* (1996), published by the National Association for the Education of Young Children (NAEYC), and developed collaboratively by NAEYC, the Division for Early Childhood of the Council for Exceptional Children (DEC/CEC), and the National Board for Professional Teaching Standards (NBPTS). These guidelines are intended to provide information and guidance to states as they reform and redesign their licensure programs for the preparation of early childhood educators.

There is significant emphasis in the guidelines and standards on preparing early childhood educators to acquire the philosophical basis, knowledge, and abilities needed to understand and implement responsible inclusion. It is important to note that these changes in what we expect candidates to know and be able to do for them to be eligible for licensure in early childhood education are substantially different from the past and will require a period of years before they are realized. Many of your professors—as well as many of the early childhood educators, early childhood special educators, early interventionists, and child care and family specialists with whom you interact—were trained in graduate or undergraduate programs that may not have had much emphasis on, for example, partnerships with parents and family-centered approaches, collaboration and teaming across disciplines, inclusion practices, attention to child and family diversity, or uses of technology in early childhood education.

Traditionally, personnel preparation programs have tended to be more self-contained; that is, they have focused on content related directly to teaching the child and commonly associated exclusively with their disciplines. Kilgo and Bruder (1997) conclude that most colleges and universities have provided unidisciplinary personnel preparation programs rather than interdisciplinary programs, and that those which were (are) interdisciplinary very often are supported by external funding. They suggest that preservice programs frequently return to a unidisciplinary approach after the funding period is complete. A significant number of both professionals and others might view inclusion of young children with disabilities as manageable only when there are substantial external resources, such as demonstration grant funding. Kilgo and Bruder (1997) note the necessity of a systems change perspective from colleges and universities in order to carry out interdisciplinary (or transdisciplinary) programs to prepare professionals in early childhood disciplines.

In the instance of early childhood education the unidisciplinary approach has meant emphasizing philosophical bases, curricula, and child guidance approaches aimed primarily at educating typically developing young children. For early childhood special education, as Bricker and Woods-Cripe (1992) have indicated has frequently meant use of traditional behavior analytic approaches that carefully structure antecedents, specify precise responses, and deliver tangible consequences. Furthermore, it meant a high degree of control by the adult(s) and very often one-on-one intervention. It is not difficult to see why the disciplines of early childhood education and early childhood special education have struggled to find common ground in their efforts to understand and implement inclusion settings and processes. We are going to briefly and generally discuss ways in which personnel preparation programs are being reformed to more effectively meet the needs of all young children and their families, as we move into the twenty-first century. Before we do so, it might be helpful to delineate what is meant by personnel preparation in the present context.

In the simplest of terms, it is possible to think of personnel preparation as occurring at either the preservice or in-service level. Generally *preservice* refers to formal undergraduate or graduate classes, offered for credit by colleges and universities and leading to a degree and/or licensure (for example, licensure or certification in early childhood education). *In-service* refers typically to a variety of ongoing training and learning experiences and opportunities provided to teachers and other professionals while they are on the job. Another way of differentiating between the two is as follows (McCullum & Catlett, 1997): "The term preservice refers to professional development efforts that prepare individuals to perform the entry-level functions of their disciplines or professions, whereas inservice refers to professional development activities undertaken to assist the more experienced professional in expanding and growing within the profession." As you probably know, many school systems and other employers have requirements regarding how much in-service, or continuing education, their employees must complete on an annual basis.

There is a substantial amount of attention in our early childhood and early childhood special education literature given to the kinds of training and support needed and desired by educators on the job in order to be successful with the inclusion process. For our purposes in this chapter we are going to limit our discussion primarily to issues and future trends of personnel preparation at the preservice level.

However, here is one example of what you might expect in the future when you are "on the job" and are the recipient of in-service education. Olson, Murphy, and Olson (1998) have developed and implemented a model for the delivery of in-service to persons working on behalf of young children and their families, including, for example, Head Start staff, early childhood educators, and early interventionists. This model is entitled Building Effective Successful Teams (BEST), and in it, in-service participants are required to work closely together in exercises aimed at fostering cooperation, team building, and shared problem solving in family-friendly ways. As we move more successfully into inclusive processes and programs in early childhood, professionals must develop and refine in practical and applied ways their skills in collaboration, partnering, and working in the context of a team.

There is, of course, a great deal of overlap with regard to the content covered at the in-service and preservice level. It is also important to keep in mind the perspective of lifelong learning as it relates to the relationship between preservice and in-service training. As professionals who serve young children and their families, we have an obligation to continue to grow professionally, to keep up with changes in our discipline by continuing our education.

Miller and Stayton (1998), in a national study of teacher programs in which early childhood education (ECE) and early childhood special education (ECSE) have been blended (interdisciplinary), found that respondents (faculty in the disciplines of child development, early childhood, and early childhood special education) considered the primary benefits of blended programs to be the values and beliefs about preparing educators to understand and implement inclusion. Primary barriers to blended programs included administrative and interpersonal relationship issues. Additionally, Miller and Stayton concluded that faculty members have a need for "retooling," that in field experiences associated with blended programs children with disabilities and families are not adequately represented, that there is a need for continued dialogue about blended content in ECE and ECSE programs, and finally that future research to identify effective structures and practices is needed.

Preservice training is rapidly moving toward more blended or interdisciplinary programs, especially related to the disciplines of early childhood, early childhood special education, and child and family studies. These changes bring with them substantial challenges for university administrators, faculty members, and practitioners to develop greater commitment to and competence in collaboration and teaming. Reform in personnel preparation is essential if we are to prepare early childhood educators and interventionists who can work together to achieve responsible inclusion.

One fundamental assumption about the relationship among disciplines related to early childhood special education, and applied at the institution in which the author works, is embodied in these statements: "In order to be an early interventionist/early childhood special educator, you must in essence be an early childhood educator. And in order to be an early childhood educator, you must have a strong foundation in and a working knowledge of child development and families." While these statements may seem a bit extreme or oversimplified to some, the message is rather straightforward. The specialized knowledge and skill needed by the early childhood special educator is only relevant if it can be applied as extensions of the best and effective practices assumed for all young children. And the ability of an early childhood educator to carry out developmentally appropriate practice is significantly constrained if she/he is not prepared to make the accommodations and adaptations necessary to include children with diverse learning needs, such as a specific disability. One of the more commonly applied practices in interdisciplinary programs is team teaching of courses by faculty members in different disciplines.

Another innovative practice increasing in use and acceptance is the partnership with faculty members in the planning and delivering of college coursework. You have studied about the importance of family-centered services. Think about what the family-centered perspective might mean if applied to how professionals are trained in undergraduate and graduate courses. Innovative personnel preparation models in early childhood special education (Capone & Divenere, 1996) are more frequently using family-centered approaches in their programs. It is reasonable to assume that in the future there will be a continued movement toward team or co-teaching between professionals and family representatives (not just mothers or fathers).

While this approach brings about challenges for university administrators, the advantages related to preparing professionals in best and effective practices are numerous. One obvious advantage is that faculty members are provided the opportunity, with students, to model collaborative relationships and partnerships with families. In addition , a large percentage of the individuals completing preservice programs in early childhood and early childhood special education have limited exposure to families through their field experiences and student teaching. This approach will add substantial, varied, and ongoing opportunities to develop a commitment to and skills in applying family-centered services. Finally, a significant number of preservice students in these disciplines will enter the profession at a comparatively young age and with limited adult, personal experience related to families. Besides affecting their beliefs, knowledge, and skill, learning directly from family members will enhance the credibility of these entry level professionals. Capone and Divenere conclude that there are three fundamental ways in which a partnership with families in personnel preparation will enhance early intervention: Service programs will have employees who are trained in family-centered practices, university programs will be enhanced, and the field of early intervention will benefit as more interventionists expand their ability to translate family-centered philosophy into practice.

There is reasonable evidence and experience at this point in the development of personnel preparation programs in early childhood and early childhood special education to assume that the blending of these disciplines will continue to occur. As the disciplines of ECSE and ECE learn more from each other and collaborate more extensively at the level of professional training, state licensure designs and requirements, and processes and practices of inclusion, the articulating and valuing of the specialized needs of young children with disabilities will be enhanced (McCullum & Stayton, 1996). While we have not dealt here with the roles of other disciplines—such as child and family studies, nursing, or therapy specialties—(for example, physical, speech/language, occupational)—in future directions of personnel preparation, they are obviously of great importance. The reforms and innovations in these disciplines—and the positions they take with regard to developmentally appropriate practice, positive behavioral supports and activity-based intervention—will directly impact our ability to further the goal of responsible inclusion for young children with disabilities and their families. A book edited by Diane Bricker and Anne Widerstrom (1996) entitled *Preparing Personnel to Work with Infants and Young Children and Their Families: A Team Approach,* provides a thorough introduction to the future roles of various disciplines in the preparation of personnel to serve young children and their families.

Summary

This chapter has provided the reader with an exploration of future directions in the field of inclusive early childhood education. Although not a comprehensive review of future issues, the chapter identified future directions from the perspective of foundations, policy, research, intervention practice, and personal preparation. Foundations for future directions in these domains were explored. Next the emergence of research in guiding the practices of early childhood educators and related professionals in the future was examined. Specific areas of research to practice included the advances of technology and early brain research and their relationship to improved practices and quality-of-life issues for young children. Finally, future perspectives in the areas of practice were explored, including the areas of assessment, intervention, and planning.

Chapter 9 Suggested Activities and Resources

Suggested Activities

1. Students might consult the journal *Exceptional Parent* for its annual issue devoted to the areas of early childhood and technology to keep abreast of the areas from a "families" perspective.

2. Identify "model" early childhood education programs in your communities, and ask to visit and observe the program. While there, document specific examples from your observations that reflect best and effective practices.

3. Attend a parent-to-parent meeting, if available, in your state to gain additional knowledge in how parents and families can assist one another when confronted by the challenges associated with parenting a child with a disability. Relate their perspectives to issues identified in the chapter.

4. Consult the emerging literature from suggested journals in the fields of early childhood education, early childhood special education, and child development and family to keep informed on current issues and specifically projections about the future.

Selected Resources

The following list of resources will provide the reader with more information concerning future directions in the field of inclusive early childhood education as they unfold.

1. *Websites*

   Division for Early Childhood of The Council for Exceptional Children: http://www.dec-sped.org

   National Association for the Education of Young Children (NAEYC): http://www.naeyc

   The Association for Childhood Education International: http://www.udel.edu/bateman/acci/

   Head Start http://www2.usf.dhhs.gov/programs/hsb/

National Early Childhood Technical Assistance System:
http://www.nectus.unc.edu

Special education resources on the Internet
http://www.hood.edu/seri/serihome.htm

Early Educators On Line LISTSERV:
http://www.ume.maine.edu/~coled/eceol/welcome.shtml

United States National Library of Medicine:
http://www.nlm.nih.gov./

2. *Publications*

   DEC Recommended Practices: Indicators of Quality in Programs for Infants and Young Children with Special Needs and Their Families. See www.dec-sped.org for ordering information.

3. *Journals to consult regarding research and innovative practices*

   The Journal of Early Intervention

   Young Exceptional Children

   Topics in Early Childhood Special Education

   Journal of Applied Behavior Analysis

   Exceptional Children

   Young Children

References

Blackman, J. A. (Ed.). (1995). *Technology in Early Intervention.* Gaithersburg, MD: Aspen Publishers, Inc.

Blackman, J. A. (Ed.). (1995). *Identification and Assessment in Early Intervention.* Gaithersburg, MD: Aspen Publishers, Inc.

Borgia, E. T., & Schuler, D. (1996). *Action Research in Early Childhood Education* (Report No. ED401047). Urbana, IL: University of Illinois. ERIC Clearinghouse on Elementary and Early Childhood Education.

Bricker, D., & Widerstrom, A. (1996). *Preparing Personnel to Work with Infants and Young Children and Their Families: A Team Approach.* Baltimore, MD: Paul H. Brookes Publishing Co.

Bricker, D., Woods-Cripe, J. J. (1992). An Activity-Based Approach to Early Intervention. Baltimore, MD: Paul H. Brookes Publishing Co.

Bronfenbrenner, V. (1979). The Ecology of Human Development. Cambridge, MA: Harvard University Press.

Capone, A. M., & Divenere, N. (1996). The Evolution of a Personnel Preparation Program: Preparation of Family-Centered Practitioners. *Journal of Early Intervention, 20*(3), 222–231.

Children's Defense Fund (1998). *The State of America's Children Yearbook 1998.* Washington, DC: Author.

Fallon, M. A. & Sanders Wann, J. A. (1995). Incorporating Computer Technology into Activity-Based Thematic Units for Young Children with Disabilities. In J. A. Blackman (Ed.), *Technology in Early Intervention*. Gaithersburg, MD: Aspen Publishers, Inc.

Garbarino, J., & Kostelny, K. (1995). Parenting and Public Policy. In M. H. Bornstein (Ed.), *Handbook of Parenting, Vol. 3: Status and Social Conditions of Parenting*. Mahwah, NJ: Lawrence Erlbaum Associates.

Guralnick, M. J. (1997). Second-Generation Research in the Field of Early Intervention. In M. J. Guralnick (Ed.), *The Effectiveness of Early Intervention*. Baltimore: Paul H. Brookes Publishing Co.

Hart, B., & Risely, T. (1995). *Meaningful Differences in the Everyday Experience of American Children*. Baltimore: Paul H. Brookes Publishing Co.

Haugland, S. W., & Wright, J. L. (1997). *Young Children and Technology: A World of Discovery*. Boston: Allyn and Bacon.

Kilgo, J. L., & Bruder, M. B. (1997). Creating New Visions in Institutions of Higher Education. In P. J. Winton, J. A. McCollum, & C. Catlett (Eds.), *Reforming Personnel Preparation in Early Intervention: Issues, Models and Practical Strategies*. Baltimore, MD: Paul H. Brookes Publishing Co.

Kontos, S., Moore, D., & Giorgetti, K. (1998). The Ecology of Inclusion. *Topics in Early Childhood Special Education, 18*(1), 38–48.

Lesar, S. (1998). Use of Assistive Technology with Young Children with Disabilities: Current Status and Training Needs. *Journal of Early Intervention, 21*(2), 146–159.

Linder, T. W. (1990). *Transdisciplinary Play-Based Assessment: A Functional Approach to Working with Young Children*. Baltimore: Paul H. Brookes Publishing Co.

Lombardi, J. (1993). *Beyond Transition: Ensuring Continuity in Early Childhood Services*. ERIC Document OERI 88-062012.

McCullom, J. A., & Catlett, C. (1997). Designing Effective Personnel Preparation for Early Intervention: Theoretical Frameworks. In P. J. Winton, J. A. McCollum, & C. Catlett, (Eds.), *Reforming Personnel Preparation in Early Intervention: Issues, Models and Practical Strategies*. Baltimore: Paul H. Brookes Publishing Co.

McCullom, J. A., & Stayton, V. D. (1996). Preparing Early Childhood Special Educators. In D. Bricker and A. Widerstrom (Eds.), *Preparing Personnel to Work with Infants and Young Children and Their Families: A Team Approach*. Baltimore, MD: Paul H. Brookes Publishing Co.

McGregor, S. L. T., & Goldsmith, E. B. (1998). Expanding Our Understanding of Quality of Life, Standard of Living, and Well-Being. *Journal of Family and Consumer Sciences, 90,* 2–6.

Miller, P. S., & Stayton, V. D. (1998). Blended Interdisciplinary Teacher Preparation in Early Education and Intervention. *Topics in Early Childhood Special Education, 18*(1), 49–58.

National Association for the Education of Young Children (1996). *Guidelines for Preparation of Early Childhood Professionals.* Washington, DC: NAEYC.

National Association for the Education of Young Children (1997). *NAEYC Summit: Preparing for the Next Millennium: Influencing Education in the Future.* NAEYC's Leadership Summit, Atlanta, GA, April 3–6, 1997.

National Association for the Education of Young Children Position Statement on School Readiness (1990). *Young Children, 46*(1), p. 21.

National Education Goals Panel (1997). *The National Education Goals Report: Building a Nation of Learners.* Washington, DC Government Printing Office.

Odom, S. L., Horn, E. M., Marquart, J. M., Hanson, M. J., Wolfberg, P., Beckman, P., Lieber, J., Li, S., Schwartz, I., Janka, S., & Sandall, S. (1999). On the Forms of Inclusion: Organizational Context and Individualized Service Models. *Journal of Early Intervention, 22,* 185–199.

Olson, J., Murphy, C. L., & Olson, P. D. (1998). Building Effective Successful Teams: An Interactive Teaming Model for Inservice Education. *Journal of Early Intervention, 21*(4), 339–349.

Roberts, R. N., Rule, S., & Innocenti, M. S. (1998). *Strengthening the Family-Professional Partnership in Services for Young Children.* Baltimore: Paul H. Brookes Publishing Co.

Rogers, S. J., & White, L. K. (1998). Satisfaction with Parenting: The Role of Marital Happiness, Family Structure, and Parents' Gender. *Journal of Marriage and the Family, 60,* 293–308.

Shore, R. (1997). Rethinking the Brain. New Insights into Early Development. New York, NY: Families and Work Institute.

Zirploi, T. J., Wieck, C., Hancox, D., & Skarnella, E. R. (1994). Partners in Policymaking: The First Five Years. *Mental Retardation, 32,* 422–425.

Section IV
Applications

OVERVIEW

The last three chapters of this book (Chapters 10, 11, and 12) provide you with fifteen vignettes that will illustrate practical applications of the principles and major themes, concepts, and procedures detailed in the previous nine chapters. Each of these three chapters will include five vignettes, or "sketches," about the experiences of young children, families, educators, caregivers, and other professionals. You will note that we have in these chapters, as well as throughout the book, avoided use of the term *case*. Families and their young children with special needs are consumers of and participants in the services provided by professionals. They are not cases to be studied or managed, or to be neatly stored in file cabinets or on someone's hard drive. This is a perspective and belief that the authors not only hold as a professional best and effective practice but also feel strongly about and have confirmed in their partnerships with families and in their personal roles as parents and family members. It is unlikely that professionals will be able to fully comprehend family-centered approaches to inclusive and natural environments-based early intervention and early childhood service delivery, much less carry them out in practice, if they maintain a view of families as cases.

The vignettes you will read in the following chapters are either taken directly or modified from the authors' past experience and work with young children and families, or they combine significant elements of the authors' professional and personal lives. Names and other identifying information have, of course, been changed to preserve confidentiality.

You are cognizant by now that the foundation of this book is that the desirability of inclusion is not in question. What is at issue is how to make it a successful process. The authors have argued that the merging of the principles and strategies of activity-based intervention, positive behavioral supports, and developmentally appropriate practice, and the incorporation of other themes and concepts introduced in Chapter 1 and elaborated on throughout the book, will allow us to plan and implement successful environments for inclusion. As you read the following fifteen vignettes, you will have opportunities at the end of each chapter (in the activities) to discover how they illustrate applications of recommended and effective practice for inclusion. However, not everything in the vignettes describes positive and successful experiences. You will find some evidence of the problems and constraints—the "real world" challenges encountered by families, children, and professionals—in the early childhood education inclusion process.

The vignettes are divided equally among age ranges, including five each for the infant/toddler (early intervention) period (Chapter 10), the preschool age range including kindergarten (Chapter 11), and the early primary grades (Chapter 12). While the authors have in the interest of continuity and readability maintained the sequence and content organization introduced below, obviously there is a significant variability between and among these vignettes with regard to the setting(s), the age of the child or children with special needs, the type and severity of the disabilities, the resources and constraints associated with the professionals and their circumstances, and the differences among families. One example might be the difference between an individualized family service plan (IFSP) and an individualized education program (IEP) with regard to the overall intent and design and with regard to specific things like the style and format for developing goals and objectives.

Each vignette has in general five subparts, including an introduction, goals, objectives, strategies, and evaluation. However, keep in mind that the vignettes do not follow this sequence exactly. In the *introduction* you are acquainted with the family, the child or children, and the professionals and learn something about the nature of the setting(s) in which services are delivered. The subpart on *goals* (outcomes) provides you with samples of some of the goals that have been established in the development of the IFSP or the IEP. Goals generally reflect global intents, or benchmarks, that are addressed over a period of six to nine months or more.

Following goals, most vignettes provide sample *objectives* related to the goals. The objectives will usually reflect a short term (weeks or a few months) and will lend themselves to reasonable forms of measurement and accountability. You will note the variance across different vignettes with regard to the way objectives are written. Some will be rather specific, quantifiable, and operational, while others will be "loose" and may even look more like what you think of as a goal. The assumption here is that there is no one correct way or recipe for writing objectives. The proof of the quality of an objective has more to do with whether or not it is collaboratively developed, is clearly understood by all, lends itself to judgments about whether or to what extent it has been accomplished, allows for generalization across settings, and is functional for the child, the family, and the expectations of inclusive and natural environments.

The fourth subpart is *strategies*. Here you will have detailed some of the activities, procedures, curricula, and techniques that were employed to address the goals and objectives established in the IFSP or IEP. Of course, these strategies will draw heavily from the content provided throughout your book and will illustrate the principles of ABI, PBS, and DAP, as well as the other themes, concepts, and procedures presented in the text. Sometimes the goal, objective, and strategy are addressed together. The last subpart of each vignette is *evaluation* and will highlight the ways in which the efficacy of the interventions is determined. In others words, what are the means, both subjective and objective, by which professionals and parents/families will determine the effectiveness of the interventions. You will note an effort to present methods of evaluation that are creative and "unobtrusive," as well as family and educator friendly.

Applying PBS, ABI, and DAP in Inclusive Infant/Toddler Settings

Chapter

10

INTRODUCTION

If you have taken the opportunity to read the overview to Section IV: Applications, then you know that this chapter is intended to provide the reader with examples of how the principles, methods, procedures, and best and effective practices introduced to this point in the book are applied in the provision of early intervention services to infants and toddlers with special needs and their families in inclusive settings and natural environments. Here are the objectives that the reader will address in Chapter 10. You should be able to:

- Explain the mandate for early intervention services in Part C of the reauthorization of the Individuals with Education Act, and list and define the components required in early intervention.
- Compare and contrast the provision of inclusive early intervention services to those provided to preschool-aged and early primary grade level children.
- Analyze the five vignettes and make sound decisions and judgments about the extent to which the foundations of inclusion—DAP, ABI, and PBS—have been applied and the quality and relevance of those applications.
- Identify in the vignettes the applications of other best and effective practices detailed in the text, including but not limited to collaboration and teaming, family-centered services and parent partnerships, people first perspectives, the ecological approach, self-determination and self-advocacy, service and transition planning, functional assessment, and social validity in interventions.

Summary History of and Legislative Basis for Early Intervention

The theoretical and philosophical models and applied practices that guide us in the planning and delivering of early intervention services to infants and toddlers with disabilities and their families have come to the fore over a comparatively short history. While much attention has been focused on the research and federal funding of model demonstration projects carried out since the late 1960s,

Gallagher (1997) has noted the importance of the work done in the 1950s and 1960s with regard to establishing the field of early intervention as a distinct and respected discipline. Certainly the early research and writing about the importance of the early childhood period in the development of all children, and the experiences of and support for compensatory programs—such as Head Start primarily—have an important place in the history of the field of early intervention.

In his book synthesizing the evidence for the effectiveness of early intervention, Guralnick (1997) suggests that the period of 1970 to 1995 represents a first generation of research that established the efficacy of early intervention or, stated another way, provides support for the argument that early intervention works, is justified, and makes a significant positive difference in the lives of most young children with disabilities and their families. Guralnick believes that we are embarking on establishing an agenda for and beginning work on a second generation of research in which we will look more specifically at program features, outcomes of early intervention, and characteristics of children and families. Maybe you will be a part of this second generation of research and further examination of the specific factors associated with excellence in the provision of services to young children and their families. At least you will want to keep abreast of recent research findings and their implications and applications for how you design and deliver early childhood education and early childhood special education.

You may recall that earlier in this text we introduced the legislative basis for early intervention. It might be useful here to review, especially how federal legislation relates to the deliver of services that you will read about in the vignettes. In 1986, the Education of the Handicapped Act Amendments of 1986 was passed (Public Law 99-457). Part H of that legislation provided funds to states that wanted to plan and begin implementation of an early intervention service delivery system. Inclusion of Part H in the legislation represented a landmark event and the culmination of the extensive and tireless efforts of numerous professionals, policy makers, parent/family advocacy groups, and professional organizations in focusing the attention of the federal government on the necessity of funding early intervention.

The purpose of the Part H program was to "provide financial assistance to states to help them develop a comprehensive, coordinated, multidisciplinary, interagency program of early intervention for infants and toddlers and their families" (Safer & Hamilton, 1993). Part H required that each statewide system of early intervention have fourteen components. While it is not necessary for us at this point to detail all of those components, three are briefly introduced here, since they have particular relevance for the vignettes in this chapter. Each state was (and is) required to have a single line of responsibility in a state-level lead agency to oversee early intervention. In the author's state that agency is the state department of education, and that is the case in more than half of all states. As of this writing, all fifty states are participating in Part H (now Part C), and in addition to education, lead agencies include health, mental health and mental retardation, developmental disabilities, social services, and combination or "umbrella" agencies combining two or more of the above. A second of the fourteen components requires that for each eligible infant or toddler an IFSP be developed that includes provision of service coordination for the family. As IFSPs have evolved, based on experience over the past decade and on research evidence and changing federal regulations and state guidelines, there has been a growing emphasis on family-centered planning and service delivery.

Despite the fact that the spirit and intent of the IFSP is "family friendly" to reflect family wishes and to have family-related goals, there is evidence (McWilliam et al., 1998) that they often continue to be written with a focus on child-related goals rather than family-focused goals. You will note in the vignettes some of the variations of how IFSPs are developed and carried out. Appendix B provides the authors' format for the IFSP document. A third component required that a multidisciplinary evaluation of each child be done. This focus on cross-disciplinary participation and cooperation in assessment and evaluation represents a rather significant departure from the traditional ways in which children with special needs have been identified. The requirement for multidisciplinary evaluation is also evident in some of the vignettes below. There are numerous resources available to you if you wish to have a more comprehensive review of the history of federal legislation that has impacted young children and their families. One resource is a text by Bowe (1995), which thoroughly addresses laws up to the 1991 amendments to the Individuals with Disabilities Education Act (IDEA).

On June 4, 1997, the IDEA Amendments of 1997 were enacted into law as Public Law 105-17. This statute reauthorized and made some significant changes in IDEA overall and specifically with regard to early intervention. Part H became Part C, effective July 1, 1998. In an article summarizing the 1997 reauthorization of IDEA, Senator Tom Harkin (1998) points out that the Part H initiative has "transformed the lives of tens of thousands of infants and toddlers with disabilities and their families from lives of despair and desperation to lives filled with hope, opportunity, love, and high expectations." He notes the now significant congressional and other federal government level support for early intervention as evidenced by the five-year authorization and increased funding level for early intervention. Senator Harkin also highlights the requirement in the new authorization of IDEA Part C that the IFSP must include information about how the child will be served in natural environments, or a justification of why services will not be, and to what extent, delivered in natural environments. An example of how this focus on the necessity for using natural (inclusive) environments is being accomplished can be found in the experiences of the professionals and families in the state of Texas. Through a concerted effort over several years, they now have more than 95 percent of all Part C eligible infants and toddlers and their families served in natural environments. (See Figure 10–1.)

Introduction to the Five Vignettes

In the remainder of Chapter 10 you will become acquainted with the real-life experiences of six very young children—Ethan, Alisha, James, Jesse, Anna and Ronald—their families, and the professionals and agencies with whom they have interacted as their special needs emerged, were identified and diagnosed, and services planned, delivered, and modified over time. You will see that there are very significant differences among these vignettes. While none are simple, some are rather straightforward. Special needs are identified, plans are made efficiently and collaboratively, and services delivered readily and in what are clearly

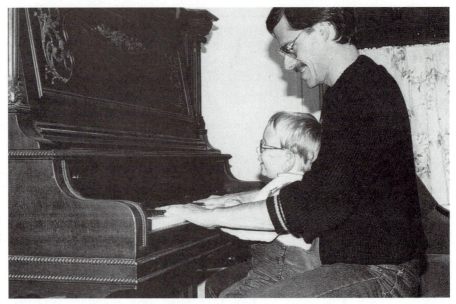

Figure 10–1 The Early Intervention Part C of the 1997 Amendment to IDEA strengthen the commitment for services in natural environments.

natural environments. In other vignettes, things don't go quite so smoothly, and that is, of course, consistent with the experiences that you have had, or will have, as professionals (or family members) in the "real world." Sometimes special needs are hard to label or to agree upon, planning processes are confusing and complicated, services and professional expertise are scarce or unavailable, and parents and families facing challenges of basic survival are not ready for or amenable to significant participation in family-centered services.

Read these vignettes with your head and your heart. That is, it is desirable for you to read with the intent of relating the experiences to the effective and recommended practices detailed throughout the book, and that is what you will be invited to do in the activities provided at the end of the chapter. But it is also desirable for you to put yourself in the places of the people described in the vignettes—including the parents and family members, the early interventionists, and the other professionals—and to consider how they might be feeling about their roles and actions. The author gratefully acknowledges the contributions to the vignettes of three colleagues and early intervention service coordinators: Mary Ebersviller, Susan O'Connor, and Filomena Walker. Also, the author appreciates the willingness of two early interventionists, Anne Johns and Lisa Davis, to share the sample development assessment.

VIGNETTE 1: ETHAN

Introduction

Ethan is the youngest for now, as his mother is expecting another child, in a Mennonite family of eight. He has three brothers—ages ten, nine, and three—and two sisters—ages eight and four. Ethan is seventeen months old. Ethan was born with Down syndrome and a hole in his heart. He was born at home, full-term, and weighed 6 lb 8 oz. The hole was repaired when he was six months old at the DeBorah Heart and Lung Center in New Jersey. His family had the surgery done there because that facility did not charge for services and allows the family to pay what they can. As Mennonites, Ethan's family does not have health insurance. The surgery appears to have been completely successful; Ethan is monitored by a pediatric cardiologist at a hospital in his home state, about 100 miles from where they live. Ethan is blond and blue-eyed with rosy cheeks; he looks very healthy and is very happy.

Ethan and his family live on a small farm about 2 miles outside the county seat of a predominantly rural county. His father builds barns and works his farm; his mother cares for the children and the home. His school-aged brothers and sisters attend the Mennonite community school; his younger brother and sister are at home with him and his mother. The family speaks German at home and English out in the wider community. The family does have a telephone and a car, so it is usually easy to contact them, and they are able to travel to appointments.

When Ethan was referred to the Part C program in his state, he was seven months old. He was referred by the hospital that monitors his heart. I (service coordinator) contacted the family by phone and arranged to visit the home for the intake. Myra, Ethan's mother, asked if her husband needed to be there, as he would take off work if needed. I said that would not be necessary, so on my first visit I met only Myra, Ethan, and his three-year-old brother. I explained to Myra what our early intervention program could do for Ethan and his family—assist them in accessing information, early intervention teachers and therapists, special equipment, support groups, and such. Myra told me that they were already connected with the Down's Syndrome Support Group within the Mennonite Church, and that they had received quite a bit of helpful information. Her main concern at that time was helping Ethan hold up his head, sit, and bear weight on his legs. She also wondered about tongue thrusting and his learning to talk. I said that we could arrange for a pediatric physical therapist and speech pathologist to do evaluations and ongoing therapy, if necessary. Myra wasn't sure about ongoing therapy, but she said they would like the therapists to do the evaluations and to give suggestions of what they could do at home to help Ethan. Myra's only other concern at the time of the intake was that if the family accepted services through Part C, would they have to send Ethan to public school. I said no, that the early intervention program covered children from birth until age three, at which time the family could continue services through the local education agency or at their church community school. I stressed that at all times the choice of services was theirs.

Goals and Objectives

On the initial plan of action, Myra decided that she would like to have physical therapy and oral-motor evaluations done, and she agreed to an assessment of Ethan's current levels of development to help us write the individualized family service plan (IFSP). The developmental assessment was done in Ethan's home. We also met at his home to do the IFSP. Ethan's father was not able to be present, so Myra, the special educator who did the assessment, a graduate student from the local university, and I developed the plan. The first outcome/goal that the family wished to address was "Help Ethan to hold his head up and develop better muscle tone." The action steps/objectives under this were (1) to have physical and occupational therapy evaluations done to determine if ongoing therapy was indicated and to provide the family with activities and exercises that could be incorporated into Ethan's daily routine; and (2) to purchase, adapt, or make equipment recommended by the therapists. The second outcome/goal was "Help Ethan with his eating, trying new foods, learning how to use his tongue to eat better." This was related to the concern Myra had expressed at intake about tongue thrusting. Ethan was successfully breast-feeding, which was already providing excellent oral-motor practice. Myra wanted to know what foods to present next and the best ways to present them. The action step/objective under this was to have an oral-motor evaluation done by a speech pathologist to determine if ongoing therapy was necessary and to provide specific recommendations for the family to use in Ethan's daily activities.

Strategies

Because the family did not have health insurance, the early intervention program was payor for the services defined in the IFSP. I made requests to therapists on contract with us for the physical, occupational, and oral-motor evaluations. The physical therapist saw Ethan in his home and found that his head control was good but that his trunk musculature needed to be strengthened. She demonstrated for Myra several options to provide Ethan with more challenging practice in sitting, including placing him in a laundry basket with a "desk" (a box cut out to accommodate his legs). She also demonstrated strengthening exercises. The physical therapist felt that Ethan did not need ongoing therapy, that periodic consultation with family would work for now. The occupational therapist to whom the original request for the evaluation was made moved out of the district before she could do it. It took several months to find another pediatric OT and get a contract with her. For this evaluation, Myra had to drive about 25 miles to a clinic site. The therapist did the evaluation on the floor with Ethan, and his mom was present. She explained what she was doing as she did it. Printed activity, play, and game suggestions were provided for the family with the written report. Again the therapist did not feel there was a need for ongoing occupational therapy.

In trying to arrange for the oral-motor evaluation, I had first bad then very good "luck." The speech pathologist that I originally sent the request to was carrying a full load, and a colleague to whom she considered giving the request was also too busy. Had either of them been able to accept Ethan as a client, Myra would have had to bring him to a clinic setting also 25 miles from home. I then asked another speech pathologist, who works for the school system, if she might be able to do the evaluation. She has many years of experience with children with Down syndrome and truly enjoys working with them, and the younger the better. She was also able to go to Ethan's home for the evaluation. This therapist recognized, as I had, that this family—mother, father,

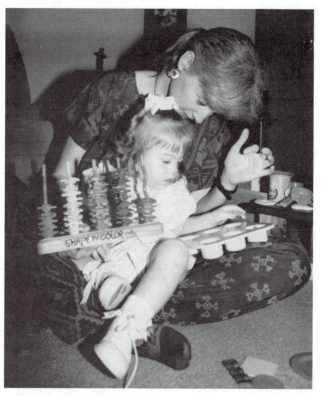

Figure 10–2 This speech therapist finds that therapy provided in the home setting is a very effective means of addressing specialized goals and developing relevant and functional speech and language.

and siblings—would enthusiastically follow through on any activities that were shown. She and Myra worked well together, to the point that the mom was comfortable with this therapist coming into her home to do early intervention therapy (incorporating gross motor, fine motor, oral-motor, and language development). So we modified the IFSP to include the speech pathologist doing home-based early intervention. It started with the therapist coming every other week while school was in session, then weekly when school let out for the summer. (See Figure 10–2.)

Evaluation

At the six-month review of the IFSP, Myra and I went over the IFSP as written, discussing what had been done and what had been delayed. I asked Myra if there was anything that she and her husband would like to add or change. She said no. They felt that quarterly consultations with the physical and occupational therapists were sufficient, since the therapist doing the weekly home-based intervention would continue to help the family incorporate the PT and OT recommendations. It pleases me that the family is very happy with the progress that Ethan is making and is comfortable with how the services he is receiving are being delivered.

VIGNETTE 2: ALISHA

Introduction

The family was full of fear when our paths first crossed. Their precious baby of less than one year was not thriving. Alisha was tiny, hovering around 15 pounds, and was not very interested in eating and was not developing at a typical rate. At nearly a year of age Alisha was not sitting and seemed weak. The family wondered if she had cystic fibrosis or muscular dystrophy or some other muscular disorder that was causing such poor weight gain and development. Such a beautiful baby with dark hair and dark eyes from her Middle Eastern heritage and such a happy baby with a smile on her face most of the time. At the point of our meeting the search had begun for the answer to the many whys that the family had about their darling baby.

Working through their local physician, their local health department, and with the early intervention system in their community, they finally had some definitive answers. It was Vanderbilt Developmental Center and the Genetics Department that finally confirmed the diagnosis of Williams syndrome. The news was devastating. Not that cystic fibrosis or muscular dystrophy would have been any better, but they had contemplated these two possibilities. Williams syndrome was new and strange, and difficult to reckon with.

Mom and dad both worked, and Alisha was at a family day care home. Strangely enough I (service coordinator) had met Alisha's day care provider at a session I was conducting for training family day care home providers the week that Alisha was diagnosed. I found that the day care provider was interested in continuing to serve this sweet baby and in playing a role in her life and her development. I found her anxious to learn more and to help in any way that she could. My role in the training was to familiarize the family day care home providers with the law and their responsibility under IDEA to serve all children including those with special needs or disabilities. More important, my role was to let them know that there are services and resources available to help and guide them and to foster the inclusion of children in settings just like theirs.

I was so surprised when the family told me that they had taken their child out of the family day care home. They had been told about a special program that was available for children with special needs where she would get individualized attention from well-trained professionals in a setting where the numbers were small and the ratio of adults to children low, usually two adults to three or four children. This description convinced the family to move Alisha to the traditional segregated early intervention program. This program was located in the same building with a traditional child care program, but the programs did not interface with each other on a routine basis although they were in close proximity.

Goals and Objectives

The IFSP was written with the family, and Alisha attended the early intervention program five days a week from 8 a.m. to 3 p.m. She saw a physical therapist and an occupational therapist, and recommendations from both of these pediatric specialists were implemented by adults during the day. Her language was beginning to develop with a high percentage of echolalia, and soon a speech and language consultation was added to the list of services. From age one to age two this little one's special needs were met by loving adult professionals and paraprofessionals in a small group setting in a largely segregated early intervention program. The outcomes and the action steps on the IFSP centered around strength building and sensory integration issues that needed attention to meet the developmental goal of sitting independently, getting into and out of sitting, getting into and out of a four point position, crawling, creeping, pulling to stand, and eventually taking independent steps—the sequence of typical motor development. There were also outcomes and action steps that addressed the need for Alisha to tolerate noise and actions and activity around her in order to smooth her learning. Much attention was given to texture and sounds and motion introduced routinely to desensitize her. Brushing and pressure were part of the routine and listed as action steps on the IFSP. But also on the IFSP was an indication of the need to have Alisha with nondelayed, typically developing peers.

Strategies

It was an interesting moment in time when the early intervention program decided that they would close for two months in the summer and it would be the role of the service coordinator—in this case me—to find settings to serve the children in the interim. The opportunity presented itself to introduce the concepts of natural environments and inclusion and the power of the peer in inclusive settings. The family schedule required day care five days per week. The changes to the IFSP were notable as the focus shifted from one-on-one adult attention to embedding the special supports in an inclusive setting. In this instance it was a day care center setting that had included children with special needs for several years and was committed to the philosophy. While the teachers changed over time, the commitment did not waiver; and as with other little ones, this smiling two-year-old with the big dark eyes and the propensity to repeat anything and brighten your day in a moment was welcomed with open arms.

The IFSP was reviewed and changed to meet the challenges and the changes. The team got a little larger and a little more multidisciplinary, now including the toddler teacher and the toddler class assistant as well as the director of the child care facility. The family had a whole new set of folks to trust and to entrust with the daily care of their child. The family also had a whole new concept to try for themselves—higher numbers of children and not so much one-on-one attention. We addressed these concerns on the IFSP. Outcomes included continuation of services through the early intervention program, but this time with the early interventionist working with

Alisha and her toddler teacher in the day care setting and within the context of the regular routines and the typical toddler day. The teacher would remain the same, providing some continuity for both the child and the family.

The action steps included the specifics of how to communicate with the family, and a journal system using a notebook was devised so that the family knew who had been working with Alisha each day, what they had worked on, and what they had observed. The family read and added to the journal what they were seeing at home, what new things Alisha was doing, and what kinds of things she was responding to. These things were then looked for and fostered in the day care center at every opportunity. Action steps included making sure that Alisha's developmental needs were included in the lesson plans for the week and that activities—including lots of practice in Alisha's goals/objectives—were also enjoyed by and needed as well by others in her toddler class, either to reinforce newly acquired skills or to promote emerging skills. Added to the action steps were paying attention to the arrangement of furniture in the classroom to be sure that Alisha had props as she began to cruise about; having several plush toys available for practice in supported walking (with others of course!); the purchase of a set of steps to foster strength on one foot; and, after an occupational therapy consult, the addition of fluorescent tape to the steps to encourage downward gaze and to give stronger cues about depth and distance, providing more security for Alisha in negotiating the steps.

The two months passed quickly, and at the end of that time the family decided Alisha had made so much progress in the inclusionary (natural environment) setting that they would like to keep her there. Modifications in the IFSP continued. Outcomes related to language development included action steps for the toddler teacher to keep a log of new words and new phrases that were clearly not echolalic in nature and to share these with the speech therapist via the journal notebook. A new action step added another team member, this time a graduate student with an undergraduate degree in music therapy. The intent was to tap into the special gift that children with Williams syndrome often have for music. This person also utilized the journal notebook to convey to the family and to the other team members her observations, her techniques, and her suggestions. The journal became an effective means of communication for all those involved and helped in the continuation of the building and maintaining of trust between the family and the team members.

In the area of sensory integration the outcome was for Alisha to tolerate the various noises and activities within the environment without major upset. While this is primarily neurological, some effort was made to address it environmentally as well as on the IFSP. Action steps toward this outcome included helping the toddler teacher understand what sensory integration is and include in the day's schedule some vestibular activities. A list of possible activities was generated and shared among those working directly with Alisha. The music therapist was sure to include songs that required turning in circles or spinning around. The playground activities included playing airplane in the swings and spinning around, and playing airplane on the ground and spinning around, all with the same vestibular motion in mind.

The classroom added a Sit and Spin to the toys, and the children took turns with it. Attention was given to supplying a wide range of textures and contact with those textures with hands and feet and body as well. Activities were generated that would be enjoyable to all the children.

In addition the action steps addressed the behavioral issues of a child trying to integrate sensory input. The occupational therapist and the early intervention teacher explained to the toddler teacher and staff that giving too much attention to the child's reaction to initial sensory overload—likely crying—could play a role in sustaining the behavior. It was important to comfort Alisha, but then move on matter-of-factly with the understanding that there was no pain involved, but rather a basic neurological response that would pass quickly. Each time the neurological reaction would likely lessen, just from the familiarity of the experience. Everyone knew that this approach would greatly help Alisha begin to tolerate noises and activities in the classroom, in the building, and on the playground.

Evaluation

There has been so much change for this baby and this family in the course of a year, and then in the course of two years as she has just turned three in recent days! The change has been most dramatic and so very rewarding for me to see. The outcomes and the action steps outlined in this vignette were evaluated in many ways, including formal assessments like quarterly physical and occupational therapy consultations that added new goals and objectives as the old ones were met. The speech pathologist shared her weekly goals and objectives with the family, who shared them with the teachers informally via their daily contact and sometimes formally via the journal/notebook, providing the opportunity for all to be on the same page. Goal pages listed the goal at the top; and then the activities, toys, and experiences that were available routinely or could be made available routinely were posted for everyone working with Alisha, with a place to put a date and the number of opportunities that Alisha had to practice the skill. The toddler teacher, the early interventionist, the family, the music therapist, and all others involved could look and see if they were including play activities to give enough practice to develop and maintain the skill to which attention was being directed.

In addition to these methods of determining if progress toward goals and objectives was being made, virtually every verbal exchange between the parents and the toddler teacher, as they came face to face two times a day, presented the opportunity to share what new or improved behaviors were observed. It is this ongoing and routine exchange that not only evaluates progress toward stated outcomes and goals but also builds the trust that is so essential for successful inclusion in natural environments for infants and toddlers with disabilities.

VIGNETTE 3: JAMES AND JESSE

Introduction

The twin boys were born two months before they were due and they were identical, with one twin weighing 1½ and the other 2½ pounds. James was the smaller one, and he had to stay in the hospital for two months. Jesse was the larger twin, and he remained hospitalized for six weeks. The hospital was a very large, comprehensive facility in the nearest metropolitan area, a two-and-one-half-hour drive from the family's home in a rural part of the state. The future for James and Jesse was, of course, somewhat uncertain, and their growth and development was predictably slower than would be typically expected. But when at age two and a half they were still grunting, mom and dad became increasingly concerned about language. Up until this point everyone, including the special health coordinator, was thrilled that the boys were gaining in skills and staying healthy after such a rough start. Everyone was just so glad that they were alive that development in some domains seemed less important. But with the onset of the frustration at not being able to communicate their needs, the call came for intervention.

James and Jesse had been followed by and periodically assessed at the hospital where they were born and spent so much time in the first several months of their lives. The developmental clinic completed an evaluation when the boys were two, and they noted delays significant enough to qualify them for Part C services for the birth to age three population in our state. The family was thrilled that there was help and that perhaps the boys were truly healthy enough to include more people on their team of specialists, who up to that point had been primarily medical. The journey to services began with a call from the special services health coordinator and a joint visit to the family. Going into a home with someone already trusted helps establish trust and credibility a little faster. It did not take long to establish a team of people gathered together to write an individualized family service plan (IFSP) for James, Jesse, and their family.

Goals and Objectives

On a beautiful spring day in April on the front porch of their home, mom, dad, and the twins—along with the special health coordinator who made the referral, the intervention teacher who completed an assessment of the developmental domains, her supervisor, and me as the service coordinator (with also an evaluation from the speech/language pathologist)—sat down to develop a plan of services that would meet the unique needs of the boys and their family. At the onset it was clear that the natural environment for these little guys was their home. They were at home with their mom and dad all the time, except when they went to grandma's or church, and so the home was where the family wanted services for their boys.

The outcomes for James and Jesse were so similar that I will treat them as one, with the primary concern and the first outcome related to language— or the lack thereof. The dialogue was open and free. Outcome number one was to improve the ability to communicate using words. The action steps to meet this goal included weekly visits for speech therapy. Unfortunately, they would have to travel to a clinic to receive these services. There were also weekly visits by the early interventionist to the home to share tips and suggestions on language development with mom and dad as well as activities and toys to foster language, following the typical sequence of development. Finally, it was important to make sure that the home visitor and speech pathologist communicated strategies, objectives, and expectations with each other on a regular basis through phone calls or joint visits, along with shared communication via the family.

Other outcomes included attention to balance and strength building to develop coordination. Again this would follow typical developmental sequence for both boys. Action steps to this end included involving an agency to provide the funds to build a playhouse that would give many opportunities for James and Jesse to go up and down steps to promote weight bearing and strength building on one foot, inclines to foster weight shifting, and uneven terrain to negotiate in order to practice balance and other characteristics to help them develop targeted skills right there in their own backyard, every day of the week, with their cousins and extended family.

The next part of the IFSP evolved as the discussion about family and frustration and language, in particular, came full circle. It was clear that mom and dad were growing weary of the constant demands of two, two-year-olds who could not communicate their needs with words and were pretty much running the roost. It was also clear that the parents were totally devoted to the little guys, but they had no time to themselves and really did not know how much to expect from the boys, since they were not talking. The parents were frustrated regarding how to go about improving James' and Jesse's quality of life.

The outcome to address this need, which really was central to everything else that we had talked about, was written in terms of improving family time by helping the family establish routines and reasonable expectations for the boys. The action steps to achieve this outcome included the early intervention teacher providing written material on child development for mom and dad to read that would help them understand what is reasonable to expect of the boys at their level of development. The parents would help the early intervention teacher understand what the current routine is and what they would like their days to look like, including meal time, bedtime, nap time, and the like. The action steps also included consultative visits by another mom of a two-year-old, now four, who could advise about the development of language skills and what works best with a two-year-old struggling to control their environment and separate from mom and dad a little as they enter "toddlerdom." The team was particularly pleased to be privy to and to help problem-solve the very real family issues this mom and dad identified as obstacles to almost anything that they tried to do. (See Figure 10–3.)

Figure 10–3 The members of the IFSP team are partners in an ongoing, family-centered approach to planning, implementing, evaluating, and revising early intervention.

Evaluation

The evaluation of these outcomes is both formal and informal. On a weekly basis both the early intervention teacher and the speech pathologist write formal objectives and note progress. They also share this information with the family. The family shares the notes with each professional, making sure that the speech pathologist's comments are shared with the teacher and vice versa, and these notes are also shared with me as the service coordinator. They are placed in the files, maybe for use in the transition to Part B (preschool) services for the boys. The progress toward the outcomes related to quality of family life is self-evident in some ways. The children are less cranky because their environment is more predictable, and they are getting more sleep, eating more regularly, and mom and dad look and feel more rested (and they indicate so) and have more energy. While these outcomes are somewhat obvious and common sense, there are also written formats (grids) that outline the daily routines and checklists to remind everyone of what comes next. There are also stars and stickers and charts used as reinforcers with the boys, and there is a menu of potential reinforcers to be accessed as the old ones become less motivating. Grids and charts are on the refrigerator, with pencils nearby to check off how James and Jesse are progressing toward particular objectives. This system seems to have made a world of difference to this family in a very short time. Life has always been good for them, and now it's getting even better.

VIGNETTE 4: ANNA

Introduction

Anna is a two-year-old girl who is the second youngest of eleven born to migrant nursery workers. She was born at twenty-seven weeks gestation with APGARS of 0 and 2, neonatal listeria sepsis, prenatal asphyxia, hyaline membrane disease, hyperbilirubinemia, sepsis, hypocalcemia, and hypoglycemia. She was transported shortly after birth to Vanderbilt Hospital for management of her respiratory distress, and she was intubated and placed on mechanical ventilation. While in the NICU she suffered a Grade 4 intraventricular hemorrhage with resulting hydrocephalus that required a ventriculoperitoneal shunt. Following the placement of the shunt, she did well and was removed from the ventilator and placed on room air.

Anna had numerous apnea and bradycardia of prematurity spells and was treated with caffeine therapy to which she responded well. After a one-month stay at Vanderbilt, she was transported back to her hometown hospital twenty-one days following the shunt placement. She was receiving a combination of oral and tube feedings. At the time of discharge from Vanderbilt, an eye exam showed the possibility of retinopathy of prematurity and bilateral esotropia. An auditory screening showed her hearing to be within normal limits. Recommendations for follow-up examination with a pediatric neurosurgeon and evaluation of retinopathy of prematurity and esotropia were made upon discharge. She was hospitalized in her local hospital for three weeks and discharged to her home on oral feedings.

During the two years since her discharge from the NICU, Anna has grown and is progressing in her skill development with the care of her family, early intervention teacher, and therapists. She has, however, begun to have seizures requiring medication. Her retinopathy of prematurity has been resolved, and she has undergone the first of two eye surgeries to correct the esotropia. She is currently being fitted for glasses and is on an eye patching routine to strengthen her weaker eye. Anna has spasticity, weakness, hypersensitivity, and hypertonicity on her left side, especially in her left arm and hand. She has been fitted with an ankle foot orthotic and is beginning to take some supported steps.

The referral to our state's early intervention system was made by the Vanderbilt NICU on the day that Anna was sent to her hometown hospital so that preparations could be made for her discharge to home. The family was contacted through the owner of the nursery where the family works. Since the family speaks no English, an interpreter was found to help with application for Social Security, medical assistance, and to help with the intake and assessment for programming, as well as accompanying the family to doctor's visits. Since Anna would be coming home on an apnea monitor and needed breathing treatments, the service coordinator's (that's me!) first assignment, after finding an interpreter, was to be sure that the family had electricity and a phone.

The family lives on the property of the nursery owner in a building that was initially a potting house. They have one large room that serves as a kitchen, living room, and bedroom for all members of the family. At various times, other family members have lived with them while coming to the nursery to work. Several of the family's children attend the local public school, and they are doing very well. Service coordination and intervention are complicated by many social and cultural difficulties experienced within the family. The family income is well below the poverty line, and although two of the children are American citizens, the rest of the family members are illegal aliens. Because of the need for Anna's mother to work in the fields, the primary caregiver and homemaker for the family was Anna's fourteen-year-old sister. She was responsible for all housekeeping duties, cooking, and care of the younger children in the family. She was also responsible for carrying out the recommendations of the early intervention teacher and therapists providing services to Anna. She fulfilled this role for approximately two years until the local school district was notified that she was in the home and not attending school. She is now enrolled in the local high school full-time. The child care now is done by all the children in the home on a rotating basis. Each child takes a turn staying home to care for the younger children in the family. Since this family does not speak English (requiring, as noted above, interpretation for all services) and the mother does not drive, the managed care organization (MCO) providing this child's medical coverage agreed to provision of services in Anna's home, rather than in a clinical setting.

Goals, Objectives, and Strategies

Goals for Anna are both child and family need directed. On the initial IFSP all goals were directed at helping the family access services needed for Anna. On the second IFSP the goals became more child-focused, although there are still some family needs to be addressed. Attending to the many needs the family has in terms of daily living, medical care, and accessing resources in the community is important to the success of Anna's intervention. The family has been connected to Children's Special Services for help with coordinating medical care, Social Security for help with expenses for Anna, the Department of Human Services (DHS) for food stamps, Family Support Services for help with getting needed equipment, and Tennessee's Early Intervention System (TEIS) for help with coordination of all services and local early intervention and therapy providers. The family has also been adopted by one of the offices at a local university for help with providing Thanksgiving dinner and Christmas gifts for the children.

The first goal/outcome to report is that Anna's family will gain access to her Social Security check and will receive help in applying for food stamps. In the action steps, the interpreter who visits the family with the early interventionist agreed to help the family with a change of recipient for the Social Security check, since neither parent has a Social Security card and cannot open a bank account for direct payment. Originally the owner of the nursery had his wife appointed, but this did not work out and another recipient had to be found. Also, the family is often short of food and cannot manage on the salary earned by the parents, so the interpreter helped Anna's mother apply for food stamps for the children who are citizens. The team felt that if the basic needs of the child for nutrition and shelter were not being met, the early intervention would certainly be less effective and the family focus would have to be on meeting these needs before addressing Anna's developmental goals and objectives.

A second goal/outcome is that Anna will continue to develop new skills in all developmental areas. Action steps for this outcome include a weekly home visit by the early interventionist and interpreter to provide activities and family training to encourage the development of skills. The early interventionist visits the home weekly and demonstrates for the family, children included, activities to help Anna learn language, motor skills, feeding and self-help skills, and cognitive/play skills, as well as ways to embed these activities in the family's usual daily routines and events. By embedding the activities in this way, the family is better able to carry them out and to see the application of Anna's intervention focus in daily life. With so many siblings in close age proximity to Anna, there are many role models for her and she has the opportunity to practice newly acquired and developing skills with children who are typically developing and near her own age. Her siblings also provide motivation to "keep up with them." In this family, all children are responsible for the care of the children who are younger than them, so by including them in the intervention and intervention teaching, they are providing a significant amount of assistance in Anna's development.

A third goal/outcome is that Anna will increase her fine and gross motor skills to allow her to move about her environment more independently and to have the opportunity to explore. In the action steps for this outcome, the team decided that a weekly visit by the physical therapist was indicated to monitor progress and to provide family training on positioning and activities to help maximize Anna's abilities and help her continue to progress in her ability to move about. The PT is also responsible for communicating with the doctor about Anna's progress and the need for equipment such as an AFO (ankle-foot orthotic brace). The team also determined that—because Anna's ability to manipulate toys, perform self-help actions, and move about has been impacted by her weakness and hypersensitivity in her left hand and arm—an occupational therapy evaluation is needed to determine the best intervention. Translation was also added to this outcome as an action step.

Evaluation

We are evaluating progress in a number of ways. The early interventionist, the interpreters, the agency providing PT and OT, and the service coordinator are in contact by phone, mail, and fax on a regular basis. They discuss how things are going and if changes need to be made, based on family and other team member recommendations. The therapists and the early interventionist perform ongoing assessment of progress, which is documented monthly. Each six months, prior to the IFSP review or annual meeting, a formal assessment is completed. Family needs and medical reports are relayed to the service coordinator by the early interventionist, the therapists, and the interpreters. The service coordinator then shares the information with the other team members.

VIGNETTE 5: RONALD

Introduction

Ronald is a two-year-old boy who was referred to Tennessee's Early Intervention System (TEIS) by his primary care physician after his foster mother expressed concerns about his speech and language development. Although the initial referral was for speech and language, during the intake visit it became apparent that Ronald's behavior was of even greater concern to the family. His foster mother described Ronald as having always been active, but explained that as he has grown and is more mobile, it is "almost as if he is driven." She said he needs constant supervision and appears to move about without regard for his own safety. He climbs excessively, sleeps unusual amounts of time, and is beginning to show aggression toward family members. He is also described as having tantrums that are "out of control." He has been observed on a number of occasions eating nonedible things, crayons in particular.

The foster parents state that Ronald does not engage in purposeful play, but rather moves quickly from one thing to another. Ronald will carry out a box of toys, dump them on the floor, and walk away, even if the other children in the house are playing with the toys. The only toy that the foster mom has observed Ronald holding is a mechanical toy, which he held up to his face to feel the vibrations as it operated. His foster mother reports that she has heard Ronald say ma-ma, bye-bye, and sounds for other words with intent. She described him as often clumsy and falling a lot. During the intake visit, Ronald's foster mother shared that he had been in their care since the age of two months and that the Department of Human Services (DHS) was working toward reunification of Ronald with his birth mother within the year.

Ronald was transferred to the University of Tennessee NICU shortly after birth, although his foster mother is not sure why. He is one of four children born to his mother, with the other three children being half-siblings. During her pregnancy with Ronald, the birth mother was known to have abused barbiturates, cocaine, and alcohol. She was also taking phenobarbital and Dilantin for a seizure disorder. Following his release to her home, he was reportedly given Tylenol every three hours, until his removal by DHS, to "keep him quiet." His mother reported that she did not know that this was not an acceptable practice.

Medical records were obtained from the DHS worker in his home county. They indicated that Ronald was born two weeks prematurely after his mother suffered a seizure. Records also indicated that his kidneys are different sizes and there is some indication that there needs to be a follow-up on this condition. He was positive for hepatitis C at birth. The mother reported at the time of his removal that Ronald was a good baby who slept through the night, but after removal, this was not found to be the case. He cried almost constantly and refused to be comforted. He was also described as listless. After a period of time without regular administration of Tylenol, the behavior was resolved. He is now described as a friendly and inquisitive child. Ronald is, however, a little shy around strangers.

Because the plan for Ronald was to have him returned to his birth mother, services were coordinated with the TEIS office in his home region, not in the region in which I (service coordinator) work. On the initial plan of action, it was decided that a developmental evaluation would be done using two agencies, one that could provide services in the area where his foster home is located (if he were to stay there) and one that serves the area near his birth mother's home, so that both agencies would have a firsthand look at Ronald's developmental status. The developmental assessment is provided here.

Developmental Assessment Summary

Name: <u>Ronald</u>

Chronological Age: <u>24 Months</u>

Sex: <u>Male</u>

Examiner: <u>A. Johns, L. Davis</u>

Test Instruments: <u>PEACH Scale of Development, Functional Vision</u>

<u>Screening Test, Insite Auditory Skills Subtest</u>

Background Information

Tennessee's Early Intervention System (TEIS) requested the following evaluation to discover current levels of development and to help in determining eligibility for early intervention services. Ronald has lived with a foster family since shortly after his birth. He has a history of prenatal exposure to cocaine. Ronald's family expressed concern regarding his speech development. They are also concerned about behaviors he exhibits at home: eating inedible objects (especially crayons), the lack of purposeful play, his need to be in constant motion as though he is "driven," lack of any sense of danger, and his aggressive play with other children in the home.

Continued on page 268

Evaluation Setting

The PEACH Scale of Developmental was used to provide current developmental information. The evaluation was performed during two home visits with the assistance of Ronald's foster mother, who provided excellent information regarding Ronald's typical behaviors in daily routines. Ronald appeared healthy and eager to participate in our games. The Insite Auditory Skills Subtest and the Functional Vision Screening Test indicated good functional hearing and vision for test purposes. L. Davis of KIDS, Inc., joined the evaluation team on 04-17-98. Interview, observation, and presentation techniques were combined to obtain observation results.

Perceptual Skills (Problem Solving)

Ronald accomplished 75 percent of the skills typical for a child in his age range. He is performing at the eighteen-month skills range at this time. STRENGTHS include places circle, square, and triangle into formboard; stacking 8+ one-inch cubes; places pegs into pegboard; makes deductions as to where hidden object can be found; imitated vertical line. RECOMMENDATIONS: Perform tasks in orderly routines. Structure and concrete manipulation of objects accompanied by hand-over-hand guide were helpful in initial presentation of new tasks. Include matching object and color; nest differently sized containers; group toys by color, shape, and size; draw simple strokes in art activities.

Conceptual Skills (Concept Development)

Ronald accomplished 85.5 percent of the skills for a child his age in this area. He is working at the twenty-one-month age range. STRENGTHS include understands the use of household objects, follows one simple direction, points to four body parts on a doll, names one object ("ball"). RECOMMENDATIONS: Again utilize very organized and concrete presentation of new tasks. Include matching picture to object, understanding of prepositions, help him begin to develop a sense of ownership ("my").

Language Skills (How He Communicates with His Voice, Understands Words)

Ronald demonstrated 45.8 percent of skills in his age range in this area. He is performing at the eleven-month age range at this time. STRENGTHS: Foster mother reports that he vocalizes "mama," "nite-nite," "bye-bye," and "ball." Ronald has several sounds that clearly tell the family specific wants and needs: "ba-a" (rolls tongue) for "bottle," "ga gone," "ba bou" for "belly button," and so forth. He enjoyed sound play presented in play routines such as "zoom" and "rooom" in car play and "pop" in bubble play (he retained this new sound and used spontaneously on our second meeting). Ronald "sings" (hums) as he goes to sleep. He indicates needs spontaneously using vocal and gestural communication. RECOMMENDATIONS: Because of Ronald's significant delay in this area, a complete speech/language evaluation performed by a pediatric speech pathologist could direct

Continued on page 269

parents and teachers to methods to help Ronald increase his use of words in everyday communication. Until then, continue to model descriptive language in daily routines (the *red* cup) and to expand sound play. Make it fun.

Gross Motor (How He Moves Around) and Fine Motor (How He Uses His Hands)

STRENGTHS: Ronald is very interested in activities in these areas. He completed age appropriate skills in both areas. RECOMMENDATIONS: Continue to encourage balance and control of movements with jumping, running, and climbing games. Use both skill areas (because they are so high interest to him) to practice sound play. For example, make a sound while jumping up and down; vary the tone and intensity. Encourage him to follow your lead; change sounds. You follow his lead (this produces even more results!).

Personal-Social Skills (How He Responds to Other People/Situations, Self-Care)

Ronald accomplished 70.8 percent of the skills typical for a child in his age group. He is performing at the eighteen-month age range. STRENGTHS: Responds to own name, plays pat-a-cake, acts to gain attention, cooperates with dressing, indicates wants, imitates another child at play, feeds self with spoon, pulls off socks, drinks from a cup, voluntarily slows down for nap, sucks from straw, and is beginning to go to the potty chair to sit. CONCERNS: Physically aggressive to other children, occasionally responds to "no" or "stop," puts all objects into mouth. RECOMMENDATIONS: Firm and fair guidelines will help Ronald know how he is expected to respond to other people. Give him clear, simple rules such as "We are nice to each other." Demonstrate physically how we are nice to one another (hug, shake hand, pat on head, smile). Include oral motor/sensory simulation questions in speech evaluation.

Summary

Ronald is an adorable little guy. His test results indicate several areas that warrant early intervention at this time. Speech/language skills represent the area of greatest concern. A thorough evaluation by a pediatric speech pathologist is recommended. This evaluation should also address oral/motor and sensory stimulation concerns (excessive mouthing). Other areas of concern, personal-social skills and perceptual skills, can be addressed in typical daily routines that are structured to provide Ronald clear and consistent expectations. Physical guides appeared to be beneficial in learning new skills. Teaming multisensory input also seemed to enhance Ronald's learning. The family might want to consider early intervention services in the home to support their efforts in building the suggestions into daily routines. A half-day developmental program could be used later to help Ronald generalize these skills into other environments. This gradual increase in structured programming is recommended because this evaluator observed overstimulation (marked breathing difficulty) during testing. An

Continued on page 270

occupational therapy evaluation may be helpful if he is unable to organize/adapt to increased sensory input after a short time in early intervention or with speech pathologist's recommendation. It was a pleasure to meet Ronald and his family. Please let us know if we can be of further assistance.

We requested that a speech and language evaluation be done by CSS (Children's Special Services), since this agency serves both counties involved. Following the intake visit, it was decided that the behaviors described by the foster mother and observed by the intake person were of significant enough concern that a request for evaluation at the University of Tennessee (UT) Child Development and Behavior Clinic would be made, with the recommendation that the evaluation be done before Ronald was returned to the birth mother. The purpose of having the evaluation done before reunification was (since his mother's parenting skills were not strong) to help develop strategies that could be undertaken by his mother for dealing with the difficult behaviors he was displaying. The social worker assigned to the reunification was very interested in having someone work with Ronald's birth mother on parenting and on following through with interventions when Ronald was returned to her.

The developmental evaluation indicated that this child had very significant delays in his speech and language development and significant delay in his social/emotional and adaptive skill development. The evaluators also recommended a sensory motor evaluation. The social worker for the family was contacted, and the IFSP was scheduled for the child's home county. The reunification of Ronald with his birth mother was moved up, and so the IFSP was written to help facilitate the move back to his home. The authorization for the evaluation at UT was obtained from the primary care physician, but at the time of the IFSP team meeting, it had not been done. The speech evaluation was changed so that it could be done at UT at the same time as the psychological, sensory-motor, and developmental evaluations.

Goals, Objectives, and Strategies

The outcomes were developed to meet Ronald's needs when he returns to his birth mother and stepfather's house. The IFSP was written by the early intervention agency in the eastern part of the state, not in my (service coordinator) region. The team meeting was attended by the foster parents, birth mother and her husband, social workers from both Ronald's home county and the county where he has been in foster care, the professional who did the assessment, a lead teacher from a state home visitor early intervention program, the early interventionist from Ronald's home county, and the service coordinator from both regions. It was a very large team!

Here are two of the goals/outcomes that were developed for Ronald and his family. One was to ensure a smooth transition for Ronald back to his birth mother and her family. The action steps established to address this goal were to have the home visitor make weekly visits and for the day care home to provide intervention and family training, to check into funds to fence the family's yard because of the concerns about Ronald's lack of fear for his own safety and the proximity of a creek to the family home, to have a developmental specialist help childproof the home and help the mother develop stronger parenting skills, and to get a referral to a local agency for early intervention services. A second goal/outcome for Ronald and his family was for Ronald to receive the evaluations that he needs. Action steps include the parents taking Ronald for periodic evaluations with the Department of Children's Services (DCS) worker monitoring these actions. The evaluations will include a hearing and occupational therapy (sensory-motor) evaluation.

The early interventionist will help both the birth mother and the day care provider with preparation for the return of Ronald to his birth home. To help in the transition to home, supervised visits in the foster home will be done on an increasing basis so that the family can learn from the foster parents how Ronald reacts to situations and how things have been handled by them. This will hopefully provide consistency. The interventionist will report to DCS, and her reports will help to determine when the family is ready to receive Ronald. DCS will closely monitor the home situation and be sure that all appointments are kept.

Evaluation

The early interventionist and therapists will do ongoing assessment of Ronald's progress, with formal assessment done prior to the six-month review and annual IFSP meetings. DCS will receive reports on an ongoing basis. The findings of the evaluation at the UT Child Development and Behavior Clinic will be incorporated into Ronald's plan with changes to the IFSP and service delivery made as needed. DHS will continue to monitor the home to be sure that Ronald is receiving what is necessary to help him grow, progress, and succeed.

Summary

What are the desirable attributes of a person who aspires to be a successful professional (for example an early interventionist or service coordinator) in serving infants and toddlers with special needs and their families? Some of the answers to this question are embedded in the content of Chapter 10. The reader understands from reading the five vignettes that the circumstances and needs of every child and family are very unique. Infants and toddlers with disabilities are served in a variety of settings, and we as professionals are mandated by law and guided by evidence of effectiveness to see that those services are provided in natural environments and through inclusive processes. It is useful to expand our view of what is meant by natural environments beyond settings such as homes and childcare programs and to include the various places in the community where families with very young children spend their time.

The successful early interventionist is a professional who is committed to forming and nurturing a partnership with families and who believes in the family-centered principles described throughout this book. As you see illustrated in the vignettes of the Chapter, the provision of early intervention services is a dynamic process that requires the ability to work collaboratively with others and to engage in problem solving. The initial development and ongoing revisions of the IFSP serve as a roadmap for early intervention. The action steps and outcomes established through this process must serve as our guidance. Certainly the successful early interventionist is someone who seeks to understand families, to respect their diversity, and to view them positively and as being in a developmental process (rather than as functional or dysfunctional). The early childhood educator, therapist, caregiver, service coordinator, or early interventionist that works with young children with special needs must have knowledge of the typical development of children and how to nurture development (developmentally appropriate practice). The vignette about Alisha and her family demonstrates that applying an activity-based approach to intervention may require some time and creative problem solving. Good communication (like their use of the journal system) and careful planning and monitoring are necessary to insure that the specialized goals and objectives of infants and toddlers with disabilities are addressed within the context of play and the routines and typical activities found in natural environments. Finally, as a part of the process of becoming a competent professional, it is important to learn how to use naturally occurring antecedents, consequences and rewards in influencing the behavior of very young children.

Chapter 10 Suggested Activities and Resources

The following activities are directly related to the five vignettes you have just read. The activities can be addressed in a variety of ways, including individual study and review, research or interviewing of a family member or professional, or meeting attendance. You might also use some of the activities in small group discussion or problem-solving sessions, and some of them are more relevant for large group or class discussion.

1. Identify and list from the five vignettes the various types of service delivery settings. How many of them would you consider natural environments or inclusive settings? Why?

2. Make a chart with the names for each of the five vignettes (maybe children's names) on the side and at the top make three columns, one each for PBS, ABI, and DAP. As part of a team or small group, identify from the vignettes the places where these principles and practices are applied. Enter a note to that effect in the chart. You may want to compare your findings and discuss them with other small groups or teams.

3. Interview a family member, early intervention teacher, service coordinator, or other professional (for example, a therapist, social worker, or psychologist) and get their views about how early intervention should be carried out. Then compare their points of view to the experiences of the families and professionals in the vignettes.

4. Review the descriptions and definitions of collaboration and teaming; then identify and discuss the vignettes with regard to how these principles and practices were done effectively, and also how they were not done so well.

5. Compare your state's current IFSP form to the one provided in Appendix B with regard to how goals and outcomes, objectives, action steps, and natural environment are included. Relate your state's form to the federally mandated content required in an IFSP.

6. Discuss what you perceive to be the role of an early intervention service coordinator in a system of early intervention service delivery. Relate your discussion to the experiences of the service coordinators in the vignettes, to the federal Part C regulations related to service coordination, and to what you find in the literature about service coordination in early intervention programs.

7. Draw comparisons between the assessment and intervention procedures, instruments, or approaches introduced in the vignettes and the assessment and intervention content presented in Chapters 6 and 7, especially related to functional assessment and social validity.

8. Examine the relationship between diversity as described in Chapter 8 and the experiences described in the vignette about Anna and her family.

9. Study Bronfenbrenner's model of the ecological systems theory of development. His work has been highlighted in several chapters up to this point, or you may want to find a more comprehensive description in the literature. Compare the model's elements and meaning to the ecological approaches applied in the vignettes. How does an ecological systems approach enhance the delivery of early intervention services?

10. Look for evidence in the vignettes of a "people first" or "families first" perspective. Where is it found, and how do you (and your small group member colleagues or your class) see it being applied with regard to recommended and effective practices in early intervention?

11. Vignette 4: Anna in the introductory section has a number of terms that are technical in nature and describe diagnosed conditions, newborn assessment or medical settings, or other professional, specialized terminology. Make a list of these words or phrases, define them, and discuss their relevance in the vignette.

Selected Resources

1. The Developmentally Appropriate Practice in Early Childhood Programs-Revised Edition document from the National Association for the Education of Young Children (edited by Sue Bredekamp and Carol Copple and published in 1997) will be useful to the reader in understanding infant and toddler development and in learning about associated appropriate and inappropriate practices.

2. Check out the Zero to Three publication from the National Center for Infants, Toddlers and Families. This bulletin has a wealth of practical information about model programs, effective practices, and suggestions for how to deliver family-centered interventions in natural and inclusive

environments. Their address is as follows: 734 15th Street, N.W., 10th Floor, Washington, D.C. 20005.

3. Use the Journal of Early Intervention and Young Exceptional Children from the Division for Early Childhood (DEC) of the Council for Exceptional Children (CEC) for ideas and information about how to successfully plan for and carry out infant and toddler inclusion. The web site for DEC is *http://www.soe.uwm.edu/dec/dec.html*.

4. The American Association for Home-Based Early Interventionists publishes a newsletter that is an excellent source on information regarding what is current practice in the delivery of early intervention service in a natural environment. AAHBEI may be contacted at 809 N. 800 E., Logan, UT 84321.

5. Numerous books and curriculum guides specific to early inclusion are available. Try Inclusive Child Care for Infants and Toddlers: Meeting Individual and Special Needs by Marion O'Brien. This book was published in 1997 by Paul H. Brookes.

6. Two curriculum guides with specific relevance for activity-based intervention and very young children are Family-Centered Intervention Planning: A Routines-Based Approach by R.A. McWilliam published by Communication Skill Builders in 1992 and Activity-Based Intervention Guide by Coling and Garrett published by Therapy Skill Builders in 1995.

7. Two textbooks published by Delmar are particularly relevant and useful as reinforcers and extensions of the content addressed in Chapter 10. They include The Developmentally Appropriate Inclusive Classroom in Early Education by Regina Miller (1996) and The Exceptional Child: Inclusion in Early Childhood Education (3rd ed.) by K. Eileen Allen and Ilene S. Schwartz.

8. The Resource Guide: Selected Early Childhood/Early Intervention Training Materials (7th ed.) document includes a wealth of resource listings under instructional content, instruction process, and curriculum guides related to the preservice preparation professionals to early childhood/early intervention practitioners. This Guide was compiled by C. Catlett and P.J. Winton and is available from the Frank Porter Graham Child Development Center at the University of North Carolina, Chapel Hill, NC 27599-8185. It is also available online at *http://www.fpg.unc.edu/Publications/Rguide/rguide.pdf*

References

Bowe, F. G. (1995). *Birth to Five: Early Childhood Special Education*. New York: Delmar Publishers.

Bronfenbrenner, U. (1977). Toward An Experimental Ecology of Human Development. *American Psychologist, 32,* 513–531.

Guralnick, M. J. (1997). Second Generation Research in the Field of Early Intervention. In M. J. Guralnick (Ed.), *The Effectiveness of Early Intervention* (pp. 3–20). Baltimore: Paul H. Brookes Publishing Co.

Gallagher, J. J. (1997). We Make a Difference: No Nobel Prizes Though. *Journal of Early Intervention, 21*(1), 88–91.

Harkin, T. (1998). 1997 Reauthorization Strengthens the Promise of IDEA. *Infants and Young Children, 10*(4), vi–x.

McWilliam, R. A., Ferguson, A., Harbin, G., Porter, P., Munn, D., & Vandiviere, P. (1998). The Family-Centeredness of Individualized Family Service Plans. *Topics in Early Childhood Special Education, 18*(2), 69–82.

Safer, N. D., & Hamilton, J. L. (1993). Legislative Context for Early Intervention Services. In W. Brown, S. K. Thurman, & L. F. Pearl (Eds.). *Family-Centered Early Intervention with Infants and Toddlers: Innovative Cross-Disciplinary Approaches* (pp. 1–19). Baltimore: Paul H. Brookes Publishing Co.

Chapter

11

Applying PBS, ABI, and DAP in Inclusive Preschool and Kindergarten Settings

INTRODUCTION[*]

The rationale, principles, and strategies of positive behavioral supports (PBS) and activity-based intervention (ABI) for providing developmentally appropriate child care, education, and early intervention in natural environments have been provided in previous chapters. As discussed in Chapter 3, PBS is "comprised of an underlying philosophy and set of strategies aimed at minimizing challenging forms of behavior and promoting positive alternative behaviors in all children" (p. 64). In Chapter 4, Bricker and Cripe's (1992) ABI was discussed and defined as the approach that is child-directed and transactional and an approach "that embeds intervention on children's individual goals and objectives in routine, planned, or child-initiated activities and uses logically occurring antecedents and consequences to develop functional and generalizable skills" (p. 2). For optimal outcomes it is appropriate and desirable to use the strategies of PBS and ABI in inclusive preschool and kindergarten settings for young children. The principles of each parallel developmentally appropriate practice (DAP) and best practices for early childhood education and for early intervention.

This chapter provides the reader with five vignettes. These vignettes are snapshots of young children's lives in homes and in educational and childcare settings. A description of the child is provided, including any special needs, and in each vignette the reader is given a glimpse of the functioning and needs of each child's family. Goals and objectives for each child are listed. The application of PBS and ABI is discussed in the context of educational environments that support developmentally appropriate practice with young children. Some constraints and resources of the families and settings are presented. A brief discussion of possible family- and teacher-friendly methods of evaluation of children's progress toward achieving their goals and objectives concludes each vignette. Here are the objectives that the reader will address in Chapter 11. You should be able to:

- Explain why children should receive educational services as children first—children who are important and valued members of families and children who may have special needs.

* Written by Linda H. Richey, Ph.D., Associate Professor of Child and Family Studies in the Department of Curriculum and Instruction at Tennessee Technological University.

- Provide examples of children with a variety of special needs in both type and severity, examples of families who exhibit the diversity of today's families, and examples of educational settings that reflect the reality of child care and education in our society.
- Discern *real* connections (partnerships) between homes and schools.
- Gain more knowledge about the specific application of PBS and ABI in inclusive and developmentally appropriate preschool and kindergarten settings and the relationships of the applications to the principles of the approaches.
- Extend your learning through follow-up activities to help increase understanding of the application of PBS and ABI in naturalistic and developmentally appropriate environments.

Five children and their families are presented to the reader. The children are Bree, Patrick, Carlos, Seth, and Sabrina. Each child is unique and each child has special needs. These children are members of five diverse families; that is, they represent an array of characteristics, including socioeconomic status, family composition, stage in the family life span, ethnicity, values, and belief systems. The child care and educational settings are accredited by the National Association for the Education of Young Children (NAEYC). They represent diverse settings, including Head Start, corporate-sponsored day care, and public school kindergarten. Each vignette containing a child's story consists of four sections: introduction, goals, objectives, and discussion. The discussion section includes a description of strategies and the evaluation of the child's progress toward achieving the stated goals and objectives.

VIGNETTE 1: BREE

Introduction

Bree is a curious, lively four-year-old with strawberry blonde hair and spina bifida. She lives with her mother and older sister and attends a privately owned day care center that serves children from the age of six weeks to five years. While Bree is in day care, her mother works full-time at a local health care agency and her sister attends a neighborhood elementary school. The family is relatively new to the rural community, having moved from a metropolitan area after the divorce of Bree's parents. Fortunately, extended family members live nearby, including Bree's grandparents, who have taken some responsibility for Bree's care.

The day care center provides high-quality care to young children as evidenced by their accreditation from NAEYC. Bree's mother was impressed by the accepting attitude of the director and caregivers at the center. Since Bree requires catherization and walks with crutches, her mother has met many roadblocks in finding care for her daughter. The director informed the family that the center has never had a child with spina bifida; therefore, it will be important for the center's children, families, and staff to learn more about the condition and, of course, to learn more about Bree.

Bree is like most children. She enjoys playing outside, especially in the water on warm days. In the winter her favorite pastime is playing in the snow. Cooking, especially recipes that require mixing ingredients with her hands, is an activity she enjoys both at home and at the center. Much to their delight, Bree frequently entertains a group of children with her rendition of the musical *Annie's* "The Sun Will Come Out Tomorrow" or her version of the "Eency, Weency Spider." Being very verbal and having an engaging smile, Bree has made friends quickly in her day care group. When Bree is absent for periodic doctors' visits and an occasional hospitalization, she is missed by the children and the staff.

With the help of the state Spina Bifida Association, the center's staff learned more about the condition. Bree's mother helped the center learn more about Bree and her strengths and specific needs. Using an expanded version of an IFSP, with the idea that an IEP would be developed for kindergarten, a staff member from the center, the director of the center, the family including Bree's mother and grandparents, and Bree's physical therapist developed goals and objectives for Bree at home and at the child care center.

Goals

Goals for Bree include the following domains of development: gross motor skills, social/emotional development, and self-help skills. It was important to Bree's mother that Bree not be left out of activities because of her motor limitations; for example, if the group sang and danced to "Hokey, Pokey," Bree should dance and sing also. Bree's mother was concerned about Bree continuing those friendships developed at school. She wanted Bree to have opportunities to play and visit with children in their homes and hoped that perhaps the child care center could be the impetus for that to happen. Bree's birthday would be celebrated in a few months, and Bree's mother wanted children to come to a party for her daughter (see Figure 11–1). She also wanted guidance in how to manage Bree's occasional temper tantrums. Bree becomes frustrated when attempting a task, such as learning to put on her T-shirt and shorts. It has been noted at the center that there are times when Bree exhibits the same type of outbursts when she is frustrated during free play. Also, periodically, Bree demands attention by being very loud, crying, and making verbal demands of her mother. These are the times that Bree's mother finds challenging, especially after a full day of work and providing care for Bree's older sister. Bree has become dependent on others, for example, her older sister, for help with dressing, and choosing to let others help her when the task becomes difficult. Both Bree's mother and her caregiver would like Bree to be more self-reliant, specifically with dressing and undressing herself.

Objectives

After reviewing the goals as a group, specific objectives were developed for Bree. Those objectives included:

- Bree will ask for items she needs instead of yelling, whining, or having a tantrum at the center or at home.

Figure 11–1 Bree celebrates her birthday. Next year she hopes to have friends at her party.

- At home and with no assistance, Bree will put on her T-shirt and shorts/pants/skirt in the morning and her nightgown after her bath at night.
- At the center Bree will take off and put on her coat/sweater as required.
- Bree will participate on the playground and at music time in the regularly scheduled activities with assistance only as needed to support her physical participation.
- Bree and her family will invite a friend with his/her parent from the center to play at Bree's house at least two times per month.

Discussion

Constraints for the center in providing appropriate care for Bree are related to its status as a private, for-profit child care setting. The financial reality of its operation is that there are no surplus funds to hire extra personnel to monitor Bree's progress in achieving her goals and objectives. It will be necessary to use personnel that are already available. The center's staff currently includes the director, various full- and part-time people, and some community volunteers (including foster grandparents from the senior citizens' center and parents). After a staff meeting it is decided that extra personnel are not really needed, just a better organization of the current employees and volunteers. Resources include the commitment the center has made to Bree and her family, including the paid and volunteer staff's willingness to seek a broader understanding of Bree's challenges and to provide appropriate care for her. The state Spina Bifida Association has also agreed to provide information and technical assistance to the center and its staff.

The plans made for Bree are developed within the context of total group planning. The center's philosophy is reflected in the plans and activities that are developed. Elements of this philosophy include the following:

- Guidance and discipline are provided nonpunitively and in a developmentally appropriate manner.
- Curriculum is play-based and developmentally appropriate.
- All domains of children's development are considered when developing schedules and activities.

Given this philosophy and after a functional assessment, certain plans and strategies corresponding to Bree's goals and objectives are developed.

Objective 1 relates to Bree's frustration level and ability to operate independently. The center's environment is checked to ensure it is appropriate for all children's accessibility, interests, and needs. Those materials, supplies, and equipment used by children independent of adult help or guidance are also checked for accessibility by all children. When Bree needs an item that is out of reach or that is being used by someone else, she will be required to ask for the item. A logical consequence of asking for an item will be that she receives it or, at least, is promised its use at a later time and redirected to another activity. Time needed for a task is considered when asking children, including Bree, to complete a task and to clean up. Enough time is allowed, and a warning of impending cleanup time is used with the group. Yelling, whining, and tantrums by Bree will be ignored. At home the same strategies will be used with regard to the environment, including Bree's personal items—such as books and toys—and with regard to ignoring inappropriate behavior.

Objectives 2 and 3 relate to Bree's independence and self-help skills, specifically dressing and undressing. Strategies that can be used include choosing clothes that allow independence—such as articles of clothing that use Velcro; allowing enough time for her to accomplish a task (both at home and at the center); reminding her that a dressing task needs to be done by setting out a clothing item; giving Bree a choice of clothing items; and reminding Bree to use her words to ask for help. Logical consequences for Bree include being able to go outside for free play with her group, wearing the clothing item she has chosen, and receiving encouragement and positive attention from adults.

Objective 4 relates to Bree's participation in activities and games that require mobility. Activities planned will include dancing and creative movement and other activities that focus on gross motor skills for the group and for Bree. She can take the initiative in many activities by demonstrating how *she* will adapt the activity. For example, during a creative dance experience, she may choose to dance with her arms and hands. At other times she may choose to dance holding on to a peer or using her crutches. For planned activities that require independent mobility—such as singing and playing "In and Out the Window"—a scooter board can be provided. The logical consequences for Bree will be the fun and the interaction she will experience being part of the group's activities, besides the development of specific gross motor skills and exercise in general.

Objective 5 relates to Bree's social competence, specifically developing friendships. Bree and her mother will invite a friend to their home once a week. The center and Bree's mother will coordinate this activity. At the center child-initiated or planned stories (at least twice a week) will be read to the group. These stories will include such topics as being friends or empathic behavior in young children. The traditional teacher-planned "Show and Tell" sharing time during a large group session will allow Bree to share her home play experience with the group. Through parent and family activities the center will provide Bree's mother with connections to other families. A logical consequence of these activities is that, eventually, Bree will be asked to a friend's home to play and friendships may develop and continue from the child care center.

Evaluation techniques for Bree's achievement of specific objectives are varied. Given that her goals and objectives relate to Bree's life in the center and at home, it is only natural that the accomplishment and evaluation of these goals and objectives would occur in both environments. Naturalistic observations with frequency and duration rates for Bree's behavior related to the number of incidents of tantrum behavior, yelling, and whining can be made. An analysis of her dressing and undressing ability can be made. A task analysis can be used to help break the self-help task into manageable steps. Does Bree participate in physical games and activities? Once again a frequency count with anecdotal notes can be used. Is Bree developing friendships both in the center and away from the center? Bree's mother can record on a calendar the playmates that visit Bree. At the center volunteers can be used to observe the activities and routines for Bree, her group, and the center.

VIGNETTE #2: PATRICK

Introduction

Mr. and Mrs. Adams are retired. With their three children grown and given Mrs. Adams' chronic health problem (diabetes), it has been a challenge to take full responsibility for raising their four-year-old grandson Patrick. They love Patrick, and because of their independent nature and their strong religious beliefs, the Adamses feel it is their responsibility and privilege to take care of and nurture him even with his demanding special needs. Fortunately, the Adamses live near many extended family members, including two sons, who provide respite care and financial assistance as needed.

Patrick's mother is in a drug and alcohol rehabilitation facility. This is her third attempt at overcoming her alcohol and drug addictions. When she is not in a residential facility, she lives with a friend and frequently visits her parents and son. When she is able to keep a job, she contributes financially to Patrick and her parents.

Patrick reminds the Adamses of their older son. Along with his blond hair, blue eyes, and light sprinkling of freckles, he has some of the classic characteristics of a child with fetal alcohol syndrome, for example, flat mid-face with wide-set eyes, short stature, hyperactive and impulsive behavior.

There is some indication of developmental delay, especially with regard to Patrick's social-emotional and cognitive development.

Patrick, at times, is aggressive toward peers. For example, when he does not immediately get a toy that he wants, he will hit the child until the toy is relinquished. His impulsivity and distractibility prevent his sustained attention on a task whether it is putting together a wooden puzzle, building with blocks, or sitting and listening to a requested story. Free play (both inside and outside) and transitions are especially difficult for Patrick. Any activity that is unstructured is a challenge. He finds it especially difficult to follow the general classroom rules that require him to walk in the classroom and to follow directions.

Child care is available in the Adamses' rural area, but it is too expensive for their budget. Because they meet the low-income guidelines, they elected to send Patrick to Head Start. Being on a fixed income the Adamses feel fortunate that Patrick is in Head Start. The teachers and staff of the Head Start Center have welcomed Patrick and his family. Head Start provides comprehensive services to Patrick and social support to the Adamses. The planned curriculum and environment at the center reflect the NAEYC accreditation the center received one year ago and include all domains of children's development. The Adamses feel involved with the center's activities, especially since Mr. Adams is a parent member of the Educational Advisory Board.

An IEP was developed for Patrick by his Head Start teacher, the Head Start mental health specialist, his grandparents, and his mother. Part of the plan includes the generalizing of Patrick's outcomes to his home. The transdisciplinary assessment team contributed information related to his behavior, cognitive and language development, and speech and hearing. This team included Patrick's pediatrician, the Head Start mental health specialist and teacher, a school psychologist, and a public school speech therapist.

Goals

Goals were established for Patrick. These included learning to use more appropriate behavior for a preschool environment, especially behavior that required more self-regulation and less aggression toward peers; increased attention span; increased compliance at Head Start; and increased participation in appropriate preacademic activities.

As objectives were developed, those professionals involved in Patrick's program gave special attention to the antecedent events and situations of his current behavior and planned to manipulate and plan those events and situations for the future. For Patrick to be successful in an educational environment it was decided that the many aspects of that setting needed to be considered. It was also decided that consideration of these elements of the preschool program would benefit all children in the program.

According to Cook, Tessier, and Klein (1996), using strategies to influence antecedent events to inappropriate behavior will help children who have been prenatally exposed to drugs. Planning for Patrick included many of these strategies, such as determining what is triggering the inappropriate behavior; reducing interruptions to class schedules and routines or to Patrick's activities; and preparing Patrick for anything that could disrupt the usual flow of the classroom routines (for example, a student observer present for the day or a parent bringing a pet to school could change the schedule or dynamics in the classroom).

Objectives

As objectives were considered for Patrick, the preschool staff evaluated their own competence in providing a developmentally appropriate experience for him. They evaluated and pinpointed necessary changes in the setting before potential changes for Patrick were identified. Objectives for Patrick included the following:

- Patrick will sit in large group sessions, such as story time, for five minutes with adult physical guidance.
- Patrick will sit at snack and lunch time with his peers for five minutes with adult physical guidance.
- Patrick will have less aggressive incidents with his peers.
- Patrick will be expected to comply with classroom rules—that is, safety rules, toy/material use rules, appropriate interaction with peers.
- Patrick's attention span will increase to five minutes for an individual activity—for example, building with blocks or painting at the easel, with adult monitoring.

Discussion

It is critical that an environmental assessment be conducted to make decisions and plans for Patrick. As stated in Chapter 3, the implementation of positive behavioral supports requires that teachers and caregivers plan and design the environment to support a child's behavior, that is, to prevent inappropriate behavior and to promote positive alternative behaviors. In developmentally appropriate preschool and kindergarten classrooms, skillful teachers and caregivers plan children's environments for optimal child outcomes. These optimal child outcomes may be specifically social-emotional (behavioral) outcomes, as in Patrick's case, or they may be cognitive, language, speech, or motor outcomes.

Planning the environment enables the teacher or caregiver to implement components of activity-based intervention. As reviewed in Chapter 4, it is important to use logically occurring antecedents and consequences when implementing ABI. A well-structured environment in a high-quality setting will provide the backdrop for those antecedents and consequences. For Patrick, complying with the request "Keep the sand in the sandbox" will result in his being able to play in the sandbox, an activity he enjoys.

Planning the environment allows teachers and caregivers to choose appropriate toys and materials for Patrick and his peers. With specific selection of these materials, a teacher or caregiver is "setting the stage" for child-initiated activities, a component of ABI. There is a relationship between planning and child-initiated activities. For example, after visiting the

Figure 11–2 A teacher can set the stage for children to share and take turns.

aquarium on a field trip, the teacher may set up a water table with plastic fish, shells, and other toys with two play spaces for two children. Patrick may or may not choose to play at the water table. If he does, he has initiated a play experience that may include another child, thus giving him the opportunity to share and take turns with a friend. (See Figure 11–2.)

The guidance technique of "Sit and Watch" (Catron & Allen, 1993) can be used with Patrick for aggressive behaviors and for noncompliance. As a guidance technique it is excellent with young children because it is nonpunitive. It is similar to time-out in that it follows inappropriate behavior, but instead of punishing a child, it teaches a child what is the expected appropriate behavior. Removed from an activity for inappropriate behavior, a child observes the appropriate behaviors of other children from the sidelines. The nonpunitive and supporting nature of this technique is in line with positive behavioral supports for children.

Teacher and parent observations of Patrick's behavior can be used to evaluate his progress toward achieving his goals and objectives. Can Patrick sit at story time (a teacher-planned activity), snack (a routine activity), and lunch (a routine activity) for five minutes each with adult help? Can Patrick stay on task for five minutes with an activity he enjoys (a child-initiated activity)? Is there a decrease in aggressive incidents? Dimensions of behavior can be measured directly, for example, frequency of hitting children, sitting duration at lunch and at snack times, the intensity of the aggressive behavior, the rate of noncompliance (Zirpoli, 1995). Observations of where the behavior occurred should be recorded, thereby helping the teacher monitor and reevaluate the physical and social environment.

VIGNETTE #3: CARLOS

Introduction

Carlos is three years old and lives with his foster family, the Millers. Even before Carlos arrived, the Millers were a busy and active family. They have four children. A son has graduated from college and works out of state. Another son is attending the local state university on a scholarship. Two daughters, aged eleven and thirteen, live at home and attend public school. Both parents are teachers. The Millers spend some of their summer with vegetable and fruit gardening, among other activities. After eighteen months with his family, Carlos feels comfortable, especially when he snuggles the family dog Woody. He is adapting to not hearing.

The Millers agreed to care for Carlos during the middle of his second year and have been appointed his surrogate parents. They felt that providing care for children is one way to positively contribute to society. At the time, they were aware of the physical abuse and neglect Carlos had experienced. The neglect indirectly contributed to Carlos' deafness. Otitis media was left untreated to the point of endangering his life with meningitis. Carlos survived, but once he recovered from meningitis, it was determined that he was partially deaf.

The local university has a child development lab that Carlos attends. The center values family participation and provides play-based, developmentally appropriate care for children. There are state funds available to help finance the cost of his care. This care is necessary during the school year while both parents are working. During the summer months he has continued to attend for the enrichment experiences and the socialization with peers. He receives intervention services at the lab within the context of his day. The lab personnel, Carlos' surrogate parents, and a teacher for children with hearing impairments, who is employed by the public schools, work closely together to ensure continuity in his total communication program at the lab and at home.

Goals

After a transdisciplinary arena assessment by Carlos' audiologist, speech therapist, pediatrician, school psychologist, child development lab teacher, and the public school teacher for children with hearing disabilities, an IEP is developed. Goals from Carlos' IEP meeting include a social- and language-focused goal of communicating more with family members, teachers, and peers; and a speech and language goal of continuing with the total communication approach. There are also goals to participate in all aspects of his preschool program (a goal related to all domains of Carlos' development) and to develop his self-help skills related to his hearing aid.

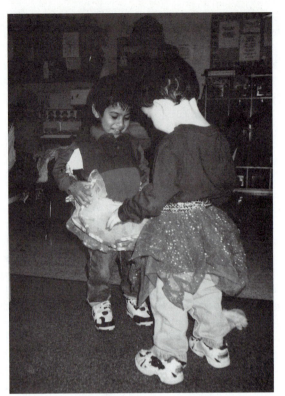

Figure 11–3
Requesting a dress-up item from a peer encourages dialogue. Receiving the costume reinforces the use of language.

Objectives

Objectives related to Carlos' goals include the following (see Figure 11–3):

- Carlos will initiate more communication, especially conversations with peers.
- Carlos will use language to make requests of adults and children.
- Carlos will use language to ask more questions at home and at school.
- Carlos will begin learning to care for his hearing aid with the help of his foster parents and teacher.
- Carlos will participate in small group activities at the child development lab, for example, finger plays during group time, playing in the sprinkler during outside free play.

Discussion

Carlos' continued development of total communication skills in the lab can be generalized to his home. The same is true for his continued learning at home. As the school and home work together, the generalizability and the functional nature of these skills increase. The ability to communicate enables Carlos to be more independent and is relevant to Carlos' life at the child development lab and at home.

During Carlos' day, there are abundant opportunities for producing and using language. As he asks for another orange slice at snack (a routine activity) or responds to a teacher's question during a cooking experience (a teacher-planned activity) or asks for help with a painting project at the easel (a child-initiated activity), he can practice newly acquired skills or learn new skills. Teacher aides, volunteers, even the child's peers can support Carlos' progress in achieving his goals and objectives.

The audiologist can teach the parents, the teacher, and the staff how to use and care for Carlos' hearing aid. He or she can also teach them how to help Carlos learn to care for and use his hearing aid. With consistent directions and support from the adults who care for him, Carlos will develop the self-help skills necessary to function independently. Just as Carlos learned to put on his T-shirt and to use "big boy" pants, Carlos can learn and take pride in caring for other personal needs.

Monitoring Carlos' language can be time-consuming. Efficient methods of data collection can be devised, however. Since Carlos is in a child development lab at the university, advanced students can be trained to assess his language use. Language samples and anecdotal notes are valuable in such situations. Measuring discrete behaviors with regard to the various behavioral dimensions can also be used productively with Carlos. Parents can report the achievement of specific objectives at home.

VIGNETTE #4: SETH

Introduction

Providing a warm and nurturing home has always been important to the Williams family. Ms. Williams is a writer and has also been involved for three years with the community symphony. She completes most of her writing at home. Mr. Williams is a researcher with the university hospital in a large northeastern city. Their son Seth, four and one-half years old, attends the day care center sponsored by the hospital for its employees. The Williamses have been happy with the hospital's child care center. Seth enjoys the sandbox, blocks, and the water table at his preschool. Both parents attend the school's monthly parent meetings.

The Williams family is concerned about Seth's future, especially the near future, when he will attend kindergarten. Currently they are debating the advisability of holding Seth back a year. He will be five years, four months when he enters kindergarten. His age concerns them, but more important is their concern for his pervasive developmental disorder diagnosed when Seth was two years old. The Williamses have many questions and much guilt, depending upon what they read or with whom they talk.

Seth seldom interacts with his peers. He is very passive when he is in small groups of children. He speaks very little, and when he does, there is some echolalic language. He becomes very anxious when routines are changed, whether at home or at preschool. There is some evidence of self-injurious behavior, such as hair pulling, but it is not excessive. Seth has average intelligence, fears strangers and loud noises, and likes ice cream, flashlights, and legos.

Goals

Various professionals have been involved in Seth's life. It started with family consultation with his pediatrician at eighteen months of age and has continued to include a communication specialist and behavior specialist in addition to his preschool teacher. At his latest IEP meeting a kindergarten teacher has been included with the intent of planning Seth's transition from preschool to kindergarten. In addition to the previously mentioned professionals, excluding the pediatrician, other people who are part of Seth's IEP team are other educators from the elementary school that he will attend, including the principal and a special education teacher, and an occupational therapist.

The personnel from the elementary school are committed at various levels to inclusionary practices in their school. All have stated their opinions and concerns, but some are more hesitant than others, especially the kindergarten teacher. The principal has essentially mandated that inclusion will occur, and has also provided the resources necessary for it to occur—personnel, time for planning, and money. Most agree that personnel and money are important and necessary, but the time for planning and developing a shared vision for inclusion in their school is extremely important. As the group gathers together to develop goals and objectives for Seth, they are also setting their own individual and professional goals for change. Some of these goals are stated.

As the IEP team discusses goals for Seth, three goals emerge as most important. Two of them are the continued development of social interaction skills with peers and adults and language instruction. A third goal is the planning for Seth's successful transition from preschool to kindergarten. His parents agree that these are goals that are important for Seth not only in school but also at home. It was agreed that a close partnership between home and school was necessary for Seth's optimal development and transition into kindergarten.

Objectives

Specific objectives related to the first two goals—development of social interaction skills and language instruction—were as follows (see Figure 11–4):

- Seth will initiate an interaction with an adult and a peer to request a toy or other object.

Figure 11–4 Mother offers a choice of clothing to wear.

- Seth will use language to make requests of adults and peers.
- Seth will take turns in the classroom and on the playground with peers.
- Seth will make choices, both verbally and with gestures, at preschool and at home.

All of these objectives will be attempted with minimal adult assistance and prompting. Objectives for the third goal will not be reviewed.

Discussion

It will be necessary to implement a systematic behavior training program for Seth. It is important to reduce the inappropriate behaviors that Seth exhibits, such as hair pulling, and also to teach Seth new skills. Fortunately, through careful and systematic observation, the caregivers and parents have noted the many objects (toys, materials) and activities that Seth enjoys. The use of this information will be necessary to plan Seth's social and physical environment.

It is important that Seth's day be predictable and that the activities allow real choices for him. For example, at snack time Seth may be given a choice of frozen yogurt flavors. At home he can be asked what color shirt he would like to wear. On the playground a child can ask Seth if he would like to play in the sandbox or on the climber.

Flashlights and legos can be strategically placed in the care room in play centers that require more than one child to play. As children move to the various learning and play centers in the room, Seth can be included. As children play, Seth can observe adults and peers making requests and taking turns.

The elements of activity-based intervention are easily integrated into Seth's day care program. Seth has specific objectives that can be embedded in his day's activities both at school and at home, whether those activities are routine or planned. Child-initiated activities are appropriate in day care. Seth's goals and objectives include child- initiated activities specifically. Because of ABI's transactional nature it provides the vehicle for child-initiation. Use of logically occurring antecedents and consequences is an element of ABI. For Seth, a logical consequence of requesting a box of legos is receiving the box and the fun and satisfaction it brings. Instead of a teacher-directed language session requiring Seth to say "I want a cookie," a more natural and functional activity for snack time at the center is the antecedent to Seth's verbal request for a cookie. The same activity sequence—seeing a plate of cookies, verbally requesting a cookie, and then receiving the cookie—can be generalized to the home.

Positive behavioral support is a specific approach that is very valuable for Seth. Of course, the nonpunitive nature of this approach is valuable for all children. For Seth, the promotion of positive alternative behaviors is especially important given the nature of some of his objectives. Reducing self-injurious behavior and echolalic language is important. Seth's passive affect and indifference to the people around him can be influenced by structuring his environment. A functional assessment of Seth's behavior may not determine causal factors, but it may determine the context in which certain behaviors do occur.

At times progress may be slow for Seth. He has already made some gains in interacting with people. Transition into day care from home was accomplished slowly, but it was accomplished. His parents have dealt with many frustrating moments in Seth's development, but they have also enjoyed Seth. Especially frustrating for them are the days when it seems that no strategy works. Then there are the days when great progress seems to be made. Evaluation of Seth's progress is important, not only for Seth but also for his parents and for the day care staff. It is encouraging to see gains, even small ones. It is just as important to document when a strategy is no longer working.

Functional assessments for Seth are especially valuable. As stated by Mindes, Ireton, and Mardell-Czudnowski (1996), a functional assessment includes observing all components of a child's environment. The preschool/day care setting consists of not only the child and his or her behavior but also the child's "environment, schedule, the routines, the rules, the personal interactions, the materials" (p. 136). With children who are exhibiting challenging behavior, it is imperative that all settings in which the child is expected to function successfully be examined and evaluated.

VIGNETTE #5: SABRINA

Introduction

Five-year-old Sabrina Maxwell is quick to smile when she sees her father coming to pick her up from kindergarten. During the school year she spends a full day at kindergarten. The Maxwells are planning for Sabrina to participate in the YMCA summer camp program between her kindergarten and first grade years. Both parents are professors at a small, private liberal arts college. They have arranged their hours to accommodate their children's school schedule. Creative scheduling and time management by the Maxwells and flexibility on the part of their employer have allowed at least one parent to be present before and after school. Sabrina has spent many hours on the campus helping her father "organize" books on his bookshelf and helping her mother surf the Internet. Sabrina is known to many of the students and faculty members on campus and at times has practiced cheers with the cheerleaders and helped a secretary with typing. Sabrina is a delightful child who adores her big brother. Sabrina's older brother frequently accompanies Sabrina on her campus excursions, but lately he is preoccupied with scouts or at a friend's house. Sabrina was born with Down syndrome.

The Maxwells consider themselves fortunate because they have a close church family. Their extended family is not near. Also, the family belongs to the International Organization sponsored by the college. The Maxwells are well known for their African culture and heritage presentations and for their support of the community's many multicultural events. They value their community and see it as a source of support.

Sabrina has been receiving speech services from the public school since she was three years old. There have been two major hospitalizations for Sabrina. Both were related to cardiac problems associated with Down syndrome. Sabrina attended a church-sponsored child care center for three years. She currently attends a public school kindergarten. Transitioning to kindergarten proceeded rather smoothly because of the planning and collaboration of the preschool personnel, the public school kindergarten teacher, the parents, and other professionals. Most of Sabrina's goals were continued with some modifications when her transition was made to kindergarten.

Goals

Although Sabrina's goals may be considered domain-specific, it is understood by early childhood professionals that the domains of child development overlap and impact each other. For example, a child who is delayed in cognitive development will most likely exhibit a delay in language development, both expressive and receptive. The following goals listed for Sabrina focus specifically on motor, cognitive, and language development. It is understood that the other areas of her development—that is, social-emotional and self-help skills—would also be considered in planning appropriate intervention for her, and that all domains of her development are important and are considered holistically.

An IEP meeting was conducted at the beginning of her kindergarten year to review the goals and objectives developed in the spring of her last year in day care. Attending the meeting were the following people: Sabrina's parents, her kindergarten teacher, the school's physical education teacher, an occupational therapist, a physical therapist, a special education teacher assigned to Sabrina's elementary school, and a communication specialist. As requested by the parents and supported by the latest legislation—namely, the reauthorization of the Individuals with Disabilities Education Act (IDEA) — a family component to the IEP was included to address the concerns, priorities, strengths, and resources of the family. It was important for Sabrina's parents that their family continue to be seen as an essential part of Sabrina's life, even at school (see Figure 11–5).

Goals for Sabrina included the following:

- To develop expressive and receptive language skills, with her skills generalizing to the home.
- To start and continue an exercise program both at school and at home.
- To develop fine and gross motor skills.
- To develop cognitive skills.

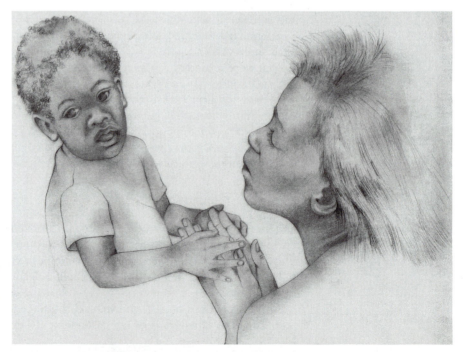

Figure 11–5 Sabrina enjoys playing, "Pattycake," especially when she can play with her mother. Artist: Cindy Mayer

Objectives

Specific objectives related to each of Sabrina's goals are as follows:

Language Development

- To increase her vocabulary to a minimum of 1,000 words, using two-word and longer phrases.
- To follow three related directions in order with no prompting or cues.
- To participate in finger plays during group time with minimal physical prompting.

Exercise Program/Gross Motor Development

- To participate in physical education class once a week.
- To throw a ball to a peer with no assistance.
- To catch a ball thrown to her after one bounce with no assistance.
- To ride a tricycle, including pedaling and steering.

Fine Motor Development

- With a model provided, copies circle with crayon with no assistance.
- With a model provided, makes shapes with play dough with no assistance.
- Balances five unit blocks in the block corner with no assistance.

Cognitive Development

- Knows her first and last names.
- Can solve a simple two-step problem.
- Can identify five parts of her body.
- Can match six colors.

Summary

These five vignettes provide information about applications of the principles of developmentally appropriate practice, activity-based intervention, and positive behavioral supports in differing circumstances. You can see that the degree to which they are relevant and the specifics of how they are applied depend on the types and severities of special needs, the resources and constraints of the environments, the educator, the interventionist, a caregiver's preparedness and willingness, the family perspective and needs, and the *nature* of the collaborative effort. The theme that you have seen consistently throughout the text bears repeating here: Young children (preschoolers in this instance) with special needs are best served in settings where the expectations placed before them by caregivers are developmentally appropriate, their specialized goals and objectives are embedded in "normal" and typical activities, and the emphasis is on planning environments to facilitate desired behaviors and on avoiding punitive consequences for undesired behavior.

Chapter 11 Selected Activities

1. Some of the indicators of poor-quality child care centers or kindergartens include the use of abstract materials and experiences (such as worksheets and workbooks); an inflexible curriculum; use of a punitive discipline policy (for example, spanking, negative and demeaning comments to children); use of only one screening or assessment instrument; large group size; high adult-child ratio; high turnover of caregivers; and caregivers/teachers not trained in child development and guidance. Choose one of these indicators. Apply it to one of the preschool centers or the kindergarten classroom in the vignettes. How would it negatively affect the outcomes for the targeted child with special needs? The child's peers? The child's family? The child care environment?

2. Choose a vignette. What aspects of the planning by teachers and/or family members reflect PBS? ABI? DAP?

3. Hildebrand and Hearron (1999) note that indirect and direct guidance techniques are important in preschool programs. Guidance techniques affect a child's development of self-esteem, self-efficacy, and self-control. They refer to indirect guidance as such aspects of the program as adult-child ratio, group size, scheduling, and the number of play spaces. They refer to direct guidance as "the physical, verbal, and affective techniques used to influence a child's behavior" (p. 92). How might indirect and direct guidance be important in optimal outcomes for Patrick (Vignette 2)? How do the guidance strategies used by the early childhood professional relate to PBS?

4. The invisible and visible curriculum is one way of analyzing a preschool setting. According to Catron and Allen (1993), the invisible curriculum includes those aspects of the program the nonprofessional or casual observer may not notice, for example, the organization and design of the classroom and playground environments, management of the classroom and guidance strategies used with children, the teacher's role and types of involvement with the children, and the partnership with parents for optimal child outcomes. Preschool teachers' planning, teaching, and evaluating embody the visible curriculum. How might the invisible curriculum impact the use of ABI? Choose a child and vignette to help explain your answer.

5. Explain why a developmentally appropriate environment is necessary for the implementation of positive behavioral supports for children and for activity-based intervention.

6. Refer to Vignette 4: Seth. Remembering Seth's goals and objectives, brainstorm other activities (routine, planned, or child-initiated) that could be implemented to help Seth achieve success. Given that an objective for Seth is to initiate more interactions, how might that be "planned"?

7. Refer to Vignette 4: Seth. What could be some of the constraints and resources for Seth to achieve success with regard to his goals and objectives? How could an adversarial relationship between school (day care or kindergarten) and home affect Seth's progress.

Selected Resources

1. *Books*

   Bredekamp, S., & Copple, C. (Eds.). (1997). *Developmentally Appropriate Practice in Early Childhood Programs* (rev. ed.). Washington, DC: NAEYC.

   Bredekamp, S., & Rosegrant, T. (1995). *Reaching Potentials: Transforming Early Childhood Curriculum and Assessment—volume 2*. Washington, DC: NAEYC.

   Bredekamp, S., & Rosegrant, T. (1992). *Reaching Potentials: Appropriate Curriculum and Assessment for Young Children—Volume 1*. Washington, DC: NAEYC.

   Bronson, M. B. (1995). *The Right Stuff for Children Birth to 8: Selecting Play Materials to Support Development*. Washington, DC: NAEYC.

   Chandler, P. (1994). *A Place for Me: Including Children with Special Needs in Early Care and Education Settings*. Washington, DC: NAEYC.

   Kaiser, B., & Rasminsky, J. S. (1999). *Meeting the Challenge: Effective Strategies for Challenging Behaviors in Early Childhood Environments*. Ottawa, Ontario, Canada: Canadian Child Care Federation.

   Neugebauer, B. (Ed.). (1992). *Alike and Different: Exploring Our Humanity with Young Children* (rev. ed.). Washington, DC: NAEYC.

   Tertell, E., Klein, S., & Jewett, J. (Eds.). (1998). *When Teachers Reflect: Journeys toward Effective, Inclusive Practice*. Washington, DC: NAEYC.

   Wolery, M., & Wilbers, J. S. (Eds.). (1994). *Including Children with Special Needs in Early Childhood Programs*. Washington, DC: NAEYC.

2. *Journal articles*

   Allred, K. W., Briem, R., & Black, S. J. (1998). Collaboratively Addressing Needs of Young Children with Disabilities. *Young Children, 53,* 32–36.

   Hanline, M. F., & Fox, L. (1993). Learning within the Context of Play: Providing Typical Early Childhood Experiences for Children with Severe Disabilities. *Journal of the Association for Persons with Severe Handicaps, 18,* 121–129.

   McCormick, L., & Feeney, S. (1995). Modifying and Expanding Activities for Children with Disabilities. *Young Children, 50,* 10–17.

   Nielsen, S. L., Olive, M. L., Donovan, A., & McEvoy, M. (1998). Challenging Behaviors in Your Classroom? Don't React—Teach Instead! *Young Exceptional Children, 2,* 2–10.

   Richey, D. D., Richey, L. H., & Webb, J. (1996). Inclusive Infant-Toddler Groups: Strategies for Success. *Dimensions of Early Childhood, 24,* 10–16.

   Schwartz, I. S., Billingsley, F. F., McBride, B. M. (1998). Including Children with Autism in Inclusive Preschools: Strategies That Work. *Young Exceptional Children, 1,* 19–26.

3. *Videos*

   NAEYC. (1994). *Designing Developmentally Appropriate Days* (video). Washington, DC: NAEYC.

NAEYC. (1996). *Early Intervention: Natural Environments for Children* (video). Washington, DC: NAEYC.

NAEYC. (1997). *Intervencion Temprana: Ambientes Naturales para los Ninos* (video). Washington, DC: NAEYC.

NAEYC. (1998). *Tools for Teaching Developmentally Appropriate Practice: The Leading Edge in Early Childhood Education* (video series). Washington, DC: NAEYC.

4. *Websites*

www.ideapractices.org	*IDEA (Individual with Disabilities Education Act) Practices*
www.dec-sped.org	Council for Exceptional Children, Division of Early Childhood

References

Catron, C., & Allen, J. (1993). *Early Childhood Curriculum*. New York: Macmillan.

Cook, R. E., Tessier, A., & Klein, M. D. (1996). *Adapting Early Childhood Curricula for Children in Inclusive Settings* (4th ed.). Englewood Cliffs, NJ: Prentice-Hall.

Hildebrand, V. and Hearron, P. F. (1999). *Guiding Young Children* (6th ed.). Upper Saddle River, NJ: Merrill/Prentice-Hall.

Mindes, G., Ireton, H., & Mardell-Czudnowski, C. (1996). *Assessing Young Children*. Boston: Delmar.

Zirpoli, T. J. (1995). *Understanding and Affecting the Behavior of Young Children*. Englewood Cliffs, NJ: Merrill.

Applying PBS, ABI, and DAP in Inclusive Early Elementary Grades

Chapter

12

INTRODUCTION

The following vignettes depict children and their families, illustrating a variety of disabilities, ages, cultures, settings, family values, and professional responses. Each example is unique to the individual child and how his/her special need impacts his/her education and independence. Although each child and family's situation is unique and individual, keep in mind the common themes that were introduced in Chapter 1 and discussed throughout the text, which included person first, family-centeredness, transdisciplinary teaming and collaboration, ecological approach, responsible inclusion, independence/selfdetermination/self-advocacy, ABI, PBS, DAP, transitions, sensitivity to diversity, and assistive technology. Some of these themes are more apparent than others in the illustrations. As you delve into the lives of these children and their families, try to determine if and where these themes are evident. Note the success when the themes are evident or challenges where they are absent. Try to identify solutions and options that might lead to the incorporation of these themes in assisting each child, family, and professional system in their situation. Here are the objectives that the reader will address in this chapter. You should be able to:

- Describe best and effective practices—such as person first, family-centeredness, teaming and collaboration—within each vignette.
- Analyze and discuss each of the vignettes and offer your own perspective on each.
- Compare and contrast the services and supports provided in each vignette.

VIGNETTE 1: CAITLIN[*]

Introduction

We were confident, as parents, that we were doing all we could to make sure we had a head start on our daughter's situation as we were planning our move to a new state. We had sent her IEP and other records ahead in June and had met with the director of special education in July before moving in August. We knew much of the transition process would be up to us, as moving to a new state made it difficult for sending and receiving programs to exchange information. We brought a wealth of information with us—as usual. Being a professional in early childhood special education, as well as Caitlin's mom, made for some interesting and, yet, frustrating times.

Our daughter Caitlin is the youngest of our three girls. She is a beautiful child, with curly brown hair, expressive brown eyes, and olive tone skin. She is nine years old and about to enter the third grade. She has been in a full inclusion program since her first "out of home" educational experience at age two, when we enrolled her in the toddler university lab preschool. She is passionate about purple. She can be *very* social and loves to talk and visit with people. She enjoys spelling and is challenged by math. She rolls very fast in her purple wheelchair and can pop "wheelies" quite well. Her favorite activities include horseback riding, swimming, playing with her sisters, using the computer, basketball, and fishing.

Caitlin was born with spina bifida. Her lesion (the "opening" on her spine) is at the T-10 to T-12 level, which is a bit higher, as most lesions of children with spina bifida are in the lumbar region of the spine. Her paralysis is from just above the navel and down. She had nine surgeries during her first year of life. She has a shunt for hydrocephalus and has some other medical needs. Caitlin requires assistance with toileting, dressing, transfers, and mobility in nonaccessible areas. Yet if the environment is accessible, she can do quite well getting around on her own in a manual wheelchair. However, she does get fatigued by the end of the day. She has several health areas that must be closely monitored (pressure sores, medication, bladder and bowel program, and shunt functioning). She has (reluctantly) begun some self-catheterization skills. Caitlin also has a colostomy. She has stated that she "never wants to learn how to change her colostomy appliances ever in her whole entire life!"

Although it is a struggle on many days, our family is quite resilient. Caitlin's father is the primary caregiver and an "at home dad." He is an artist, with a studio in our house. He had taught university-level art as adjunct faculty member, but after Caitlin's birth he was not rehired. Caitlin's sisters—Monique, age fourteen, and Abby, age twelve—are very dear to her, although sibling spats and rivalry are as common as with any family. We have organized and facilitated SIBSHOPS for the last five years and have begun collaborating with agencies to start SIBSHOPS in our new community. SIB-

---

[*] Vignettes 1 and 5 were contributed by Dr. Carol Russell. See Chapter 2 for author information.

SHOPS are support programs for "sibs" of children with special needs, developed by Don Meyer in Seattle, Washington. These have been quite helpful for our girls in dealing with the "good and not so good feelings" they have in relation to having a "sib" with special needs.

Moving has been a strain for everyone. Caitlin does not like change, and transitions can be very difficult. We have learned to prepare for transitions well in advance, and still much can go wrong. *Flexibility* is the key word for us, as is *advocacy*. We are strong on communication and we ask questions—many that professionals have a difficult time answering. I'm sure we are considered "assertive parents"—and probably some other descriptive words that should not be in print here. We love all our daughters dearly and would do anything for them. We are not strangers to pursuing our child's rights. And humor is a must—for survival!

Goals

We entered Caitlin's new school district with an IEP that had been written in the spring before the summer that we moved. We shared information about spina bifida through audio and videotapes we had made with Caitlin's former team, as well as from the National Spina Bifida Association. We had training tapes on specific techniques that a former physical therapist and occupational therapist had prepared. Caitlin's developmental pediatrician had also prepared a tape on spina bifida and how it affects Caitlin and her functioning and abilities. Goals for Caitlin included the areas of mobility, self-help, self-advocacy, visual-perception, visual memory, attention, organization, and assistance with transitions. Unfortunately, Caitlin's new team did not agree to (or perhaps understand) the goals and objectives of her incoming IEP. Although, by law, her incoming IEP was valid (and only three months old) and should have transferred with her, there was definite resistance. They decided to begin with only the OT and PT goals. We knew we were in for a struggle when one professional said, "We do things differently here." We were also told that this was all too overwhelming! Our reply was, "You bet it can be, and that's why we need support!" (See Figure 12–1.)

Although we worked through some of the other areas over the next year, I will describe only the areas of mobility, self-help, and visual-perception. This was where the team agreed to begin working with Caitlin. Needless to say, we got more information about the law in our new state and had more meetings. The following is a summary of Caitlin's present level of performance and goals formulated by the team in the areas of mobility, self-help, and visual-perception/visual motor.

Present Level of Functioning in Mobility.   In the area of mobility, Caitlin had primarily used her wheelchair to get around. She had also used a reciprocating gait orthosis (RGO), accompanied by a reverse walker for standing and walking in the classroom for about two hours a day. She was even becoming more independent with putting it on and taking it off (donning and doffing in OT lingo). However, she had a femur fracture in April before the summer we moved, which would temporarily (we thought) keep her out of her RGO. When we moved, she had just had the cast removed on her left leg.

Figure 12–1
Transitions associated with moving create the need for siblings to support each other.

Caitlin's new team was not familiar with an RGO. And frankly, they did not want to attempt to become familiar with it. "That could be done at home," they said.

She was able to get around the school if surfaces were accessible, or with the use of an elevator or lift. She experienced contractures in both legs. Daily range of motion (ROM) exercises helped prevent these from becoming more severe. Without ROM the muscles could contract to the point that they are stronger than the bone, causing a fracture. Caitlin was also working on upper extremity strengthening to improve transferring skills (getting in and out of her wheelchair).

Mobility Goal. Caitlin will increase independent functional mobility skills at school.

Present Level of Functioning under Self-Help. In the area of self-help, Caitlin was, reluctantly, beginning to assist with toileting needs and with lower extremity dressing. She assisted with self-catheterization. As mentioned earlier, Caitlin also has a colostomy and has stated that she "never wants to learn how to change her colostomy appliances ever in her whole entire life!" Caitlin required full assistance with lower extremity dressing and preferred to let someone else do this for her. It was a laborious task for her to even assist. She would cry at home saying she didn't want to do this "ever in her life." Caitlin was generally independent with upper extremity dressing, although she would ask for assistance at times and balancing was also an issue (as her lesion is at the T-10 to T-12 level). Other areas of self-help needs have had to do with adaptations in the classroom and school environment. For example, access to books and supplies, having a desk that she can access with her wheelchair, access to her locker, and so forth, have been identified as needs.

Self-Help Goal.   Caitlin will improve her self-help skills.

Present Level of Functioning under Visual-Perception/ Visual Motor.
Caitlin has full range of motion and functional strength in the upper extremity. She does have some visual-perceptual challenges demonstrated in difficulty with writing skills. There are still some reversals of letters, writing is slower than her peers, and she has trouble with spacing, punctuation, and the like. Copying from the board is challenging.

Visual-Perception/Visual Motor Goal.   Caitlin will improve writing and visual-perceptual and visual motor skills to enhance classroom performance.

Objectives

Caitlin's team (OT, PT, classroom teacher, special education teacher, school psychologist, school counselor, principal, special education director, and we, (as parents) agreed to the following objectives in the mobility, self-help, and visual-perception areas.

Mobility Objectives Included:

a. Several objectives on independent transfers: to the floor and back up and side to side, with use of a transfer board. Several short-term objectives were written, with the hope of improving from moderate to minimal assistance. She also made use of a J-seat while on the floor to prevent pressure sores.
b. Caitlin will demonstrate upper extremity muscle strength 5/5 (normal grade) to improve transfer and mobility skills by May (the end of the school year).
c. Caitlin will exhibit wheelchair push-ups/weight shifting in wheelchair three or four times per hour every school day to ensure good skin care and pressure relief.
d. Caitlin will maintain or improve range of motion (ROM) in bilateral lower extremities to ensure positioning and/or posture during school activities throughout the school year.

Self-Help Objectives Included:

a. Several objectives were written on donning and doffing lower extremity clothing. Several short-term objectives were written, with the hope of improving from full to moderate assistance required.
b. Several objectives were written regarding self-catheterization skills and self-colostomy care. Some of the objectives included learning the steps and practicing them in a simulated situation with an anatomically correct doll, as it would not be safe to perform such a procedure on herself until she had the steps and procedure down.

Visual-Perception/Visual Motor Objectives Included:

a. Caitlin will write, in manuscript, a sentence of five words using consistent letter formation, line contact, and spacing two out of three trials or opportunities by March.

b. Caitlin will write, in manuscript, three short sentences to form a paragraph using consistent letter formation, line contact, and spacing two out of three trials or opportunities by May.

c. Caitlin will write, in cursive, a sentence of five words using consistent letter formation, line contact, and spacing two out of three trials or opportunities by October (of the next school year).

d. Caitlin will write, in cursive, three short sentences to form a paragraph using consistent letter formation, line contact, and spacing two out of three trials or opportunities by December (of the next school year).

e. Caitlin will complete visual-perceptual/visual motor remedial activities in visual form constancy, visual memory, and sequential memory with 90 percent accuracy.

Strategies

Mobility Strategies

a. Transfers would take place in the natural setting (transferring to the floor for floor activities in the classroom or physical education class, transfers in the nurse's office during catheterization times). In addition, one-on-one therapy sessions would include transfer practice. The J-seat would be utilized at any time Caitlin was on the floor to prevent pressure sores. All staff working with Caitlin would be trained (by the second week of school) and be comfortable assisting Caitlin in transferring and in use of the J-seat. It's important that Caitlin also feel comfortable with those assisting her in transfers. Trust is an important element.

b. Upper extremity muscle strengthening will occur through direct PT services in a weight lifting program during one-on-one sessions before school, three days a week.

c. Push-ups/weight shifting will be monitored with a checksheet on Caitlin's desk. The teacher and paraeducator will give verbal cues to remind Caitlin, if needed.

d. ROM will occur through stretching exercises both in the classroom and during one-on-one therapy sessions before school, three days a week.

Self-Help Strategies

a. Lower extremity dressing would occur during Caitlin's catheterization times (twice a day). In addition, some dressing skill practice would occur during one-on-one OT sessions after school.

b. Self-catheterization skills and self-colostomy care would be encouraged at Caitlin's regularly scheduled times each day. A chart, with the procedure task analyzed into steps, would be checked daily. An additional session after school each week would be utilized to reinforce Caitlin's learning of the steps and practicing them in a simulated situation with an anatomically correct doll. It would not be safe to perform such a procedure on herself until she had the steps and procedure down. Additional practice on the doll could occur more frequently. An additional chart would be kept on procedure steps in this simulated situation. This time would also be used to discuss feelings and concerns about self-care.

Visual-Perception/Visual Motor Strategies

a. The OT will work with Caitlin in the classroom, in addition to consultation with the classroom and special education teachers in the area of handwriting.
b. The OT will work with Caitlin in visual-perceptual/visual motor activities after school one day a week.

Evaluation

Evaluation of Mobility Goal and Objectives

a. Objectives on independent transfers would be measured by the physical therapist and staff observation. A chart measuring the amount of assistance needed for transfers will be recorded weekly by the PT. Other staff (school nurse, classroom teacher, PE teacher, paraeducator) will record the times Caitlin transfers in the normal environment. The PT will train, supervise, monitor, and observe other staff while assisting Caitlin with transfers in a variety of settings. Staff will note any resistance to transfers that Caitlin may exhibit.
b. The PT will evaluate Caitlin's upper extremity muscle strength through a manual muscle testing assessment.
c. Caitlin's wheelchair push-ups/weight shifting will be measured by a checksheet on Caitlin's desk. The teacher and paraeducator will record the times they had to use verbal cues to remind Caitlin.
d. ROM will be measured by the PT using a goniometer (measures the degree of range of motion of joints). In addition, staff observations will be recorded on positioning and posture during school activities.

Evaluation of Self-Help Goal and Objectives

a. Lower extremity dressing can occur during natural routines at school and home (nurse, OT, parents, paraeducator). A progress chart at school and home would be utilized. If lack of motivation is an issue, it needs to be addressed.
b. Steps and procedures accomplished with simulated catheterization (with the doll) will be recorded on a chart with all the steps listed.

Evaluation of Visual-Perception/Visual Motor Objectives

a. through d. Manuscript and cursive goals and objectives will be measured by Caitlin's classroom teacher and the OT. Samples of Caitlin's daily work, in addition to her OT therapy session samples, will be evaluated. These samples will also be kept in a portfolio to share with parents and team members.

e. Visual-perceptual/visual motor remedial activities in visual form constancy, visual memory, and sequential memory will be measured for 90 percent accuracy by the OT. The classroom teacher, special education teacher, and paraeducator will observe these areas on a daily basis in the classroom (such as copying from the board, work with charts, maps, and the like).

Mobility. ABI is apparent here, demonstrated by transfers taking place in the natural setting, integrating the intervention into the daily routine. Some of these routines include "cathing" and colostomy times—which Caitlin already is not too thrilled about. PBS approach would be useful to offer some appropriate choices within the procedure, as well as determining what is reinforcing to Caitlin about the process. Independence is a major benefit, yet one that Caitlin may not appreciate quite yet, as the procedure as a whole is overwhelming. It must be broken down and celebrated in sections. One-on-one therapy sessions to work on transfers take place after school, so Caitlin is not "pulled out" of her regular routine. PBS and ABI approach could benefit Caitlin during these sessions by setting up activities and games that would motivate her to transfer down and back up. This process takes a lot of strength (try pulling yourself into a chair while using only your upper body—good luck!).

The PBS and ABI approach could be applied to Caitlin's weight lifting program. Again, developmentally appropriate activities and games that would motivate her to do the exercises might help. If music is motivating to Caitlin, then add that. Let her have some choices in the process.

The monitoring of push-ups/weight shifting appears to be a self-monitoring process. PBS approach could benefit Caitlin by offering more choices, perhaps letting her make the chart or choosing some other mode of self-monitoring. A reinforcer after completing a certain number or each chart (developmentally appropriate number) may be supportive also.

ABI is evident with ROM exercises, as they occur in the natural environment (on the classroom floor during math floor activities). Again, Caitlin should be comfortable with this routine and have some choices in the process.

Self-Help. ABI is again apparent here, with lower extremity dressing taking place in the natural setting, integrating the intervention into the daily routine. PBS would be helpful if utilized with dressing skill practice with the OT after school. The practice would increase speed, yet it would occur as part of the natural routine. For example, the areas of choice, identifying preferred reinforcers, and collaboration with the family are a few suggestions to consider.

In the area of self-catheterization and self-colostomy care, need for ABI and PBS is evident. No one is really motivated to acquire these skills, yet it is a matter of independence. The charts are effective for recording, but what is being done to motivate Caitlin? Breaking down the tasks will allow success for small steps and might assist with motivation. Practice within a simulated situation, as with the doll, is developmentally appropriate and might help Caitlin deal with some of the resistance and feelings she is experiencing.

Visual-Perception/Visual Motor. Intervention in the area of handwriting demonstrates ABI, as it is within the classroom environment and general curriculum schedule. Adjustments and accommodations should be made in the amount of work and expanded time for assignments to promote Caitlin's success. An assistive technology evaluation would be appropriate to determine the need for assistance with written communication.

The OT's work with Caitlin in the area of visual-perceptual/visual motor skills is after school and will not require Caitlin to miss any of her time in the classroom. The activities should be motivating and there should be an element of choice involved. Activities should be functional and reinforcers should be considered according to Caitlin's preferences.

Transition Issues for Caitlin

Transitions mean change. The transitions we can predict offer us the opportunity to think and plan proactively to ensure a smoother transition. Whether the transition is within school, from one school to another, from one state to state, or any other transition for young children with special needs, three elements remain important to support children, families, and professionals. They are continuity, developmentally appropriate practices (age and individual appropriateness), and parental involvement.

Caitlin's transition from second to third grade meant not only a change of school but also a change of homes, community, state, climate, medical resources, state resources, and all else that accompany such a move. We, as Caitlin's family, attempted to anticipate and plan for the changes. If you recall, we sent her IEP and other records ahead in June and had met with the director of special education in July before moving in August. We brought a wealth of information: training tapes (made by Caitlin's PT and OT and developmental pediatrician), written materials and audiotapes from the SBAA, and books on spina bifida. Although the information was taken, there was never feedback, questions, or follow-through on the strategies or methods. In-services could have included the family, written information, questions, and training in procedures such as transfers, emergency plans, and medical procedures. We learned later that the classroom teacher first learned how to help Caitlin transfer in April—after beginning school the previous August. Additional information and questions were met with resistance, and some gave feedback that "we're overwhelmed." The transition process was quite frustrating. It was as though we were giving too much— too much parent involvement.

Continuity was lacking. Caitlin's new school wanted to start with a new IEP, as they did not agree with her incoming one. We had to make requests several times before being allowed to go into Caitlin's classroom prior to the first day of school. Developmental appropriateness (DAP) in terms of the age level and group needs was apparent in her new classroom. Yet, developmental appropriateness in terms of individuality was sparse. Much of Caitlin's individuality was not acknowledged. The team refused to see many of the needs that had already been established on Caitlin's incoming IEP. Their goal appeared to be to treat her just like the other children. Our reply would be, "Equal treatment does not equal, equal opportunity." The resistance to the level of our involvement, as parents, was quite disappointing. We were very involved parents, ready to offer a wealth of information. Granted, our knowledge may have been intimidating; however, our approach was tactful and always with a smile. Parent involvement, at whatever level parents are comfortable with, is essential for successful transitions. Parents are your best resource about their individual child.

The most tragic issue here is time . . . time lost for our child . . . time we will never have back. The focus on our child was, at times, lost in the process. When continuity, DAP, and parent involvement are absent in transitions, then continued services are not in place and seamless transitions cannot occur. This may result in regression and make any progress difficult to attain.

VIGNETTE 2: DANIEL

Introduction

When I first met Daniel he was four years old. I had been asked by his mother and school-based team to pay a visit to his school and observe him in his early childhood special education self-contained classroom. Daniel was a cute little boy who appeared quite withdrawn and noncommunicative. He had been diagnosed with autism at the age of two and one-half years by a pediatric neurologist, and his family had been struggling with not only the label of autism but how to obtain meaningful educational services and supports for him in an underserved and rural community. Daniel's family included his mother and father, both of whom were very supportive and loving parents, his younger sibling, a brother named Matthew, who was two years of age. Daniel's family life was enriched by a large extended family and his enjoyment of the farm life that he was so familiar with. Daniel loved animals of all kinds, especially dogs and horses, and demonstrated a fondness for taking care of them and playing with them on most days following school. Daniel had been experiencing great difficulty in his educational placement (a self-contained classroom for young children with moderate to severe special needs). He had no contact during the day with nondisabled peers. The classroom was quite traditional in its daily operation, and in terms of behavioral supports, emphasis was placed on a traditional consequence-based approach, such as edible rewards and punishers like time-out.

Daniel engaged in a variety of challenging behaviors that included noncompliance, aggression, and tantrums. He had little or no verbal communication, and his receptive language skills were also suspect as evidenced by his inability to respond to his name or other direct verbal cues, minimal eye contact, poor peer relations, limited use of gestures, and low levels of participation in classroom activities. At this juncture, Daniel's mother wanted him evaluated to determine the best options educationally for him over the long term, and her expressed desire was that he develop greater capacities in the area of expressive communication and that he have opportunities to interact more frequently with nondisabled peers.

Daniel was given the *Psychoeducational Profile Revised (PEP-R)*, which is an inventory of behaviors and skills designed to identify uneven and idiosyncratic learning patterns in young children within the age range of one to twelve years (Schopler, Reichler, Bashford, Lansing, & Marcus, 1990). This test explores the child's learning capacities in seven developmental areas including perception, fine motor, gross motor, eye-hand integration, cognitive performance, and cognitive-verbal skills. The test also provides a developmental profile of the child's current learning strengths and emerging skill areas as a basis for curriculum development (Schopler et al., 1990).

Daniel obtained an age-equivalent of 1.8 years and displayed splintered development, a pattern typically observed in children with autism. Specific areas of strength included eye-hand integration and fine motor development, with language and imitation falling well below age level norms. At this point, Daniel's family elected to change his educational placement and enrolled him in an early childhood special education classroom that placed emphasis on total communication.

Goal

The goal most critical for addressing Daniel's current and future educational strengths and areas of need was to increase the structure in his learning environment in order to better accommodate his learning style and to promote increased task engagement.

Objectives

In an effort to obtain increased levels of task engagement, objectives were developed and implemented within the classroom. Daniel's team increased the level of structure and consistency within his daily routine. This was accomplished through the development of a photo activity schedule for Daniel that depicted the daily classroom activities. His teacher and teaching assistant devised a greater array of developmentally appropriate activities that incorporated visual cues, once again as a means of accommodating Daniel's visual learning style. It is quite common to note that children with autism process visual cues much more efficiently given their level of communication challenges.

Finally, Daniel's teacher and teaching assistant made specific environmental modifications to better accommodate Daniel's need for visual clarity in the classroom. They divided the classroom into designated areas for individual and group activities and also developed separate areas within the classroom for leisure, music, and snack.

Specific objectives for Daniel included the following:

a. *Acquiring the skills necessary to utilize his individual photo activity schedule independently.*
   The purpose of the photo activity schedule was to provide a visual means of communicating to Daniel his daily routine while also including his preferences and affording him the opportunity to make

choices—most important, communicating to him the concept of "what comes next." It served as a concrete means for not only communicating the order of activities but also assisting him in anticipating changes in activities. The longitudinal educational purpose of such a teaching tool is that it will promote increased levels of independence for the child and generalize to new settings over time.

b. *Increasing his task engagement through the use of his individual photo activity schedule as demonstrated by his ability to independently locate necessary materials for a task, completion of the task with 80 percent accuracy, putting away materials upon completion of the task, and self-reinforcing after successful completion of the activity by locating his preferred toy.*

Strategies

The strategies that were applied with Daniel were illustrative of positive behavioral supports, developmentally appropriate practice, and best and effective practices in early childhood special education with respect to children with autism. Given Daniel's challenges in the areas of expressive communication (approximately one year, five month level) and receptive communication (approximately one year, two month level), it was determined after consultations with his family and team members and assessment results that he was communicating at the picture level. He did not respond to verbal cues during instructional or play periods. Transitions were extremely difficult for him, often resulting in challenging behavior. Taking these facts into consideration, the decision was made to develop a daily schedule for Daniel consisting of photographs depicting the activities that were part of his typical daily routine. Additional strategies included the creation of visible areas within the classroom for specific activities such as individual work, group activities, play, leisure, snack, and circle time. These areas were labeled with pictures; the walls were also painted different colors in each of the separate areas, and carpet squares matching the colored walls were used to assist with discrimination.

The teacher provided Daniel with instruction in the use of his daily schedule, relying on a combination of modeling and gestural cues such as pointing, paired with verbal cues, to assist Daniel in the acquisition of this very important skill. Coupled with instruction on how to use the schedule was the enhancement of Daniel's curriculum to include developmentally appropriate activities that built on both Daniel's current and emerging skill development. Some of these activities included shape recognition, labeling colors and objects, responding to his name upon being asked, drawing shapes, printing his name, counting from one to ten, expressively identifying familiar pictures, and responding to simple one- and two-step directions. These tasks were interspersed with preferred activities and built into independent activities, small group activities, and individualized instruction in those skills that he was just beginning to acquire. In addition, a daily communicator was developed that accompanied Daniel to and from home each day and kept his parents informed as to his daily progress and also afforded Daniel's parents the opportunity to communicate any of their feelings or concerns.

Evaluation

The results of Daniel's intervention were very positive. Data were taken daily by his classroom teacher as a means of evaluating his ability to follow his schedule and also on specific skills that were part of his daily routine. Data were scored as number of occurrences/total number of opportunities. An example of this would be as follows: Daniel was given five opportunities as part of his daily schedule to independently get his folder. If he performed this skill independently five times for that specific day, the teacher would score 5/5, which then could be converted to 100 percent for that specific skill on that day.

Data indicated that the multicomponent intervention package, including the individualized photo activity schedule, resulted in an increase in independent task engagement, appropriate social interactions with teachers and peers, and increased eye contact. Data obtained during the preintervention or baseline phase indicated that Daniel averaged 29 percent on independent performance of scheduled tasks. However, during intervention—which consisted of direct instruction in the use of his individualized photo activity schedule, classroom modifications, individualized work tasks, and self-administered reinforcement (upon completion of five tasks, Daniel checked his schedule, noted the visual cue, a picture of a lion, and thus obtained his preferred toy, a lion figurine)—his level of independent performance of scheduled tasks increased to an average of 87 percent spanning a two-week period. Probes conducted during week four of the intervention phase indicated performance levels at 100 percent, an additional week follow-up probe conducted at four months indicated performance levels at 86 percent.

Other results from this intervention included social validity statements from his teachers, family, and other related professionals that addressed the efficacy of this intervention procedure. Postintervention follow-ups conducted at six months indicated an increase in performance on the PEP-R resulting in an age equivalent of 3.10 years. These scores reflected a performance increase on this assessment instrument of over one year. In addition to these measurable increases, Daniel began to receive educational services in a half-day inclusive kindergarten setting during afternoons while still receiving preschool services during the morning.

Long-Term Educational Outcomes

Daniel's performance in the kindergarten class remained consistent with his previous performance levels. The instructional and classroom modifications utilized in the preschool setting were also implemented within the kindergarten with only minor modifications. Daniel's daily schedule began to have photographs paired with simple words. Teacher interviews reported high levels of satisfaction with both Daniel's rate of progress and the intervention package.

Daniel's educational program was enriched the following year with his full-time placement in the kindergarten class. We were gratified to see Daniel continue in the use of his schedule, his emerging abilities to read words, and his increased levels of communication. His peer interactions were quite good, and he interacted very appropriately with his classmates.

As a positive long-term educational outcome, Daniel has recently successfully completed first grade. He will be attending an inclusive second grade classroom in the following year. As a final note, the author is reminded of a visit paid to Daniel's school not long ago. As I observed him in his inclusive first grade classroom at the board one day, he came upon a point where he needed teacher assistance. He had completed his assignment and his teacher had been busily assisting another student. Daniel turned and made eye contact with her and said, "So now, what do you want me to do?" Upon witnessing this memorable event I smiled and felt overcome with emotion. For here was this little boy—who many had thought would be limited in his ability to communicate verbally with others, predestined by some to spend the rest of his educational career in a self-contained classroom for children with moderate and severe disabilities—now in a classroom full of children with and without challenges in his local community, communicating his needs and desires so well, and finding success as a result of positive behavioral supports and activity-based interventions utilized by a committed team of professionals and Daniel's family as well. Indeed, this was a victory for Daniel, his parents, his teachers, his school, and also for those of us who have the pleasure to know and work with him.

Need for Positive Behavioral Supports, Activity-Based Intervention, and Developmentally Appropriate Practice

One should note the successful merger of PBS, ABI, and DAP in this vignette. The development of child-specific behavioral supports included managing the antecedents associated with Daniel's challenging behaviors. This involved restructuring the classroom environment to take into account Daniel's learning style and need for visual clarity; the development of an individualized schedule for Daniel to assist in communicating the occurrence of activities and transitions; and, finally, the active teaching of skills that were developmentally and age appropriate given Daniel's learning style, individual strengths, and emerging skill areas. ABI and DAP are consistent throughout as well. The use of developmentally appropriate activities and instruction in these skills within natural settings, as well as within inclusionary settings, is noteworthy. Choice was also a major component in Daniel's educational program as teachers and his parents attempted to take into account personal preferences in his daily schedule. The development of relevant skills is also a point worth mentioning. Daniel's educational program placed emphasis on skills that were developmentally appropriate, authentic, and relevant in his current and future educational placements. Comments received from his teachers and parents validated not only their perceptions concerning his progress but also their satisfaction with his total program. This program component is often not reflected in individualized educational programs (IEP).

Transition Issues for Daniel

The attention given to transition issues and longitudinal educational outcomes for Daniel was quite obvious. A major component was the development of the individualized photo activity schedule for Daniel and instruction in its use. This intervention component represents the teaching of a "process" that enabled Daniel to self-manage his behavior in the classroom success-fully. The process took into account Daniel's learning strengths and com-munication needs. The strength of this approach is that like any process, it will remain over time, across teachers, and within different classrooms. We witnessed how Daniel's schedule progressed from using only photographs to pairing photographs with words. Finally, at this point Daniel's schedule consists of words indicating activities with an occasional picture/symbol to illustrate a new or novel activity. It is likely that as Daniel ages, he will grow from this approach to perhaps a daily planner that he will carry in his pocket to assist him in self-managing his daily routine.

The stepwise and systematic exposure to the next educational setting was also very helpful in facilitating successful inclusions. Daniel's teachers carefully considered and referenced skills around future needs as well as those in the immediate educational and home environments. Communica-tion and consultation among all team members and Daniel's parents was also a strong point in terms of promoting successful transitions for him. The "big picture" maintained the focus for Daniel's parents and educational team as they developed Daniel's educational goals and objectives. Finally, support among team members, administrators, and relevant others served to promote smooth and effective transitions. Without question, Daniel was the centering point for all team members, and his overall well-being and development served to guide each and every member of the team in the development of a long-term educational plan.

VIGNETTE 3: TIMMY

Introduction

Timmy is a six-year-old boy who is in the first grade. He attends a regular classroom, but his teacher has noticed that he has been displaying some be-haviors of late in the classroom that have become somewhat of a concern. Timmy seems to have difficulty paying attention in class, following through on instructions, and is generally distracted. His teacher, Mrs. Jennings, is also concerned with his loud talking, hitting other children, and impulsive behav-iors such as getting out of his seat and running about the room. She has also observed that Timmy appears to experience some difficulty in completing his seat work; however, he thoroughly enjoys working on the computer in the classroom. Mrs. Jennings recently met with Timmy's parents to voice her con-cerns about his behavior. Timmy's mother and father recently divorced but are committed to his welfare. As a group, Mrs. Jennings and Timmy's parents decided that they should schedule a meeting with Ms. Kinsey, the special ed-ucation resource consultant, and Mr. Albertson, the school counselor.

The meeting was scheduled for the following week, and immediately the concerns for Timmy's well-being were presented by his mother and supported by his teacher, Mrs. Jennings, and Timmy's father. Ms. Kinsey, the special education resource consultant, asked Timmy's classroom teacher if she had employed any prereferral strategies with Timmy related to specific academic tasks, such as modifying assignments, adapting materials, using individualized schedules, and providing choice for Timmy in terms of assignments. She replied that she really had not done anything formal yet because she wanted to consult with Timmy's parents as well as a professional in special education. Mr. Albertson, the school counselor, brought up the issue of adjustment for Timmy given that his parents had just undergone a divorce. He stated that when he visited with Timmy about the situation, Timmy expressed anger and frustration about the divorce and mourned the separation from his father. He continued to see his father often during the week and on weekends, but missed the daily overnight contact. Mr. Albertson strongly encouraged Timmy's parents and teacher to rally around Timmy and offer him as much support as possible as he tries to deal with his feelings in this major life transition. Timmy's parents immediately liked the idea of trying some adaptations in the classroom and agreed to be as supportive as possible to Timmy to ease his postdivorce transition.

Ms. Kinsey, the special education resource consultant, offered to collaborate with Timmy's first grade teacher, Mrs. Jennings, in recommending some prereferral strategies to assess their effectiveness before recommending a referral for a complete educational evaluation. It was also decided by Timmy's parents that Mr. Albertson would continue to do weekly follow-along sessions with Timmy to assist in identifying some of his emotions. Timmy's teachers began to collaborate on the development of some strategies to employ within the classroom to determine if Timmy's performance would improve. The team agreed to meet in two weeks to discuss their progress.

Specific classroom strategies employed by Timmy's teachers included the following: Ms. Kinsey, the special education resource consultant, asserted the need for information to first confirm the extent of the problem. She developed a scatter plot recording form (refer to Chapter 6) for determining the frequency of Timmy's impulsive behaviors and also to determine if there were any patterns associated with these behaviors and specific times of day and/or content areas in which the behaviors were at their highest or lowest in terms of frequency. She also asked that Mrs. Jennings and Timmy's parents complete a Functional Assessment Interview Form (refer to Chapter 6) to obtain background information on Timmy's behavior.

Results after three days of collecting data using the scatter plot recording form revealed that there was a high frequency of disruptive behavior and inattentiveness scattered throughout the day. Specific examples included Timmy stating that his eyes hurt too much and that he could not work, excessive talking aloud to himself and others during work time, breaking his pencil thus not allowing him to complete his assignment, and getting out of his seat on numerous occasions. Finally, Timmy fell out of his chair a number of times, which resulted in his being upset and reporting that he was too upset to finish his written work. Data obtained from the structured interviews conducted with Timmy's parents and Mrs. Jennings did reveal a consistent pattern of loud and disruptive behavior across times and events, home and school. Timmy also displayed frequent episodes of frustration that was expressed through yelling, crying, and a refusal to follow through on directives by his parents and teacher. Data obtained through the structured interview revealed that Timmy enjoyed art, especially drawing, as well as playing with action figures. It was during these times at school (during art) and at home (while engaged in art or playing with his preferred toys, in this case, Timmy's action figures) that the behaviors were not present.

Meanwhile, after Ms. Kinsey completed her initial assessment and offered some prereferral instructional strategies, Mrs. Jennings sought to modify her instructional practices, such as using visual organizers for Timmy, providing him with more choice-making opportunities, and providing him with praise for completing assignments and for appropriate behavior rather than verbal reprimands for displays of challenging behavior. Despite the well-intentioned effort on the part of Timmy's teachers, problems continued in the area of behavior and academic performance. The team reconvened after two weeks and discussed progress and future options. At this point, Timmy's parents asked that he be given a comprehensive evaluation to determine eligibility for specialized educational services and supports. They suspected that Timmy might meet the criteria for attention deficit disorder and that he might also have a specific learning disability. The team supported this decision, referral procedures were completed, and an evaluation was scheduled.

Timmy was evaluated by the school psychologist from the district and by Ms. Kinsey, the special education resource consultant. He was administered a battery of tests that included a standardized measure of cognitive skills, in this case the WPPSI-R (Wechsler Preschool and Primary Scales of Intelligence-Revised). The *Woodcock-Johnson Psychoeducational Battery-R* (1989) was also administered to assess academic achievement. Results of these assessments indicated that Timmy was above average in terms of intelligence, but the presence of specific learning disabilities was noted in the area of reading. In addition, the evaluation revealed some concerns in terms of Timmy's auditory processing. Delays were evident in the areas of expressive and receptive language. Hearing was assessed by an audiologist to rule out any hearing loss. Further observational assessments were conducted at home and at school. Behavior rating scales were administered to both Timmy's parents and his teachers to determine if Timmy met the criteria for attention deficit/hyperactivity disorder (ADD/ADHD). Attention deficit/hyperactivity disorder is characterized by a persistent pattern of inattention and/or hyperactivity-impulsivity that is more frequent and severe than is typically observed in individuals at a comparable level of development (DSM IV, 1994). These behavioral characteristics typically are evident across multiple environments including home, school, and social settings.

Also associated with ADD/ADHD is a chronic pattern of impulsivity as evidenced by erratic behaviors in and about the classroom, such as general inattentiveness, responding to questions in a hurried manner, and often blurting out responses or answers that are inaccurate.

ADD/ADHD is neurologically based and has been linked to the frontal lobes, basal ganglion, brain stem, as well as one of the major neurotransmitter systems (Riccio, Hynd, Cohen, & Gonzalez, 1993). Distractibility is often another characteristic associated with ADD/ADHD that is made worse by the presence of auditory processing disorders such as we have witnessed in this vignette.

Goals

After determining that Timmy did indeed have a specific learning disability and that he also met the criteria for ADD/ADHD, an M-team meeting was scheduled. In attendance at the meeting were Timmy's parents; Ms. Kinsey, the special education resource consultant; Mrs. Jennings, Timmy's first grade teacher; the school psychologist; and the school counselor. The coordinator of specialized educational services for the district was also on hand and served as facilitator for the meeting.

Results were shared by the professionals and opinions expressed about Timmy's performance and the presence of a specific learning disability and ADHD. Timmy's parents expressed their greatest concern: that educational and behavioral supports be exhausted before the use of stimulant medications to deal with Timmy's periods of inattention and impulsivity. They wanted to avoid the use of medications if at all possible. Their second concern was that, if at all possible, Timmy have services and supports provided to him within the context of the regular classroom. Timmy's team concurred with these recommendations as well.

The goals selected for Timmy were as follows:

1. Increase task engagement during scheduled classroom activities.
2. Increase Timmy's socioemotional abilities to recognize and express feelings about himself and others.
3. Increase Timmy's abilities to decode words through the use of rhyme and movement.

Objectives

The following objectives were developed to accompany the goals that were identified by Timmy's educational team.

1. To assist Timmy with task engagement, he will be provided with teacher delivered instruction in the area of self-instruction and self-recording.

   Objective 1. Upon receiving verbal instructions and modeling from the teacher, Timmy will utilize self-instruction when confronted by words that he does not recognize for twenty consecutive trials/probes without teacher assistance. The steps he will use consist of a language experience approach (Miller, Miller, Wheeler, & Selinger, 1989) designed to teach Timmy to (*a*) ask "What is the sound of the first letter?" (*b*) ask "Does it look like any other word that I do know?" and (*c*) "blank it out" and read the rest of the sentence.

   Objective 2. When given a visual cue in the form of a compact picture/written schedule, Timmy will independently follow each item on his schedule eight out of eight trials daily for ten days without teacher assistance.

Objective 3. When presented with a "List of Things to Do" each morning by the teacher, Timmy will independently check each item off the list upon its completion without assistance, 100 percent of the time daily.

2. To increase Timmy's ability to recognize and express feelings in himself and others. In order to accomplish this goal the guidance counselor and Timmy's parents collaborated to develop the following objectives for Timmy to receive instruction once per week with the guidance counselor. The program would also be followed up at home and within Timmy's classroom and is designed to utilize both a structured teaching approach (McGinnis & Goldstein, 1984) and also the teaching of language associated with feelings (Giddan, Bade, Rickenberg, & Ryley, 1995).

Objective 1. After being provided a rationale for learning the chosen behavior, and a model demonstration, Timmy will:

  a. Identify the expressed feeling by name (e.g., anger, sadness, happiness).
  b. Demonstrate socially acceptable nonverbal responses.
  c. Model appropriate behavior.
  d. Vividly role-play facial, vocal, and body movements and characteristics of an emotion while labeling it.

Art therapy and journaling will also be used as a means for expressing feelings. Writing about how Timmy feels on a given day will be conducted daily both at home and at school settings.

3. To increase Timmy's ability to decode words, his teacher utilized a learning through rhyme approach (Dye & McConnell, 1997).

Objective 1. When given three single-syllable, short /a/ vowel sound words, Timmy will change the initial consonant and create a list of five new words at 100 percent accuracy across ten trials.

Objective 2. When given three single-syllable, short /a/ vowel sound words, Timmy will change the final consonant and create a list of five new words at 100 percent accuracy across ten trials.

Strategies

Ms. Kinsey, the special education resource consultant, provided instruction to Timmy in her office on how to use self-instruction for word attack in the area of reading. The quiet setting was deemed most conducive to minimize the distractions in the regular classroom and also to not draw undue attention to Timmy. Ms. Kinsey developed a checklist to assist him in learning the steps of the self-instruction approach.

The method that Ms. Kinsey employed was adapted from Miller, Miller, Wheeler, and Selinger (1989). Ms. Kinsey provided daily instruction in the use of the procedure until Timmy could self-instruct independently for twenty consecutive trails with follow-up probes. She combined this approach with an exercise designed to increase Timmy's ability to decode words by changing the initial consonants and creating families of words that make similar sounds (Dye & McConnell, 1997). The same exercise was also adapted to change the final consonants to create words that sound similar.

Figure 12–2
Computer assisted instruction is a preferred mode of learning for many children.

Timmy's Self-Instruction Checklist

1. ASK "What sound does the letter make?"
2. ASK "Does it look like a word that I know?"
3. "BLANK IT OUT" and read the sentence.

Timmy's Daily Checklist

Timmy's To Do List

1. ABC's — √
2. Lowercase Letters — √
3. Writing — √
4. Math — √
5. Recess — √
6. Lunch — √
7. Art — √
8. Science — √
9. Library — √
10. Play — √

Sessions were conducted daily to develop Timmy's capacity to learn the skill and to generalize it across words.

Ms. Kinsey also provided Timmy with individualized instruction on how to use a compact picture/word schedule, similar to following a pocket calendar throughout the day, to pre-cue him before transitions, to help him maintain task engagement, and to assist in completing all scheduled activities. Attached to the schedule was a daily reminder sheet that listed activities and assignments for Timmy to check and mark off as he proceeded through the day's activities.

Timmy was provided with direct instruction in each of these strategies. Instruction consisted of providing him with a rationale, modeling the skill for Timmy, allowing Timmy the opportunity to practice the activity, and providing him with reinforcement and corrective feedback.

Finally, as previously mentioned, an intervention was collaboratively designed with Timmy's parents and the school counselor. Timmy met one day per week with the counselor. During that time, they did structured role play and individual counseling to help Timmy in identifying how he felt that day. The role play consisted of Timmy identifying a feeling of his choice by name, demonstrating appropriate nonverbal responses, modeling appropriate behavior, and demonstrating the facial, vocal, and body movements associated with the emotion. Timmy was also encouraged to keep a journal of feelings and thoughts that he cared to express and to illustrate the journal with pictures of his choice. The journal and art therapy were continued at home as well.

Evaluation

Evaluation of Task Engagement and Reading Objectives

1. The self-instruction and self-monitoring activity will be evaluated in daily sessions by Ms. Kinsey, the special education resource consultant, with follow-up evaluations conducted by Mrs. Jennings, Timmy's first grade teacher. Data will be recorded as occurrence/nonoccurrence with the level of assistance needed by Timmy to complete each of the steps.
2. Portfolio assessment will serve as another form of evaluation. Materials for the portfolio will consist of Timmy's completed assignments before, during, and following intervention. Additional materials will include completed copies of the daily checklist.

Evaluation of Socioemotional Objectives

1. Mr. Albertson, the school counselor, will maintain a log with progress notes related to Timmy's sessions with him.
2. Notes will also be kept on how these sessions assist Timmy in defusing some of his stress and anxiety.
3. Timmy's journal will also serve as an indicator of progress and will contain any homework assignments that Mr. Albertson gives him.
4. Finally, Mr. Albertson will list in detail the activities conducted during each session in his progress notes.
5. A home/school communicator will be developed that will travel to and from school each day with Timmy and will serve as a source to inform Timmy's parents of his progress and any concerns. It will also allow Timmy's parents to communicate their concerns, questions, or information to the school as a means of keeping Timmy's team members informed. Timmy's first grade teacher will be responsible for maintaining this.

Need for Positive Behavior Supports, Activity-Based Interventions, and Developmentally Appropriate Practice. Timmy's situation presents a unique challenge to both his educational team and his parents. He is challenged by a specific learning disability coupled with ADD/ADHD and socioemotional issues related to the divorce of his parents. The need for positive behavioral supports is very evident. Timmy's teachers first need to identify the functions of Timmy's behavior. Is Timmy disruptive because of his need for attention? Clearly some of his behaviors are directly related to his need to escape some demand situations such as specific academic tasks. Thus, positive behavioral supports are needed in the form of modified lessons, reducing the volume of in-seat paper and pencil worksheets, providing Timmy with choice pertaining to academic tasks such as the teacher identifying the objective for the week, and permitting Timmy the opportunity to select three of five options (e.g., skills-based activity, whole language activity, computer-assisted instruction). See Figure 12–2.

Timmy's preferred learning mode is through the computer. He enjoys the computer, and increased access to the computer should be provided. Reinforcement should also be consistent with Timmy's efforts at positive behavior. The teacher should make every attempt to teach Timmy positive alternative behaviors and reinforce him for good behavior while ignoring and using natural consequences for challenging behavior. Positive behavioral supports are also evident in the development of an intervention designed to teach Timmy how to identify his feelings and label them. This intervention combines developmentally appropriate practice and activities-based intervention through the use of natural settings and activities that are developmentally appropriate.

The ecological model is also evident in this vignette. Collaboration across home and school environments is obvious as is the development of interventions that are not only aimed at Timmy's learning new skills and behaviors but involve Timmy's teachers and parents in the learning and behavioral change process.

ABI and DAP are evident in the development of the language experience activities; however, some instruction does occur in the context of a segregated environment. Perhaps one method for modifying this would be to incorporate the teaching of the self-instruction/self-monitoring and language experience approaches in the context of Timmy's first grade classroom.

VIGNETTE 4: BRANDI

Introduction

Brandi is a seven-year-old girl who attends a special education self-contained class for children with severe disabilities located within her neighborhood elementary school. Brandi displays some significant challenges physically in that she meets the criteria for multiple disabilities and has been diagnosed with visual impairment and speech/language delays. Her current placement is in a classroom of ten children, all who display moderate and severe disabilities including children with mental retardation. Brandi is of average height and weight for a child her age and appears to have a level of comfort in her classroom environment. Her orientation and mobility skills within the classroom are quite proficient as she is able to find her preferred toys and classroom materials without assistance. Brandi is generally a very agreeable child who responds well to teacher directives. Brandi's teacher is challenged by the level of Brandi's disability—her communication skill deficits coupled with her visual impairment—and by her desire to enrich the curriculum for Brandi. The current educational program consists of a variety of tasks to enhance Brandi's fine motor skills and discrimination abilities, yet is not functional or developmentally appropriate given Brandi's age. Brandi's mother has stated that areas of primary concern include Brandi's need for increased levels of independence both at home and at school, enriched opportunities for learning and personal growth, and, most important, increased self-help skills such as brushing teeth, dressing, and expressive communication.

Brandi's teacher and mother have decided to make a referral to the statewide assistance team for children with low incidence disabilities to assist them in the redesign of Brandi's individualized education program. A major issue of concern for Brandi's mother and teacher is that Brandi will frequently tug at her hair throughout the day. Fortunately, the force has not been enough to result in any damage, but the behavior is of concern. In order to fully understand Brandi's educational needs the following assessments were conducted: functional assessment structured interview conducted with Brandi's mother and teacher, *Vineland Adaptive Behavior Scales-Interview Edition* administered to Brandi's mother, and, finally, an analog assessment of behavior in which Brandi's teacher worked at varying levels of instructional and behavioral supports in order to ascertain precisely the level of supports needed by Brandi.

A summary of the assessment revealed that Brandi displayed several strengths, including her ability to work on a variety of tasks with multiple instructors, the ability to follow verbal directions, an ability to work independently for an extended period of time, and the ability to make choices and seek assistance. During the analog assessment of behavior it was noted that Brandi demonstrated a preference for specific activities and was stimulated by music and noises in her environment. She demonstrated periods where she would engage in joint attention with her teacher while performing tasks. She also displayed the ability to anticipate transitions. Although previously believed by some to not have any language, Brandi was observed by the team to use language that was appropriate given the context. A specific example of her language usage was her saying "dropped it" while picking up some work task materials that she had dropped on the floor. She also used the words "push it" to request the teacher to push a button on a toy to make it play a tune.

An analog assessment was conducted to determine the level of structure and type of positive behavioral supports most needed by Brandi in the classroom. Of course, these same strategies could be applied in Brandi's home setting as well. Specific instructional conditions were presented to Brandi in which her teacher worked directly with her as she performed class-room work and leisure activities that were part of her typical day. Examples of the changing instructional conditions include specific directions, choice, and access to a preferred toy or activity. Each of these conditions was im-plemented for a period of five minutes. Brandi's behavior was observed and recorded during each of these sessions. The conditions were replicated three times each to ensure reliability.

On the basis of the information obtained through the team-based as-sessment and input from both Brandi's mother and the teacher, the follow-ing was noted: Brandi's performance on the *Vineland Adaptive Behavior Scale* reflected an adaptive behavior composite score in the low range for Brandi's age, suggesting moderate to severe levels of mental retardation. Her highest scores were reflected on the socialization domain. This meas-ure supports the findings from the analog assessment, which showed that Brandi maintains the ability to transition easily across activities and is re-sponsive to directives from her mother and teacher. The results from the analog assessment indicated that Brandi appears to disengage from tasks that are not specific in terms of directions and that are repetitive. This re-flects much of her previous curriculum, the cause of concern. During play activities and activities where choice is present, Brandi maintains levels of task engagement. Her highest levels of task engagement during work ac-tivities occurred during tasks that had specific directions and that afforded her choice-making opportunities in the selection of the task. Naturally, one of the findings from the assessment was that Brandi's environment at school needed to be enriched and also more relevant to Brandi's needs and learn-ing strengths.

Goals

The following goals were developed for Brandi given the outcomes of the assessment and from input by her mother and each of the team members.

1. To increase Brandi's expressive communication skills through the use of single-word models paired with behaviors that are typically used by Brandi to obtain her needs.
2. To provide Brandi with increased choice-making opportunities as a means for developing her expressive communication skills and as a means for allowing her to exercise her right of choice within the context of her daily routine.
3. To enrich Brandi's curriculum through the enhancement of functional and developmentally appropriate activities that coincide with her preferred learning modalities (i.e., auditory and tactile).
4. To increase Brandi's independence through the use of an object schedule on a daily basis within the classroom and home settings.
5. To increase the level of positive behavior supports to Brandi through the following means:

- Modifying setting events—such as enhancing Brandi's curriculum through the provision of increased choice-making opportunities, increasing the tactile clarity in the classroom, and reinforcing her in the absence of hair pulling.
- Teaching Brandi to verbally communicate her needs with single words.
- Ongoing data-based instruction should be developed in order to be fully able to determine the rate of Brandi's progress.
- Consultation with the vision specialist and speech/language therapist.

6. To provide direct instruction—using task analysis, most-to-least prompt hierarchy—in acquiring basic self-help skills such as brushing teeth, tying shoes, washing hands, and using utensils. This will be implemented at school and followed up at home.

Objectives

1. Given a functional context—such as the classroom during individual instruction, recess, lunch time, play, snack, and bathroom breaks—single-word models will be used to teach Brandi functional word usage. These words will be paired with naturally occurring activities and nonverbal behaviors typically exhibited by Brandi. Examples of words include *yes, no, more, bathroom, happy, sad, music, play,* and *toy.* These words will be paired with activities, and Brandi will be given verbal praise for any approximate verbalization.

A. Given the functional context across activities (instruction, music, play, recess, and the like), the instructor will provide Brandi with a question to teach choice making and yes/no responses. Example: "Would you like more to drink Brandi?" "Would you like to play with the toy? " Brandi will be presented with a minimum of ten opportunities per day. Reinforcement in the form of verbal praise and a pat on the hand will be given for any approximation. Evaluation will be conducted by maintaining a record of occurrences/nonoccurrences divided by ten (the total number of opportunities) resulting in a percentage. Performance criterion: 90 percent across consecutive sessions.

B. When presented with or engaged in an activity, the teacher will attach single words as labels for the activity or behavior as a means of teaching functional vocabulary words to Brandi. The teacher will then provide Brandi with an opportunity to say the word. An example of this teaching strategy would be as follows: "Throw me the ball Brandi." "Can you say ball, Brandi?" "Show me the ball Brandi." Evaluation will be conducted by maintaining a record of occurrences/nonoccurrences divided by the total number of opportunities resulting in a percentage. Performance criterion: 90 percent across ten consecutive sessions.

2. In order to promote communication, all work areas, materials, and personal belongings will be marked with meaningful symbols to assist Brandi with discriminations and also the labeling of items.

A. Given the verbal cue, "Brandi it is time to do *(activity),*" Brandi will independently retrieve the necessary materials needed for the activity. Evaluation will be conducted by maintaining a record of occurrences and nonoccurrence yielding a percentage. Performance criterion: 90 percent across ten consecutive sessions..

3. Given a daily schedule consisting of objects, Brandi will acquire the ability to self-manage using her schedule as a means of prompting the beginning and end of each activity.

A. Upon receiving the verbal cue "Please check your schedule Brandi" paired with a light physical prompt (a touch on the back of her hand), Brandi will grasp the appropriate object on her schedule as a cue designed to inform her as to "what is next." Evaluation will be conducted by maintaining a record of occurrences and nonoccurrences yielding a percentage. Performance criterion: 90 percent across ten consecutive sessions with only a verbal cue from the teacher. The same format will be applied within Brandi's home by her mother.

Evaluation

Brandi's classroom teacher will monitor her performance on each of the objectives by maintaining a record of her occurrences and nonoccurrences and dividing by the total number of opportunities to yield a percentage. This will provide her with information as to the rate of Brandi's progress. She must be sure to maintain the same number of opportunities related to some of the goals to minimize any measurement error. Brandi's mother will also maintain a similar record as to Brandi's progress on the use of the object schedule at home.

A home/school communicator will be developed and sent to and from school each day in Brandi's backpack as a means of maintaining notes on her progress and any potential concerns that Brandi's mother or teacher might have. Brandi's teacher will also maintain any evaluation measures that itinerant consultants such as the speech/language therapist, vision specialist, or school psychologist might provide.

VIGNETTE 5: MARWA

Introduction

Marwa came racing down the school hallway two days before the first day of school. I was getting the last-minute preparations ready in my first grade classroom. Marwa is a striking young six-year-old girl with beautiful black hair and gorgeous black eyes. Her skin is a glowing cinnamon shade of brown. As I told her to slow down a bit and use "walking feet" inside, I soon realized that she did not speak English and I was unsure if she understood any either. She stopped suddenly when she saw me. I greeted her with a cheerful, "Well, hello." She replied, "Moeo." Her mom, dad, and brother followed quickly down the hallway after her.

Marwa and her family moved from South Africa just a week ago. Their native language is Zulu. Marwa's dad is just beginning graduate school in the engineering department at the university in town. He told me that his wife knew a few words in English, but counted on him to be there to interpret. When he is gone, she refuses to answer the phone, as she is uncomfortable when a person speaking English is on the other end.

Marwa was six years old, and her little brother was two. Her health and immunization records substantiated her obvious excellent health.

I was just beginning my second year of teaching. This was my first real experience with a student who was non-English-speaking. As a student teacher, I worked with a second grader who knew English as a second language. His name was Juan. He spoke English very well, and we really made few adjustments for him. It was a very positive experience. This was different. This child knew, literally, no English. Someone else had done the intervention with Juan before my student teaching experience. I reaped the benefits of the teacher before me in that situation. Now I guess it was my turn. I wasn't sure where to start.

Marwa's father was available the first days of school to stay if needed. I didn't want to limit my communication with Marwa's mother, but talking to Marwa's father was the only way for now. I tried, whenever possible, to talk with Marwa's mother through her father's interpretation. However, her father often came alone, as her mother would be home with the little brother.

After talking with the principal, I contacted our district's English as a second language (ESL) teacher (we only had one) for assistance. Her schedule was so busy, and she couldn't make it to our school until the second day of classes. When I asked her for suggestions for our first day, she replied, "She'll watch and learn from you and the children. Use gestures. Ask Marwa's dad for a list of 'survival words' from their native language for the first day (Monday). I'll see you and Marwa on Tuesday."

This sounded reasonable. "Survival words"—what a good idea. I could handle this.

Things went pretty well in the morning of the first day of school. Although Marwa appeared very cautious, she kissed her dad goodbye at the door and sat down at her desk (she had found her name printed on it, as I had shared it with her the day she visited before school started). Her father handed me a list of words with two columns, one headed Zulu, the other English. Then he was off to class. Marwa and I exchanged smiles. "Moeo," I said. She quickly replied, "Moeo," with a nod. With the use of many gestures, pictures, and the survival words, we made it through the morning. She did not interact with the other children, nor they with her. She definitely had an observing eye and closely watched my every move. I decided someone should be with her at lunch, so I assigned a classmate to assist her in the lunch line and I sat at her table (across from her). She ate a few bites, then picked at her food during the rest of the lunch period.

After lunch more children were approaching Marwa. During the free choice time right after lunch, Marwa began to manipulate the unifix cubes in the Math Center. Two other children also chose the Math Center. Together, they began constructing a long unifix line on the floor. They must have had at least 200 various colored cubes connected. I was pleased to see the interaction and cooperation. Then a fourth child approached the center. As she began to touch and move the construction, it broke into pieces. Marwa quickly turned to her and bit her arm! It all happened so fast, and right in front of my eyes! All I could say was, "No, no Marwa! Biting hurts!" as I comforted the crying child who had been bitten.

Goals

Marwa appeared to have needs in the areas of language and social skills. The team (the ESL teacher, the principal, Marwa's parents, and I) decided Marwa would be best served by integrated English instruction in the natural setting, as it would be more functional and she could practice her language skills in typical interactive opportunities with her peers.

Present Level of Language. In the area of language development, Marwa was quite articulate in her native tongue, as reported by her father. However, English is just being introduced. She appears to grasp words quickly, as each day we see progress. The team decided to start with survival words, then short sentences, while also introducing written English.

Language Goal. Marwa will increase her verbal and written knowledge and usage of the English language.

Present Level of Social Skills. It appears that Marwa wants to interact and join in activities with other children. She is often watching the other children and does not object when they are around her, unless they disrupt something, as demonstrated by the example on the first day of school. However, when language is required, it becomes more difficult, particularly if she is frustrated. Marwa has demonstrated this frustration with inappropriate behaviors (biting).

Social Skills Goal. Marwa will have positive social interactions with her peers.

Objectives

Language Objectives

a. Marwa will use single English words for requests and responses 90 percent of the time, by October 1 (within one month).
b. Marwa will use two- to three-English-word sentences for requests and responses 90 percent of the time, by November 1 (within two months).
c. Marwa will write, in manuscript, five new words (starting with survival words) per day, using consistent letter formation, line contact, and spacing two out of three trials or opportunities.

d. Marwa will write, in manuscript, three short sentences (three-word) to form a paragraph using consistent letter formation, line contact, and spacing two out of three trials or opportunities by December.

Social Skills Objectives

a. Marwa will be reinforced for all positive interactions she has with peers 100 percent of the time (teacher effort).

b. Marwa will appropriately express her feelings and needs to her peers, verbally and nonverbally, during four out of five interactions by October 1 (within one month).

Strategies

Strategies for Language Goals and Objectives and Strategies for Social Skills Goals and Objectives.

Each of these goals would best be implemented in conjunction with the other. Using positive behavioral supports as part of her English language program would impact both language and social skills. Collaboration among the ESL teacher, the classroom teacher, and the family is essential. In addition, the school environment must represent a diversity-friendly setting (see Figure 12–3).

Strategies that might be utilized include:

a. Working in small groups in the natural environment.

Figure 12–3
Sensitivity is needed on the part of teachers for children who are non-English speaking and for the sometimes overwhelming challenges that they confront.

b. Pairing Marwa with children who are particularly strong in language development.

c. Utilizing peer assistance; pair children.

d. Fostering all peer interactions.

e. Creating an environment that welcomes Marwa and her family.

Some strategies in creating a diversity-friendly environment include:

a. Having teachers and staff learn key words in Marwa's language and learn about her culture.

b. Having Marwa's peers learn certain key words in Zulu.

c. Creating a diverse environment with materials depicting various cultures (posters, books, art materials (such as multicultural markers, paper, crayons, clay, and the like).

d. Introducing a variety of cultures through books, dolls, pictures.

e. Countering any misconceptions or stereotyping.

Also refer to Chapter 8 on multiculturalism and *The Anti-Bias Curriculum: Tools for empowering young children.* by Derman-Sparks (1989) for additional ideas and strategies.

Individualized strategies that would welcome and benefit Marwa and her family could include:

a. Inviting Marwa's family to share food, photos, and various items from their country.

b. Inviting Marwa's family to teach the key words in Zulu.

c. Having an interpreter for stronger partnership with parents.

d. Keeping a list of English words that Marwa has mastered and those she is currently working on. This list could go home each day with her (perhaps in a journal that would go back and forth, between home and school).

Additional strategies and creative solutions would certainly emerge during team discussions. It would be essential to explain and demonstrate both PBS and ABI to Marwa's parents so that they can understand and also utilize these strategies at home. In addition, the Circle of Friends approach might be helpful to start off the school year. This would address both language and social skills goals. Also utilize Personna Dolls, as illustrated in *The Anti-Bias Curriculum* by Derman-Sparks, in dealing with possible bias behavior. The teacher introduces a new doll friend (culturally diverse) and creates with other dolls appropriate ways for the dolls to interact, play, and help each other. The teacher can set up situations for the children to create solutions. This strategy is particularly helpful for peer problem solving and reflection of behavior. Additional cultural awareness activities of Marwa's choice could be used.

Evaluation

Evaluation of Language Goals and Objectives

a. Marwa's use of single English words for requests and responses will be measured by utilizing frequency charts and written anecdotal observations by the ESL teacher and the classroom teacher.

b. The above method will also be utilized to measure Marwa's use of two- to three-English word sentences for requests and responses.

c. and d. The ESL teacher and the classroom teacher will save daily examples of Marwa's manuscript writing of five new words per day and three short sentences (three-word) to form a paragraph using consistent letter formation, line contact, and spacing.

Evaluation of Social Skills Goals and Objectives

a. Adult reinforcement for all positive interactions that Marwa has with peers will be charted, also recording antecedents, the specific behavior, and detailed responses.

b. Marwa's expression of her feelings and needs to her peers, verbally and nonverbally, will also be charted, including the recording of antecedents, the specific behavior, and detailed responses.

Summary

The purpose of this chapter was to provide the reader with applications of the themes discussed throughout the text. These themes included family-centeredness, transdisciplinary teaming, collaboration, ecological intervention, activities-based intervention, developmentally appropriate practice, and positive behavioral supports. Specifically, this chapter sought to explore how ABI, DAP, and PBS can be applied with various children within inclusive early elementary grade levels. One major objective within the chapter was to provide the reader with the opportunity to compare and contrast the services and supports provided within each of the vignettes.

There were five vignettes presented in this chapter. Each addressed the individual needs of a child specific to the relative learning style, strengths, and areas of challenge. In Vignette 1, we see the example of Caitlin, a nine-year-old about to enter the third grade. Caitlin is a bright and energetic child with a very supportive family; however, she is physically challenged by spina bifida. After reading the vignette, the reader comes to the realization that Caitlin demonstrates a resolve to fully participate in all aspects of her educational experience despite the challenge. The reality of this vignette is how professionals and family members must then collaborate in the provision of supports for Caitlin to attain a meaningful inclusive educational experience in spite of these obvious challenges.

We see similar themes applied within each of the remaining vignettes. Vignette 2 explores the challenges that Daniel and his family confront due to the diagnosis of autism. Here ABI, DAP, and PBS are applied as professionals and family members develop an individualized educational program that matches Daniel's visual learning style to the development of emerging skills.

In the example of Timmy, Vignette 3, we see a six-year-old child who is experiencing various learning difficulties and behavioral excesses. Upon closer examination, we realize that Timmy has a lot going on in his life in addition to what appears to be a learning disability and deficits in attention associated with ADHD. Timmy's parents are in the process of a divorce, which serves to confound Timmy's challenges even further. The vignette is illustrative of how ABI, DAP, and PBS strategies are employed across teachers and parents, home and school. Timmy's challenging behaviors are addressed through the active teaching of alternative behaviors that serve to meet his needs in a more acceptable fashion. Ecologically based supports are provided that span across environments to provide wraparound supports for Timmy to ensure his emotional well-being.

Finally, in the remaining two vignettes, ABI, DAP, and PBS are incorporated and applied with a child with multiple disabilities, and a child who is non-English-speaking. In both examples, the reader witnesses the convergence of these approaches as they are applied within the context of the inclusive classroom setting, recognizing the individualized support needs of every child and the element of ongoing collaboration among professionals and families.

Chapter 12 Suggested Activities

The following list of suggested activities is directly related to the five vignettes you have just read. The activities may be done individually or in class as a group during a discussion period or as a problem-solving activity.

Activities

1. Make a list of the five vignettes, and classify them by types. How many of the vignettes would you consider to be inclusive settings?

2. Create a matrix that contains the children from each of the five vignettes, and categorize the presence or absence of ABI, DAP, and PBS. Are best and effective practices reflected for each of these within your matrix? Where are the gaps and why? Discuss your findings as a group.

3. Interview a regular classroom teacher, a special education resource consultant, a parent or family member, and a special education teacher trained in severe disabilities, and ask a series of questions related to what they consider to be best and effective practices for early elementary-aged children. Then contrast their viewpoints with each of the vignettes.

4. Identify the degree in which consultation and collaboration occurred in each of the vignettes. Consider collaboration and consultation between professionals and parents and family members. In which of the vignettes was it best demonstrated, and why?

5. Review your matrix developed from each of the vignettes, and identify the level of positive behavioral supports that was provided in each. How many consisted of both modifying environmental and instructional setting events and teaching positive alternative skills?

6. How was the issue of cultural diversity dealt with in the vignette describing Marwa?

7. Was there evidence in the vignettes that the assessment and intervention procedures reflected a child/family-centered perspective?

8. Select one vignette, and identify the constraints faced by the child and family and educational personnel. How well are the constraints minimized by the professionals and families within this vignette?

9. What are your feelings about the decision to not encourage the use of stimulant medication at this point to minimize Timmy's behaviors? Identify how an ecological model was used to provide ABI, DAP, and PBS to Timmy and his family.

Selected Resources

1. *Books/curricula*

   Derman-Sparks, L. (1989). *The Anti-Bias Curriculum: Tools for Empowering Young Children*. Washington, DC: NAEYC.

   McGinnis, E., & Goldstein, A. P. (1984). *Skillstreaming the Elementary School Child: A Guide for Teaching Prosocial Skills*. Champaign, IL: Research Press.

   Pierangelo, R. (1995). *The Special Education Teacher's Book of Lists*. West Nyack, NY: The Center for Applied Research in Education.

   Wolery, M., & Wilbers, J. S. (1994). *Including Children with Special Needs in Early Childhood Programs*. Washington, DC: NAEYC.

2. *Articles*

   Koontz-Lowman, D. (1998). Preschoolers with Complex Health Care Needs in Preschool Classrooms. *Young Exceptional Children. 1,* 2–6.

References

American Psychiatric Association (1994). *Diagnostic and Statistical Manual of Mental Disorders*. Washington, DC: Author.

Derman-Sparks, L. (1989). *The anti-bias curriculum: Tools for empowering young children*. Washington, DC: National Association for the Education of Young Children.

Dye, G. A., & McConnell, J. L. (1997). Learning through Rhyme. *Teaching Exceptional Children, 29,* 72–73.

Giddan, J. J., Bade, K. M., Rickenberg, D., & Ryley, A. (1995). Teaching the Language of Feelings to Students with Severe Emotional and Behavioral Handicaps. *Language, Speech, and Hearing Services in the Schools, 26,* 3–10.

McGinnis, E., & Goldstein, A. P. (1984). *Skillstreaming the Elementary School Child*. Champaign, IL: Research Press.

Miller, M., Miller, S. R., Wheeler, J. J., & Selinger, J. (1989). Can a Single-Classroom Treatment Approach Change Academic Performance and Behavioral Characteristics in Severely Behavior Disordered Adolescents: An Experimental Inquiry. *Behavioral Disorders, 14,* 215–225.

Riccio, C. A., Hynd, G. W., Cohen, M. J., & Gonzalez, J. J. (1993). Neurological Basis of Attention Deficit Hyperactivity Disorder. *Exceptional Children, 60,* 118–124.

Schopler, E., Reichler, R. J., Bashford, A., Lansing, M. D., & Marcus, L. M. (1990). *Psychoeducational Profile Revised (PEP-R).* Austin, TX: Pro-Ed.

Woodcock, R. W., & Johnson, M. B. (1989). Woodcock-Johnson Psychoeducational Battery—Revised. Allen, TX: DLM.

Appendix

A

NAEYC Position Statement: Guidelines for Decisions about Developmentally Appropriate Practice

Guidelines for decisions about developmentally appropriate practice

An understanding of the nature of development and learning during the early childhood years, from birth through age 8, generates guidelines that inform the practices of early childhood educators. Developmentally appropriate practice requires that teachers integrate the many dimensions of their knowledge base. They must know about child development and the implications of this knowledge for how to teach, the content of the curriculum—what to teach and when—how to assess what children have learned, and how to adapt curriculum and instruction to children's individual strengths, needs, and interests. Further, they must know the particular children they teach and their families and be knowledgeable as well about the social and cultural context.

The following guidelines address five interrelated dimensions of early childhood professional practice: creating a caring community of learners, teaching to enhance development and learning, constructing appropriate curriculum, assessing children's development and learning, and establishing reciprocal relationships with families. (The word *teacher* is used to refer to any adult responsible for a group of children in any early childhood program, including infant/toddler caregivers, family child care providers, and specialists in other disciplines who fulfill the role of teacher.)

Examples of appropriate and inappropriate practice in relation to each of these dimensions are given for infants and toddlers (Part 3, pp. 72–90), children 3 through 5 (Part 4, pp. 123–35), and children 6 through 8 (Part 5, pp. 161–79). In the references at the end of each part, readers will be able to find fuller discussion of the points summarized here and strategies for implementation.

1. Creating a Caring Community of Learners

Developmentally appropriate practices occur within a context that supports the development of relationships between adults and children, among children, among teachers, and between teachers and families. Such a community reflects what is known about the social construction of knowledge and the importance of establishing a caring, inclusive community in which all children can develop and learn.

A. The early childhood setting functions as a community of learners in which all participants consider and contribute to each other's well-being and learning.

B. Consistent, positive relationships with a limited number of adults and other children are a fundamental determinant of healthy human development and provide the context for children to learn about themselves and their world and also how to develop positive, constructive relationships with other people. The early childhood classroom is a community in which each child is valued. Children learn to respect and acknowledge differences in abilities and talents and to value each person for his or her strengths.

C. Social relationships are an important context for learning. Each child has strengths or interests that contribute to the overall functioning of the group. When children have opportunities to play together, work on projects in small groups, and talk with other children and adults, their own development and learning are enhanced. Interacting with other children in small groups provides a context for children to operate on the edge of their developing capacities. The learning environment enables children to construct understanding through interactions with adults and other children.

D. The learning environment is designed to protect children's health and safety and is supportive of children's physiological needs for activity, sensory stimulation, fresh air, rest, and nourishment. The program provides a balance of rest and active movement for children throughout the program day. Outdoor experiences are provided for children of all ages. The program protects children's psychological safety; that is, children feel secure, relaxed, and comfortable rather than disengaged, frightened, worried, or stressed.

E. Children experience an organized environment and an orderly routine that provides an overall structure in which learning takes place; the environment is dynamic and changing but predictable and comprehensible from a child's point of view. The learning environment provides a variety of materials and opportunities for children to have firsthand, meaningful experiences.

2. Teaching to Enhance Development and Learning

Adults are responsible for ensuring children's healthy development and learning. From birth, relationships with adults are critical determinants of children's healthy social and emotional development and serve as well as mediators of language and intellectual development. At the same time, children are active constructors of their own understanding, who benefit from initiating and regulating their own learning activities and interacting with peers. Therefore, early childhood teachers strive to achieve an optimal balance between children's self-initiated learning and adult guidance or support.

Teachers accept responsibility for actively supporting children's development and provide occasions for children to acquire important knowledge and skills. Teachers use their knowledge of child development and learning to identify the range of activities, materials, and learning experiences that are appropriate for a group or individual child. This knowledge is used in conjunction with knowledge of the context and understanding about individual children's growth patterns, strengths, needs, interests, and experiences to design the curriculum and learning environment and guide teachers' interactions with children. The following guidelines describe aspects of the teachers' role in making decisions about practice:

A. Teachers respect, value, and accept children and treat them with dignity at all times.

B. Teachers make it a priority to know each child well.

(1) Teachers establish positive, personal relationships with children to foster the child's development and keep informed about the child's needs and potentials. Teachers listen to children and adapt their responses to children's differing needs, interests, styles, and abilities.

(2) Teachers continually observe children's spontaneous play and interaction with the physical environment and with other children to learn about their interests, abilities, and developmental progress. On the basis of this information, teachers plan experiences that enhance children's learning and development.

(3) Understanding that children develop and learn in the context of their families and communities, teachers establish relationships with families that increase their knowledge of children's lives outside the classroom and their awareness of the perspectives and priorities of those individuals most significant in the child's life.

(4) Teachers are alert to signs of undue stress and traumatic events in children's lives and aware of effective strategies to reduce stress and support the development of resilience.

(5) Teachers are responsible at all times for all children under their supervision and plan for children's increasing development of self-regulation abilities.

C. Teachers create an intellectually engaging, responsive environment to promote each child's learning and development.

(1) Teachers use their knowledge about children in general and the particular children in the group as well as their familiarity with what children need to learn and develop in each curriculum area to organize the environment and plan curriculum and teaching strategies.

(2) Teachers provide children with a rich variety of experiences, projects, materials, problems, and ideas to explore and investigate, ensuring that these are worthy of children's attention.

(3) Teachers provide children with opportunities to make meaningful choices and time to explore through active involvement. Teachers offer children the choice to participate in a small-group or a solitary activity, assist and guide children who are not yet able to use and enjoy child-choice activity periods, and provide opportunities for practice of skills as a self-chosen activity.

(4) Teachers organize the daily and weekly schedule and allocate time so as to provide children with extended blocks of time in which to engage in play, projects, and/or study in integrated curriculum.

D. Teachers make plans to enable children to attain key curriculum goals across various disciplines, such as language arts, mathematics, social studies, science, art, music, physical education, and health (see "Constructing appropriate curriculum," pp. 20–21).

(1) Teachers incorporate a wide variety of experiences, materials and equipment, and teaching strategies in constructing curriculum to accommodate a broad range of children's individual differences in prior experiences, maturation rates, styles of learning, needs, and interests.

(2) Teachers bring each child's home culture and language into the shared culture of the school so that the unique contributions of each group are recognized and valued by others.

(3) Teachers are prepared to meet identified special needs of individual children, including children with disabilities and those who exhibit unusual interests and skills. Teachers use all the strategies identified here, consult with appropriate specialists, and see that the child gets the specialized services he or she requires.

E. Teachers foster children's collaboration with peers on interesting, important enterprises.

(1) Teachers promote children's productive collaboration without taking over to the extent that children lose interest.

(2) Teachers use a variety of ways of flexibly grouping children for the purposes of instruction, supporting collaboration among children, and building a sense of community. At various times, children have opportunities to work individually, in small groups, and with the whole group.

F. Teachers develop, refine, and use a wide repertoire of teaching strategies to enhance children's learning and development.

(1) To help children develop their initiative, teachers encourage them to choose and plan their own learning activities.

(2) Teachers pose problems, ask questions, and make comments and suggestions that stimulate children's thinking and extend their learning.

(3) Teachers extend the range of children's interests and the scope of their thought through presenting novel experiences and introducing stimulating ideas, problems, experiences, or hypotheses.

(4) To sustain an individual child's effort or engagement in purposeful activities, teachers select from a range of strategies, including but not limited to modeling, demonstrating specific skills, and providing information, focused attention, physical proximity, verbal encouragement, reinforcement and other behavioral procedures, as well as additional structure and modification of equipment or schedules as needed.

(5) Teachers coach and/or directly guide children in the acquisition of specific skills as needed.

(6) Teachers calibrate the complexity and challenge of activities to suit children's level of skill and knowledge, increasing the challenge as children gain competence and understanding.

(7) Teachers provide cues and other forms of "scaffolding" that enable the child to succeed in a task that is just beyond his or her ability to complete alone.

(8) To strengthen children's sense of competence and confidence as learners, motivation to persist, and willingness to take risks, teachers

provide experiences for children to be genuinely successful and to be challenged.

(9) To enhance children's conceptual understanding, teachers use various strategies that encourage children to reflect on and "revisit" their learning experiences.

G. Teachers facilitate the development of responsibility and self-regulation in children.

(1) Teachers set clear, consistent, and fair limits for children's behavior and hold children accountable to standards of acceptable behavior. To the extent that children are able, teachers engage them in developing rules and procedures for behavior of class members.

(2) Teachers redirect children to more acceptable behavior or activity or use children's mistakes as learning opportunities, patiently reminding children of rules and their rationale as needed.

(3) Teachers listen and acknowledge children's feelings and frustrations, respond with respect, guide children to resolve conflicts, and model skills that help children to solve their own problems.

3. Constructing Appropriate Curriculum

The content of the early childhood curriculum is determined by many factors, including the subject matter of the disciplines, social or cultural values, and parental input. In developmentally appropriate programs, decisions about curriculum content also take into consideration the age and experience of the learners. Achieving success for all children depends, among other essentials, on providing a challenging, interesting, developmentally appropriate curriculum. NAEYC does not endorse specific curricula. However, one purpose of these guidelines is as a framework for making decisions about developing curriculum or selecting a curriculum model. Teachers who use a validated curriculum model benefit from the evidence of its effectiveness and the accumulated wisdom and experience of others.

In some respects, the curriculum strategies of many teachers today do not demand enough of children and in other ways demand too much of the wrong thing. On the one hand, narrowing the curriculum to those basic skills that can be easily measured on multiple-choice tests diminishes the intellectual challenge for many children. Such intellectually impoverished curriculum underestimates the true competence of children, which has been demonstrated to be much higher than is often assumed (Gelman & Baillargeon 1983; Gelman & Meck 1983; Edwards, Gandini, & Forman 1993; Resnick 1996). Watered-down, oversimplified curriculum leaves many children unchallenged, bored, uninterested, or unmotivated. In such situations, children's experiences are marked by a great many missed opportunities for learning.

On the other hand, curriculum expectations in the early years of schooling sometimes are not appropriate for the age groups served. When next-grade expectations of mastery of basic skills are routinely pushed down to the previous grade and whole-group and teacher-led instruction is the dominant teaching strategy, children who cannot sit still and attend to teacher lectures or who are bored and unchallenged or frustrated by doing workbook pages for long periods of time are mislabeled as immature, disruptive, or unready for school (Shepard & Smith 1988).

Constructing appropriate curriculum requires attention to at least the following guidelines for practice:

A. Developmentally appropriate curriculum provides for all areas of a child's development: physical, emotional, social, linguistic, aesthetic, and cognitive.

B. Curriculum includes a broad range of content across disciplines that is socially relevant, intellectually engaging, and personally meaningful to children.

C. Curriculum builds upon what children already know and are able to do (activating prior knowledge) to consolidate their learning and to foster their acquisition of new concepts and skills.

D. Effective curriculum plans frequently integrate across traditional subject-matter divisions to help children make meaningful connections and provide opportunities for rich conceptual development; focusing on one subject is also a valid strategy at times.

E. Curriculum promotes the development of knowledge and understanding, processes and skills, as well as the dispositions to use and apply skills and to go on learning.

F. Curriculum content has intellectual integrity, reflecting the key concepts and tools of inquiry of recognized disciplines in ways that are accessible and achievable for young children, ages 3 through 8 (e.g., Bredekamp & Rosegrant 1992, 1995). Children directly participate in study of the disciplines, for instance, by conducting scientific experiments, writing, performing, solving mathematical problems, collecting and analyzing data, collecting oral history, and performing other roles of experts in the disciplines.

G. Curriculum provides opportunities to support children's home culture and language while also developing all children's abilities to participate in the shared culture of the program and the community.

H. Curriculum goals are realistic and attainable for most children in the designated age range for which they are designed.

I. When used, technology is physically and philosophically integrated in the classroom curriculum and teaching. (See "NAEYC Position Statement: Technology and Young Children—Ages Three through Eight" [NAEYC 1996b].)

4. Assessing Children's Learning and Development

Assessment of individual children's development and learning is essential for planning and implementing appropriate curriculum. In developmentally appropriate programs, assessment and curriculum are integrated, with teachers continually engaging in observational assessment for the purpose of improving teaching and learning.

Accurate assessment of young children is difficult because their development and learning are rapid, uneven, episodic, and embedded within specific cultural and linguistic contexts. Too often, inaccurate and inappropriate assessment measures have been used to label, track, or otherwise harm young children. Developmentally appropriate assessment practices are based on the following guidelines:

A. Assessment of young children's progress and achievements is ongoing, strategic, and purposeful. The results of assessment are used to benefit children—in adapting curriculum and teaching to meet the developmental and learning needs of children, communicating with the child's family, and evaluating the program's effectiveness for the purpose of improving the program.

B. The content of assessments reflects progress toward important learning and developmental goals. The program has a systematic plan for collecting and using assessment information that is integrated with curriculum planning.

C. The methods of assessment are appropriate to the age and experiences of young children. Therefore, assessment of young children relies heavily on the results of observations of children's development, descriptive data, collections of representative work by children, and demonstrated performance during authentic, not contrived, activities. Input from families as well as children's evaluations of their own work are part of the overall assessment strategy.

D. Assessments are tailored to a specific purpose and used only for the purpose for which they have been demonstrated to produce reliable, valid information.

E. Decisions that have a major impact on children, such as enrollment or placement, are never made on the basis of a single developmental assessment or screening device but are based on multiple sources of relevant information, particularly observations by teachers and parents.

F. To identify children who have special learning or developmental needs and to plan appropriate curriculum and teaching for them, developmental assessments and observations are used.

G. Assessment recognizes individual variation in learners and allows for differences in styles and rates of learning. Assessment takes into consideration such factors as the child's facility in English, stage of language acquisition, and whether the child has had the time and opportunity to develop proficiency in his or her home language as well as in English.

H. Assessment legitimately addresses not only what children can do independently but also what they can do with assistance from other children or adults. Teachers study children as individuals as well as in relationship to groups by documenting group projects and other collaborative work.

(For a more complete discussion of principles of appropriate assessment, see the position statement "Guidelines for Appropriate Curriculum Content and Assessment in Programs Serving Children Ages 3 through 8" [NAEYC & NAECS/SDE 1992]; see also Shepard 1994.)

5. Establishing Reciprocal Relationships with Families

Developmentally appropriate practices derive from deep knowledge of individual children and the context within which they develop and learn. The younger the child, the more necessary it is for professionals to acquire this knowledge through relationships with children's families. The traditional approach to families has been a parent education orientation in which the professionals see themselves as knowing what is best for children and view parents as needing to be educated. There is also the limited view of parent involvement that sees PTA membership as the primary goal. These approaches do not adequately convey the complexity of the partnership between teachers and parents that is a fundamental element of good practice (Powell 1994).

When the parent education approach is criticized in favor of a more family-centered approach, this shift may be misunderstood to mean that parents dictate all program content and professionals abdicate responsibility, doing whatever parents want regardless of whether professionals agree that it is in children's best interest. Either of these extremes oversimplifies the importance of relationships with families and fails to provide the kind of environment in which parents and professionals work together to achieve shared goals for children. Such programs with this shared focus are characterized by at least the following guidelines for practice:

A. Reciprocal relationships between teachers and families require mutual respect, cooperation, shared responsibility, and negotiation of conflicts toward achievement of shared goals.
B. Early childhood teachers work in collaborative partnerships with families, establishing and maintaining regular, frequent two-way communication with children's parents.
C. Parents are welcome in the program and participate in decisions about their children's care and education. Parents observe and participate and serve in decisionmaking roles in the program.
D. Teachers acknowledge parents' choices and goals for children and respond with sensitivity and respect to parents' preferences and concerns without abdicating professional responsibility to children.
E. Teachers and parents share their knowledge of the child and understanding of children's development and learning as part of day-to-day communication and planned conferences. Teachers support families in ways that maximally promote family decisionmaking capabilities and competence.
F. To ensure more accurate and complete information, the program involves families in assessing and planning for individual children.
G. The program links families with a range of services, based on identified resources, priorities, and concerns.
H. Teachers, parents, programs, social service and health agencies, and consultants who may have educational responsibility for the child at different times should, with family participation, share developmental information about children as they pass from one level or program to another.

Note. From Developmentally Appropriate Practice in Early Childhood Programs (rev. ed.) (pp. 16–22), by S. Bredekamp and C. Copple (Eds.), 1997, Washington, DC: NAEYC. Copyright 1997 by the National Association for the Education of Young Children. Reprinted with permission.

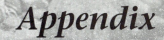

Appendix

Sample Format for an Individualized Family Service Plan

INDIVIDUALIZED FAMILY SERVICE PLAN

Child's Name:_____ IFSP Meeting Date:_____

Birthdate:_____ IFSP Type: Initial   Annual

Designated Service Coordinator:_____

Service Coordinator Phone #:_____

	Date Due	Date Completed
Six Month Review	____	____
Annual IFSP	____	____
Additional Review Dates		

____   ____   ____   ____   ____   ____

m/d/y   m/d/y   m/d/y   m/d/y   m/d/y   m/d/y

Transition Dates

	Date Due	Date Completed
Notification of Local Education Agency (LEA) by age two.	____	____
Planning Conference with Parent/s, Lead Agency, LEA and other Service Providers, as appropriate. (At least 90 days, or up to 6 months prior to child's third birthday)	____	____
Transition to LEA, as appropriate.	____	____

Natural Environments/Settings

To the maximum extent appropriate, services will be provided in natural environments, including the home, and community settings that are natural or normal for the child's age peers who have no disabilities. Natural environments for young children are those environments/situations that are within the context of the family's lifestyle — their home, their culture, daily activities, routines and obligations. Services will only be provided in settings not identified as the natural environment when it is determined that the desired outcome/s cannot be satisfactorily achieved within the natural environment of this child and family.

The natural environment for _____ included the following places/settings:

_____

_____

_____

_____

339

IDENTIFYING INFORMATION

Child's Name: _____

Child's Birthdate: _____ m/d/y

Child's Social Security #: _____

Child's Address: _____
Street _____ TN _____ Zip: _____

City: _____ Phone: _____ County: _____

Parent's Name(s): _____

Parent's Address: _____ Street _____

(if different from child) _____ TN _____ Zip: _____

City: _____ Phone: _____

	Part C/TEIS/TIPS	DMR	CSS
	From Tennessee's Definition of Developmental Delay Meets: (check if applicable)		
Eligibility	% of Delay ☐ Diagnosed Condition ☐ Informed Clinical Opinion ☐	DMR ☐	CSS ☐
Referral	_____ m/d/y	_____ m/d/y	_____ m/d/y
	_____ Source	_____ Source	_____ Source

DOCUMENTATION

IFSP Team Member—If present, sign. If not present, list member's name	Agency/Title	Date	Contributed/ not present/method	Full Agree	Area(s) of Concerns/Comments
(Service Coordinator who organized this IFSP meeting)					
(Parent)					
(Parent)					
(Evaluator/Assessor)					

Designated Service Coordinator/Agency and Rationale

Name	Agency	Address	Phone#	Rationale

Informed Parental Consent

yes   no

☐   ☐   I am the parent/legal guardian/Department of Education trained surrogate parent of this child.

☐   ☐   I have been informed of & understand my rights as a parent in Tennessee under Part C Regulations. I have received a copy of Rights of Infants and Toddlers with Disabilities.

☐   ☐   I have participated in the development of this IFSP and understand its contents.

☐   ☐   I agree to its implementation to the degree noted above.

_____   _____   _____   _____
Parent   Date   Parent   Date

PRESENT LEVELS OF DEVELOPMENT
(Include a statement of <u>functional</u> strengths & needs in each area)

Child's Name _____

Health

	By		
Date	Chron. Age	(Adj. Age)	<u>Needs</u>
	<u>Strengths</u>		

Vision

	By		
Date	Chron. Age	(Adj. Age)	<u>Needs</u>
	<u>Strengths</u>		

Hearing

	By		
Date	Chron. Age	(Adj. Age)	<u>Needs</u>
	<u>Strengths</u>		

Physical Development-Gross Motor

	By	Instrument	
Date	Chron. Age	(Adj. Age)	<u>Needs</u>
	<u>Strengths</u>		

Physical Development-Fine Motor

	By	Instrument	
Date	Chron. Age	(Adj. Age)	<u>Needs</u>
	<u>Strengths</u>		

PRESENT LEVELS OF DEVELOPMENT (Continued)
(Include a statement of <u>functional</u> strengths & needs in each area)

Child's Name _____

Communication Development (Speech/Language) By | Instrument

Date   Chron. Age   (Adj. Age) | <u>Needs</u>
                        <u>Strengths</u>

Cognitive Development   By | Instrument

Date   Chron. Age   (Adj. Age) | <u>Needs</u>
                        <u>Strengths</u>

Social/Emotional Development   By | Instrument

Date   Chron. Age   (Adj. Age) | <u>Needs</u>
                        <u>Strengths</u>

Adaptive Development   By | Instrument

Date   Chron. Age   (Adj. Age) | <u>Needs</u>
                        <u>Strengths</u>

Other   By | Instrument

Date   Chron. Age   (Adj. Age) | <u>Needs</u>
                        <u>Strengths</u>

Child's Name _____

SUMMARY OF FAMILY RESOURCES, PRIORITIES, AND CONCERNS RELATED TO ENHANCING THE DEVELOPMENT OF THE CHILD

yes   no

☐   ☐   Family agreed to a voluntary family-directed assessment.

☐   ☐   Family agreed to the inclusion of the voluntary family-directed assessment in the IFSP.

Type(s)/method(s) of Family Assessment Used: _____

Date(s) of Family Assessment: _____

Participants _____

Family Resources	Family Priorities	Family Concerns

OUTCOME/ACTION STEPS

Child's Name _____

Major Outcome # ☐ _____ Timeline (Target Date) _____

Action Steps	Person(s) Responsible

Review/Changes

Comment

*☐ Review Status _____ Date: _____
                                                                         m/d/y

*☐ Review Status _____ Date: _____
                                                                         m/d/y

*☐ Review Status _____ Date: _____
                                                                         m/d/y

*☐ Review Status _____ Date: _____
                                                                         m/d/y

*Review Status Key (1) on going (2) completed (3) delayed (4) unavailable (for non-required services only) (5) modified

OUTCOME/ACTION STEPS

Child's Name _____

Major Outcome # ☐_____ Timeline (Target Date) _____

Action Steps	Person(s) Responsible

Review/Changes

Comment

*☐Review Status _____ Date: _____
m/d/y

*☐Review Status _____ Date: _____
m/d/y

*☐Review Status _____ Date: _____
m/d/y

*☐Review Status _____ Date: _____
m/d/y

*Review Status Key (1) on going (2) completed (3) delayed (4) unavailable (for non-required services only) (5) modified

OUTCOME/ACTION STEPS

Child's Name _____

Major Outcome # ☐ _____   **Timeline (Target Date)** _____

Action Steps	Person(s) Responsible

Review/Changes

Comment

*☐Review Status _____   Date: _____
                                                                        m/d/y

*☐Review Status _____   Date: _____
                                                                        m/d/y

*☐Review Status _____   Date: _____
                                                                        m/d/y

*☐Review Status _____   Date: _____
                                                                        m/d/y

*Review Status Key (1) on going (2) completed (3) delayed (4) unavailable (for non-required services only) (5) modified

OUTCOME/ACTION STEPS

Child's Name _____

Major Outcome # ☐ _____   **Timeline (Target Date)** _____

Action Steps	Person(s) Responsible

Review/Changes

<u>Comment</u>

*☐Review Status _____   Date: _____
m/d/y

*☐Review Status _____   Date: _____
m/d/y

*☐Review Status _____   Date: _____
m/d/y

*☐Review Status _____   Date: _____
m/d/y

*Review Status Key (1) on going (2) completed (3) delayed (4) unavailable (for non-required services only) (5) modified

SERVICES

Child's Name _____

Service	Outcome #/s	Provider	Required or Non/Req	Starting Date	Expected Duration	Environment	METHOD Frequency	Intensity	Payor	Review Date	*Review Status

Justification for Provision of Service in Environments/Settings Not Identified as the Natural Environment

Service:_____ Options Considered _____
The desired outcome could not be achieved in the natural environment because:

Service:_____ Options Considered _____
The desired outcome could not be achieved in the natural environment because:

Service:_____ Options Considered _____
The desired outcome could not be achieved in the natural environment because:

*Review Status Key (1) on going (2) completed (3) delayed (4) unavailable (for non-required services only) (5) modified

SERVICES   Child's Name _____

Service	Outcome #/s	Provider	Required or Non/Req	Starting Date	Expected Duration	Environment	METHOD Frequency	Intensity	Payor	Review Date	*Review Status

Justification for Provision of Service in Environments/Settings Not Identified as the Natural Environment

Service: _____ Options Considered _____
The desired outcome could not be achieved in the natural environment because:

Service: _____ Options Considered _____
The desired outcome could not be achieved in the natural environment because:

Service: _____ Options Considered _____
The desired outcome could not be achieved in the natural environment because:

*Review Status Key (1) on going (2) completed (3) delayed (4) unavailable (for non-required services only) (5) modified

OUTCOME/SERVICE SUMMARY PAGE (Optional)

Child's Name _____

Key C-Child
F-Family
C/F-Child and Family

Non-req. Services	Services to be Provided (required by Part C)											
Vision												
Transportation												
Speech/Language												
Special Instruction												
Social Work												
Service Coordination												
Psychological												
Physical Therapy												
Occupational Therapy												
Nutrition												
Nursing												
Medical (for diagnostic purposes only)												
Health												
Family/Training/Counseling/Home Visits												
Audiology												
Assistive Technology												

MAJOR OUTCOME

# # # # # # # # # # #

REVIEW/CHANGE FORM

Child's Name _____

Date of Current IFSP _____

Review Date
_____

Review Type
___ six month
___ parent request
___ provider request

Review Status
___ continue IFSP
___ change IFSP
___ inactive IFSP

Inactive Status _____ Date inactive status began _____
___ no longer eligible
___ transition (Part B/Other) _____
___ parent declined further service
___ whereabouts unknown
___ other (specify)

Enter reference of page/outcome#/service where changes/additions have been made.

yes   no
☐   ☐   I have participated in the review of this IFSP.
☐   ☐   I approved the review status indicated and
         ctonsent to the changes of outcome(s) and/or
         service(s) as noted in the IFSP.

Parent _____   **Date** _____

Parent _____   **Date** _____

Designated Service Coordinator _____   **Date** _____

Other IFSP Team Members Contributing to Review

Name	Title/Agency	Date	Method

TRANSITION FROM PART C SERVICES PLAN

Today's Date _____   Child's Name _____
                m/d/y   Date of Birth _____

Current Program _____ _____
                         Name   Type

Anticipated Date of Transition: _____

Planned Transitioning Procedures	Implementor	Timeframe	Date Completed

Transition Plan (cont.)

Child's Name _____

Transition Page # _____

Planned Transitioning Procedures	Implementor	Timeframe	Date Completed

Index

A

Accountability, collaboration between professionals and families and, 58–59

Activity-based intervention (ABI), 103–23, 140
assessment and, 164–67
child-initiated activities and, 106–9, 119
concerns regarding, 121–23
cultural diversity and, 214–15
definition and components of, 5, 104–5, 187–88
in early elementary grades, 120–21
family-centeredness, collaboration and, 65
family day care homes and, 112
Head Start programs and, 114–16
home-based services and, 109–11
in infant and toddler nursery and child care settings, 113–14
merging PBS, DAP, and, 96
planned activities and, 106
positive behavioral supports (PBS) and, 182, 188
in preschool/kindergarten settings, 116–20
routine activities and, 105

theoretical foundations of, 103–4

Adjustment, of family of children with special needs, 32–35

Administrators, future of inclusive early childhood education and, 234–35

Advocacy (advocates), 43
parental, 60–61
siblings as, 43, 45

AEPS (Assessment, Evaluation, and Programming System for Infants and Children), 165–66

Ages and Stages Questionnaires: A Parent Completed, Child Monitoring System (ASQ), 166

Akesson, E. B., 74, 150

Allen, J., 284, 294

Alston, F. K., 112, 113

Americans with Disabilities Act (ADA) (1990), inclusion and, 16–17

Anderson, M. A., 57

Anecdotal recording of behavior, 87–89

Antecedents, activity-based intervention (ABI) and, 106, 119

Anti-Bias Curriculum, The: Tools for Empowering Young Children (Derman-Sparks and the A. B. C. Task Force), 211, 218, 326

Appropriateness, meaning of, 132–33

Arndorfer, R. E., 83

Arrango, P., 57
Artistic expression, 36–37
ASQ (Ages and Stages Questionnaires: A Parent Completed, Child Monitoring System), 166
Assessment
  activity-based intervention (ABI) and, 164–67
  authentic, 167
  defined, 153
  educational and intervention programs and, 168–69
  family participation in, 167–68
  functional, 163–64
  future of inclusive early childhood education and, 231–32
  importance of, 153–55
  instructional goals and objectives and, 190
  interdisciplinary, 162
  models of, 155–67
    traditional assessment, 155–57
  multidisciplinary, 162
  team-based approaches to, 162–67
  transdisciplinary, 162–64
Assessment, Evaluation, and Programming System for Infants and Children (AEPS), 165–66
Assessment competencies, 152
Assessment of children, 148–70
  diagnosis of a developmental disability and, 148–52
Assistive technology, future of inclusive early childhood education and, 234
Atkins, M., 73
Attermeier, S. M., 165
Attitudes, inclusion of young children and, 196
Atwater, J. B., 215, 217
Audiologists, assessment process and, 157

Authentic assessment, 167
Autism, 196–98
Autonomy versus shame and doubt stage, 81

B

Bade, K. M., 75, 315
Bailey, D. B., 57, 60, 62, 110, 164
Bamberra, L. M., 186, 187
Bandura, A., 76, 81
Banks, C. A., 218
Banks, J. A., 209, 210, 218, 219
Barbour, L., 41
Barnard, W. S., 57
Barrara, I., 78
Barry, E., 34, 35
Bashford, A., 306
Behavior
  developmental age and, 80–81
  operational definition of, 87
  recording, methods of, 87–95
    anecdotal recording, 87–89
    challenges in, 94
    hypothesis statement, 95
    interobserver reliability, 94–95
    Motivation Assessment Scale (MAS), 91, 94
    scatter plot analysis, 89–91
Behavioral development of children
  ecological influences on, 74–76
  parental influences on, 76–78
  sociocultural influences on, 78–79
Bennett, C., 210, 218
Berk, L. E., 104, 117, 130
Bérubé, M., 151
BEST (Building Effective Successful Teams), 239
Billingsley, F. F., 196, 197

Binkard, B., 45
Bioecological theory,
    Bronfenbrenner's, 49
Bishop, K. K., 57
Blackman, J. A., 234
Borgia, E. T., 226
Bossert, K. W., 83
Bowe, F. G., 251, 274
Bowman, T., 214, 215
Bradley, R. H., 74, 75
Bradshaw, J., 75
Brain research, 230, 231
Bredekamp, S., 114, 117, 121, 131,
    133–35, 139, 140, 194, 215, 218
Bricker, Diane, 64, 103–5, 108, 111, 121,
    165, 166, 179, 187, 196, 198, 200,
    214, 239, 241
Brinker, R. P., 62, 64
Brisby, J. A., 74, 75
Brito, T., 208, 212
Bromwich, R. M., 110
Bronfenbrenner, U., 10, 49, 74, 80, 81, 97,
    127, 129, 130, 236, 243, 273, 274
Brotherson, M. J., 45
Bruder, M. B., 238
Building Effective Successful Teams
    (BEST), 239

C

Capone, A. M., 240, 241
Caring community of learners, 135–36
*Carolina Curriculum for Infants and
    Toddlers with Special Needs, The*
    (CCITSN), 165
*Carolina Curriculum for Preschoolers
    with Special Needs, The,* 165
Carta, J. J., 72, 76, 215, 217
Catlett, C., 239
Catron, C., 284, 294

Cerebral palsy, 149
Chan, S. Q., 79
Child Care Law Center, 17
Child-centered learning environments,
    designing, 193–95
Child development, 128–32. *See also*
    Developmentally appropriate
    practice (DAP)
    basic principles of, 130–32
    developmentally appropriate practice
    (DAP) and, 141
    teaching to enhance, 136–37
    theories of, 129–30
Child-initiated activities, 106–9, 119
Children's Defense Fund, 225
Choice-making opportunities, 186–87
Chronosystem, 49
Clark, P., 210, 215
Classroom schedules, 185
Cleveland, D. W., 41, 43
Cohen, M. J., 313
Collaboration, professional/family,
    51–54
    accountability and, 58–59
    communication and, 54, 59
    defined, 6–7
    due process and, 56–57
    focus on the child and, 57–58
    implementing effective, 57–59
    mediation and, 55–56
    negotiation and conflict resolution and,
    54–55
    recommendations from parents, 47–48
    trust and confidentiality and, 59
Communication, collaboration between
    professionals and families and,
    54, 59
Conditions of objectives, 189
Conference, parent/professional, 158–60
Confidentiality, collaboration between
    professionals and families and, 59

Conflict resolution, 54–55. *See also* Mediation

Connors, L. J., 8

Consequences, activity-based intervention (ABI) and, 106, 119

Cook, R. E., 282

Cooper, J. O., 95

Copple, C., 114, 117, 121, 131, 133–35, 139, 194

Corderio, P., 208, 218

Council for Exceptional Children (CEC), 14–15

    Division for Culturally and Linguistically Diverse Exceptional Learners (DDEL), 209

    Division for Early Childhood (DEC) of. *See* Division for Early Childhood (DEC) of the Council for Exceptional Children

Crimmins, D. B., 91

Cripe, Juliann J. *See* Woods-Cripe, J. J.

Cross-cultural competence, 79

Culbertson, J. L., 158

Cultural differences, defined, 208

Cultural diversity, 207–19

    activity-based intervention (ABI) and, 214–15

    defined, 208

    developmentally appropriate practice (DAP) and, 215

    early childhood education and, 210–11, 217–19

    multicultural education in schools and, 209–10

    positive behavioral supports (PBS) and, 212–13

Culture, defined, 208

Curriculum

    developmentally appropriate practice (DAP) and, 137

    inclusion of young children and, 196

Cushner, K., 208, 218

D

Deal, A., 7, 51

DEC. *See* Division for Early Childhood (DEC) of the Council for Exceptional Children

DEC Recommended Practices: Indicators of Quality in Programs for Infants and Young Children with Special Needs and Their Families, 15

DEC Task Force on Recommended Practices, 111, 211

Deiner, P. L., 113

Demchak, M., 83

Derman-Sparks, L., 210, 218, 326

Development. *See* Child development

Developmental age, behavior and, 80–81

Developmental delays, 148–49

Developmental disabilities, diagnosis of, 148–52

Developmentally appropriate practice (DAP), 127–41

    assessing children's learning and development and, 137

    concept of, 5–6

    cultural diversity and, 215–17

    curriculum and, 137

    merging PBS, ABI, and, 96

    relationships among caregivers and children and, 137–39

    shared philosophy and similarity of recommended practices, 139–40

    teaching to enhance development and learning, 136–37

Developmentally Appropriate Practice in Early Childhood Programs (NAEYC), 6

Developmentally appropriate
  programs, 139
Developmental psychologists, assessment
  process and, 156
DeVillar, R., 218
Dewey, John, 104
Diagnosis of developmental disabilities,
  148–52
Dinnebeil, L., 122
DiVenere, N., 8, 30, 241
Diversity in the Classroom
  (Kendall), 218
Division for Culturally and Linguistically
  Diverse Exceptional Learners
  (DDEL), 209, 219
Division for Early Childhood (DEC) of
  the Council for Exceptional
  Children, 4, 182
  activity-based intervention (ABI)
    and, 111
  on assessment competencies, 152
  cultural diversity and, 211
  on inclusion, 15
Dodd, J. M., 79
Dowdy, C. A., 195
Down's syndrome, 149
*DSM IV (Diagnostic and Statistical
  Manual),* 90, 196
Due process, 56–57
Dunham, J., 32
Dunlap, G., 182
Dunlap, L. L., 51, 53, 54, 57
Dunst, C. J., 7, 51, 74
Durand, V. M., 73, 83, 91
Dye, G. A., 315

E

Early childhood education, cultural
  diversity and, 210–11, 217–19

Early childhood educators, assessment
  process and, 156
Early childhood special educators,
  assessment process and, 156
Early elementary grades
  activity-based intervention (ABI) in,
    120–21
  vignettes, 297–327
Early identification/child find, 231
Early intervention, summary history of
  and legislative basis for, 249–51
Ecological approach, 10
Ecological model (ecological influences),
  74–76
  family systems approach and, 75
Education of the Handicapped Act
  Amendments of 1986 (PL 99-457),
  18, 250
Education of the Handicapped Act (PL
  94-142) (1975), 18
Effectiveness of Intervention, The
  (Guralnick), 228
Elementary grades, early, activity-based
  intervention (ABI) in, 120–21
Embarrassment of siblings, 38
Empowerment, of families, 7, 60–64
  family concerns, 61–62
  family priorities, 62
  family resources, 62–63
  model for, 60
  parental advocacy, 60–61
  response to family concerns, priorities,
    and resources, 63–64
Epstein J. L., 8, 27
Erikson, E., 80, 81, 97
Ethnic groups, defined, 208
Evaluation, 165
  defined, 153
  of intervention effectiveness and
    outcomes, 198–99
  of progress and outcomes, 190

typical, 157–58
Exosystem, 49
Extended family, 46, 48

F

Fallon, M. A., 234
Family(-ies), 32
   behavioral development of children
      and, 76–78
   collaboration with. *See* Collaboration,
      professional/family
   empowerment of, 7, 60–64
      family concerns, 61–62
      family priorities, 62
      family resources, 62–63
      model for, 60
      parental advocacy, 60–61
      response to family concerns,
         priorities, and resources, 63–64
   future of inclusive early childhood
      education and, 236–38
   impact of a child with a disability on
      adjustment process, 32–35
      grandparents and extended
         family, 46
      siblings, 37–46
   need for professionals, 51
   participation in assessment, 167
   reciprocal relationships with, 137–39
   relationships in, 50
   responsibilities of, 50
   roles of members of, 50
   as a system, 49–50
Family-centered approach (family-
      centeredness), 50–51
   characterizing and defining, 51
Family-centered services, 8
Family day care homes, activity-based
      intervention (ABI) and, 112–13

Family-first language. *See* Person and
      family-first language
Family systems approach, 75
Fantuzzo, J., 73
Farber, B., 41
Feldman, R. D., 130
Fetal alcohol syndrome (FAS), 149–50
Fisher, R., 54, 55, 68
Flagler, S. L., 166
Florio-Ruane, S., 214
Focus on the child, 47, 57–58
Foley, G., 61
Folio, R., 110
Ford, B. A., 208, 209
Forest, M., 179, 180
Fowle, C., 41
Fox, L., 182
Frost, J. E., 111
Functional analysis, functional assessment
      distinguished from, 84
Functional assessment of behavior,
      163–64
   components of, 84–85
   defined, 84
   positive behavioral supports (PBS)
      and, 83–87
Functional skills, activity-based
      intervention (ABI) and, 108
Future directions in inclusive early
      childhood education, 224–41
   families and, 236–38
   personnel preparation and, 238–41
   public policy, 229–31
   research, 227
   service delivery practices, 231–36

G

Gaffaney, T., 83
Gallagher, J. J., 250, 274

Garbarino, J., 237

Garcia, E., 208

Gath, A., 41

Generative skills, activity-based intervention (ABI) and, 108

Gestwicki, C., 131

Giangreco, M. F., 172

Gibson, M., 209

Giddan, J. J., 75–78, 315

Giorgetti, K., 228

Goal 1 Early Childhood Assessments Resource Group, 128

Goals and objectives
  developing, 189–93
  socially valid, 175–78

Goldsmith, E. B., 236

Goldstein, A. P., 315

Gonzalez, J. J., 313

Grandparents, 46, 48

Granlund, M., 74, 150

Gresham, F. M., 84

Gronlund, G., 167

Grossman, F., 43, 45

Guidelines for Appropriate Curriculum Content and Assessment (NAEYC), 218

Guidelines for Decisions about Developmentally Appropriate Practice (NAEYC), 331–38

Guidelines for Preparation of Early Childhood Professionals (NAEYC), 238

Guidry, J., 118

Guilt of siblings, 38–39

Guralnick, M. J., 228, 250, 274

H

Hacker, B., 165

Hall, L., 41

Hamby, D., 74

Hamilton, J. L., 250, 275

Hanson, M., 72, 76, 78

Hanson, M. J., 219

Harkin, T., 251, 275

Harry, B., 209, 212, 213, 219

Hart, B., 77, 225

Haugland, S. W., 234

Hawaii Early Learning Profile (HELP), 166

Head Start, inclusion and, 17

Head Start programs, activity-based intervention (ABI) in, 114–16

Hearron, P. F., 294

HELP (Hawaii Early Learning Profile), 166

Hemmeter, M. L., 96, 183–84

Heron, T. E., 95

Heward, W. L., 95, 177

High demand activities, alternating low demand activities with, 186

Hildebrand, V., 294

Hobbs, N., 74

Hofferth, S. L., 112

Hogdon, L., 184

Holden, C., 208

Home-based services, activity-based intervention (ABI) and, 109

Hooper, S. R., 119

Horner, R. H., 182

Hummel, L. J., 83

Humor, sense of, of siblings, 45–46

Hynd, G. W., 313

Hypothesis statement, 95

I

Identification of children with special needs, 231

Impact of a child with a disability on

Implementation, future of inclusive early childhood education and, 232–33

Inclusion, 195–98
  defined, 4
  merging disciplines and, 21–23
  rationale for, 12–13
    advocacy groups and professional organizations, positions of, 14–16
    ethical and commonsense arguments, 14
    legislation, 16–19
    research support for early inclusion, 19–21

Inclusion: Moving beyond Our Fears (Phi Delta Kappa), 16

Individualized family service plans (IFSPs), 19, 250–51
  ecological model and, 74–75

Individuals with Disabilities Education Act (IDEA) Amendments of 1991 (PL 102-119), 18–19, 251

Individuals with Disabilities Education Act (IDEA) Amendments of 1997 (PL 105-17), 19, 251

Individuals with Disabilities Education Act of 1990 (IDEA) (PL 101-476), 4
  assessment process and, 153–55

Infant-Preschool Assessment Scale (IPAS), 166

Infants and toddlers, 249–71
  activity-based intervention (ABI) in nursery and child care settings for, 113–14
  history of and legislative basis for early intervention with, 249–51
  learning environment for, 194
  vignettes, 251–71

Initiative versus guilt stage, 81

Innocenti, M. S., 237

Insight of siblings, 41–43

Instructional cues, clear and consistent, 186

Instructional goals and objectives. *See* Goals and objectives

Integration, 12–13

Interdisciplinary assessment, 162

Interobserver reliability, 94–95

Intervention goals, selecting, 175–78

Interview, structured, functional assessment and, 85–86

IPAS (Infant-Preschool Assessment Scale), 166

Ireton, H., 290

Isolation, of siblings, 39–40

Iwata, B. A., 84

Izard, C., 77

J

Jalongo, M. R., 215

Jens, K. G., 165

Jipson, J., 215, 216

Joe, J. R., 79

Johannson, C., 74

Johnson, B. H., 68

Johnson, M. B., 313

Johnson-Martin, N., 165

Juul, K. D., 74

K

Kagan, S. L., 128

Kaiser, A., 122

Kaiser, C., 110, 122

Kanthorwitz, B., 116

Kantos, S., 32

Karagiannis, A., 120
Kaufman, R. K., 61, 63
Kazdin, A. E., 94, 176
Keeley, B., 118
Keenan, M., 113
Kendall, F., 211, 213, 218
Kilgo, J. L., 238
Kindergarten settings, 276–93
    activity-based intervention (ABI) in,
        116–20
    vignettes, 277–93
Kisker, E. E., 112
Klass, S., 110
Klein, M. D., 282
Koger, F., 187
Kontos, S., 228
Kostelny, K., 237

Linguistically and culturally diverse,
    defined, 208
Lockwood, R., 208, 213
Lombardi, J., 181, 235, 236
Loneliness, of siblings, 39–40
"Long Haul, The" (Moyer), 65–66
Longitudinal educational planning
    (LEP), 180–81
Losardo, A., 122
Loss, siblings' sense of, 39–40
Low demand activities, alternating high
    demand activities with, 186
Loyalty, of siblings, 45
Lubeck, S., 215
Lusthaus, E., 179, 180
Lynch, E. W., 78, 79, 101, 209, 219
Lynch, J., 222

L

Labato, D., 41
Lally, R. J., 113
Language development, 77–78
Lansing, M. D., 306
Learning environments, child-centered,
    193–95
LeFrancois, G. R., 80
Legislation, 16–19, 249–51
LeLaurin, K., 63
Length of activities, developmentally
    appropriate, 186
Lennox, D., 83
Leonard, B., 63
LEP (longitudinal educational planning),
    180–81
Lerman, D. C., 84
Lesar, S., 234
Linder, T. W., 157, 161, 164, 200, 232

M

McBride, B. M., 196, 197
McCaig, G., 132
McClelland, A., 208, 218
McConnell, J. L., 315
McConnell, S. R., 215, 217
McCubbin, H. I., 35
McCullum, J. A., 239, 241
McGinnis, E., 315
McGonigel, M. J., 70
McGregor, S. L. T., 236
Macrosystem, 49
McWilliam, P. J., 60
McWilliam, R. A., 251, 274, 275
Mainstreaming, 12
Malach, R. S., 101
Mallory, B. L., 215
MAPS (McGill Action Planning
    System), 179

Marcus, L. M., 306

Mardell-Czudnowski, C., 290

Martin, G., 78

Martinez, L., 208, 218

Meaningful Differences in the Everyday Experience of Young American Children (Hart and Risely), 225

Mediation, 55–56

Mesosystem, 49

Meyer, D. J., 35, 38, 41–43, 45, 68

Meyer, L. H., 209

Microsystem, family as, 49

Miller, C. T., 41

Miller, M., 314, 315

Miller, N., 41, 43

Miller, P. S., 240

Miller, R., 139

Miller, S. R., 314, 315

Miller-Lachman, L., 209, 218

Miltenberger, R. G., 83

Mindes, G., 290

Modeling, behavioral development of children and, 76–78

Moore, D., 228

Morgan, J. L., 51, 52

Motivation Assessment Scale (MAS), 91, 94

Moyer, Jeff, "The Long Haul," 65–66

Muenchow, S., 115, 116

Multicultural education, 209–10

Multicultural society, United States as, 208–9

Multidisciplinary assessment, 162

Multiple disabilities, 150

Multiple Voices for Ethnically Diverse, Exceptional Learners (Division for Culturally and Linguistically Diverse Exceptional Learners), 219

Munkres, A., 171

Murphy, C. L., 239

N

National Association for the Education of Young Children (NAEYC), 4, 193, 194, 226
    on assessment competencies, 152
    cultural diversity and, 210, 218
    developmentally appropriate practice (DAP) and, 5–6, 15
    Guidelines for Decisions about Developmentally Appropriate Practice, 331–38
    Guidelines for Preparation of Early Childhood Professionals, 238
    inclusion and, 15
    Position Statement on School Readiness, 236

National Association of Early Childhood Specialist in State Departments of Education, 218

National Association of State Boards of Education, 16

National Down Syndrome Society, 16

National Education Goals Panel, 236

National Information Center for Children and Youth with Disabilities (NICHCY), 149

Native American families, 78–79

Negotiation, 54–55

Nelson, J. R., 79

New, R. S., 215

Nieto, S., 210, 218

Noah, T., 128

Notari-Syverson, A. R., 199

Novick, R., 96, 104

Nurse (practitioner), assessment process and, 157

O

Objectives. *See* Goals and objectives
O'Brien, C. L., 120
O'Brien, J., 120
Occupational therapists, assessment process and, 156
Olds, S. W., 130
Olson, J., 239
Olson, P. D., 239
O'Neill, R. E., 85
Operational definition of behavior, 87
Orelove, F. P., 157, 162
Overidentification of siblings, 38

P

Papalia, D. E., 130
Parent/professional conference, 158–60
Parents. *See also* Family(-ies)
    role in development of the child, 76–78
Partnerships with families, 7–8
Patterson, J., 35, 62
Patterson, J. M., 35
Patton, J. R., 195
PDD/NOS (pervasive developmental disorder/not otherwise specified), 90
Pear, J., 78
Peck, J. T., 132
Performance component of objectives, 189
Performance criteria statements, 189
Perske, R., 32–35, 61, 62, 67, 68
Person and family-first language, 11–12
Personnel preparation, 238–41

Peters, J., 195
Peterson, N. L., 62
Phelps, P. C., 113
Phi Delta Kappa, 16
Philbrick, L. A., 182
Physical therapists, assessment process and, 157
Physicians, assessment process and, 157
Piaget, Jean, 104
Piazza, T. P., 195
Planned activities, 106–9
Planning, future of inclusive early childhood education and, 232–33
Polloway, E. A., 195
Positive behavioral support plans, 95
Positive behavioral supports (PBS), 5, 72–73, 82–96, 140, 183
    activity-based intervention (ABI) and, 182, 188
    choice-making opportunities, 186–87
    clear and consistent instructional cues, 186
    cultural diversity and, 212–13
    developmentally appropriate length of activities, 186
    family-centeredness and collaboration and, 65
    functional assessment and, 83–87
    future of inclusive early childhood education and, 233–34
    individual schedules, 184
    matching level of instruction to child's abilities, 185–86
    merging ABI, DAP, and, 96
    principles of, 82
    varying activities, 186
Potter, W. J., 128
Powell, D. R., 215–17

Practices, 133–35

Preparing Personnel to Work with Infants and Young Children and Their Families: A Team Approach (Bricker and Widerstrom), 241

Preschool
   activity-based intervention (ABI) in, 116–20
   multicultural education in, 210–11

Pretti-Frontczak, K., 165

Pride, of siblings, 43

Prizant, B. M., 73, 83

Professionals
   collaboration with. *See* Collaboration, professional/family
   families' need for, 51
   preparation of, 238–41

Program evaluation, 198–99

Psychoeducational Profile Revised (PEP-R), 306

Psychosocial development, Erikson's theory of, 80–81

Public Law 94-142. *See* Education of the Handicapped Act

Public Law 99-457. *See* Education of the Handicapped Act Amendments of 1986

Public Law 101-476. *See* Individuals with Disabilities Education Act of 1990 (IDEA)

Public policy, future of, 229–31

R

Reaching Potentials: Appropriate Curriculum and Assessment for Young Children, Volume 1 (Bredekamp & Rosegrant), 218

Reagan, T., 208, 218

Recommended Practices: Indicators of Quality in Programs for Infants and Young Children with Special Needs and Their Families, 211

Recording behavior, methods of, 87–95
   anecdotal recording, 87–89
   challenges in, 94
   hypothesis statement, 95
   interobserver reliability, 94–95
   Motivation Assessment Scale (MAS), 91, 94
   scatter plot analysis, 89–91

Reichle, J., 84

Reichler, R. J., 306

Relationships, in the family system, 50

Reliability, interobserver, 94–95

Repp, A. C., 94

Research, future of, 227–29

Resentment, of siblings, 40–41

Resources, inclusion of young children and, 196

Responsibilities, of families, 50

Rhinehart, P. M., 63

Riccio, C. A., 313

Riche, M. F., 208–10

Richey, D., 110

Rickenberg, D., 75, 315

Risely, T., 77, 225

Roberts, R. N., 237

Rodd, J. C., 211, 214, 215

Rogers, S. J., 237

Rortvedt, A., 83

Rosegrant, T., 139, 215, 218

Routine activities, 105

Rowland, C., 122

Ruef, M., 182

Rule, S., 122, 237

Russell, C. L., 31n, 42, 45

Ryley, A., 315

Ryley, A. T., 75

S

Safer, N. D., 250, 275
Sampon, M. A., 110
Sanders Wann, J. A., 234
Sandler, A., 35, 46, 48–50, 60
Sapon-Sevin, M., 209
Sapp, M. E., 132
Sarracino, C., 128
Scaffolding of children's learning, 104
Scandinavian countries, 74
Scatter plot analysis, 89–91
Schedules
    classroom, 185
    individual, 184
Schopler, E., 306
Schuler, D., 226
Schwartz, I. S., 196, 197, 215, 217
Self-concept, 75
    of siblings, 43
Self-determination, concept of, 9–10
Selinger, J., 314, 315
Service delivery practices, future of,
    231–36
Shearer, D. E., 110
Shearer, M. S., 110
Shepard, L., 128
Shuster, S. L., 199
Siblings, 37–46
    as advocates, 43, 45
    embarrassment of, 38
    guilt of, 38–39
    increased responsibilities of, 41
    isolation, loneliness, and loss of,
        39–40
    loyalty of, 45
    maturity and insight of, 41–43
    overidentification of, 38
    pressure to achieve, 41
    pride of, 43

resentment of, 40–41
self-concept of, 43
social competence of, 43
strength, resiliency, and sense of
    humor of, 45–46
suggestions from parents, 39
suggestions from siblings, 40
tolerance of, 43
vocational opportunities for, 43
SIBSHOPS, 39, 45, 68, 71, 298
Simeonsson, R. J., 60, 110
Skirtic, T., 45
Slentz, K., 165
Slentz, K. L., 64
Smith, D. J., 79
Smith, T. E. C., 195
Sobsey, D., 157, 162
Social competence, of siblings, 43
Socially valid goals and objectives,
    175–78
Sociocultural influences, on behavioral
    development, 78–79
Speech/language pathologists
    (SLPs), assessment process
    and, 156
Spina bifida, 150
Spodek, B., 216
Spoon, teaching how to use a (vignette),
    191–92
Squires, I., 166
Stafford, P., 208, 218
Stainback, S., 120
Stainback, W., 120
State of America's Children Yearbook
    1998, The, 225
Stayton, V. D., 240, 241
Stott, F. M., 214, 215
Strain, P. S., 96, 183, 184
Straus, M. A., 76
Stress (stressors), 75–76

Structured interview, functional
    assessment of behavior and,
    85–86
Summers, J. A., 45
Swan, W. W., 51, 52
Swartz, L. C., 55
Sweden, 74

T

Target behavior, activity-based
    intervention (ABI) and, 106
Taylor, C., 209, 218
Teachers, preparation of, 238–41
Tessier, A., 282
Thomas, R. M., 130, 135–38
Thurman, S. K., 74
Toddlers, learning environment for,
    194–95
Tolerance, of siblings, 43
Torres, Y. L., 113
Touchette, P. E., 89
Training, of professionals, 238–41
Transdisciplinary assessment, 162–64
Transdisciplinary Play-Based Assessment
    (TPBA), 232
Transdisciplinary teaming, concept of,
    8–9
Transitions, 235–36
concept of, 10–11
Trivette, C., 7, 51
Trivette, C. M., 74
Trout, M., 61
Trust, collaboration between
    professionals and families and, 59
Trust versus mistrust stage, 80–81
Turnbull, A. P., 45, 54, 56, 57, 75,
    150, 182

Turnbull, H. A., 54, 56, 57
Turnbull, H. R., 75, 150, 182

U

U. S. News and World Report, 208
Udell, T., 195
Umansky, W., 119
United Cerebral Palsy Association, 16
Upshur, C. C., 64
Ury, M., 54, 55, 68

V

Vadasy, P. F., 35, 38, 41–43, 45, 68
Values, 212
    defined, 208
Value systems, defined, 208
Van den Pol, R., 118
Varying activities, 186
Veltman, P., 171
Vold, E. B., 215
Voltz, D. L., 209, 218
VORT Cooperation, 166
Vygotsky, L. S., 78, 175

W

Wacker, D. P., 84
Waddell, M., 165
Waite-Stupiansky, S., 104
Walters, R. H., 76
Wayman, K. I., 213, 219
Weatherby, A. M., 73
Wheeler, J. J., 175, 179, 185, 314, 315
White, L. K., 237
Widerstrom, A., 241

Williams, L. R., 215, 216
Willis, D. J., 158
Wingert, P., 116
Winners All: A Call for Inclusive Schools
   (National Association of State Boards
   of Education), 16
Winsler, A., 104
Winton, P. J., 8, 30, 60, 68, 274
Wolery, M., 164
Woll, J., 57
Woodcock, R. W., 313
Woods Cripe, J. J., 103–5, 108, 111, 121
Woods-Cripe, J. J., 103–5, 108, 111, 121,
   165, 187, 214, 239

Woster, S., 83
Wright, J. L., 234
Wurtz, E., 128

Z

Zigler, E., 115, 116
Zirpoli, S. B., 193
Zirpoli, T. J., 76, 231, 284
Zone of proximal development
   (ZPD), 104